AUTOBIOGRAPHY OF JOHN YOUNGER.

AUTOBIOGRAPHY

OF

JOHN YOUNGER,

SHOEMAKER, ST. BOSWELLS,

AUTHOR OF "THOUGHTS AS THEY RISE," "RIVER ANGLING FOR SALMON AND TROUT," "THE LIGHT OF THE WEEK" (PRIZE ESSAY ON THE SABBATH), "CORN LAW RHYMES," ETC.

KELSO:
J. & J. H. RUTHERFURD, 20, SQUARE.
JOHN MENZIES & CO., EDINBURGH AND GLASGOW.
1881.

All Rights Reserved.

Publishers' Note.

THE Publishers, in issuing this Autobiography of a man altogether out of and above the common ranks in which it was his lot to be born and to live—the publication of which, they are aware, has been awaited by many with considerable interest and curiosity—desire to explain that in passing it through the press it has not been subjected to any extensive editorial pruning or toning. Here and there sentences which were considered unduly involved or extended have been simplified or broken up into two, in order to avoid tediousness to the reader, and occasionally a word of the author's own coining has been changed so as to remove ground for hypercriticism; but these changes have been so extremely few that the reader need not have any misgivings lest he is not in contact with John Younger's own genuine thoughts expressed in his own frank and forcible manner. There was an originality and individuality about John's way of viewing things as well as in his mode of expressing his thoughts which imparted to him and to them an additional interest and attraction, which it has been the object of the Publishers to preserve.

In order to understand some of the allusions readers must remember that the Autobiography was originally written in the form of "epistles addressed to Mr. Robert Riddell at London, by his friend and relative," to which, in their collected form, the author had given the title "Obscurities in Private Life Developed; or, Robinson Crusoe Untravelled."

The Publishers would take this opportunity of expressing their obligations to Mr. William Brockie, Bishopwearmouth, an intimate and attached friend of John Younger's, for reading the proofs as the work passed through the press, and for several notes which supply information regarding some of the individuals named in the text, as well as for the valuable supplementary chapter, which, as it were, completes and crowns the work.

20, SQUARE, KELSO, *Oct., 1881.*

Contents.

	PAGE
INTRODUCTORY	ix
CHAPTER I.	1
CHAPTER II.	10
CHAPTER III.	17
CHAPTER IV.	28
CHAPTER V.	40
CHAPTER VI.	50
CHAPTER VII.	60
CHAPTER VIII.	70
CHAPTER IX.	81
CHAPTER X.	103
CHAPTER XI.	114
CHAPTER XII.	123
CHAPTER XIII.	137
CHAPTER XIV.	149
CHAPTER XV.	169
CHAPTER XVI.	189
CHAPTER XVII.	199
CHAPTER XVIII.	211
CHAPTER XIX.	220
CHAPTER XX.	235
CHAPTER XXI.	246
CHAPTER XXII.	257
CHAPTER XXIII.	280
CHAPTER XXIV.	297
CHAPTER XXV.	314
CHAPTER XXVI.	328
CHAPTER XXVII.	345
CHAPTER XXVIII.	362
CHAPTER XXIX.	372
CHAPTER XXX.	396
CHAPTER XXXI.	407
CHAPTER XXXII.	416
CHAPTER XXXIII.	434
CONCLUSION	446

Autobiography of John Younger.

INTRODUCTORY CHAPTER:

AN EPISTLE TO MR. ROBERT RIDDELL, LONDON, A FRIEND AND RELATIVE OF THE AUTHOR.

MY DEAR FRIEND,—To a mind more at ease, in respect of present comfortable circumstances, there might have been a greater solitary pleasure in the embodiment of such a vision as the life of your friend, in retracing the movements of a human heart throughout the incidental occurrences in general life, and under various excitements of affection, through the flowery braes and sunshiny lanes of rambling childhood and youth, still shadowing on the memory the soft reflection of

"A light which ne'er can shine again
On life's dull stream,"

often enough sobered into tinges of the sallower hues; sometimes verging into the clouded envelopment of melancholy. However, in so far as memory will at present supply, I determine here to give you a faithful transcript of incident, excitement, and consequent feeling throughout the monotonous tenor of my evanescent existence—evanescent, indeed, in comparison with the mass of the wonderful through the course of time. It will supply very little or nothing of amusement to those accustomed, according to the fashion of the day, to riot in the pages of war, blood, and murder, or to sport their imaginations like hunting horses over the fields of novel vagary and romantic fiction.

My narrative will present little indeed of war or shipwreck, or "hair-breadth 'scapes by flood or field." Yet some curious phenomena relative to the history of common and middle life in this age of comparatively free thought, still very ill explained, may be here evolved as cud for the rumination of your future philosophy; for I have long considered that the true and simple philosophy of humanity is quite overlooked. Being, the most common of all things, is taken for granted as generally understood, while comparatively few who live understand the main end for which life is conferred, any more than they comprehend the nature and quality of that breath of air by which it is supported, and thus the main comforts of existence are entirely neglected for things more foreign, and of infinitely less intrinsic value.

Most of the pictures of common life that we meet with in books are drawn in the shape of novels, with the view of attracting the attention of indolent readers; the question with authors being, not of what can I inform my neighbour by which he may be improved in head or heart, mind or morals? but what is the fashion of public taste? that by pandering to it I may secure sale and applause! Hence the present jumble of brains, the rack of invention to excite, supply, and cram the public appetite, all so agape after tales of the marvellous, till the picture of life is overwrought, and the image of nature bedaubed to disgust.

That notion, so common amongst writers even of greatest name, that humanity stands classified in general *castes*, agreeably to particular stations in life, is taken up and held upon very shallow observation, and implies a very slight research into the nature of mind and character; for, to a close observer, individuality of character is easily perceptible, as existing greatly independent of outward circumstances, and this not only in all the human species, placed by Providence under the exercise and direction of the reasoning faculties, but even in creatures of merely instinctive existence. So much does creative wisdom seem to delight in variety, that, tame only a nest of small birds—starlings or sparrows—and you will soon perceive that these birds will not only be distinguishable by bodily appearance, but also by individuality of temper. The same diversity of disposition pervades all creation, even the vegetable and mineral kingdoms, and is far more perceptible in the human species, where the variations are endless and minute, between the two extremes of greatest and least ability and aptitude.

Education will always do a great deal; yet where, by infinite labour, you can excite and impress the dull faculties of one brother or sister till they have got versed by rote in any lesson of art or science, another will catch up the idea at once with such aptitude as might make you suppose it intuitive in his or her constitution.

Many of our great philosophical writers, such as Locke and Dr. Johnson, in their passion for general principles, lose sight of individuality of character; although you may suppose it confessed somehow in their general view, yet it is never understood and carried out as a received principle. The idea seems taken up of a *class* or *caste*, as if every statesman must necessarily be a Solon, and every shoemaker a Souter Johnnie; and thus, although Locke himself had broken through the cobwebbery of the great *alma mater* and the old philosophy, into the most liberal sentiments of the Bacon school—having the perception to note that "many a good poetic vein is buried under a trade, and never produces anything for want of improvement"—still, he seems not to have perceived clearly with Rousseau that "true genius will educate itself, and, like flame, burst through all obstructions." For though education, in the true sense of the word, is necessary to excellence, yet a question still lies open, What is education? Is it certain old rules of thinking which require to be forced on the individual by others, more particularly than those which, by the exercise of his own faculties, he perceives in nature and life within and around him, and seizes, concentrates, abstracts, and digests for himself? Some do this spontaneously with unaccountable facility, such as Shakespeare, Burns, and Ebenezer Elliot; while others never can be tutored into any method of it by old rules, and often, when even stuffed in "the schools" to repletion, feel only besotted from a mind full of old abstruse indigestibles. For instance, it does not appear that Mr. Locke could have conceived it possible that a *self-taught* (or, as some would have it, an untaught) day-labouring village cobbler, who has scarcely ever seen beyond the circle of uplands that bounds his village prospect, nor more than the outer walls of a seminary of regular education, should be able to appreciate at a glance the extent of his research in the philosophy of mind, detecting the weaker fancies of the theorist in the bosom of the philosopher.

I have been pelted through life with the word *classic* by paltry, brainless *scholars*, who do not themselves perceive that the word is by them misused; since, in its first and proper sense, it is applied to ancient authors who copied from nature, being "the classics of an age that heard of none." Without studying them at all, I just start where they started, conceiving that I may as well also copy at first hand, from nature and life, as copy from them; while those who spend their time in endeavouring to read such ancients, may find themselves less truly classical at last, however they at present may stupidly claim a monopoly of all common rationality, and sputter Latin now, to distinguish themselves, as the Roman fashionables in their day made themselves classically ridiculous by lisping *Greek*.

Classics, properly understood, were the few amongst the ancients who had improved the language and philosophy of their respective countries, and arrived at considerable proficiency in that which constituted the polite learning, the arts and sciences of their age. The decay of their countries having left their language unalterably fixed at a pretty full stage of its growth, it has been thought convenient to be taken as a standard of example for present ages, as well as a sort of fund or quarry from which to take materials wherewith to build up succeeding languages. Their discoveries and advancements in arts and science also, being ready materials fitting for fabrics of modern construction, have been found convenient as models for imitation, and they are held precious from that veneration which the human mind ever pays to antiquity. Man, being the child of imitation, has a general tendency in life and in religion to follow the creed and tastes of his fathers, whether in the ways of wisdom or folly—perhaps more readily in the latter.

Whatever ideas of life, fancy, or philosophy had come within the sphere of ancient perception, the classics expressed these in their language, now fixed as in a frost; and the knowledge of these ideas by such as patiently devote their time to the acquirement of the original language makes up a second-hand stock-in-trade, which answers well enough for modern scholars, who have not vision sufficient to discover for themselves; therefore, it becomes fashionable for such to depreciate all knowledge, however useful, unless it has been ferreted from among the rubbish of the dead languages.

Hence, we seldom find very good conversible companions on topics of real every-day life in these very dead-language men; and hence, also, the truth of Goldsmith's remark—"Take the word of a man who has seen the world, and has studied human nature more by experience than precept; take my word for it—I say, that books teach us very little of the world." If classic literature is absolutely necessary to enable a person now to write well, it must be from its giving an intimate acquaintance with the models of antiquity. In this view, then, models must be necessary for the production of whatever is excellent, as deductions from the experiences of life. From whence had the sons of antiquity their models so necessary to produce these specimens of theirs, now esteemed so excellent? From whence had they their arts and language, which are, by the fashion of our day, considered so essentially necessary to the opening of the mouth in human conversation, to our pen in writing, our brush in painting, or our chisel in statuary?

Though such specimens are not to be despised, any more than a graceful garment of ancient construction for human clothing, yet I cannot consider them so absolutely essential to the direction of present ingenuity as some seem to suppose, not having been necessary to that genius which originally produced them from the mere exercise of those human powers which are as fresh to-day in the living individual as in the sons of Noah ten years after the flood. Classical learning may be necessary to trace, to follow, to comprehend and explain former works of genius; but the genius able to produce, sees the form of the attainable excellence in idea, and brings it out into existence by individual labour. Classical learning is more necessary to enable ordinary minds to perceive and follow the soarings of genius than to direct genius in its flights; and it never will enable an ordinary mind to invent or execute any original grand work. Genius will do much without classical acquirement now, as in former ages; but classical learning without inventive genius will not gain an inch upon art or science in seven ages. Good common sense is the same through the course of time.

Nothing, indeed, seems to be yet less understood by the great and classically scientific than the common path of life, through which pass on to eternity those who are by fashionables accounted the *low vulgar*—though, indeed, the productive portion of humanity: those whom the fortunate, in the vanity of their heart, often despise, are yet the very roots, bones, and sinews, supporting and holding together the framework of society. Our carrier's two strong, old horses are of more real utility than these two fence-crashing hunters, on which our fox-hunting Duke (according to that learned writer, Mr. Nimrod,) made such a saving by purchasing them for £900! —a sum that would have put eighteen poor village families into a comfortable position in various lines of useful occupation for life, or educated as many poor village children.

It is quite amusing to perceive how our aristocracy carry out their distinctions regarding blood and breed in the human, as in the race-horse and game-cock, creation. One inconsistency, however, has always existed in the latter—the brute case. Your connoisseurs very properly choose the best bone, figure, and general symmetry from which to propagate and improve the kind; whilst in the human, fashion places improvement entirely upon wealth, estate, entail, and court dignity, so that these have hitherto been considered your best human blood refiners.

In novels, and past tales of fancy and fiction, when

you meet with a "Cuddie-Headrigg," or any other son of *Mause, Madge,* or *Jenny Nettle,* as a necessary appendage to the filling up of a plot, he must, of course, be described as a chubby, round-headed, flat-faced-looking rascal, with no quality of mind higher than, perhaps, low cunning, and a continual mischievous appetite for "coarse commons," solid, liquid, and fiery, to heat his *base* phlegmatic blood withal; whereas, walk out of fiction into the common path of real life, and you will likely meet with the honest-born sons of any of these *plebeian* females—strapping, boardly, and athletic—wanting nothing earthly but the creative touch of a sword royal, with an alphabetical insertion of name on the State beggar list, to cause them spring up absolute miracles of symmetrical perfection, most fascinating to the eyes of courtly beauty and quizzing-glass scrutiny; compared with whom, your in-and-in blood-bred courtier, whose tree of generation forms a chronological and legal puzzle, might by no means shew such a marked distinction of visage as in the standard statuary imaginations of your novel authors! For, in the very truth of life, there are to be met with in the pathway of productive labour as few, proportionately, of what we may suppose apish-faced and shamble-shanked, as in the House of Lords, and, I believe, fully more possessed of that fine conjunction of soul and body requisite to distinguish Solomon's "man amongst a thousand."

Your great gentleman author knows nothing at all about ordinary life or its constituents—just about as much as of the manners of the inhabitants of Saturn. He is precepted in his youth that he may not mix amongst the children of common human-kind, as if there were contamination in the slightest contact; and by precept and example he is taught to look on not only the poorest class of labourers, but the middle class of the community, tradesmen, merchants, and mechanics, as a sort of inferior beings, whose interests and sympathies of life are, if not disgusting, at least to him of no moment or account whatever. All he knows of life, therefore, below those who drive reckless over earth to their graves in coaches, is picked up amongst his own grooms, gamekeepers, huntsmen, and hostlers—classes of men who too often think it their duty, or feel it their interest, to shew an acquiescence in his honour's judgment, will, or opinion in a general and passive way; reserving the expression of their experience to escape the risk of being cashiered.

Swift, on "Modern Education," observed that "education is worse in proportion to the grandeur of the parents. If the whole world were under one monarch," says he, "the heir of that monarch would be the worst educated mortal since the creation." Now, supposing an improvement in this matter since the days of Swift, I will observe that your present gentleman may acquire at college, perhaps, some knowledge of Latin and Greek grammars, mathematical or other science; and in courts, camps, and aristocratical coteries or assemblies, he may sound and bottom the current interests, intrigues, and hourly vapours of the fashionable insignificance of his own class. He may even have a knack of writing his own observations in all the delicate *minutiæ* of refined taste, like Lord Chesterfield, to the admiration of his son, or his own *caste;* and yet, after a sixty years' respiration of common atmosphere, go into his family vault having lived as ignorant of *life,* according to the broad, true meaning of that word, as he is of the present situation of the soul of his great grandfather, or the production of his own life's daily bread under the curse.

And what is still more pitiful, the same absurd ideas about classicality, gentility, vulgarity, and all that, are insensibly instilled even into those children of common life, who are destined by their parents for some literary profession by which to attempt gaining an easy, labourless livelihood, or, according to fond parental hope, even make a fortune or a figure in the world. They are sent early to school, and in many cases the rest of the family are curtailed of common comforts, sometimes even of a sufficiency of daily bread, in order to save the means wherewith to promote the laudable purpose of carrying forward this favourite to great learning and respectability—perhaps to fortune and to fame. There is the young man, walled in amongst college-gowns and perukes, to feed his hungry heart upon old Greek and Latin authors—the fust, the lust, and rust of antiquity—often as unpalatable as indigestible; and in this way the days of his prime are spent, learning simply to convey his ideas in *proper language,* without having acquired any ideas worth conveyance; as, in fact, this sort of seclusion loses him the chance of the knowledge gained by every-day experience in the active business of life in contact with the real world. He has become of age, still as ignorant of God and man, heaven and earth, the main great essentials, the use and end of this world, with all its wonderful phenomena, or of his own individual being, purpose, or position in it, as was Julius Cæsar, Bonaparte, George IV., or the Emperor of China; and often as helpless as a suckling, as ignorant of the methods, as unaccustomed to the labour requisite to force daily bread from the elements of earth, air, fire, and water, particularly as these are restricted and spider-webbed around from the touch of the poor by the legal snares of the lawless, as if he had been in dungeon-seclusion for life. And what is worse, these scholars too generally shew a tendency to fly off from their own family circle, and to ape the *great*, though not one of a thousand ever gets forward so far as to shine in their train, like a moon feather in a peacock's tail, to be cast off in the moulting season. For it is very ludicrous to hear it cast in a poor scholar's teeth, that "there is no law in our free constitution to hinder him from rising by genius and industry to the highest offices of the State." He may as well be told that there is no law against his rising to the moon, which is as conveniently to be come at by a corn-billed son of a cobbler, and where, I understand, there may be about three millions of square miles of various soil yet *unentailed*.

If ever you, my friend, help to spoke a ladder by which such aspirant climber may ascend, escape when you perceive him reach the top—so far below, you will be despised anyway; and as weak heads get giddy on heights, your *protege* is apt to leap or fall at risk of your bones or life below. I have learned this! Experience is the most cunning teacher! I may still yet, now and then, be giving a gentle hoise up, from a constitutional sympathy that way; aye, even occasionally lend my back to his foot to facilitate his ascent; but I never look up after him for fear of his dust in my eyes. Just escape until he may be fairly again fallen, and requiring that assistance which, to the credit, and discredit, of human nature, is often more readily bestowed from the sympathy of some half-despised old maiden aunt than from the whole fraternity of his classical brethren taken together.

From one or other of these classes of *classics* generally spring forth the authors of all works commonly approved by the reviews and journals as worth notice. Hence that sameness of gloss given to all descriptions of life, however circumstantially varied, since the close of scripture biography downward. Such authors as have classical authority to write, cannot write but what they have seen, read, or dreamed; and the actors in my condition of life, who feel their state, and, self-taught or inspired, attempt to describe what they feel, are neglected, or instantly borne down by the plodding reviewer of the day, who, like my lord's gamekeeper, must do his duty in strapping off the unlicensed vulgar as poachers on the assumed manor of this same classical community.

Nor, though a newsmonger editor were personally charmed, dare he express his feelings in praise, approval, or due credit, for fear of loss occurrent on the censure and scorn of the fraternity of his *classical* supporters. Hence, if we read at all, we are just obliged to take the polished dreams of these gentry as pictures of life, which they consequently never are—as far at least as poor and middle life is by them written at. For instance, excellent as the "Waverley Novels" may be imagined in this respect, they are in a great measure only amusive dreams of the author's imagination; since, as a picture of Scottish life and manners, even that of our forefathers, they may as properly be called a graphic description of the "man o' the moon" and his feudal tenantry. No, no; real Scottish middle life is a very different affair, as I well know, from a fifty years' day and daily experience, and my hale old father for forty more years prior to that period. The "Scottish peasantry," forsooth! What do such authors know about the souters, tailors, weavers, blacksmiths, alewives, shopkeepers, and labourers about St. Boswells and other villages? What know they of the lives, cares, joys, sorrows, hardships, personal and family feelings, sufferings and sympathies, even of their own farmers', hinds', and cottars' families? They will loll past in their open coaches, and take notes of the rural pleasures, and beauties of the fine harvest fields, and social sportive bliss of the happy reapers, never perceiving that such labourers are generally *hamstrained*, wire-wrought, through wet and dry, often without the conveniency of pure water to slake their parching thirst, though it flows free in the next field, till their blood is inflamed, and their passions in a ferment, which sometimes results in sudden death on the spot, and often in rheumatic and pleuritic fevers. They may say this is the folly of the individual, who often over-exerts himself; but I can tell them that their college philosophy would not preserve them a day uninflamed under the operation and pressure of the last thirty years' general farming system.

Thomson, in the "Seasons," talks smoothly sentimental of the rural pleasures of the reapers' field. Well, I suppose the fields might be more *rural* in his day, as well as in his Palemon's scripture times; but, what is more likely, Jamie Thomson, my favourite poet, never straddled ten hours a day for a month on a harvest field, carrying forward his *ridge*, as I have done, with a young pupil partner, against such a rough, rugged rustic as Will. Robson and his yoke-fellow, else would he have sung quite another song on the subject. No man ought to write on these subjects who has not reaped at least one harvest before one of our high-rented Border farmers.

Yes, my dear friend, it was a very pleasant thing for a man of fortune to drive up in his light calash on a forenoon airing to the height of Bowden Moor, and, gaining the top of Eildon Hills, there overlook the Merse and Teviotdale, with the romantic vales of the Tweed and Teviot all below his eyes, with all their tributary streams—to the distant Carter-Fell and the blue Cheviots—and, retiring at leisure, give you a fairy description of hill and vale, wood and stream, towering mansions and scattered villages, starred over between with smoking hamlets, surrounded with pasture fields and waving corn; the romantic beauty of old wood-bined abbeys, the hall of the peer with all its grandeur, and the habitations of their modern tenantry, little inferior in splendour; the rural elegance of their farms, from adoption of approved modes and machinery in their husbandry—their drainings, manurings, ploughings, sowings, reapings, huntings, singings, dancings, in a circle of rural magnificence of life. From the impression of such a picture on the reflective eye of a poetic imagination—agreeably, also, to the state of inward feeling of a well-fed writer!—such a description as could be given of the whole scene must look charming, making the gentlemen suppose themselves all Palemons, "generous and rich," and the ladies rural nymphs, lovely *Lavinias*. And then comes a fine imaginative tale, drawn in the windings of a fox-run, through the whole scenery of wood, stream, cliff, and glen; nicely done up in the Ballantyne hot-press; received and applauded, agreeably to bargain, by all the periodicals, reviews, and journals throughout London, Dublin, Edinburgh, and Paris!—read over England, her easts and wests, and two or three continents, with *such* satisfaction and delight, till the fame of our author returns again into our own very vale where the scene was laid; and where we, the very poor—flattered out of our consistency with our goose's golden egg—join in echo of praise, without considering the falsity of the whole picture, in as far at least as we ourselves stand represented.

Ah! my dear friend, the lives of the poor in these valleys are, from the cradle to the grave, a very different affair from all this, or from anything yet written by these high-flying novelists and imaginative tale-tellers; as the following recollections of the simple life, observations, and reflections of one of these humble individuals will give you a tolerably fair sample in proof—that is, if you will peruse it, after your late romancing, as you would a draught of plain, cooling water after a heating fuddle.

Autobiography of John Younger.

CHAPTER I.

"I would not give my free thoughts for a throne!"—BYRON.

IN beginning to write a life, it is necessary to say we have been born; and yet in a world where there are born at an average 82,000 a-day, one is almost ashamed to notify an individual birth, even of a common-place king or superior, or any one of less account than some patriarchal progenitor, or father of a marked race, or saviour of a people—such as Noah, Abraham, Moses, Wallace, Washington, &c. And yet again, if we take it into serious consideration, we must perceive in such a creative work of divinity, as the production of any single human being, an act of power and providence equally as great as any of those miracles against which infidelity has kept up such an insignificant carpation for nearly two thousand years. Therefore, it would indicate a false delicacy to tamper further with the idea of telling you that I was born on the 5th day of July, 1785, at

Longnewton, then a considerable village of the olden fashion, now almost swept from the face of the earth —a picture of the Auburn so beautifully described by Goldsmith.

The days of childhood and early youth, which, according to his proper view, the wisest of men justly denominated vanity, may not be worthy of remark further than as they tend to shew the native force of the mind, and to explain and account for the casual direction given to its original impulse, on which seems to depend so many of the issues of our future life—which latter, alas! may generally be accounted equally vain, usually more wicked, than the ways of childhood.

But there may be a pleasure, to a mind jaded and harrassed amidst the toils and trammels of life, to throw back an occasional glance of reflection over the sunny hours and flowery fields of our simplest delights, when the opening roses of life were enjoyed in their freshness, their prickles yet undiscovered. And of all else that we meet with in this world of sound and sympathy, what can touch our ear with half the pleasure which that simple air evokes, by which we were sung asleep in our cradle? recalling a glow of associations, the earliest endearments of a fond mother's ardent caress—the clambering over her lap, with fresh little hands grasping her neck in the full vigour of our whole heart's love? Yes, what a review is it, back through the shadows of long intervening years, to trace from memory the sunshine on the inner walls of the cottage of our youth; the moths journeying on the window panes; the twitter of the swallow under the eaves, and the chitter of the sparrow in the thatch; the green grassy knoll, where first we culled gowans, crawflowers, and wild clover; the very spots and freckles of the eggs in the first bird's nest we discovered in our earliest rambles; the varied tinges of the small pebbles picked up by the pathway sides, as washed out of the earth by the summer spate;* and the rowans† and other berries? And of all other starts of sudden joy, that of our little hearts at the sound of our first penny whistle! And of our tiny wanderings, when, astray amidst scented bean-fields, we have anticipated the wild bee by untimeously rifling much sweet blossom. Meanwhile, a-missing by our guardian, all probable spots, particularly those of danger, are eagerly searched till hope is beginning to die away in flickering shadows over the palpitating heart of the anxious parent, when lo! the fluttering butterfly, unconsciously tempting the wicked pursuit, leads the little adventurer happily again forth into open discovery. These are all worth a remembrance, and much more. And who can slightingly forget the lovely visions which took fairy forms in the vivid imagination of youth at that sensitive age, when even inanimate objects appeared to the eye, like Ezekiel's wheels, instinct with the moving spirit of life? Who does not regret when these visions are chased away by the stubborn realities of cold, calculating experience? The light of information, with all its blessings of wisdom, brings nothing equivalent to the loss of the "silver spoon" ever to be found at the end of the rainbow! And oh! the freshness of the green heart. Age, that

---

* *Spate*, a heavy fall of rain.
† *Rowans*, red berries, fruit of the mountain ash.

steals it away, has no equivalent to bestow. The leaves and flowers of youth seemed to breathe and to feel. In childhood I have conversed with them as with sweet little sisters; and so I yet believe that they do breathe and feel, though imperceptibly to the callous senses and purblind philosophy of age. Yes, and the appearance of that pretty bush of sives,* shooting up their pod-heads into blossom and seed, beside which, an arm-child, I was first laid to sprawl on the grass, has left the shadow of its life and hues on my soul, still unobliterated by all the sad impressions of fifty intervening years' experience of life. I love its kind still, and can lie down beside them here, but cannot array them in the colours of my former imagination, nor return in retrospect into the fancy of the first feeling. And then that first red polyanthus, a flower to be loved indeed—the planting and watering of it, with a flock of little neighbours assembled, all in gaze, like Indians worshipping the sun, and with various expression of admiration. What a queen was little Betty, who could say, " It is mine in gift!" The charm of these recollections lies in their naturalness to the heart. No amusement of wealth can give such delight to the eye of manhood, because the pleasure lies more in the simple susceptibility of the mind than in the greatness and glory of the acquisition. No proprietor since Noah's flood of the barony in which I was born has ever had half the pleasure in his appropriation of the soil that I have had, a child tumbling about amongst its grass and willows.

But then came our schoolboy days, of sore trial,

* *Sives*, cive; Lat., *cibium*.

task, and discipline. Into a small schoolroom, crowded with some threescore young commoners of both sexes, is led forward by the fond parent to the foot of the village teacher's small old table-desk our bare-headed little self, rising five years old, eyeing, with some palpitation of alarm, the sagacious face of "the master," as, placed at his knee, by the foot of his exalted chair, he lays his hand on our head, and kindly pronounces us "a fine *brood*,"* and says we must not be afraid, as he will let no one harm us. Gathering confidence from his friendly condescension, we soon grow trustful and almost familiar. And then what an exertion of judgment and memory takes place, between the time we can certainly distinguish the letter O, "round like the moon," till we have learnedly mastered the "Reading made easy." Here came to be committed to memory "The Shorter Catechism" of our Church of Scotland, at the rate of a question or two a day; first singly, then with scripture proofs attached; a psalm, or portion of one, repeated from memory every Monday morning; while our lesson reading was the Scriptures, first through the New, then the Old Testament. And well I recollect the great interest excited in a class of about a score, standing all around reading "verse about," through a course of three or four chapters, with the full liberty of trapping the reader at every wrong expression, and taking his higher place; the same vigour and anxiety in spelling in classes words from memory, as given out by the teacher, and the emulation in every exercise, particularly in a fair-written copy.

* *Brood*, a Scotch word now obsolete, signifying child.

Here an anecdote may be worth noting, as it illustrates a principle of the mind so prevalent in more mature life by no means creditable to our common human nature. We imitated our teacher in writing particularly slow, which, though perhaps a good mode for beginners, kept up an awkward stiffness in the writing. I was at *half-text* when the master declined to mend my pen, observing that it was still good enough. This I felt an affront, and, in petulance of spirit, set about to convince him by writing my copy very quickly and more carelessly than usual —determined, in case of a challenge, still to blame the pen. When I presented the half page for his examination, he immediately called up the oldest lad in the school, who was far advanced, and superior to us all in everything—the son of our landlord's factor, and cock of the school. Sensible that I had written too carelessly, I felt alarmed at the uncommon proceeding; when he laid our copies both down to my superior, saying, "Look at that, and say whether you are not ashamed to let a *brood* like that beat you." The free dash I had carelessly given to the writing had produced a cast of improvement beyond expectation, of which I was not then sensible, and Scott felt keenly affronted; the consequence of which I felt out of doors, when there was no play-fellow strong enough to deliver me from the terrors of his revenge for this unconscious offence against his pride. In later life I have observed that I might have met with much of this treatment had I not exercised a necessary and easy caution in evading every visible cause of it.

Mason's spelling book, with eight rules for syllabic

pronunciation, gave the high finish to my grand *course of education.* Ague, small-pox, measles, &c. (so prevalent and severe in this south of Scotland in those days of wet, marshy, and unimproved clay soil) interrupted in their turns my school attendance, and about my ninth year it was considered necessary, as nothing better seemed attainable, that I should tie about a small leather apron and commence with my father his craft of a shoemaker. My parents thought that time might improve their circumstances, and that I should get to school to my arithmetic at a future period, which, like most things of future hope or promise, never arrived. My mother particularly had a taste for education; and had circumstances possibly permitted, it was signified as her desire to have had me qualified for a clergyman, or some such literary profession, but supreme necessity imperiously overrules all.

I may here observe that though I was doomed to lose my mother before I was able to ascertain or appreciate her taste or constitution of mind, yet, from what I can recollect of her whole way and manner, I am led to conclude that her heart must have glowed with the feelings and sympathies peculiar to the poetical temperament, corrected by a strong impression of moral responsibility. Her perceptions were of the clearest, and her sensibilities of the most delicate and acute order; even her softest look was the most penetrating in reprehension. There was little need of coercive measures with her children. She could have melted our hearts by the tenderest expression of reproof. I have heard these qualities of hers since dilated on by individuals who had ability to perceive and appreciate them. Nothing seemed to delight her more than my attempts to con her over a lesson of scripture, or to repeat a psalm, or anything of the ballad kind common in those days.

My father once brought home from some town a copy of "The Gentle Shepherd," which had been bought at her request; and while he sat reading it to her, spinning at her wheel,* though I understood not a word of the matter, I saw my mother was electrified with delight, occasionally suspending her work, and involuntarily dropping her hands idly on her check-aproned lap. Here was a scene for a painter, perhaps as truly poetical as any in that sweet pastoral itself, and my mother was perhaps as interesting a female figure as even the Peggy of Allan Ramsay's imagination, although she could claim no alliance with what Allan or others would, in the language of their day, have called *house* or *family*, being only one of the five daughters of a blacksmith in Roxburgh.

I may observe that while there is a positive honour in belonging to the house or family of those who have been remarkable for the quiet faith and virtue of their lives, when, in a religious point of view, the

* Down to the beginning of the nineteenth century, or a little further onward, to about the end of the French war, when steam-loom power and machinery came into general use, spinning lint yarn on the small wheel and woollen yarn on the long wheel was the occupation that filled up all vacancies of time left from other necessary employments, engaging every country woman's earnest attention early and late. Throughout my mother's married life she was accustomed, when at all in ability, to rise very early, by five or six o'clock, even in cold winter mornings, for the purpose of spinning yarn to provide clothes for the family use. The *boom* of her large, and the *birr* of her small, wheel were music to my young ear on awakening in the mornings. Handloom weaving was then a thriving occupation for men throughout country villages; now a *done-up* business.

blessing of God descends, according to promise, upon the children of the just, who are taught to love and fear Him, yet that blessing is not always attached to earthly inheritance—to the possession of lands, houses, goods, and chattels, which articles are often the portion of minds qualified to enjoy nothing of a higher or more intellectual quality or character. It seems indeed a law in our nature to claim respect and authority upon this principle of notable descent, and also to concede the same to others; yet no principle seems more liable to abuse, since many we see are so degraded in sentiment as to worship any fellow who can claim much earth, or seems otherwise rising to estate, although on the ruin of others. And this they will often meanly do, even though his wealth may have been accumulated from the plunder of their own fathers. I like to respect the man for his moral worth, not for his clay soil or fine clothing.

And so, agreeably to my view of the case, my mother possessed all the real honour which house or family can confer.

CHAPTER II.

A WORD on my father's family circumstances—how he came to that spot, and managed to exist upon it—may here be proper to account for my position.

My great grandfather, John Younger, was lineally descended from Younger of Haggerstone, in Northumberland; so that I might trace family as far back as any duke in christendom were it worth while so to honour men who have had too much world-disqualifying honesty or too little of the Border-raid principle to rob, thieve, and secure to their descendants lands, cattle, and other plunder. But I do not conceive it would do me any honour to prove my ancestor Percy's flagstaff-man at the battle of Chevy Chase! where he may probably have had the honour of getting his bowels warped amongst the fetlocks of Douglas's war-horse, to his exceeding great *glory*—more particularly as the rude proceedings of savage life are fast failing to produce any interest in civilized society, and the memory of those feudal times is dying away in the distance into uncertain dreams, while the fables and lying novels intended to support them fade also, and will make but a slight impression on the improved intellects of the coming generations.

Well, we find our great grandfather, John Younger, with his "loving spouse," Isobel Collingwood (most likely of the family of the great Admiral), from fellow servants in Pringle of Stitchel's house, came to be tenants in Stitchel Mill farm, there, from clod and dust, propagating a numerous family of sons and daughters, all of whom they somehow contrived to educate well for their condition of life. While Henry, the eldest, became factor and land steward to the then Sir William Scott of Ancrum for that estate and the barony of Longnewton, John, his brother, my grandfather, bred a gardener at Ancrum, went in that profession to seek fortune in England; married a Mary Yates, somewhere about London, who before her early demise had to him two children, a son and a daughter, who were by their father, at the time a widower, sent down to Scotland to be kept by grandpapa and mamma till their father should further pursue his purpose of bettering his fortune before his return. The expiry of their lease of Stitchel Mill caused the old people to retire and live with their son Henry at Longnewton-Place House, to which they brought along with them my father, then about four years of age, a brisk little fellow, amusing the village children with his sharp London accent. The old people dying soon afterwards, were interred in Longnewton churchyard, within the walls of the old church then standing, their feet close to the easter gable end; and their place of rest may still there be distinguished by the raised mound from the rubbish of the old wall. Let us speak of my grandfather first, and come down by regular succession. He had pursued his gardening about England to advantage, till, in the course of some years, he had realized about £900, when he wrote his brother Henry to purchase for him some plot of good land, as he intended to come home and commence nurseryman, as people were then beginning to show a desire of inclosing the then open country with thorn hedges, and he might realize a fine business by furnishing them with plants of thorn, and forest, as well as fruit, trees. The land was selected, very suitable, of the fine croft lands about the village of Ancrum, and the price agreed on. Nothing was wanting but his further letter of final agreement, when, in place of this, he wrote that he had made another marriage, and broke up his capital in some stupid speculative attempt at commencing a brewery in London, when, being taken in with his first bargain of the vats and barrels, he was unable to go forward with his project, and all finally came to nought, so that, I suppose, he returned to his gardening.

Had his first nursery scheme been effected, my father's earliest prospects might ultimately have been considerable, as this occurred just prior to the time that the weaver of Hassendeanburn, Mr. Dickson, commenced that fine nursery business there, on the very smallest scale, in his cabbage garden, by following out which that family has since realized a vast fortune.

At that time, about the year 1760, my father informs me there was no plantation in the country here, nor fence, except of drystone dikes about gardens, or those reared of turf for march enclosures of estates, and farm fences; and, except about a stationary laird's old mansion-house, there was not a tree between Longnewton House and village all along that beautiful range of ten miles down Tweedside to Springwood Park, near Kelso. My father then used to ride along that height by Rutherford without let of tree or fence, save two turf march dikes, easily got over.

My father having an aunt then married at Oxenham, then a kind of village Border pass, to Walter Rutherford, who, besides keeping an inn, carried on the business of a shoemaker to a considerable extent, and with a far-spread moorland fame in his line, kept six or eight hands, my father was apprenticed to him by his uncle for five years.

From the mirth and cheerfulness of his situation amongst these young men and the young people of his master's first family about his own age, the time flew lightly by, while he became an excellent workman. And his father's death occurring at London before the expiry of his apprenticeship, he continued with his master four years more as journeyman, during which nine years he had the folly, or credit, or glory, such as it was, of keeping the pass against all Border competition in putting the stone, wrestling, and jumping.*

When he became of age and experience to commence for himself, he did so, with his uncle's advice, at Longnewton. That village, then in a state of decline from its original, was still considerable, and was a feasible enough situation for a tradesman, taking into account the agricultural population around it. In short, he there found plenty of feet requiring comfortable shoes, though too little money in circulation to pay for them.

* He died lately at ninety-four years of age, having kept sound in lith and limb to the last.

Shortly afterwards he married Jean Henderson, my mother, from Roxburgh. One of the small village farms by-and-by becoming vacant, my mother advised the taking of fourteen acres for as many pounds of yearly rent, from the idea, no doubt, of acquiring milk and meal for her rising family. This did not turn out a judicious speculation, as two occupations, each requiring particular personal labour and attention, go not well on together. They kept a cow, sometimes two, and a pet sheep (and *Pet Nanny* was little behind a Highland cow, quality and quantity of the milk considered); but then the horse market, where my father was evermore cheated with cheap worn-out *hiphalts*,* kept him horse-doctoring and skinning continually; while the best of his days were exhausted in draining, ploughing, and tugging through the day, and shoe-making half the night without due rest or intermission. However, being of an excellent constitution, he wore well!

I was the youngest of their six children, two of whom had died in infancy, and my mother had fallen into a weakly state of health before I saw the light; yet still, over and above her household employment, she grew lint, and carded and span late and early to keep us clothed, and, excepting for the frequent days of the most excruciating headache, was, in spirit and in temper, cheerful to the last. The youngest of my three sisters was five years older than myself, and, as the only son and youngest child, I was, in spite of my mother's philosophy, a favourite.

The village at that time consisted of about five or

---

* "Wrung or sprained in the haunch or hip, so as to relax the ligaments that keep the bone in its due place."—*Bailey*.

six more small farmers, renting from thirteen to thirty acres a-piece, of what, in more ancient times, had constituted the croft lands, originally let in small *feu** acres; and these, with some twenty other householders, then constituted the population of the village, where, although the forms of religious duties, in a family-devotional point of view, were kept up more strictly and methodically than now, yet I cannot perceive that the population were any more correct in their dealings, or that they more pointedly fulfilled their moral obligations. One-half of them were as careless in endeavouring to pay for their shoes as any class of people can be in any age or country—of which the following observation (though perhaps rather delicate to express here) is fully indicative. One winter night my father and mother had talked over their affairs at full length, which led them into a free review of the circumstances, and consequently the characters, of all their neighbours —how they had by them been ill-paid and ill-treated, cheated, and disappointed through the piece, till, removing to bed from the dying embers of their peat fire, she sealed up the disagreeable review with this emphatic reflection—"'Deed, Willie, I think there's nae honest folk left now in the world but oursel's *twa*."

My father's uncle, Henry the factor, with whom he had been partly brought up, dying about that time, left my father his executor, to collect and pay his accounts and debts, which ran so near to a counter parallel that he never could clearly ascertain from

---

* *Feu*, in Scots law, a possession held of a superior on payment of a certain yearly rent. French and English, *pif*; Latin, *feudum*.

recollection whether he was a half-crown out of pocket or into pocket, but that it was within the half-crown the one way or the other he never had any doubt.

CHAPTER III.

ALTHOUGH it would be trifling and tedious to go through all the school-green sports or amusements which excite such interest in the breasts of youth as to cause them "awake impatient with the gleam of morn"—the clubs and shinties, tops and peeries, bows and arrows, jumpings, swingings, wrestlings, racings, with other vain *stravagueries,* such as our solitary summer moonlight attempts to trace and catch the *craik* (landrail) amongst the dripping wet green corn or clover; yet nice observation might perhaps trace much of the future character of the man as developed in these childish exercises, as perhaps something of future ruling passion and principle may be here formed, or take at least the bent of their future peculiar direction. This is a little in consistence with Wordsworth's idea, when he calls the child the "father of the man," though perhaps not calculating on the same strict degree of phrenological principle. However, with the greatest pleasure I took the restless trouble of introducing in their turns, and leading the alternate change and fashion of these, as well as various other games of amusement on the large school green, not only through my school-boy term, but of a year or two after I had assumed my leather apron, not having been required to sit very close; or rather perhaps it might have taken more trouble to watch and confine me than my work was worth. Yet all the while some ideas of a very different character were so strongly impressing my youthful mind as to be still distinctly remembered, and may, to you who delight in the minute philosophy of mind, be even worth remarking.

The most unaccountable thought that then frequently, perhaps daily, shot across my mind, affecting me with a deep thrill of inexplicable feeling, was, what is all this world? or, where would we all have been if the world were not? For I felt such a tenacity to life that I could not agree to calculate upon non-existence. This idea, as then felt, cannot properly be conveyed in language to the informed mind of manhood, nor conveyed at all, except through the medium of similar memorable recollections, being then simply a strong impression on the untutored mind and feelings of a child. Only, if I knew it to have been a pretty general thought of youth, I might conclude it certainly to indicate something of an innate proof of the immortality of the soul, although we have still more acknowledged proofs at hand. It has had one effect, however, of all along preventing my wonder at finding people influenced with eccentric ideas, hopes and fears, beliefs and opinions, which seem to be taken up and held agreeably with the exact balance between the degree of their general information and the strength of their intellectual conception.

The next thought that then followed in general succession indicated how strongly the youthful mind clings to the natural protection of some guardian—

what will become of me should my father or mother die? for I thought that though I even were grown up to be a man in the great world, I could not in such case live comfortably, if live at all. And brisk of heart as I then was, I sometimes became suspicious that I had not the strength of mind, the fortitude of scorning fears in danger, the confidence to dash forward at visible risk like some neighbour boys, and my own suspicions that perhaps I might naturally be a coward, gave me more pain of heart than even occasionally to be called so by any playmate.

Though I could have climbed trees with any one, yet no effort was necessary to make me calculate on the folly of risking life by incautious footing on slippery precipices; or if I had occasionally risked, I was, on extrication, exceedingly vexed at my own stupidity. As, above all things, I had an innate feeling of aversion to quarrel, I used to exhaust every effort of my rhetoric and ingenuity to settle school-green disputes by fair concessions and reasoning of matters, though, to do myself justice, whenever worn* up and impelled to resistance, I was always successful in securing honourable victory. So I cannot be out-Wellingtoned on the defensive side of warfare, were there honour at all in it, which I cannot see that there is, any more between men than between bulls, mind and muscle being alike the gift of a common Providence over which we have no control, the favour of which Providence should call up no feeling of pride, but rather a sublimed sentiment of gratitude to the beneficence which could as well have withheld the favour, and left us weak and helpless.

* *Worn*—Scotch, driven into a corner, from *wear, weir.*

My first idea respecting the shape of the earth, from its being said to be *round*, was that it was flat and circular like a large table, and full of hillocks, and could not extend very far beyond the upland ridges which bounded my prospects. I used to trouble my friends with interrogations respecting its boundary at the edge; but their answers generally tended to confound my notions, without in the least clearing up the matter. I could get no light into the dark mist which I supposed hung continually over the gulph in which the verge of my circle terminated, and horrible was the idea of falling over, as I supposed the poor little fellows like myself must sometimes do in their morning or evening rambles, who were so unfortunate as to live near the edge.

It is not easy to account for ideas attached to certain sounds; for while the names of India, Egypt, China, and Japan conveyed no idea of great distance, I conceived *Birgham*, a village not twenty miles distant, to lie so far off as to be on the very verge of creation!

But the idea of how we came all here, by what power, or for what express purpose, was the most awfully puzzling, as much so to me as to any great infidel philosopher, if such there ever were! And my world on that scale was as interesting and difficult to account for as is now our relation to the star *Sirius*, the phenomena of gravity, centrifugal impulse, or the acting cause of our earth's diurnal motion.*

---

* May our earth's diurnal motion not be caused by the sun's rays poured constantly upon her like a stream of water on a mill-wheel?—their force, of course, greatest at the equator, and lessened in proportion as her diameter contracts towards the poles. And may not the sun have a greater degree of attraction for the colder particles of her atmos-

I looked out on nature around, on the snows of winter, on spring, bud and blossom, and on the animated creation, beast and bird, with wonder and

phere and surface, drawing them under his influence, than for those which are constantly receding back into night, as already rarefied by the intense action of his rays of light (since it certainly is the forceful action of his rays of light poured into our atmosphere which excites heat by electric motion?)

Agreeably to this idea, the moon's having little or no atmosphere may be the reason why she makes only one diurnal revolution in the time she runs the whole circle of her orbit (27 days, 7 hours, 43 minutes, 11 seconds, 5 of our time.) Therefore, it is not unlikely that the time in which she so slowly performs her diurnal rotation may be in exact proportion to her quantity of atmosphere and surface on which the sun's rays can act, in comparison with that of our earth.

May the above cause not have also a tendency to propel and keep up the action of centrifugal motion? And why not this be a general law in the order of nature? even extending to comets, which, as they travel outwards towards the extremity of their elliptical orbits, may thus gradually lose projectile force until reaching the point of distance where the influence becomes inoperative; the sun's attraction—still proportionately active—will cause their return again within the effect of this propelling principle.

If, according to the received opinions in astronomy, the projectile motion is simply the effect of a *first* impulse, without any more continued application of force, and if, as is asserted, the speed of a body is necessarily increased as it nears towards its perihelium, in counteraction of the power of the attractive principle as increased by vicinity, how then should bodies which move to such immense distances, in orbits so extremely oblong, return around such comparatively sharp curves, unless they had lost somewhat of the effect of the originally propelling power, which, if continued in equal force, must of necessity give them still a greater tendency to proceed straight forward, in proportion as their *gravity* becomes the less effective, agreeably to their extension of distance?

It appears that there must necessarily be a propelling power of motion constantly kept up, as well as the already acknowledged power of centripetal inclination, and that it must also be invested in some second cause, standing in strict analogy with all the rest of the works of God in creation and providence.

It is not enough to deny such *second cause*, because philosophers have yet failed to discover it.

You may think the foregoing note is impertinent here; still it is curious as a thought! And as all we enjoy of life above the capacity of the beasts of the field is this active power of thought and of reasoning—conception and communication—let us, by all means, be so rational as to improve and enjoy the pleasure arising from the free use of such sublime faculties.

admiration!—listened to the redbreast and the lark with rapture, enchanted with the cheerful liveliness of their manner, traced by degrees into their haunts and habits, found their nests, attempted to tame their young for the purpose of making them my most intimate companions—a most preposterous idea, of course, to think of gaining a reciprocity of affection, or any rational satisfaction, from the slavery of any creature to whom God had given wings, with the whole earth and air for a habitation. This is as ridiculous as it would be to confine a winged angel, had we the power.

When just old enough to stray a field or two in breadth from the village, I took a particular delight in observing the lark ascend the air in song, and used to lie on the grass, enjoying the fine flutter of his wings and his circling motion, till he became a mere speck in the upward distance. The first time I perceived him in his descent drop from a considerable height I ran in on the place, thinking him fallen dead, but observed that he had recovered his wings near the ground, and, skimming around, was alighting at his pleasure. I soon perceived that it was the bird's very frequent habit, and thought that if I could fly I would also delight to do the same thing. The first opportunity, I took out a young play-fellow, who, I supposed, had not made the same discovery. We lay down on our backs, when I fixed his attention on the lark in air, remarking to him that it would be an awful thing if he should suddenly lose power of his wings and fall from that height. The bird, descending by degrees, at last suddenly folded his wings and dropt head-foremost into the lap of earth, when my fellow seemed much struck with the event, while his wonder was increased by my anticipation of the catastrophe. I enjoyed his astonishment with satisfaction, until discovering a new pleasure in undeceiving him. And so light is our share of what we may call positive pleasure in this world, that I cannot recollect of a moment of my existence in which my capacity of immediate enjoyment was more filled to perfect gratification. My delight might be as great, though not so pregnant of essential consequence in its results, as was that of Sir Isaac Newton with the glowing idea that struck him on the fall of the apple.

What then puzzled me to very great uneasiness was an idea arising from mere childish ignorance of the appetites and habits of wild animals, birds, and insects. From their figure and plumage I conceived a high delicacy of taste and constitution quite irreconcilable with their apparent means of support through all seasons. How they should subsist on mere accidental gleanings of coarse raw field materials was past my comprehension. Yet their lively sprightliness seemed ever maintained.

But some succeeding severe winter storms, particularly that of the beginning of 1795,* threw a little more light on the matter, as their pressure brought a variety of field birds into the village barn-yards and cottage shelters, which were too easily caught, as "necessity's sharp pinch" made them forego their usual watchfulness. Hence, by strict observation I began to trace a little further into their

---

* That storm came on on the 15th January, 1795, and lay about thirty inches in general depth of snow till the 5th of April, while deep-blown wreathes lay here and there till the middle of June.

appetites and particular habits. And here began to open on my view a new field of inquiry suitable to my taste. This was a vague sort of arrangement in my own mind of that small portion of the animated creation with which I had become acquainted, into kinds and classes. It was impossible I should have then conceived that any one had ever before done so as a study, far less that books had been written on the subject; but about that time a neighbour boy had been presented with an octavo volume containing the plates with a description of 300 animals. I could not conceive that there was another copy of the same in the universe! And had I been heir to India, I most certainly had given him the rights in eternal entail for that particular volume.

Having no other regular course of means to arrive at second-hand information, I was driven back on my own resources to discover for myself. Therefore, it was some years before I had gained knowledge enough on the subject to be enabled to strike out into a rapturous hymn, rather of heart-swelling sensibility than of outward expression, which may be thus embodied.

How beautiful is nature in all, and particularly in this respect, that, with so little apparent labour of preparation, all creatures find subsistence! Stray where we will into the wilds of nature, field or forest, even amidst apparent sterility and savage wildness, the field tenant is supplied with general abundance for the necessities of its nature. From the pelican of the Egyptian wilderness to the smallest bird that wings our Scottish moors and morasses, all is healthful and cheerful under the eye of heaven, and even in the depths of winter enjoying generally the simple requisites of existence, if not a full supply of feast. Such are the provisions of God, that even these twittering small birds, which one might suppose too fine to exist on anything less than what man would account a delicacy of atmosphere and provision, briskly disport in health and pleasure amidst the branches of the rude forest, flitting with the rapidity of thought up and down the trunk of the rough, and apparently barren, fogged fir tree. Yea, see the bold-eyed *redbreast*, with appetite as fierce as the lion, prey as voraciously; and, when the earth is bound over with frost and buried in snow, the small *wren* flisk avidiously through the tangled roots of bank-growing trees, or below the eaves of house and shed, securing her prey in their close retreats with unerring choice—banqueting as assuredly as the fanged tiger, or the eagle of Ben-muich-dhui.

Though this was rather a subsequent conclusion, yet pleased with gaining any such as I considered definite, I then began to find a new pleasure, which was this:—When any individual object in nature perplexed me to form a precise idea of, as regarding its production or use, I began to shift from the perplexities of deep reasoning, always sure that it would be for some grand purpose in the economy of nature, and that at some future leisure I should have it considered and found out some way or other. And, as but few of the newest objects, or the ideas they excited, occupied my attention at one and the same time, it did not occur to me that the task to get to the bottom of all that was mysterious in nature would be either very difficult or tedious.

On such reflections when a-field alone, I used to get very brisk in spirits, sometimes taking longer and firmer steps in ideal imitation of manhood, for I thought that by the time I should come to be a man I would have all things found out. What a folly to ever lose the present by anticipation of the future; for I was then more of a man, in the true sense of the matter, than I have ever found myself since. However, in this light-hearted way I got over many a staring difficulty, winding up my conclusions with this, that all things in creation were certainly very good, answering their end so well, and withal so curiously; that it was a very grand world, and so delightful to live in, only for people being liable to trouble and uncertain death; for every recurrence of the thought that all must die, and I myself, used then to give my heart a touch like a slight electric shock, which passed over my nerves, to toes and fingers, in an instant. And though what I frequently heard regarding a future state of existence, where all the believing, good livers in this world should be made so very happy, I felt to be all very well; yet then I was so pleased with this world, and all my friends, and most of my play-fellows, that the thought that I might die before I could get to the other, was so awful that I always dismissed it as fast as I could, just in the common way. It never then entered into my mind that old men could be ignorant of these things that so puzzled me to find out and account for. They must know them all, only I was diffident in making inquiry, thinking they did not wish to be troubled; and when I did venture a curious question, their answers were generally indefinite, or delivered in words of which I could not comprehend the import, and there I remained in the mist of my ignorance. Indeed, I never began to suspect the weakness of full-grown men till about thirteen or fourteen years of age, and then it was only suspicion, for I had never the face to put it to the test on my own score till about sixteen. I saw often, indeed, enough of weakness, and sometimes what I even knew to be gross ignorance, in men, but thought this to be—what, to be sure, it partly was—individual. I had now, however, got all my then visible world pretty well settled, partly with what I thought I understood, and partly with what I laid over till I should get it more fully considered. And so I felt more comfortable than I have ever perhaps done since.

CHAPTER IV.

PREVIOUSLY to this time I had marched over the hill-tops with "Jack the Giant Killer" in his seven-league boots; braved "the Græme" with "Sir James the Rose;" wept with robin redbreast over the sweet little "Babes in the Wood;" and travelled in friendly sympathy with poor "little Whittington" by the side of his waggon! Yet none of all my early readings, not even the shepherd David mastering the blustering Goliah in the valley of Elah, had half the charm to my soul of the fable of the "Lion and the Mouse," one of the selections in our school-spelling book. The magnanimity of the lion in granting "the little suppliant's" petition of mercy, at the time when he had his paw upon him, and "just about to put him to death," for the trespass of having run over his body while asleep in the forest: this showed such greatness of soul as could be excelled by nothing but the fine gratitude which filled the whole heart of the little mouse. When afterwards the lion had "fallen into the toils of the hunters, and, unable to extricate himself, set up a hideous and loud roar," nothing could equal the charm I felt in repeating the following sentence:—"The mouse hearing the voice, and knowing it to be the lion's, ran to the place and bade him fear nothing, for he was his friend!" The idea here naturally arose, whether I would like to have been the lion or the mouse. Oh! there was no comparison at all; the mouse was decidedly the hero in my imagination—to feel strong in those powers which enabled him to bid the great lion "fear nothing, for that he was his friend!" And then such a glorious opportunity of showing not only his gratitude, but his ability to do what the "king of the forest," with all his terrible powers, could not accomplish—to "fall to work with his little sharp teeth," to "gnaw asunder the knots and fastenings of the cords, and set the royal brute at liberty."

These two principles of generosity and gratitude, bearing such a mother and child relation, show so well everywhere, when in an active state of juxtaposition, that, like attraction in the material world, they seem to hold together the framework of moral society. They take hold of the affections with such a kindly sympathy that it is difficult to imagine any state of moral life beyond the circle of their influence.

People may occasionally wonder at a boy's impropriety in breaking out in a burst of laughter when they cannot see a cause why. But I durst not then have risked my gravity in the church if the idea had crossed my mind of seeing in imagination the little sleek mouse nutting amongst the forest grass, and pricking up its ears to listen when it heard the lion's roar, and then the glance of its clear round eye as it scampered off through amongst the withered leaves in hurry to the place on its errand of gratitude.

About this time an affair occurred rather harassing to our poor family—though I say "*poor* family," we were yet considered amongst the most independent of our villagers. So much for comparative greatness! My father and John Wallace, a village tailor and small grocer, had taken it into their heads to purchase a quantity of growing corn at a sale in the neighbourhood, and "billed" for the price conjunctly and severally. The corn had been sold to defray some debt of suretyship, but exposed in the man's own name, and not under a legal form of bankruptcy. The farmer showed them afterwards that he personally held their bill, and warned them of their danger in being cozened or threatened over to pay the money to his prosecutors. He then for some considerable time absconded, when the law agent for rent or other debt demanded payment from them as of bankrupt stock; but shuffling the matter regarding their *bill*, pretending that *he* held it, only could not lay his hand on it at the moment, but that his receipt should be good when the bill might cast up. This they knew to be all fudge or palaver; but, so terrified for law, would yet have been puzzled how to act, had not their inability to raise the money at the time determined their course of conduct. They *must* decline payment; therefore were forthwith prosecuted by the law agent as if upon the bill. Then followed officers with "charges of payment," which, being disregarded, a considerable time elapsed; then a new *charge* repeated. A considerable time further, and then letters of *horning;* and long after, when my father was soothing himself that they had settled down, arrived at last a messenger with his captain and band of *beagles* to haul them to jail. This roused the village to a spirit approaching personal resistance, which was overruled by the cool advice of the messenger, together with that of Mr. Scott, then the Longnewton land factor, who was duly respected as the poor man's friend, when they forthwith proceeded jailwards eight miles to Jedburgh. Then one of the outfield farmers, who was known to possess some small *pose* of original capital, came in to comfort the families, with assurance that the *gudemen* should not lie long in jail, although he should strain himself to do some very great thing! The appearance of friendship and sympathy works miracles of comfort in such cases, and a flock of neighbours assembled in the evening, and sat till late at night with us, which was agreeable, as going to bed under bolted doors, and our father out or in prison, was not to be thought on. I listened, and heard him coming at last; knew him in the starlight at some distance, and ushered him in, when he related the adventure thus:—

"Jean, I'm here yet, safe and sound, lass. Od, I gae yon chaps a sweat in to Jeddart. If it hadna been for John Wallace, poor falla, I wad have had mair fun wi' them still. They thought I had been meaning to run awa', and got into a fluster. 'Come on,' says I, 'or ye'll never see mair o' me.' However, when we gaed in, Reid, the lawyer, had gane out, and we were ta'en in afore blind Fair, his neighbour. I had charged John Wallace not to speak ava, if possible, for fear he should stammer out something that might gi'e them hopes o' making mair o' us, or some clause against us; for I wasna sure what they might still ha'e i' their power—and thae lawyers are just as bad as mad dogs when they get ought to bite at. And then Peggy's greetin' when John came awa', an' his ain fears thegether, put him in sic a pickle that I was fear'd he might just promise onything, or maybe agree to even sign some new bill to gar them let us hame th' nicht again. However, he managed brawly through the piece, for when the lawyer attacked us, I took speech in hand mysel', an' aye carried on, to prevent John frae the necessity of opening up. 'What's the case?' says Mr. Fair. 'What's brought you here?' 'Your officers have brought us against our will, sir,' says I; 'and for perfect nonsense after a', for can onybody think o' us as either able or willing to pay our *banking* corn twice o'er?' 'Paid it already, have you? Who did you pay it to?' 'O, Sir, Willie Brown claims the payment himsel', and wha else should we ever ha'e thought o' paying it to but the man belang'd the corn?' 'That's very strange,' says he; 'but I maun go down to the Black Bull, where Mr. Reid's dining, and inquire about the case; you will stop here with the officer till I return.' So we sat there starving, for we had been sweating afore, and I thought John Wallace would sigh his heart out wi' fatigue and suspense thegither; and I turned sae wearied mysel' that I wad ha'e been glad to ha'e shifted position, even if it had been to the prison—for a lawyer's room aye brings me i' mind o' Daniel's den o' lions. However, in he came at last, halden his hands out afore him, as blind folk 'ill whiles do. But I saw he had gotten mair than us in his heid sin' he gaed out, for they wad be bousin' an' drinkin' in the Black Bull Inn! 'Well, gentlemen,' says he, 'I find there is nothing for it but that you must agree to pay the money or go to jail.' So I got up to my feet, an' shuffled about to let him hear, for his room floor was newly sanded. 'Weel,' says I, 'we maun just go, then; there's nae help for't, it seems——.' 'Stop a minute,' says he, 'and consider yourselves a little; the jail is a bad affair; you'll not like it.' 'I daresay that,' says I; 'but poor folk get sae muckle i' this world that they dinna like that we're just used wi' misfortunes o' a' descriptions, tho', to be sure, we never were 'prisoned before——.' 'Had you not better agree to pay the money?' 'To pay the money twice ower,' says I; 'the thing's clear nonsense! It's as ridiculous to ask it as it's needless to expect it! I can tell you, Sir, we're ower glad to think o' gettin' it once paid, an' a' the powers o' earth couldna raise the sum frae us twice ower—no! though ye wad roup us out o' house an' harbour to quarter wi' the peaseweeps.' 'Well, but you will assuredly find the jail a worse concern than quartering wi' the peaweeps, and you may lie there long enough—indeed, until the money be paid.' 'Od, Sir, ye'll no get a shillin' o' siller by keeping us jailed till doomsday.' 'Well, but, after all, the prison is a horrid place. It will be much better, and, indeed, I would advise, to settle it otherwise. See what money you have got about you; we will take that in part, and give you some time yet to pay the remainder, and let you home to-night to your own firesides.' 'Money, Sir; I have just a sixpence by mere chance, and the chaps brought us away without our dinner; and I'm wearyin' to get out o' your room to ony other place ye like to get a bottle o' ale and a *bap* wi' this last sixpence, as I'm growin' mad wi' hunger, and our wives an' bairns 'ill be here, a' roaring an' greeting up the causeway, in an hour or less, an' the Lord knows how I'm to pacify them!' 'You speak all yourself; have not you a neighbour here?' (For John Wallace had sat as cosh as a mouse in the corner, poor falla.) 'Ou, aye, Sir, John Wallace is here.' 'John, you are very quiet.' 'Yes, Sir,' says John. 'Have you got a family, too, John?' 'Yes, Sir, a wife and three daughters.' 'What money have you got about ye now, John?' 'Not a farthing, Sir.' 'Oh, nonsense! You must have got some pound or two, certainly.' 'Not a farthing, Sir.' 'You are poor devils.' 'Yes, Sir,' says John, 'we are that.' 'Go home to your wives, an' be curst t'ye.' 'Thank ye, Sir,' says John; 'good night, an' God bless ye, Sir.' So off we came, and hump-backed Mungo, the beadle, showed us to the door, an' harkit—'Od, Will Younger, ye're a queer falla.' 'Od, I'm as queerly dealt by wi' you Jeddart crew,' says I. 'Weel, but,' says Mungo (for he's a sleeky body, yon Mungo), 'I ne'er saw Mr. Fair sae match'd i' my life.' 'He hasna met wi' mony active folk, man, Mungo; but he couldna find the bill!—that was the grand point o' the hale farce. But nae mair aboot it. I'll gi'e ye a bottle o' ale the next time I come into the market, and maybe tell ye the main curiosity o' the hale story; for we're far ower late the night; they'll be in an unco pickle at hame.' Sae John an' me left Jeddart just laughin', an' I'll assure ye we've let nae dirt stick to our heels i' the road hame. Od, we persuaded oursel's that we just fand the air finer after we came past the *Scaa,* up by the Woodhead, an' heard the miresnipes booming in perfect freedom east about Ancrum Moss.

"But, save me, Jean, woman, I'm cuttin' o' hunger an' drouth baith. I'll warrant, John Wallace an' Peggy's bedded by this time: her an' the bits o' lassies were out list'ning for us at the head o' the liggate as we came up, an' I ne'er saw folk as daft happy as when Peggy grap John a' in her arms, an' grat like a bairn. An' sae may we be, an' thankfu', too. It's e'en better here than Jeddart prison. Gude keep us out o' their black holes.

"An' now, Sirs, I maun thank ye a' afore we say gude nicht, for we never ken how we're likeit by our neighbours till some bit strushin' like this takes place. Misfortunes are no just sent for naething; for I believe our hearts would grow case-hardened a'thegither an' it werena thae bits o' spouthers to stir up our kindlier feelings now an' then."

So the neighbours retired, and then my mother began telling him of auld Jamie Gray o' the Greenend coming west and vowing so heartily to have them released. I saw the tears start to my father's eyes while he observed—"Jamie's a kind auld heart, Jean, tho' he's nae great philosopher mair than mony o' us; but the heart's the thing, woman, as ye've aften said yersel'. I think we'll be nae mair fasht wi' this affair, ony way, for yon crew sees we ha'e nought they can make a prey o'." And they never were, and William Brown soon appeared himself, after having taken a sail across to America, and again returned with their bill in his pocket, when they got the money scarted together somehow, and had their bill recovered and burnt. Thus was likely a small reversion saved to William Brown of the wreck of his general substance, so foolishly risked by that kind of suretyship, against which his old friend, Solomon, had given him such a friendly caution, "Be not surety for a stranger, lest thou smart for it." And all are strangers of whose honesty and circumstances we are not aware.

About this time harvest wages to reapers had somewhat suddenly advanced so high as to a shilling a day for women, without victuals, which my mother conceived to be little short of a coinage, and, supposing herself stouter than for some years previously, she would set out to earn a few shillings before commencing our own little harvest. She went to Bewlie Hill, about a mile's distance, where the farmer was in want of hands, and paid his *day tales* every evening. The second night she found only sixpence remaining of her first day's deposit, in the place of her shilling. On inquiry, my father confessed how he had disposed of it:—"Indeed, Jean, I was this morning sae dowie my lane, an' sae glad when Piper Hastie drappit in wi' his drones, an' his auld haveral stories, which were mair amusin' than even the din o' his pipes, that I enticed him to sit a' day, an' couldna offer him less than that saxpence. I have aye been fond o' the pipes sin' that rascal, Jamie Allan, the grand Northumberland piper, used to come about Oxenham when I was a 'prentice there." My mother discovered that he had bespoke Hastie's company for next day also, providing she was to be out; so she good-humouredly took the hint, and declined her distant hard labour, resolving to rather bear him company herself, and spin at home, than sweat herself out of doors to pay the piper.

Old Hastie, who was then town piper in Jedburgh,

wore a coat with red neck and sleeves, gun-knee'd breeches, large brass shoe buckles nearly the size of your hand, and a three-cocked hat. Thus, with the pipes he cut an alarming figure on his sallies out to the country villages. On first sight of him the children screamed with affright, then would sigh themselves down into the quietude of secret suspicion, until catching up some idea of the ludicrous, they would almost go wrong-headed with bursts of laughter. I can yet almost feel the terrors of his first entrance, and imagine the horrific grunts of his drones, while he began to inflate his bag with wind, which seemed like a stuck pig snorting for breath. It was ten at night; he had left the Place-house (where good old Mr. Scott of bagpipe sympathy used to lodge him), in dudgeon and terror of rats, of which rats he gave us an alarming account, having heard them squeaking in every corner and cranny, felt them nibbling about his ankles in the chimney seat, and actually seen a large white Muscovy one dash out by a broken pane in the kitchen window. And then his huge wind-bag must have been eaten to tatters had he remained all night, as it was of leather, and just newly mellowed with best goose grease, the "dreepings" of some then election dinner, and had no cloth covering at the time.

After he had bolted from the Place-house kitchen, Mr. Scott's lads, who, by means of a white kitten, had raised the rat alarm, from ticklings of fun and kindness together had followed him down, and after an hour of his roaring pipes and clatter by our fireside, entreated him to return. But an idea once impressed is not so easily erased: no, the white kitten was most certainly of the Muscovy race, if not itself personally imported. And in relating his history of rats, he took such mouthfuls of his subject that his lips seemed as if literally made of piper's old bags.

But, alas! "O why so oft should goodness wound itself?" My mother's discretion cost her that night the credit of her whitest blankets; for, laying the old piper in her bed-clothes, which were kept sacred to hospitality, he rolled up his pipes, bag and all, in the blankets above him for fear of the rats of his imagination—which bag imparted that election-dinner stain to her best white *unlaids*,* which never could, by any chemical process then in the knowledge of country practice, be taken out.

Though this to one in her situation was a serious matter, as much so as the burning down of his old Palace at St Petersburg, and the scourging back of his slave troops by the brave Circassians, is at present to Nicholas, yet my mother had more philosophy than this Emperor of All the Russias, for she showed no symptoms of running mad about the matter. And there is not so much disparity of interest in matters thus taken in comparison as may at first sight be supposed—that is, when our view is taken from a proper point of distance—that point where philosophy can throw her sunlight beam upon the object with proper effect. As at one time, when the fate of empires seemed in a great measure to be hanging on the influence of two leading characters in our British Parliament—opposed in principles, and

* *Unlaids* are blankets made of wool from sheep that had not been previously besmeared with tar, &c., to repel disease or the winter cold.

a view of interests, and the world agape in wonder at their eloquence, or what might be the probable and ultimate effects—Burns, our poet, observing from the true philosophical point of distance, remarked—

> "The tulzie's hot 'tween Pitt and Fox,
> And our good-wife's twa birdie cocks."

This was a view of the matter worthy of the philosophy and satire of Burns.

CHAPTER V.

IN our village at that time, nearly next door to my father's, lived an old woman, the widow of a respectable farmer, with her only remaining son, the youngest of her dispersed family, on whom she depended in her age—her two oldest sons having gone out a negro-whipping to Antigua, in the West Indies.

In sympathy with her present state, in comparison to the better days she had seen, my mother used to treat this old woman with rather particular respect. In return for this marked kindness—as I was the youngest of the family—old Jean Harkness used to show me no small kindness, and sometimes took me in to amuse myself about her cottage fireside, where generally in the evenings assembled, along with her son, four or five other young men to amuse themselves with cards or draught-board.

Her son, John Thomson, was what was then reckoned a good scholar, having had a longer course of school education than generally fell to the lot of our villagers, and was therefore by his neighbour young men esteemed very profound, knowing, and witty. Though now, from recollection, I cannot perceive that he ever took any pleasure in reading, except the newspapers, which were then all in a blaze of the bloody revolution in France—Robespierre, Billaud, Collot d'Herbois, Couthon, Danton, St. Just, Carnot; the guillotine, and the "Tree of Liberty;" Pitt, Fox, and the flight of Palmer, the Kelso newspaper printer; the trials of Muir, Gerald, and others; Liberty, Slavery, Reform, Revolution, and the hurry and horrors of war.

I could comprehend none of these matters, and as my father seemed to take no notice of them, I wondered at the interest and enthusiasm of these men, whom, around old Jean's fireside, I considered the finest, kindliest beings in the universe. They were all staunch Republicans, yet I believe they did not perceive, any more than I did, that it was the hydra of fanaticism writhing beneath the knife of infidelity, while rational religion wept over the wretched extremes of human frenzy. Although they could justly estimate the excited reaction of the human mind under the insufferable pressure of absurd aristocratic tyranny, yet I doubt whether they had Christian humility enough to prevent them from glorying in such revenge.

As this John Thomson turned out a desperate character, involving many companions, particularly a family of these his neighbours, in his unlawful practices, to their general ruin, it may be proper to introduce him here more fully, and then to touch on the sequel, in its proper place, agreeably to point of time.

John was bred a stone-mason, and wrought throughout the summer season, hewing stones at a quarry at Troneyhill, some three or four miles distant; but all the winter he lay off idle, and along with two of these companions, sons of a neighbouring farmer (James Gray of the Greenend), poached with the gun throughout the winter to a considerable extent. About that time, differing with his quarry-master, he had gone on a summer jaunt to the south, ostensibly in search of employment, where, as it was afterwards understood, he had fallen in with some forgers, and learned the art of making false coin. This false coin in some succeeding years became so plentifully mixed with the plain, worn, old silver currency, that people all around, however desirous of money, durst hardly receive silver in payments.

This had been for some years carried on in old Jean's cottage before the villagers, amidst all their scantiness and poverty, suspected a mint so near their own doors. The false coin was clipped out of copper plates, rounded smoothly, and watered over with quicksilver. And so John lived freely, though he had discontinued all visible employment, and only poached for pleasure, which poaching, between his long jaunts of sometimes months from home, appeared to be his only out-of-doors amusement.

The whole party who tried the gun yielded the palm of superiority, for shooting and other adventure, to the youngest of the farmer's sons before mentioned, who, indeed, was the most personable and athletic fellow I have ever seen in life, always excepting James Douglas, your cousin, then of Nisbet. Reports occasionally reached our village of their depredatory prowess, as exercised around the country at a distance, in which this young man, George Gray, out-did all casual competition, such as acting the gentleman on the moors, where, with one dog (a trained collie) and gun, he achieved feats of slaughter equal to what we now see boasted of in the newspapers by lordly shooting parties with all their "appliances and means to boot." He was of a social turn, and of all the rest the most kindly in his attentions to the village youngsters, and twice or thrice as he passed by with his gun he allowed me to follow with him across a few fields, which in his search for hares he did not, like the mediumly skilful shooter, traverse all over, but took only at points and corners, going directly to the spot, and finding the hare within a ridge-breadth as certainly as if he had seen her take her seat there in the morning. Sometimes, indeed, in fresh, grey weather, he would have circled round about the hare in her form, closing so gradually without lifting his eye from her, until by degrees he bent over her, seizing her with his hand. In fact, there seemed a sort of magic in his address, or, as it might now be called, animal magnetism. And by one method or other he would have cleared a wide track of lands in a day, which track he would not cross again for a month or two. When out far a-field, he would have given any one a hare who would return him the skin. Old David Ross, then innkeeper, St. Boswells Green, who had seen more of this young man's manners than was known at Longnewton, told me long afterwards that amongst other feats, George called on passing, one fresh-weather winter morning, to cross by Dryburgh ferry for the Mertoun lands, a distance of five miles from his own home, and again calling on his return in the evening, told out from the bag below his plaid the skins of sixteen hares and rabbits, which he had shot and stripped in the course of five or six hours, leaving the carcases in the fields; the skins being about that time suddenly raised in value from sixpence to a shilling a-piece, and they then sold very little higher with the carcase than without it. It hurt George Gray's sport then very little for any old trusty protector of gentlemen's game to follow him a whole day. He would have shot over the Maxton lands all the day a field's breadth a-head of David Fiddes, General Carre's old faithful keeper, labouring and sweating after him until lost in the shadows of gloaming. Yet he and his brother Andrew were caught together by the fox-hunters, and fined of eleven pounds, which, in place of deterring them, made them only increase their diligence to gain as much over as to cover that loss.

I then panted eagerly to come at some imitation of these their amusements, draught-board and playing cards, which articles I contrived to manufacture for myself out of wood, paper, and so on. But then paper was an article by no means to be come at in anything like a sufficient quantity for my various means of consumpt. A sheet of clean white paper was then a great prize, and stirred up in my mind ideas as comparatively interesting, though less mischievous, than the map of Europe did in the mind of Bonaparte at the same time, or a very little afterwards. And then the desire to have shot birds or crows in winter about the village stackyards, but a gun or pistol was un-come-at-able; therefore I must be content with moulding and re-moulding at a small imitation lead pistol in the blacksmith's shop, for which accommodation I must repay him by using the fore-hammer in striking out his nailstrings—whenever he was at leisure to work up his broke iron to that purpose and could procure—no stronger hammerman. Thus occasionally in his service I laboured with patience, pride, and vigour, until I became somewhat handy and expert in it. Indeed, the old man's smithy was the favourite winter-evening rendezvous for a number of our young villagers, whenever the moon did not allow us light for our favourite play of "bogle about the stacks" in some of our village stackyards, or of sliding with pike-staffs on the meadow ice, then sheeted all around the low situations of the village lands. In the smithy, when free of horses, we played at "blind man's buff," or, clustering on the forge hearth, told stories of ghosts, bogles, robberies, and fairies until we often durst not go home alone in the dark.

About this time a village farmer's servant, on his journey to the Lothian coal hills, had found a military pistol which a horseman had dropped, with which he astonished all our village youth. We had never seen such like before, so clear, strong, and beautiful to our imagination, and too new-looking to have yet shot any men! So I made agreement with him for a single shot of it, and charging hard, he added my lead pen, with some small pebbles for shot, showing me how to *vizie* to hit a small board placed out in the barn-yard. I aimed and fired, but heard not the report, only came to myself staggering, the pistol lying glancing on the ground, two of my fore-teeth knocked by the brass butt into my throat, and a gash in my forehead by the doghead of the lock. The stupid young fellow, who had slunk with the rest of the lads behind till I should fire, came up, and examined his pistol, quite charmed that it "had stood such a shot," and praised it, as David did Goliath's sword, "there is none like it."

Thus was experimental philosophy knocked into my skull with a vengeance, yet it had not such a passion-cooling effect as one might suppose, for still "bray a fool in a mortar," &c.—the ruling passion of the hour is not so easily beat out as the fore-teeth; and field sports—shooting, fishing, &c.—become a passion, particularly when learned in youth. Being about the *teeth-casting* age, mine soon grew again.

The before-mentioned sportsman, George Gray, trouted also occasionally, where, with permission, I followed him west to the stream of Ayle-water, saw him angle, and carried his trouts. First agreeably amused, I soon became passionately fond of the sport, as it is called; and then tried it for my own hand—the outfit being a simple acquisition, a rowan-tree sapling, and a fly-hook, with which he presented me; and the first penny I became master of went, not to Margaret Wallace, the village shopkeeper, as usual, for ballads or paper, but was sent a distance for fly-steels, which I made shift to dress for myself, and soon afterwards I became a more dexterous and successful angler than my prototype. But as this latest amusement could only be then followed in certain seasons and states of the water, my attention became divided amongst a variety of pursuits, which each in their turn promised great pleasure.

Three sons of Blythe the joiner's family had each, as they grew up, a taste for limning, which, with the scantiest means imaginable, they industriously amused themselves with, without seeming to relish anything else. The two oldest died as they reached manhood; and Gavin, the youngest, of my own age, a very innocent, *sackless*, thumb-sucking creature of a laddie, seemed to seek no other amusement than "making pictures," as he termed it. He drew to it just like a butterfly to a flower, and though, from the pining state of the simple family, who seemed, old and young, to be living out of their native element, he never had means to get further than a few pence-worth of the very cheapest water colours, China ink, gamboge, and a snuff of vermilion, with a pennyworth of green, yet it was amazing what likenesses of living things he produced on stray leaves of schoolboys' copy-books. He showed some niceties of taste for the curiosities of cabinet work, but had neither bone of body nor muscular energy ever to make bread by anything wherein physical exertion was necessary. It appears to me, on reflection, as if Nature had designed him for an artist who might rival all antiquity, while Fortune inadvertently dropped him on her journey to starve in the desert, where, in truth, "many a flower is born to blush unseen."

I took occasional freaks of painting in imitation of Gavin, but could never contrive to produce any original touch of life like him. Mine were all dead and fearful-looking faces, and never shaped so as to sit easy in their skins; while I could suppose I saw his asses just about to bray, and his sedate cats actually purring. He did just exist on, up to something like manhood, a kind of dwarf imitation of a country joiner, when, to the admiration of all the natives, he was discovered to have fallen deeply in love with a gill of whisky, by the fireside of Bett Melrose, then innkeeper of the half-deserted village, where an acquaintance of mine had frequently perceived him cowering beside a three-footed stool, and averred that it was impossible to estimate whether there was more spirit in Gavin, the living creature, or in the newly-filled pewter gill-stoup, deserted of its lid.

Gavin's father's family becoming soon afterwards all dead or dispersed, he resisted not being taken out to America by a brother-in-law, his sister's husband, and not since being heard of, has likely by this time evaporated. What reflections these recollections breed now in my old age!

> Oh! where fly the pleasures our manhood discards?
> When scar'd frae our youth's haunts by tacksmen and lairds;
> As men we can ne'er get a will o' our ain
> As we'd ha'e could we a' become callants again.
>
> In manhood there's nae way o' livin' at a',
> Thus warpéd in net-warks o' rude landlords' law;
> Our rights of existence we cannot retain
> Unless a' bewitch'd back to laddies again.
>
> The laddie has pleasures that dukes canna share;
> He's born by his nature the wide warld's heir;
> The bounds to his freedoms we're apt to count sma',
> While plain to perceive they ha'e nae bounds ava!
>
> He's lord of a' round him as far as he sees;
> The rivers are his, and the tall forest trees:
> Our lairds may entail them, an' ca' them their ain;
> But our first parents' rights does the laddie maintain.
>
> He's free as the lav'rock that mounts to the cluds;
> Scare him frae the streamlet, he starts to the wuds
> Enjoys with the squirrel crab, nut, bush, an' tree;
> It can spang but a twig or twa higher than he.

Oh! now to reflect on the pleasure, the cool
Half-wading, half-swimming in clear sunny pool,
A-hunting the wee parrs around the grund stane:
What wadna I gi'e to be callant again?

We may talk o' our lang saumon rods, reel, and line;
Write essays on angling our friends may call fine;
But a rowan-tree sapling, lang string, and bent preen
Gave visions to boyhood in age never seen.

Still as in a dream I can see the first flee
George Gray by the Ayle-water kindly gave me;
Such "pleasures of hope" as it rais'd in my breast
Have never by poet on earth been exprest.

"Where was ye a' day, laddie? What been about?"
When joyful I held out my first little trout!
To utter the feeling a' language is vain,
But just it is what I can ne'er feel again,

Except in idea as we rub in life's rust,
Wearing down into age ere we drop in the dust;
The thoughts of a new birth may weel make us fain
Were it only a hope to be younglings again.

CHAPTER VI.

AND now, amidst what was called my work in the shop, and my school-green and other out-of-door amusements, another kind of philosophy slipped in upon my ease of mind. This was to account for the evil arising from the untoward disposition of mostly all with whom I came in contact. What could make people so cross, ill-natured, selfish, and unreasonable? and do such foolish and wicked things, at which even themselves were afterwards so vexed and miserable? And what could have made myself yesterday stand out so bitterly, even though Bob Gray was so very wicked and unreasonable? And what was it that stirred up all my mischief, and made me so obstinate, even when my mother wished to reconcile me? Here was a strange absurdity: how should people be so bad in such a good world? For though in my school lessons, and sometimes at home, I had been reading about original sin, corruption, and perversion of the heart, and every day hearing something of such things either in my father's evening worship or my mother's private conversation, it somehow had never come to my mind as applicable to myself individually. I was certain that, except when in a passion, I loved everybody but those whom I heard spoken of as robbers, cheats, or murderers, who mostly lived far away, I knew not where. I forgave my playmates so soon as they would agree again, yet still what was the sense or meaning of getting into an angry passion? On inquiry, I believed what my mother said about original sin, and consequent disorder of the will, because she said so, but could not clearly comprehend it; for though by the very simplest method of communication such doctrinal points be preached to youth daily, there seems just as it were only a lucky moment when the idea can be taken up by the understanding, and fixed upon the heart and memory as a principle of data for future reasonings. I do not recollect when or how the idea was fixed in me; but it was a long struggle between the belief of the principle and the assent of the will that it should be so, and for several years more I always kept labouring to settle matters in my own mind, and arrange all the apparent anomaly of life independently of such consideration, conceiving two-thirds of all moral mischief to flow from mutual misunderstandings. And, worst of all, I hated that bull-dog spirit that would not make mutual concessions; for even then I considered that the better-informed mind should be conscientious in making fair allowance for honest prejudices, and thought coercive means the worst, or at least the most sorry, way of impressing rational convictions. Indeed, I never through life could bear to act or work under coercive restraint, and in like proportion have ever hated to exercise it. Many feelings and sympathies run in these counter parallels; as, for instance, in the same degree that our ear is delighted with good music will we feel disgusted with bad, and easy virtue will be content with a coarser quality of enjoyment.

Though even then, in school-green playtimes, I used to labour at such reasonings in my own mind till they often became perplexing, I felt as if I should be laughed at to moot them amongst my play-fellows, and was much puzzled to determine whether several of them might not stand privately in my own predicament. I thought it natural that they should, and yet could seldom make any progress in ascertaining that they did. Here was another dilemma: did not every one privately conceive and think alike? It seems natural that they should, yet somehow it appeared that they did not. And what was the reason? This was an insolvable case; nobody could inform me! Even my mother, who, I conceived, knew most things, could make little of it, further than observing that some just naturally had more *rummlegumption* than others, which I afterwards somehow discovered to mean *common sense*. The only ideal solution I could reason out of my main question at last was, that knowledge was a thing of acquirement; that one question rose naturally out of another, and that every one resolved matters agreeably to their degree of perception and information on any particular subject, and that there must certainly be some unknown original quality in the constitution of mind that caused diversity to considerable degrees in the strength of intellect. And when I think of it even now, I believe that it was as good a solution as has to this hour been given by the best philosopher.

The last of these positions is consistent with the present doctrine of phrenology; and the preceding one is the datum upon which the apostle Paul's Christianity and David Hume's Deism seem both to have been founded.

When by divine grace the apostle was brought to understand the scriptures, he believed from conviction. David Hume, in the hurry and pride of his mere human philosophy, slighted the New Testament and that spirit with which its truths must be discerned, taking his view of it principally from the diversity in opinion of its disagreeing professors, rather than from a due consideration of the spirit of the text; consequently he lived uninformed of those revelations of which a yet deeper search in philosophy than that of his or of the present day, on the true inductive principle, will tend more fully to corroborate and elucidate.* I got confirmed in my

---

* The revelations of God, in His message of grace, the same as His revelations in material nature, seem to be adapted to the full exercise of our most reasonable faculties, both alike requiring our cool and minute investigation in order to comprehend them. Many complain that the scriptures are not clear to their present understanding, and that after eighteen hundred years the truths of Christianity are disputable, nor at all perceptible or explicitly demonstrable to their common sense; but they never seem to consider even their own deficiency in the comprehension of language in its various party translations. And far less do they make sufficient allowance for this, that the simple facts of the positive order and organization of material nature, the surface of the earth on which they tread, and which has been trodden over by the foot of all the generations of men, is never yet so investigated as that even the mechanism of its outer coatings can be clearly accounted for or definitely understood, far less so explained, by even the best philosophers of our race. Shakespeare casually hit a good idea when he said, "There are more things in heaven and earth than are dreamt of in your philosophy."

I'll conceive that when, from a more full and careful investigation, under the exercise of a more healthful and mature philosophy, the works of God *in nature*, and the words of His inspirations *in grace*, shall be duly investigated and more clearly understood, they will be found to be the two grand fitting parts of one great whole, perfectly adapted to each other, in their constitution, figures, and proportions, fitting each other as the mind and the body, and productive of one great and glorious end.

opinion by finding that the psalms and other scriptures often bore relation to the affairs and principles of our common life, and that boys who hummed them over as a school task without perceiving this were also often behind in reasoning on even the simplest matters. Some could not even understand how the sudden pull of the string from their *peerie*,* as it darted from their hand, should give it the tendency to whirl, and that the effect was in exact proportion to the impulse.

I felt anxious to ascertain the cause of every little thing, and frequently discovered it; and thus, musing on with my boyish philosophy, I never dreamed of books on such subjects, as, if I had, I must certainly have conceived them fully as much to the purpose as I have since found them.

In this way, however, I rolled on through the day, starting out a-musing here or there around the poor village, vigorous after any variety of pursuit, retiring to sit and work between-hands, with soundest sleep a-nights, and glorious visions of the joy in projected pursuits of to-morrow—just then, as now, the pleasure lying more in the prospect than in the enjoyment, generally more successful in dreams than in my day's operations, particularly in trouting, for the day trouts were never so large as the dream ones, which I felt tugging to the bottom of the deep, curling pools. And thus yet below the storms of life, I understood nothing of the machinery that moved the affections of men! The breezes of passion which give impetus to the tide of human affairs, though blowing around, were yet to me im-

* Boys' spinning top.

perceptible; as hitherto I had been like a bird frisking by the sunshiny hedges, and taking shelter for rest and security with the wild daisy, beside

"The random bield o' clod or stane;"

and though often, like little Whittington when "his father and mother had died, as ragged as a colt," of this, I doubt, I took as little care in proportion as my mother took much "with her needle and her shears" nightly; to my discomfort in one respect, as, the more torn and loose in my garments, the more free I felt for play of muscle in all exercise, of which I took to the extent of my whole strength daily. But clambering trees was the clothes' particular ruin, and there was no getting whistlewood, clubs, bows and arrows without much climbing, besides the pleasure of swinging on the topmost branches, or looking thence around—the only way I could ever take of rising in the world, although I was then vigorously in love with life.

Our family life was, upon the whole, a kind of redbreast nest concern, both alike on nature's common, only that robin could pick his worm or his grain with more security and less responsibility, having no landlord's rent on his head. For this he sang his note of praise to heaven the whole year throughout, except an occasional month or two of winter's frost, and could scarcely even then keep silent.* He had, to be sure, another advantage over us, wings with which to fly away at pleasure; while we had a smart rent to pay for fourteen acres of land, flooded all the

* I should like to have robin-redbreast's recipe for keeping up the spirits even now; and what hurry of circulation in these small legs of his keeps them from freezing is past my comprehension!

winter for want of a large main drain, some time since mined below ground at the landlord's expense, then only a weedy ditch bordered with green willows.

Farming improvements were not then generally begun on our Border. Mr. Low was just commencing land-doctor, projecting for the country gentry the improvement of laying six or ten small farms into one. Then, indeed,

> "Tenant bodies, scant o' cash,
> How they maun thole a factor's snash."

My father's "gear" was actually "poinded," more by way of giving colour to the ejectment than for the purpose of securing the trifle of back-rent, when old Adam Small—bless his memory!—(then tenant of Belses Mill), never conceiving the full extent of their lordly plan, spoke to Mr. Low, proffering to pay my father's debt up to the instant, and be his future security, providing he would let him continue in his tenement, enforcing his argument with my father's industrious habits and family; also, how he had improved the spot till now it would pay by cross-draining with his own hands. But the factor on horseback rode away without further reply than the emphatic "No," thrown in a spittle manner half over his shoulder. So Willie Younger's crop was rouped on the ground by order of the Sheriff, when it luckily paid the last shilling—law expenses and all—that the world could claim of Willie, though with as little reversion as justice generally will permit, and his heart was light from considering himself the freest man in the universe! with

> "All the world before them where to choose
> Their place of rest, and Providence their guide."

Not exactly so my mother. I well recollect her sublime submission to the Providence of the case, while the natural gleam of indignation stood only half repressed in her eye. To comprehend the ideas floating on the surface of a baronet's fancy under the tuition of a land-doctor expounding his projections of improvements was what my mother could not then be expected to calculate on. No, her genius lay on the other side. She was more like a partridge startled in the field where she had fondly nestled her yet half-feathered brood in the centre of a few acres, which she supposed to belong properly to the Maker of heaven and earth, God's bounty to man, of which the proprietor was the dispenser; and the new factor's order to quit bore too near a resemblance to the tremendous mandate in the first garden to be heard with indifference by a mother so rich in affection and so sensitive as mine was.

"Some natural tears she dropt, but wip'd them soon."

The shadings of this rural picture were a little deepened by some trifling incidents, which, in spite of our country philosophy, took the appearance of aggravations; as, after the ejectment was effected, and four or five of these small tenements had been thrown into the Place-house portion of farm, the whole was let to one of their own number, the preference to whom seemed to proceed upon our Church-creed definition of the principle of free-grace election; as it was not considered that he was chosen for any superior worth in himself, either in quality of faith or manners, or even superior ability to stock his new large farm, being conceived the barest amongst them; but generally acknowledged as by far the best qualified to cast glamour in the eye of the new factor, who, I yet believe, acted honourably, so far as his perception of individuality of character qualified him to distinguish amongst the group as strangers. And duplicity is not so easily detected below a very smooth surface; therefore, a man of such description is generally in such cases preferred.

From want of determination where to move, and still amongst their old customers, with some small debts still due to them about the place, they felt inclined to linger in the village; and, as the house they occupied was then to let singly, they took it still for the coming year, and became simply cottars, retaining nothing of their former stock but some three or four barn-door hens, a fowl considered indispensable with every ancient cottar. But the green, gowany plot around the door was now laid into the surrounding field, and closely ploughed into the sewer—that spot where formerly fed "Pet Nanny," who now, like her of Skinner's old song, "The ewie wi' the crooked horn," was literally "sell'd awa';" and the parting tears of her friends we children again dried. But before my mother had got considered how to dispose of her fowls, our new great man came stalking across, gun in hand, over the new-sown field, and at once showed both his dexterity and new-fledged consequence by shooting my mother's whole three hens at one smart crack. This, from being done without even previous warning, was worse taken than all else, as she declared in her lowest serious tone of voice that, with all her perception of character, she could not have divined that Tam Smail would have shown so much of the emperor so early in the commencement of his auspicious reign—the more particularly as he had borrowed eggs (which was the same thing as begging them) to help to scrape up a luncheon to grace himself with the new factor on one of his first visits to the grounds.

These matters, so frivolous in comparison with the crash of empires, were yet as great in our little cottar family as the loss of North America just previously was to the British crown; and I am not certain but that, as viewed by a superior intelligence from some higher sphere, it might be considered the greater *moral* event of the two.

However, my father's attention being thrown into one point—his shoe-making—they began to entertain hopes of yet being able to exist on by diligence, more particularly as my three sisters were now fit for service, and two of them already engaged out to farm places, while the youngest was left to do our house-work, to let my mother remain diligent at her spinning.

CHAPTER VII.

How sweet were my hours of childhood's day,
   How the sunny time flew by,
When I wove fond dreams of bliss to come,
   Nor felt the weight of a sigh:
O then my locks were the blackbird's wing,
   My young limbs were lithe and free,
The thrill of joy dirl'd o'er my heart,
   And the world seem'd made for me.

To emotions new my youthful soul
   Soon expanded like the sky—
The lovely flame of the rainbow's hues
   Then shone on my raptured eye.
The hills so blue in the distant view
   Rais'd thoughts I could not express;
With love of nature, and love of life,
   Love of the power to give bliss.

Then far, far west in the tinted clouds
   Fancy fondest dreams would weave
Of heavenly fields and bowers of love,
   Where the sun might sleep at eve.
And young hope then shed her glow o'er all,
   My heart danc'd light in its beam;
Winds sang the songs of life to my ear,
   Music of love sang the stream.

But now my locks confess the cold touch
   Of winter's approaching grey,
While the sweetest of my life's spring flowers
   Are withering all away;

And memory through my soul still wakes
  This fondly reflective power;
Oh! where are the joys that thrill'd my heart
  In my life's young morning hour?

WELL, I would rather now again be the simple laddie on the old school-green at Longnewton, or gathering slate pencils by the Ha'-hill at Aylewater, than be lord of all I can see in the wide prospect from Tweed bank-head here, at fifty-five years of age, along with some of my old associates (reduced, of course, from our present bulk and world-contracted selfishness), back into the fine, free, fairy-footed activity and social warm-heartedness of six and nine years old. For most minds acquire a steel magnet quality from the friction of a forty years' grinding on this whirling planet, and often a north polar sort of gravity by fifty, with a Greenland bearish selfish-sullenness of disposition. Two or three of my still living old companions, who were poor, and ragged as colts, or even as myself, on the school-green, are grown wealthy, lumpish, lazy, and selfish—not at all the same free, bright chaps they were.

Oh! the days of youth were such that even in a condition where family-poverty pinched of bread, the ills of the period seldom gave more of trouble than was necessary to correct or rectify the excess of pleasure that touched the young nerves so thrillingly. And then on occasional misdemeanour the responsibility was a mere household affair, parental clemency being so propitiable by juvenile ingenuity.

The greatest evil of those days was an occasional heartache, which it required a burst of tears to relieve and make sufferable; when blamed on some unworthy suspicion of some misdeed, for which one would rather have been scourged than have entertained the low, wretched idea, and, indeed, to have been beaten on suspicion was the preferable infliction, as it more effectually excited the animal resistance, to relief of the heart's bitterness.

The open and generous affection of the young heart is often miscalculated on by the cold, pedantic morality of age; for, notwithstanding the truth of all the evil springing from the original attaint of the heart in hereditary succession, men yet act very absurdly in blaming the young on mere suspicion; they consider not the ungardener-like rudeness of wounding the best buds of proper feeling in the young heart. Keep a child long on that level of slavish suspicion and consequent coercion, and, ten to one, you will work him down till he become the very thing you at first very falsely only suspected him. A slave can get acted only a slavish part. Yes, the proper nurture of youth is not yet at all well understood, nor the best mode of education promulgated. How should we suppose it while we see old men dying fools daily?

Dr. Johnson talked of beating as the best mode of infixing education. However wise he might be esteemed, this was a coarse idea. A bull would hardly as a parent or tutor agree to such a mode of calf education, and the beaten calf would get sulky and revengeful, even to goring. But the doctor was of a political party who have always had a desire for coercive government in all things, as if men should not at least attempt at a general rationalization. If a man suppose his own wisdom so superior as to give him an exclusive right of property in the government of another, why not then govern so as in reversion he would wish himself to be governed? This is seldom, perhaps never, done; it having always been an assumed case with the State party, of which the doctor was an approver, that the man of wealth has a right to coerce the man of poverty, or the man of strength to bear down the man of weakness; for, talk of it as you will, it amounts to nothing more, and is subversive of all life upon moral principle. I do not think much of a frivolous statesman, or great land proprietor, greedy or arrogant, claiming such privileges, which have hitherto been far too simply conceded; but that Dr. Johnson, a learned bully, as poor as seclusion from natural right of property and a voracious animal appetite for victuals could make him, should have entertained and propagated such absurdities in his common philosophy, shows the weakness of our general nature with a witness! But the doctor was then hungry for a pension from "the powers that be," as well as for fame, which too many authors have been before his time and since. It never seems yet to have entered one of their minds, as a primitive moral fact, that every man born into the world has a natural share of right to the means necessary to support that existence which his Maker has given him, and this whether he have any aggrandizement forming a charter claim to the soil of the planet or not. Nor do they seem capable of reasoning that if *any one* have a right, *legitimately*, as they term it, to overrule and coerce another, every other man must have it as naturally and as *legitimately;*

and hence, even on the highest ground, there is no getting out of the level upon which this rational conclusion comes to be inferred, that necessary government for the general good must be adopted and exercised by the general suffrage, or that otherwise it must always be liable to the objection of being a party usurpation, or if *all* are unqualified to choose what is best for *all*, how shall a part of that *all* be specially qualified, not at all to speak of every individual right? For, as to natural right, any man born into the world, although the child of a wandering beggar, has as just a right to his natural food from the fruits of the earth, according to his just proportion of labour for the general production, as has the *legitimated* heir to an entailed dukedom. The right of the former to untaxed daily bread is even more, for we see it asserted in the general law of nature, even "the fowls of heaven will vindicate their grain;" and hence, while the right to acquired property and legal succession must be held inviolable, yet laws of *entail*, and prohibitory taxes upon entail product, such as corn and other staple necessaries of general subsistence, so affecting the right in the former case, must, in a moral point of view, be considered as in direct opposition to the ordinance of God.

Very early in life I felt antipathy to what appeared to me as the mainspring of general action—a strong, selfish principle amongst mankind, and a rude desire towards retaliation of offence or supposed aggression. That spirit was so disagreeable to my feelings that the dislike of it became a fixed principle before I knew that it was an enjoined precept and distinguishing characteristic of Christianity. The dislike with me felt as constitutional and intuitive, for which I not only never thought of taking credit, but glad when not laughed or hooted at for the *unmanliness* of its exercise, often feeling a false shame for what I perceived others thought of me, even in their visible ignorance. And such feeling is a hard task for the young mind to despise, particularly when an implication of pride of singularity is insinuated as the cause.

But what in the time of youth, or, I may say, through life, has given me particular vexation and most unhappy feelings, was when I found that I had, through inadvertency, given offence in saying or doing something unguardedly, to the pain or just reprehension of others, or in unwittingly committing myself with a proud person of avengeful spirit, or to feel misunderstood by those whom the ill-usage or hard pressure of the general world had rendered suspicious; and, when words failed in explanation, wanting the power of wealth, what Sir John Falstaff would have called "the testimony of an angel," to convince them of the honesty of my intentions. In youth, under such unfortunate casual occurrence, or when the selfish ways of individuals, influenced by unfeeling pride or the spirit of oppression, filled my heart with bitterness, I would have shrunk away to solitude, giving vent to feeling in a gush of tears over the apparent wreck of human affections.

It is perhaps a necessary pity that we should thus harden by age, and assimilate with the coarser affections. Necessity makes fashion, and fashion is servilient to necessity; for yesterday it gave me no uneasiness to be told by an acquaintance, while discussing the propriety of passive acquiescence in the state of manners as they may prevail at any given period, that he had no doubt I would be a very imperious tyrant were I placed high in the entailed aristocracy. I excused his observation on two grounds—first, that I know the human heart is deceitful as well as assimilative, and recollected the words of the ancient Jewish king to the prophet, "Is thy servant a dog that he should do this thing?" and yet came to do it; and, next, that I conceived my acquaintance had not a proper understanding of this positive principle, that in proportion as the mind resists oppression to its own enslavement will it scorn all false desire to the oppression or enslavement of others. And I have never seen a petty tyrannical master, as farmer, tradesman, or mechanic, who was not the most fawning, cringing, lick-foot thing alive with his landlord or other proud, assuming superior. Hence my friend's mistake ran principally on this, that he was very honestly estimating my mind and principles by the measurement of his own. It is a pretty general way of calculating, but than which nothing gives a more uncertain estimate.

Many think this sort of submission is humility of character: it is no such thing; it is the snake spirit of tyranny crawling helpless and disgustingly at the foot of Ambition's ladder, when it would fain slime itself up by the spokes if possible.

Is it humility to concede that power of assumption to every Caligulian slave of all lust, and to pay him that bending devotion of soul and body which is due only to the Maker of heaven and earth?

The Author of the pure doctrine of Christian humility came to *save*, and by precept and example to reform, the world from such errors, and their sad, their ruinous, consequences, from this as well as from every erroneous principle of the corrupted mind under the habits of false, earthly tuition. He taught to "give honour to whom honour is *due*"—to render to Cæsar his penny, his image and superscription, the dross of earth to those who claim it as their portion, but to reserve the devotion of the heart and soul to God.

Whilst, therefore, we respect every individual virtue in every individual person, from king to wandering beggar, we must proportionally disrespect every vice, though decked out in Babylonian scarlet; and true humility lies in assimilating our heart and conduct under Christian precept and example to this proper feeling—always aware that to worship the ideal majesty of an assuming neighbour of our own species bespeaks a degradation of mind unworthy the proper dignity of humanity. And of all degrees of improper servility, that of worshipping the presumptuous swellings of our own little heart by claiming the abasement of others is the most disgusting to all who can feel as a man; therefore, whoever can think and feel as a sensible man cannot be guilty of such presumption.

Slavery to our own heart's lusts is indeed in some degree a more degrading and unwholesome servility than even to be the slave of a West Indian fortune-hunter. For as to the heart to which I have been referring, in nothing are we more apt to err than in our partial conclusions respecting its nature and affections. Indeed, we feel much bewildered when we cast our thoughts inward in endeavour to fathom the bottom of our own human heart. Here is a breed and concentration of affections, sympathies, and propensities, under the impression of principles pure and polluted, and these often in a state of inexplicable effervescence, a complete *melee*. "The heart knoweth its own bitterness;" but who is so simple as to conceive that he knoweth his own heart, "deceitful" as it is, and "desperately wicked?" We are often misled regarding this matter by reasoning from feeling, under any present casual impression; and while the finer sympathies are awake, we are apt to doubt the apostle's asseveration, that "from the heart proceeds murders, adulteries," &c.; for when on the calm, unruffled surface of the heart all is smooth and placid, and sensitive of the softer touches of mutual affection, the mirror-surface reflecting the seeming sensibilities of even a flower, conceiving that flower to breathe some expression of heavenly beauty —even language!—we are apt to forget the effect of such storms of passion as tide it into flood until the settlings at its bottom are stirred up in the fitful commotions of lurking principles—like Macbeth's witch-pot, full of unsightly ingredients; the ghosts of former joys, the blackening corpses of abortive ideas; the sad wrecks of former pearls of thought tumbling up from the bottom amongst the sickening images of decaying hopes. Here comes the stir of momentary madness, too often swelling over in reckless daring and ruthless deed.

It is perhaps the surest sign of ignorance, folly, pride, and presumption to say that we can ascertain any correct knowledge of our own heart, or the various phases to the full extension of the human faculty denominated by the name of heart. It is much in this case as in some other views of nature, where we may discern the outward appearance of her productions, and little more is discoverable by the best human philosophy. We know but very little of her secret workings. From a fine combination of vegetative principles springs the primrose amongst the grass in all its silent, simple loveliness; and what can philosophers say of the matter? For who has been favoured with a peep into Nature's private chambers? or detected the subtle influence in its germination of principles? What chemist can discover the necessary combinations, not to mention the sympathy of their attachments? And what can all mankind perceive regarding the production of a blade of grass? not to say the form of parts, and the infusion of the principle of life into that active mass of matter required to the production of a gnat? Indeed, human language is inadequate to convey even our faint perceptions on such subjects. For

> There's a poetry in Nature which words can ill express;
> A loveliness of feature, an easy sort of grace;
> The play of light on leaf and stream, the shine and lovely dipple,
> With soft-reflected tints of gleam on curl and on ripple.
>
> The poetry of thought is flown ere words can it impart,
> For words can never full express the feelings of the heart;
> Impressions cannot be convey'd as on the soul they're made,
> Nor can the painter give the hues of quivering light and shade.
>
> There are sympathies of soul which we cannot bring to birth,
> Apparently too fine for the climate of our earth;
> These are the seeds of virtues that bear no date of years,
> But wait the time to bud and bloom in more congenial spheres.

CHAPTER VIII.

MY DEAR FRIEND,—I doubt I have already drawn too deeply on your patience throughout these last seven chapters of childhood, having dwelt on them like one returned from a life's weary pilgrimage hanging over the scenes of infancy and the grave of parents, loath to leave "that greenest spot on memory's waste;" yet, as I have no other means of accomplishing the purpose with which I started, of explaining the growth of mind, in its branchings out like a forest tree, under the influences of that soil and climate on which it was casually cast, I will venture yet to proceed, the more particularly as I am feeling a certain pleasure in thus recalling the memory of those scenes which so interested at the time, and which to me can never again return.

To proceed, then: I was now fully ten years old, though not yet properly begun to find out my situation as a being cast on this world of mutation, where, whether learning fast or slow, we have only a very fleeting and uncertain time allotted for the rational occupation of this life, or for inquiry after, and preparation of heart and affections for, whatever other scene of future existence may eventually be awaiting us. And as then, in our family capacity, we were settling into a still more circumscribed sphere of action, yet it was with spirits cool and reviving, and nothing immediately apparent to distract our minds, or draw us out of our narrow limits.

The first bestir was in the winter following, when a person from a neighbouring village came and commenced an evening dancing school in ours, which raised the spirits of all our youths; and a request from my sister Anne and myself to attend this for a month was successful with our father through our mother's acquiescence. She had certainly the true art of recommending propriety to youth by putting the harmless amusements in their proper place amongst the more necessary duties of life, thus making instruction in duty and religion so perfectly agreeable to the feelings of youth as to appear what it really is, a high privilege conferred on our nature.

I was then allowed to try my hand at making a pair of slim pumps, and to skip over the old barn floor at shantrews "on the light fantastic toe." This was indeed a new and spirit-stirring exercise, which amused through the month, and for some weeks afterwards, but of which I never became so passionately fond as many of my compeers seemed to be, although occasionally afterwards I delighted to make one at a New Year's dance or harvest-home merriment, feeling a pleasure in seeing so many fresh faces shining cheerfully through the dews of active excitement and social mirth—yes, and lovely faces, too.

One strange trait in my mother's character I may mention here before I come to the last sad scene in regard to her, and which I can never to this moment fully account for. Notwithstanding all her power of comprehension, foresight, care, and caution, she seemed no way scrupulous in allowing me to roam at large, even into dangerous situations. I might occasionally go alone, and wade the long summer afternoon in Ayle-water, often enough stuck fast in the gullies of the stream above the whirlpools at such risk as that it appeared a miracle to myself how I should possibly have got out. Or I might have swung like a squirrel on the topmost boughs of the great old trees then around us without incurring more of her censure than a simple observe, "Laddie, ye'll climb till ye fa' and fell yoursel' some day, and then ye tear your claes to tatters." Whether her care had actually been so slight as to me it appeared, from her not understanding all the risk, from her want of a like experience, or from her actually not seeing personally the greater part of my risks; or whether she had higher notions of that instinct which we naturally possess, an involuntary tendency of muscle to grasp for self-preservation; or whether her ideas of an active, protecting Providence amounted to something bordering on fatalism, perceiving, like the sailor in the song,

> "A sweet little cherub who sits up aloft
> To watch o'er the life of poor Jack,"

I cannot say; but most likely her mind was imbued with a mixture of all these together. However, that trait in her character seemed at variance with her almost second sight in regard to whatever came under the character of moral caution; for the least appearance of any dereliction of moral propriety, such as a seeming desire to possess what was not my own, even a longing eye to the merest trifle, could not pass her suspicion and well-timed reprehension, and bad words were, above all, with her intolerable. She, no doubt, had perceived that spirit of impatience and vigour with which I then went on every pursuit, and it must have cost her some address to restrain or direct it in the manner she did; for whether her restrictions were laid in the shape of commands or persuasions, or simply as recommendations, it is not easy to define; but generally they were pleasingly effective, and without any apparent effort on her part, which is wonderful to me even now, considering the ardour of my mind at the time. For throughout youth, when an idea of some new object had struck me at night, I felt as if it were impossible to wait till the light of morning to have it pursued; and then no dull vacuity of mind, but always vigorous on some main object in view. In nothing have I changed more than in this; for by the time I reached manhood I became all patience, perhaps too passive, and could forego the attainment of an object in distant contemplation for seven years, with very little solicitude of spirit in regard to the issue for or against. This change I conceive to be as much owing to a contraction of the feelings under the cold chillings of life, as to the influence of a moral and reflecting power of mind.

At this time I was, very unsuspectingly, on the verge of the greatest change in my whole life, and which seems principally to have cast the die of my life's fortune.

Being all settled down into a very contracted sphere of life, yet in comfortable circumstances in regard to present family health and hopes for the future—more particularly as for a month or two past my mother had got much relieved of her very frequent excruciating headaches, when we would all have taken our turn in holding her head, pressing it till our arms and hearts were like to break—her spirits rose a little with her better health, when the reading school was again projected for me, and to start also with arithmetic. I had scarcely got entered and commenced with my multiplication table, in the beginning of March, when one morning my sister and myself were awakened by our mother looking on us with an eye in which calm, melancholy reflection seemed mixed up with some serious alarm. She had risen in her apparent ordinary health, kindled the fire, and set about making my father's breakfast to let him get proceeded on an errand from home; but while talking comfortably together she declined answering him in turn, when, looking round, he perceived that she had seized the table to support herself, and could not speak. It was palsy had deprived her of the power of the whole left side, and while my father had hurried out to bring in a nursing neighbour, my mother, aware of her situation, had awakened us to give her last advice, while yet she felt some small remaining power of utterance. This advice, lisped out rather inarticulately, was in such a calm, affecting seriousness that, though I have long forgotten most part of the matter, the manner is still fresh in my remembrance—"Praise your Maker while ye have a tongue to speak," being the main injunction, is all I can recollect. Her voice then sank down into silence, and my father returning supported her to her bed, while her eye hung over us in some sort of prophetic solicitude until it sank in shadow. The disease pervaded her frame, and on the tenth day she expired. It was then that new and strange sensations seized me: the awful solitude of her lifeless face; my father in grief; my three sisters sobbing around—the youngest of them five years older than myself; the ever and momentarily recurring feeling of the want of her to whom I had ever still applied in all states of matters—in all distress; the being from whom I felt as if I could not possibly stand detached and yet still subsist, as if from her I yet solely held existence—here was distress of a new kind, and she was not to appeal or apply to. My uncles and friends assembled to her sober funeral. I gazed, awe-struck, and felt as if bereaved of heart. They shook my hand, and gave me sixpences, calling me a good boy, inquired whether I could read, hoped I would behave well, and remember the many good advices my affectionate mother had given me, do my father's commands willingly, and be thankful he was still left to protect me.

It is forty-two years since at this date I am here writing, and the sound of the first spadeful of earth which was thrown in on her coffin has maintained the particular tone of its sound on my ear, different from all other sounds, to the present hour, and that in despite of all the noise of folly and idle din of life to which one's ears are subjected. But mine was (what every one may likely suppose of their own) a very particular mother.

You must have seen Longnewton old churchyard

sometime in your youth; yet no one who is not interested in it by attachments such as mine would pay the least attention to such a lonely, deserted spot. Though in former times it had extended down the declivity to the north, it has long been contracted into about a quarter of an acre, fenced by a thorn hedge, out-faced by a drystone dyke, with a large ash tree or two at its east corner, left standing out of respect to the spot when all the large hedgerow trees around the place were cut down and rooted up, with a younger one or two also left on the south and west points. The area of the old church, where lies the dust of my mother, is on the very north side, where the rubbish of the old church wall forms the latest-drawn north fence, and that area is still a hollow place, where on occasional summer visits I lie down, and find myself alone, secluded from the world, and, as it were, in a double sense, reclining on my mother's lap. The place is so solitary that a few years ago a partridge had her nest amongst the long grass on my mother's bosom! My father discovered it and told me. I am sorry she was startled from her numerous hatch of eggs. I blessed the bird in my heart, and thought how such a circumstance would have affected "the poor inhabitant below" in her life-time—for she was of a reflective, as well as of a nestling, nursing turn of mind. On one of my visits to this sacred, solitary spot, I conceived the following:—

THOUGHTS OVER MY MOTHER'S GRAVE.

My mother's grave! My mother! Oh! that word
Stirs up associations sadly pleasing—

The fondling images of childhood's day,
Which thrill'd my little heart to joyous swelling!

I recollect when thou hadst hapt me in,
Listened my prayer, and told me holy things
Of Him who lov'd and died for my salvation
Pictured His lowly birth and manger bed
Where first He slept and hallowed humble life!
Till my young heart would throb with sacred love
And youthful aspirations inexpressible:
Grasping thy neck I claimed the approving kiss,
Then sank to dreams of high perceptive bliss.

Here let me ponder on thy last advice,
Then lisp'd so earnest from thy yearning heart
When scarce that power of utterance was left:
"O praise your Maker while you have a tongue
To speak," for thine thou knew'st I saw was taken from thee.
This Christian mandate from thy soul presageful
Of much then feared that *may* have followed since
I yet desire to live but to obey
And please thy spirit in the realms of bliss;
And cause have I to praise Him who has been
God of my life, my hope, and my salvation.

When Death, who stalks our globe in gloomy terror,
Closing the film o'er thine eyes, quenching their stars!
And wresting round their whites with damp, cold fingers
In dire disgust and mockery of life,
When like a tyrant giant he is slain,
And all his human prey remanded up
To light and view from dreary, dismal hidings—
When, by omnific word, the scattered parts
Material, with more nice and subtle skill
Than lagging slow philosophy conceives,
Howe'er commix'd in water, air, earth, fire,
Shall dancing move! dilated or condens'd,
By virtual influence, and meet affinity,
And forms reanimated start to view
With bright eyes sparkling immortality.

> Then, as the Godhead's pledg'd for faithful deeds
> And virtuous, thou shalt shine with kindred spirits,
> And prove that blissful ecstasy of feeling,
> That swelling, pure felicity of thought,
> Which thrill'd thy heart with joy to dream of here.
>
> Oh! let me hope, this dream of life once o'er,
> To meet thee happy where we'll part no more.

It delighted me much some few years ago to find that the lady of the late Sir John Douglas of Springwood Park, the proprietor of Longnewton, on some of her first visits to the place, had caused the planting of some young trees about the hedges around the churchyard's adjoining grounds, which are shooting up into beauty, supplying in part to my imagination those beautiful hedgerows that have been rooted out since the days of my youth.

And blessings on the heart in possession of such good feeling (but the feeling itself is a blessing) as to conceive the planting of young yews, where the thorns had originally been missed, along that piece of the fence formed by the mound of the old ruined church back wall, which yews will, by-and-by, shadow my mother's grave from the north. No wonder if these fine touches of human sympathy should delight angels, as they are the best traits of our human character. And this lady could have as little notion of whom she was then delighting on earth as she could have of an unseen flight of blessed spirits overlooking and gratulating each other on the germination of these finer traits of human feeling.

For the last thirty years I have had a wish to put up a stone to commemorate my mother and other relatives, such as great grandfather, mother, grand uncles, aunts, &c., as well as to secure my more palpable claim to a longer preservation of the nearly deserted spot, but hitherto I have had so much to do with the living that I never yet could spare that expense in regard to the dead.

And what you may consider strange as a piece of false delicacy (which, perhaps, it is), though my father is now fully ninety years of age, and yet active in body and mind, with many of the simplicities and sensibilities of youth still apparently green about him, I never dare risk the feelings to ask whether he would wish his remains carried thither, or to be laid in this St. Boswell's churchyard, where we have now been settled the last thirty-six years; hallowed also now in our hearts by the mortal remains of my second sister, Betty, being there deposited.

By the way, although in feeling I am a strong advocate for the Utilitarian system of life, and improvements generally, as that which is calculated to produce the diffusion of the most general comfort, yet there is something so hallowed and hallowing in churchyards, and to me, or to any reflecting mind, not the less so that such may be an old monitory relic of some long-deserted village or other rural population, the decays of which may be there gathered even to the last individual, that I would wish to see such preserved, and to feel convinced of their being so by the fences being kept up, and the spots held sacred from "the tearing plough" throughout all generations.

In June last, 1837, when musing through St. Boswell's churchyard (where lies the dust of your parents) while the people were assembling for public worship, I perceived a little blue flower blooming on a very low grave where no stone of remembrance had been set. This suggested a reflection which I endeavoured to embody in the following verses:—

FORGET-ME-NOT.

Oh! 'tis a lovely little flower
   That blue "forget-me-not,"
I see it blooming on the grave
   Of one who seems forgot;

And Nature's nightly tear has wet
   Its pretty azure eye,
But morning's sun again returns
   To smile and kiss it dry.

Oh! as in sympathy it seems
   To love the grassy tomb,
So even in Paradise it may
   Perhaps unfading bloom.

So modest the appeal it makes
   To Fancy's list'ning ear,
I must suppose some gentle heart
   Lies lowly mouldering here.

And though the slumbering tenant be
   On earth remember'd not,
The fond request in heaven is heard,
   Where there is none forgot.

St. Boswell's Churchyard,
   4th June, 1837.

CHAPTER IX.

MY father's jaunt, which was interrupted by the sad occurrence in last chapter, was to have received an account for shoe work with which to have settled his last principal debt, some five pounds, which would again have cleared him with the world; but this money being now most necessarily otherwise expended, with perhaps a trifle of more debt incurred, family prospects took a dusky hue, and my oldest sister, now quite a woman, was brought from her out-service home to be our housekeeper.

All things for a while continued to look chill and sad in my view, and even amidst all attempts at my usual amusements the idea of a blank ever and again recurred. But the young heart, buoyant and flexible, is never long the stationary residence of grief. The intervals between qualms of reflection gradually lengthened and lightened in their compressure, and my school scheme being delayed, like the "most noble Festus's" considerations of Christianity, was at last, amidst the multiplicity of family difficulties, neglected altogether. My out-door amusements were still, however, occasionally permitted, when I began to amuse even my father with my trouting, he having never seen anything like my success in his generation, even in Oxnam and Kale waters.

An old woman who was left a solitary widow with some hundred and fifty pounds of money saved by a life's careful scraping and holding of herself and husband, an old shepherd, was destined to become the "abuse" of a brother's son about Newcastle, who, on her application, was written to by my father. This individual, Tommy Fala, being bred a shoemaker, no sooner read the letter intimating such prospects than he set out and landed at Longnewton, stumping on a wooden leg, engaged to become my father's journeyman, when for a while he shaped to do well, but was soon discovered to have acquired tippling habits about Newcastle, which occasionally disconcerted his old aunty, who was disgusted with any irregularity of conduct, having, with her husband, led a shepherd's quiet life of prayer and temperance. Yet Tommy was in other respects of honest principles, for although he mixed with the fore-mentioned John Thomson's band of young men in their evening sedentary games and careless habits, yet never participated in anything relative to their secret unlawful pursuits, which it is likely he suspected and avoided.

We now tugged on for two years more at Longnewton, with very little variety of occurrence from one day to another, unless I were to note down some laughable anecdotes of an eccentric door neighbour weaver, out of whom Tommy contrived to extract the most ludicrous scenes of amusement for every day in the year. His natural bravery of spirit led him continually into trifling scrapes of word or deed, which Tommy would waggishly describe as laying him directly under the tiger paw of the law, and then succeeded long faces, and curious grimace of bitter repentance, with some complicated contrivance of plan to ward off the danger and get himself ideally extricated—likely an imaginary examination of witnesses, some multiplication of circumstantial points, with a general asseveration in denial of all evil intentions, which would very likely all end in a new scrape, requiring at last a solution of Meg Wallace's ale to wash off the remembrance.

One little occurrence that made a day or two's fun amongst us I can well recollect. No militia had been raised in Scotland from the date of the Union until after the commencement of the Pitt war with France, when a militia was set afoot, and this contrary to what the people, the principal sufferers in all such cases, understood as the terms of the Union. When the names of those within the age of ballot, therefore, were taken in a list by the parish schoolmasters, the people began to remonstrate, and then to attempt to right themselves in their own way, which has hitherto been certain to be always the most preposterous way imaginable, or next thing to it.

In this case a commencement was made in some of the country parishes by the aggrieved parties assembling on a given evening at the parish schoolmaster's door, and enforcing the delivery up of his list of their names, after which they kindled a bonfire, and had the list burnt in imaginary due form, and then went home and slept in supposed security.

This was then done at Ancrum, where John, our village weaver, had been present, and taken a bold and manful hand in the operations—when he had speechified and gestured to great purpose and effect, with universal unbounded applause.

Next day John was a great man in our village, a hero in miniature; and Tommy Fala, the wooden-legged veteran, was his secretary-elect, to whom he delivered the history of his yesterday's campaign with all its bearable interest. Tommy's admiration of John's ability in tactics, and approval of the general principle, led John out to the very eminence of his fame, in admiration of which, no doubt, all the world was supposed to be in the echo of! John felt himself the very Danton of the reforming parish, and in what distant cloud the sun of his fame should eventually sink into shadow there was really no saying. But, destiny! oh, supreme destiny! John, our weaver, had his destiny as well as the next greatest hero of his time, the once famous Bonaparte.

Our Tommy was a wag, and next day, observing a Jedburgh law beadle—hump-backed Mungo Glendinning—enter the village, he stumpled in to John the weaver on his loom, and briefly alarmed his fears, that the county court officer was at hand, and had been earnestly inquiring after him as the leader of the desperate band of Republican rascals who had mobbed and nearly frightened to death the schoolmaster and the drummer's wife of Ancrum, outraged the king's laws, and made breaches in the peace too horrible and tedious to mention. John at first stared and looked agape, then hem-hemmed, and began to plead off to Tommy by lightening the transaction of at least more than two-thirds of its former weight of fame, and finished by observing that as for his part he had seen the tumult, but hardly knew what it was, having had so little to do or say in the matter. "Why, John," says Tommy, "did not you tell me yesterday, as well as this morning, that had it not been for your bravery the thing would never have been got effected? that not even the drum could be got to beat the people into forming order till you forced the old village drummer's wife to give it out in spite of all her desperate termigancy; and that by saying, 'You old hag, if you don't bring out the drum immediately I'll make a drum of yourself, and beat till I raise the seven devils that came out of Mary Magdalene to dance ye round and round, and run ye over the back-brae scaurs into the Ayle water, as they ance did the swine about the Red Sea?'" "Oh! Tammy, ye've misunderstood me widely, my man. I tell'd ye that some o' the wild callants about Ancrum were talking that kind o' nonsense; but nae decent body could ever hear me say sic things. She's a fine body, auld Ann Dunlee, the drummer's wife; at ony rate, she'll never say sic an ill word o' me. Annie an' me was ower weel acquaint for that lang syne. An' as to the 'Tree o' Liberty' that I was telling ye about me helping to set up on Ancrum Green—hout, man, it was just an auld winter fish leister that the callants stuck in the grund, wi' the lang shank up in the air, an' a wheen colourt clouts fleein' at the tap o't. I had vera little either to do or say i' the hale matter, that's i' the main, ye understand, Tammy, my man; an' that I can assure ye." "No, no, now, John; you was there, with your own confession, and was considered the main ringleader, as the officer tells me, and as I acknowledged to him that ye said yourself; and ye'll be nabbed this night on a summons, and laid in jail to await trial, and I'll be obliged to be a witness of your confessions to me, or else be hanged for resisting the law, as well as you are almost sure to be." "Gracious, man, Tammy, have ye been tellin' him thae stories already? That was perfect ridiculous blasphemy. Od, d'ye think I should hide i' the *baux* amang the *hiddles*, or slide out up to the braidside plantin', or west to the auld kirkyard, till sic time as he leaves the town? An' ye could come stumpin' yont in the gloamin' to tell me how things may be lookin'." "Ye have no time to consider now, John, for there is the officer past your loom window, and at the door already."

Here John had sprung from the loom, and stood on the floor, his bushy head and black-bearded countenance looking confusion twice confounded, when beadle Mungo was at his hand in an instant with an open paper, at which John gave a glance, not so much of suspicion and fearful presentiment, as of awful aghastment. He felt as if the rope noose had been already slipping over his luggs—for hanging was the county town's order of that age, and a *Jeddart* beadle brought one always in mind of a rope. Indeed, the two ideas were hardly then and there separable. "I see I've hit on the right place at the nearest," says the officer. John, dumfoundert, could not mutter a sentence in reply. "Will ye be sae kind, honest weaver, as to favour me wi' a bit clag o' your flour-dressing paste to batter up this adverteesement of a roup on your smithy door? I'm sure I'll be muckle obliged to ye." "Od, ma man, ye sal be welcome to as muckle paste as 'll plaister a' the doors o' the town o'er wi' adverteesements! Tammy, I ken this man now; this is Maister Glendinning, an honest man. No the least like yere ratch kind o' rif-raf constables that comes about gliffin' honest folk out o' their wits, if they ever have ony, about naething but some o' their lawyer contrivances that they ca' *malversions, whoverifications,* captions, an' confoundry. Losh, man, an' ane werena a' the stranger, or mair bull-horn minded, it wad put a man out o' his judgment just to dream o' getting into their claws, or ahint their stanchel windows. A weaver can hardly stand the thought o't. I believe it wad put a tailor screaming mad to think on't ava —that is, if we could suppose a tailor capable o' thinking seriously on sic a thing." "But what, after a'," says Master Glendinning, the officer, "what gars ye think tailors sic silly-minded men?" "Oh! I ance asked Willy Smith, the tailor, that very question, an' he tell'd me the reason off-hand: he said they were a' mair than half women i' the mind, an' the cause o' that was this, that forby that theirs was a kind o' woman's wark, that in our country situations particularly, where they for the most part wrought out in ither folk's houses, frae the day they first began apprentice laddies, they were mair *conversationt* wi' the women folks of a' kinds than wi' ony other human creatures, and they just grew up through time into a kind o' likeness o' their mind, as if it were naturally." "It may be," says Mungo, "though I've lang thought that, as tailors are a kind o' second-hand makers o' men—that is, the most part o' what we account men o' the warld—tailors should rather be reckoned to ha'e a bit knack o' something like creative demi-godhood about them, for the maker of even the outward appearance of a creature that we ca' a man might surely be reckoned something at least as great, if not far greater, than the creature itsel'." Here Mungo had got his paste, an' wi' kindly thanks bade John good day. When so relieved, John broke out into a vehement burst of admiration of the wisdom, sagacity, and kindly feeling of Master Mungo, whom he had found a superior human creature of the kind commonly called Jeddart Beadles.

As I feel in the spirit and recollection of a few matters, I had better just here note you down one or two more of many anecdotes of our old friend, John, now otherwise forgotten, as to lose them for ever may be considered like the loss of a once-observed cluster of stars to an astronomer. They are particularly characteristic of the taste, information, and eccentricity of one who figured, as many other hero who has made even a greater noise in the world, as "a lad in his day." John gave frequent innocent amusement to a whole parish, for it would have argued a parishioner or even a neighbouring parishioner himself unknown, not to have known John, our weaver.

In the youth and manhood of his days, and of my father's days, John had been a neighbour villager in Longnewton. He had removed to Ancrum for some years, in which time my father was wont to declare, without knowing that a prince had previously declared the same thing of another all fun and famous character, that he could better have spared a better man. John returned to reside in Longnewton again, however, in the time of my youth, and his return was to our village what we may suppose the opening up of the places of public amusement would be to London after the sad and devastating ravages of plague and fire. He gave a zest, a mirth, and a character to the place, as, because "a wonder lasts only nine days," John, very unintentionally on his part, supplied his near neighbours with something grand every week at least. Had he meant it for fun, it would have been no fun at all; but amusement to others proceeded as naturally out of his manner, his motions and actions, as the bray from the ass or the low from the cow! The fact was that John was a natural hero, and whatever phrenologists might have said or supposed of the cause of the matter (had any lived in his day), it was quite clear that John would have undertaken anything undertakable, and even a little beyond that, such as to jump over a kirk-steeple, without seeming to awaken his caution that the possibility of danger might be considered. Indeed, the bump of caution must have been the only sleepy organ in his brain, though when it did awaken it became imperious among the faculties, and that might have happened even in the middle of a ram-race to spring over a peat stack.

One early spring morning, sometime in the morning of my days, an alarm was, not sounded, but whispered through the village that a stranger who had slept in the room of the village inn had decamped about daybreak with the incautious landlady's purse from the cupboard containing twelve pounds sterling, when immediately out sallied three or four of the boldest young men of the village to as many points of the compass, determined in imagination to run down the rogue somewhere. After all were gone clear out, and the wondering and inquiring about circumstances was beginning, like a soughing breeze, to sink into quiet, the lame-legged village dominie, Tam Tamson, came to John, our weaver, who had then got an old beast to try the eggling, or cadgering, a little around the country (having supposed some one to be succeeding better in that line than he had found himself doing on the loom.) "Now, John," says he, "lay the sunks on your yellow mare—she carries double like a decent old madan as she is—and here is a horseman's pistol has done some execution in its day, and I'll lay you a guinea to a green gooseberry that we shall overhie and down the thief ere twelve o'clock at noon. They're all off on wrong scents, man, and I've a notion where the rascal's gone." "Od, Tam, I ken ye're a gey queer falla, forby that you book-learned scholars ha'e sic great advantage o' ither poor ignoramusses: where, think ye, he's gane?" "Don't talk just now, John, man, but get the sods girthed on." The dominie mounted foremost himself, as he best knew where he was going, and John, with the advantage of a *hirst*, sprang on behind him. "Now, get up, ye auld jade; ca' her on, my man; keep ye the stick at wark, and I'll carry the pistol. Od, Tam, ye're a queer falla, an' aye was. I mind ye sin' ye was a mere cock-bird, an' game frae the shell—a pity ye had gotten yoursel' lamed, yet better yere limb than yere neck-bane. Od, ye've taken down the liggate; the thief can never ha'e gane that Jeddart airth, the straight road to the gallows." "Come on, Mallbrooks," says Tam, addressing his sapling to her sides, and the poor mare, though no hunter now, raised her old-fashioned trot in a manner quite surprising.

They were down by the *Scaa*, past Bell's Butts, and over Teviot Bridge while the day was yet in the blush of its sweet sunny youth. Tam was one of those shrewd characters who could in an instant lay out the skeleton of a scheme, and trust to occurrent circumstances and his own ingenuity of the moment to fill up the outline into a grand scene of life.

Instead of pursuing the Jedburgh road over the hill, to John's amazement Tam now took the turn west the Hawick road for Lanton, and got on like five ell o' wind. "At leisure, ye devil's limb," says John, "or ye'll swirl the hale lading o' us into the ditch, as ye may be sure I'll no gang down by masel'; ma fingers is just made for grippin." The dominie dashed on a little further, then drew up to a quiet walk, when the mare and he both began to seem rather contemplative. "What ails ye now?" says John; "but I needna ask that, for I wad rather a' the thieves on earth should escape than my poor auld yellow should be broken down i' the hunt o' them. Od, Tam, I doubt ye're ridin' out o' yere wits, ye mad buckie. What i' the wide warld are ye gaun to do up Lanton Moor?" "Did ye not see that man hurry ower the height," says Tam; "yon's the thief: I ken him—I'll warrant him." "Od, an' if it be, will there no be a den o' them i' the thick whins ayont the tap? I couldna take in hand aboon twa or three at ance, ye see, an' if there should be the matter o' fifteen, as I've often heard tell o', living in caves in a band, we may get oursel's murdered, an' never be mair heard tell o' till our banes be bleached white after they're a' pikeit bare wi' the corbies." "John, you must not *hen* now, lad; for yonder we ha'e our chap, head and shouthers ower the height, the very thief, making up for the Stell plantin', an' a dog wi' him." "Gonshins," says John, "I dinna like the dog." "An' ye take the man, John; I'll fight the dog." "Od, as lang's there's but ane there's nae fear about takin' him; we'll hae'm enow or he make the bit hirst. Pit on, mak' in at him or he notice us; the mare's fit's no heard here." "Now, John, spring off, collar him, an' man yoursel' fairly." And John had verily made up within a tether length of the musing shepherd ere ever he was aware of a human being near him. "Good morning," says the shepherd. "The morning's weel enough," says John, advancing and collaring the man of some foot or more above his own height; "but be the morning what it will, ye're in the habble ony way, ma man. Ye're ma ta'en prisoner i' the King's name, and the Shirra o' Jeddart's, be that name what it like! Ye needna startle, lad, for ye're just i' the clams o' them that can manage ye, an' take the stown siller frae ye, an' ye dinna gi'e it up in a minute." "Ye're perfectly wrang," says the shepherd, although it was plain that he rather thought our John perfectly mad! "What do ye mean about stown siller?" "Aye, ye'll make it strange if ye can, billie—nae doubt o' that. Where's the twal pound ye took out o' the cupboard this morning, where ye sleepit a' night, frae poor Isobel

Young's at Langnewton?" "The bodie's gane wood crazy," said the shepherd, wakening up a little; "I never was in Isobel Young's at Longnewton in my life. Let me go, ye wabster-looking creature, or ye'll maybe rue't." For half a minute John's fingers began to act a curious, undetermined kind of part, agreeably to the uncertain impulses of the mind— not that he could be frightened off with threats, in which case he would only have grasped the tighter —but from some qualms of suspicion that he was on the wrong scent. This was sufficiently confirmed when he glanced aside and saw the dominie dismounted, and rolling himself on the ground, fit to burst his sides with gusts of laughter. He then quitted the man, began to look simple or bamboozled, and moving towards the dominie—"Oh! ye cripplet deevil, have ye been rinnin' the rig ona me again?" Tam answered only by another burst of laughter, and then remarked, "Od, John, I believe it's the wrang man, but it's as weel so, as I see you're but a coward after all." "A coward," says John; "ye ill-haired urchin, I've a good mind to nooze your ribs there where ye lie, an' leave ye to hirple hame on your ae foot. A coward! ye latin o' ye; d'ye think I couldna grippit that lang chield round the middle an' faulded him in a minute like twa yards o' raw plaidin', an' it hadna been that I began to smell that I was begunkit wi' you, ye ill-dessented, slee sinner ye?"

The shepherd, forgetting to be angry, now began to suppose some curious ploy, and, entering into the humour of the thing, observed that John's great old rusty pistol wanted a lock! "Od, ma man, it's the first I've observed that mysel', for if I had needed to have used it ava, it wad ha'e been in another way than firing it. I took it just because that dominie creature put it in ma hand. It wad be a fine thing for breakin' a cheild's head in a case o' absolute necessity. Just as it is though, whenever it wad come to nettle earnest I wad readily thraw it doon, an' grip in wi' ma hands. Gi'e me just the ten fingers in a hurry, my man, I've been sae weel used to them." John then turned off to catch auld yellow Mall, who had begun to stray about in search o' tufts o' grass, while the dominie took an opportunity very briefly to satisfy the shepherd in regard to the nature of the outrake, and told him that he was going to see a particular friend, the neighbouring farmer beyond the height, to the south-west—namely, Rewcastle—and had taken advantage of the circumstance of the robbery, which was actually real, to get a ride on John's old mare, and as much fun by the way as possible. The shepherd, who had once began to feel angry, and even to mutter about prosecution for such a rude attack, now entering fully into the spirit of the joke, forgave all, and kindly showed them the nearest outlet, west the moor way for Rewcastle. When Tom telling John that they should not be disappointed of their dinner, and a dram at any rate, with perhaps a feed of corn to the mare, they both got remounted, and rode west to the dominie's friends, where all matters were again soldered up for a still more close acquaintance or a lasting friendship. And home they returned in the evening bright as crickets, when, landing in Isobel Young's, they found "all going merry as a marriage bell," from the thief having been taken on another point of the wind by John the mason, the dominie's younger brother, the same person who became so notorious some years afterwards as "coiner Jock Tamson." Jock was then only a poacher, besides working as stone mason through the summer, and had skill to trace a footprint amongst the early rime of the morning. He had marked the thief's foot-print a very short way from the door, and followed him like a slough-hound south across the Ayle water, about three miles out to Belses Moor, where he got him in sight, and ran him within cry till, on the back of Troneyhill, he downed him on the leap of a stone dyke, and *knoozing* him well, then and there took the money off him, whole and entire, when the thief begged him just to take what further revenge he wished on the spot, and, for God's sake, not to give him up to justice. "I've neither time nor inclination to give ye ony mair than Troneyhill justice—ilk ane their ain again," said Jock. "I'm thinking that if I were to put myself to the trouble of hacking you on to Jethart, it is likely I would have to leave the wife's siller wi' the law crew in security and witness against ye, and the pleasure or pain of seeing you hanged would be all that either her or me might then expect to see again for this twal pound sterling that's to pay her house rent again Wednesday. Na, na; I would rather see you live for ever, thief as you are, and the Jethart justice starved out o' memory, than part wi' the honest woman's siller, now that I've got such a fast grip o't, and after such a race for't. Gude morning to ye, thief; and if your memory winna retain the eighth commandment, dinna let it forget the gallows.

Ye'll find vera few thief-catchers as wise as to let ye off, nearly hale scart, at the back of a moor dyke, though it's my favourite way and manner of seeking and finding justice. Ye'll make Hawick to your breakfast, and if ye have fourpence left, ye may drink my health at the first ale-house ayont Gilnockie auld hall as ye pass through, to tell ye're Yorkshire friends how ye came on this morning at Longnewton." Here Jock came away over the hill crooning a stave of his favourite ballad, "Johnnie Armstrong":—

> "Up then spake his bonnie young son,
>   As he sat on the nurse's knee;
> An' if ever I live to be a man
>   My father's blood revenged sall be."

John, the weaver, being quite a favourite door neighbour, my father on a Sabbath evening went in, as village neighbours will sometimes do, to ask for the family. He found Jean and John alone at opposite sides of what had lately been the peat fire. "I set forward a chair," says he, "and sat down in the front of the fire-place between them. How are ye baith the night?" says I. "Are ye no lookin' unco demure like? Is a' weel enough wi' ye, sirs? Jean, what ails John? for I watna whether he's sour-like or sorry. Ye're unco dull yersel', Jean. John, ye're no right some way; say what's the matter, man." "Willie, my man, there's muckle the matter wi' me. Man, I'm doomed till a wife there that would just put ony man that were trystit wi'er out o' his judgment. She's used me this blessed day as never man was used wi' a woman—she's affronted me afore my ain family, Willie, till I canna bide to think on either her or mysel'; but I've been just tellin' her that, an'

I had the morn, she sal get the house to hersel' a'thegither, an' then she'll can use her guests as she likes for me, and see whether she'll need ony knife or fork to eat their dinner wi' when the head's gane of the house. We did weel eneuch wantin' the chimla after the wind blew it down; the reek was little better, little waur, wantin' that, except for the rain fa'in' a hantle freelier into the pot; but she'll look a gey deal queerer-like wantin' a pot ava, when she has naebody to work for either meal or meat to put in till't. Od, Willie, I've hadden the house up aboon that woman's head this seven and twenty year, foughten for her livin', an' worn a' the mischief i' the warld aff her. An' what think ye's the reward she's gi'en me this day? Na, but ye needna try to guess, for ye could never figure sic a thing. Ye've been differently trystit, my man: ye've fa'en better on yere feet than me; your wife's a mense to ony man, an' to a' woman kind. Aye, lad, she has sense an' discretion—no like that auld runt o' mine, wha has lost ony rummlegumption that ever I thought she was possessed o'. I wonder what tempted me to buckle wi' her lang syne, or to let her gang on as she's likit. But an' I be spared till the morn's mornin', I'll gi'e that auld clocker, there where she sits, Scotland for her dowry: an' I had my foot on the bent, od, she'll skirl louder than ever she's done yet, an' she whistle me back for ae twalmonth to come." "What airt are ye gaun, John, man?" interrupted my father. "I'm no sure o' that till I see what airt the wind is in the mornin'; for I'm determined to be out o' the smell o' the Longnewton peat reek, ony way, and then she'll see whether I'm like ane that should ha'e been affronted or no." "But stop now, John; I canna see what ye're to do out i' the frem'd now at your age; there's nane 'ill take ye now for a journeyman webster, an' ye're ower auld for a sodger or sailor, or even to begin the warld anew by setting up a loom o' your ain in ony faraway part o' the country, and that eggling never seems to do onything for ye after a' your trials at it." John "clew his lug," sleeked his loof across his beard, an' made a verra queer face, looked considerate, like no' verra far frae his wit's end. Jean ventured a sidlins look across the fire-place; but whether in the least degree expressive of matrimonial sympathy and contrition, or of a "do-as-ye-like" kind o' defiance, John no seemed verra clear to determine on, therefore did not seem to slack the least thing in his outward-bound deliberations. "Though I dinna like to meddle," says I, "wi' family matters, particularly between man and wife, yet, as you twa ha'e agreed sae lang thegether as my door neighbours, I canna bear to see ye cast out now when ye've weathert sae weel through the warst half o' the blasts an' storms o' life; sae I ha'e ta'en a thoucht that if ye'll baith submit the matter to me I'll be glad to gi'e ye my opinion. An' sae, Jean, as we like aye to gi'e women the preference, out of a kind o' respect an' civility, as ye're the mistress o' this house, I wad like to hear you first; sae just tell me, if ye please, what's makin' this uncomfortable difference between your ain man an' you?" "I wad like better for John to tell you himsel'," says Jean. "Now, John, that's a fair an' modest concession on Jean's part, sae proceed ye, my auld neighbour." "Weel, Willie, ye see, this morning the twa lads, Pate an' Will, came ower frae where they're servin' to see us, a' binkit up i' their new Sunday's claes: they nae sooner landit in than Jean set to fleeing about the house, gat on the mickle pat, wi' the mart sheep-head an' pluck. It was nae sooner come a-boil than to the meal-box she goes wi' twa dishes, an' in wi' a spang neevefu' oatmeal in ilka dish, an' than to the lea side o' the pat wi' the ladle, an' makes them bowlfuls o' brose wi' the fat a' soomin' like moons and stars, or livin' sheep's een, on the tap o' them, an' clankin' them down to the twa chields, never had the mense to say, John, will ye take a spoonfu'? Aweel, I lets that pass without lettin' on that I was careiñ'; an' lang, lang I waited, till dinner-time came at last, about twa o'clock, when we were a' set to the table, when she clinks down the knife an' fork to Pate to cut down the meat wi', an' a spoon to Will, and there I'm left sitting at the open end o' the table, just like an orra body that had nae say i' the house ava. Now, just think o' that, Willie! Just see them a' set up in that fashion, an' me, that's keepit the house ower a' their heads sin' lang afore they could step ower the kailstick fa'en the i' floor, the real head o' the house, left to eat wi' ma fingers! Na, na! I canna digest it ava. Od, an' I had the morn, I'll let them a' ken wha's wha." "Now, Jean, is that the hale truth, and nae mair than the truth? What do ye say about it?" "It's just the way," says Jean; "John's tellin' verra true; I deny nane o't—oh, whow me!" "Now, John," says my father, "in the first place, I'll understand that ye was lang o' risin' this morning, and got your bowl of parritch in your bed, when Jean an' the lesser bairns got theirs." "Aye," says John. "An' ye was not even up when Pate an' Will came in." "I b'lieve no," says John. "Now, ye see that after being sair wrought throughout the week, the twa lads, instead of lying socking up in their beds, resting on the Sabbath morning, had risen wi' the sparrow, fond to start out to see their auld mother an' father, and cam' a lang jaunt, the ane frae the Rawflat and the other frae Raperlaw. And there's their mother, sae fond to see her twa auldest, grown up frae bairns to men, out in the warld at the plough, was nae doobt desirous to show them a' the motherly kindness in her power. She kenn'd they would be hungry, coming sae far in the open air, wanting their breakfasts, and what was sae ready or sae wise-like of a' she had in their father's house to set afore them, as a wheen brose out o' the skim o' the pat? It was impossible for her to think o' you needing twa yitmeal breakfasts ony mair than hersel'. Now, John, my neighbour, ye see that clearly. And there's, again, at dinner-time, when the sheep-head and draucht was set up, there ye're sitting down wi' your auld creeshy-weaver breeks, that ye dicht aye ye're fingers on in ordinary, and there's the lads wi' their good Sunday's claes—wad it ha'e been mensefu' or rational-like for Jean to ha'e stappit the knife an' fork in your hand, seeing that there's but ae knife an' fork in the house, an' left the lads to file a' their bits o' Sunday's claes wi' eating wi' their fingers? But I've mair to say atween ye than that, John, for ye see ye used to tell me what a queen Jean was when ye first ran sweet-hearting her! when a' her arms, bare to aboon the elbows, for ewe-milking, or other wark, were sae clear an' bonnie—spangled and freckled wi' fresh good health an' fairnitickles, as weel's her mild-looking face, that ye could hardly reach up to get a kiss o' without a kind o' climbing, unless she had kindly becked a little down out o' modest condescension. And now, after raising a braw, promising family to ye, that ony man might be proud of, and still every hour consulting in her ain mind, and frae day to day, diligent to keep a' things richt, what may be her feelings, poor woman, to see you the only petted bairn in the house? Od, I'm sure, if Jean could wean her lang-used love an' regard frae you, an' let ye rin away like a gowk and seek for yoursel' in the frem'd, that wi' a very trifling help o' Pate and Will's half-yearly wages, added to her ain activity, she would make a better shift to keep the family than ye wad do for your ain single sel'." Throughout the latter part of this discourse John had been stealing some slant looks across to Jean, when at last her een met his with a very kind and serious-like expression. "Jean," says John, "what's come o' the cutty pipe, woman?" "It's here," quo Jean, "on the cathud-stane; but there's naething in't, John." "Find your pouch an' ye ha'e a bit end o' 'bacco, an' fill the pipe, and we'll ha'e a blast wi' Willie; he's been lang a good neighbour o' ours: we'll get mair 'bacco, my woman, an' we be spared till the morn." Jean charged the cutty pipe, and set up a reek that changed the atmosphere of the whole house, and seemed to excite a train of new and sociable feelings and ideas, which set John to his apostrophising in a very different style of spirit. "Od, Willie, an' I be spared till the morn I'm thinking of beginning a new life a'thegither, and being just verra extraordinary diligent; an' if I'm spared till another year, I'll let ye see I'll no ware my harvest fee and ither gains as I've done this year, a' on flesh meat. It was perfect nonsense o' me to gang up to the Hawick fair wi' Will Douglas the hackler and lang Jock the tailor, and ware a' on these five draucht mart ewes. It's been naething here but haggises an' heads an' drauchts sin' syne, till the bread meal's run out, an' I dare say, Jean, there's no aboon a stane an' a half o' the yitmeal left either. Now, there's naething to the fore to buy bread to eat the sheep's bouks wi'—and it looks daft-like to see the bairns tearin' at banes an' sennents o' lean sheep flesh without a bite o' bread till't! Od, I'm feared they'll turn cannibals. But an' I be spared till another Martinmas term, I sall ha'e corn to make meal an' bread-meat, though we should never see flesh in this warld again." And John was as good as his word, for next Martinmas he bought three bolls of raw pease, on which he expended his all again, and was in the same predicament—with the one thing alone, the kiln-dried peasemeal bannocks and porridge—that he had been the previous season, with what he had deplored as the constant and unvaried flesh, flesh, flesh—now changed to boiled pease, peasemeal bannocks, and peasemeal porridge, morning, midday, and evening everlastingly.

CHAPTER X.

I WAS now learning to work as a shoemaker's apprentice; but otherwise sorely cramped in the means of following the bent of my natural tastes; and I made less progress in acquirements of general knowledge in these two years than in any two months previously. Not a germ further in school education, and without either example or enticing books, or other excitement to read; so except what was acquired in use of hand in shoemaking, these two years were a blank in as much as mind was concerned.

Tommy Fala was the only being who showed any sympathy with what he perceived as my tastes, and he insisted that if I had lived in Newcastle-on-Tyne to have got proper instruction in certain things—singing, for instance—I might have made my bread by it; and in the lighter stitching and lining parts of our business I used to plague him with comparisons of work, when he would blame his spectacles and eulogize my sharp, young sight. I soon became altogether in his view, as with his provincial *burr* he expressed it, "a *curious laddie*." Tommy had read some poetry, and spoke frequently of Pope, and Thomson's "Seasons," which I kept entreating him to explain to me, and to repeat such passages as had clung to his memory. Such were but short sentences, the meaning of which I thought I perceived "as through a glass darkly." These two years slid by, when my father determined to leave Longnewton, where, with the general poverty of the falling village, he found it next to impossible to make a scanty subsistence, even without lessening his few pounds of debt—indeed, they were rather increasing. So as Mr. Tulloh, having bought the estate of Elliestoun, about a mile and a half north of us, some few years previously, was there rearing a fine young family, and improving the place, and as my father had been employed by them, he built for him a cot-house beside the blacksmith's shop and the joiner's at the end of his avenue—the Loanend, as it is called. To this we removed at Whitsunday, 1798. This remove, so short, left my father still contiguous to the best of his old customers, besides throwing us into the chance of some new ones—at least, so we thought. We entered this new cottage of bare outer walls, roofed with red tiles, like the rest then adjoining it, and fell to work, dividing it into apartments by making partitions of home fir spokes, plastered up with *claut and clay* (straw dubbed with mortar of clay hung over the spokes and sleeked down with the hand), which makes a cosy wall of partition. In the same way we made a kitchen chimney, with its *hallan* (or sheltering angle), and the shop and another small apartment were thus also neatly divided, covering the joists over-head with small, round fir trees overlaid with green sod.

I here felt most delighted, having fallen in amongst young woods, and birds, and burns of clear water all around, and the green plantations so pleasant to wander in, whenever I went out of doors. No cushat cooing in clump of shade felt more happy than I did rambling through these thickets, seeking pleasure in an ever-green shape of—I could not tell what. I fixed on forming my nest like the rest of the birds, a seat in a large spruce fir which on the sunny side of the north plantation overlooked our dwelling. This was soon accomplished, by turning up the tops of the under branches and tying down to them those above all around, and lining over with fog (green moss); but, like most things else, here the pleasure lay more in the idea than in the real enjoyment of the aerial bower. It being understood by all concerned, as well as by myself, that I must now settle to work in the house really for bread, except on mornings or evenings occasionally, or for a Sabbath afternoon seclusion for a lesson, I seldom could visit my woodland nest, and indeed I found I was too restless to sit in it unemployed when I had a liberty of strolling. In the novelty of this wood-wandering I felt a boundless pleasure for the first two summer months, always, however, keeping a sharp eye about me for fear of meeting with the laird, for he was represented by the people around as very terrible to be offended; and though I was conscious I would do no real harm in his plantations, yet I reasoned that he was not obliged to understand so. I soon found, however, that he had discovered my summer-seat in the tree, for he had been inquiring about it at the forester, as a neighbour boy—a little chap I had once or twice invited to sit with me in it—informed me. I felt somewhat in Robinson Crusoe's situation, when he thought of defacing his grove and other improvements to elude the attention of the savages, and then it was reiterated in my hearing that "the laird was not to creel eggs with." But no reprimand followed, though I had made up my mind not to deny it. My next project was to work out and enclose a small plot of waste front ground between our kitchen window and the road, which cost a labour something like said Robinson Crusoe's cave-house in the rock, as it was entirely stones, broken tiles, and rubbish of a former house, which I quarried out to about eighteen inches depth, and carried all away in a bucket to a distance, then carried in good earth from behind the house to fill up the space—it might take several hundreds of bucketsful—next laid all out in what I supposed a true garden style in miniature, with its box-edged gravel walks of a foot-breadth, &c. On the main plot I planted early cabbages in the fall, which were so soon ready in the succeeding spring that I dug and planted again and again, cutting three successive crops from the same ground that season. About the commencement of this operation the laird surprised me sweating in it, and it made me very happy to find that he highly approved of my plan and work, and projected some improvement of the fence, allowing me to cut broom, briars, &c., to weave the paling, which, making it thus as thick as a board, excluded all trespass from without, even that of the neighbours' poultry. It charmed me to hear the laird talk quite plain and pleased, and as confidentially as my own father, and this the more so from the terrible character some of the boys around had given of him. And if gentlemen could conceive (what they seem never to be taught at their colleges) that there are many honest and ingenuous, though sometimes erring, hearts amongst the children of the poor, and would treat them with open kindness rather than with those thief-making terrors of prosecution, sign-boarded in threatenings at every turning, they would find that their harvest of regard, respect, and love from boy and man together would be worth the reaping, and this generally, except in a very few scoundrelly instances. I afterwards learned that my cabbage had been an object of attention, the laird having rallied his gardener about the shoemaker's *laddie* beating him till the man peevishly lost temper.

On a summer day, which I had selected after a heavy fall of rain for a solitary trouting excursion, I sallied out, but just met the laird in the avenue. "Where are you going?" says he. "To Ayle water, sir, to fish." "Where is your fishing-rod?" "Oh, sir, I was thinking of cutting a rowan-tree wand in the plantin'." "How dare you think of doing so, and to tell me to my face?" "Oh, sir, I would not cut a young tree, but these bushes of stock-shots, growing out from the tree roots, should be pruned away at any rate." Well, go, cut what ye like, but lose no time, and recollect to bring me in your trouts, or I'll blow you up." So off I flew, thinking, if you like trouts I'll get an extension of commission from my father also. It blew at the water an almost defeating gale of wind, but I got into a sheltered spot, and succeeded in bringing into Elliestoun House just fifteen, which might stand half-pounds at average. I now took great courage, determining never again to skulk from the laird, or from any person, even should my vagaries lead me into a trespass amongst private walks, woods, or hedges. And to a former observation that one-half of the mischief of life arose from mutual misunderstandings, I added this as a maxim, that plain dealing, and free acknowledgment of error, would not only often avert displeasure, but sometimes even secure friendship. My occasional movements in these charming plantations and fields were afterwards made with open freedom, and I would not have hurt a fence or growing tree, if for no other reason than the violence I found I would do my own mind, making me despise myself, for about this age I grew very sensitively tender in feeling, and besides I had really begun somehow privately to conceive that very likely my mother's spirit might be in a situation to perceive me; at all events, I took strong resolutions to behave as I thought would please her, if such should be the case. This, added to my general notions of religion, proved a stronger check to my conception of evil thoughts than even the idea of displeasing my still surviving parent, who, though sometimes a little high-tempered with me in my vagaries, was generally confidential, and upon the whole indulgent.

Tommy Fala, who had come daily across the plantations and wrought with us for the first two or three summer months of which I speak, at last got his aunt to purchase for him some leather, and so set up for himself where we had left, and though a poor, tasteless workman in the main, might yet have made his living comfortably, having the use of a little money, a very superior advantage to us, with the name of having come from Newcastle, which was as great in a country village as "from Paris" is in Edinburgh. And, indeed, I have always observed that tasteless, bad hands in our craft make most money, because they push on their jobs solely for the money, no way hampered by an over conscientiousness or delicacy of taste. And Tommy was as little troubled with delicacy as any person I have ever known. He might have made even a rational marriage, with his aunty's consent, had not his drunken propensity quite overcome him, and defeated every attempt at well-doing.

Though my father's delicacy of disposition had hitherto prevented him from discharging Tommy, whose work he had found never did him due credit, so that he was glad when he withdrew of his own accord, yet the part of custom which he at first took from us was felt, while I was not come the length of doing half a man's work, nor duly careful of the business, nor indeed could thoroughly comprehend the necessity of particular exertion at the time for the purpose of gaining customers, or quickly serving, so as to secure them. Besides, there were few leather-merchants in this district of country, not one then for ten now, leather very high in price and still then rising, and my father's credit with them but limited, while his debts were rather increasing. The French war was beginning to make impression on all markets, victuals rising daily; all taken together gave matters a sickly appearance to us. Only about half gains were actually earned, from which, when the occurrent losses were deducted, little indeed was left for our daily living.

It is a curious phasis in the constitution of our

human mind that in such family circumstances a man's power of action has a greater tendency to fall below his ordinary standard taste, even to fail him, than to rise in energy equal to the necessity of the case. Such was the way with my father. He grew thoughtful, shame-faced, and fearful to see his creditor; and, in as far as I understood matters, I became smitten with these his disqualifying affections. Still, however, the winter was setting in, and my mind was too young to rest long on gloomy prospects. I read up all the old ballads I could lay hands on, and could not conceive that any of the then living generation could ever attempt to write books of any kind. All these I supposed to have been the study of the wise old people of former generations. In respect of these things I was then just at the point where our Lords, Parliaments, and law courts seem to be at now; I durst not decide out of the precedents of former ignorance, as sanctified by the cobwebbery of years and customs. Such was the pitiful state of my mind when one day the hedger came into our shop, quite tickled with some little crambo poem he had picked up from some newspaper, which he repeated to us with wonderful spirit and particular emphasis, averring that the author was certainly just going to be another Burns! "And who is Burns, Jamie?" says I. "Bless me, man, a'body's surely heard o' Burns by this time, the Ayrshire ploughman, who's beat Allan Ramsay and Ferguson, and the rest o' the Scotch poets, a' to nonsense. But I havena heard ony o' his poems so often as to be able to repeat them, and I havena the book." Having never once heard such names, I felt something like a chill of ignorance pass over my nerves; and as I was in raptures with the simple verses he had compared to Burns, I cast about where in all my circle of known world any such books might possibly be to be found, but could get no clue to lead to such treasure until the feeling again subsided, and I settled into the pursuit of my former amusements.

The blacksmith's shop next door was a winter rendezvous, where I sometimes warmed on the forge hearth, and heard him (who was a young man) talk to the ploughmen and others as they occasionally came in with their horses to shoe, or ploughshares and coulters to repair. This blacksmith was a clever fellow in his own line, as well as ingenious in other respects: one who had sucked in a considerable stock of general information, and could have twisted an argument into any fold with the same address as he could twist a hot nailstring. Such a scatterment of good sense, general knowledge, novel imagination, and desire of fun, even to any risk of mischief, with a fertile power of inventing offhand a complicated story, which, before it was closed, would most likely involve some one of his audience assembled at the forge hearth in some strange dilemma regarding himself, or friends, or some girl, for whom he would cunningly suspect his young listener might likely have a prepossession. Though in religious profession he was a strict sectarian, yet he was loose in his walk, and unboundedly so in his conversation, indulging in a tissue of intrigue scarcely possible to be unravelled. It was amazing to see how he would have made a young rustic stare with astonishment at his anticipation of a train of his ideas, particularly where a private love affair was by him suspected. I have never met with any man through life who had a deeper insight into the propensities and affections of human nature, or more able to define their workings, and who, at the same time, had as little of the real poetry of nature in the composition of his mind, that quality with which the other faculty is most usually accompanied, although it is plain that they can subsist in considerable perfection independent of each other.

What I have often thought strange was, that although that man (Robert Wight) was continually "running the rigg" on some one, and never without a ploy on hand, he scarcely ever attempted such with me, seeming to consider me simply as the observing party, amused at his skill in his manœuvre with others, and whenever we talked alone, either at that time or on occasional meetings long afterwards, he invariably threw aside all his levity and became ingenuous, when, after some detail of stratagem or farce in which he had previously been engaged, where he had drawn out any particular trait of personal character, with the reflections natural on such observations, or with whatever discourse we casually started, we generally fell souse into the old question of free-will and necessity, at which we would hammer, till, like Milton's Adam and Eve, "of our vain contests appeared no end." But he was "cunning of fence," and could perceive the clinch-end of my argument often in the distance, and would dash in with an interference of some foreign matter to break the arrangement of my ideas, and drive off at a tangent without any decision. Though a dozen years older than myself, he had been too throng with the action of life to be deeply read in books, and therefore at the early time of which I speak had little advantage of me in respect of book knowledge or even in the use of words, of which I felt woefully deficient.

CHAPTER XI.

IT was at this Martinmas of 1798 that the band of forgers formerly mentioned was detected and broken up; and a fearful band it was, considering all who were privately understood to stand connected with it, besides those who were publicly implicated. John Thomson was the first who was taken up in Jedburgh market, on the Martinmas Fair-day, and there committed to jail. He was no sooner seized than one of his chief accomplices ran home and had all his household coin and apparatus carried out from his old mother's cottage and hid in the fields. Considerable quantities of the base coin have since been found in the foundation of their old garden dyke at its removal. The occurrence made a great noise with us, so near the scene of action, and I had various strange ideas on the occasion, from my so late immediate vicinity to the whole party, who from my infancy I had conceived to be the finest, kindliest men in existence, and from another circumstance which had occurred that morning, which altogether combined to make that the most wonderful day I had yet seen in life.

Several in our hamlet had arisen some hours before daylight, amongst them being my two sisters, to set out to Jedburgh for the hiring market, when a loud talk arose about the doors of something very wonderful going on in the heavens. I ran out half-naked, and witnessed the finest show of fiery meteors that I have ever seen, all of the kind taken together. Some present called them "flaming swords," which indeed they resembled upon an awful scale, somewhat like the "flaming brand" hung over the gate of Paradise lost. They rushed from a small southern cloud head foremost eastward along the sky, with a hissing sound; and then, as if arrested in middle flight, seemed to fix against the sky till they faded into faintness, and died away by slow degrees, and was immediately succeeded by others, till, from the time I was first alarmed, perhaps a score had thus appeared *fearfully portentous.** So in the evening, when the news was brought home from the burgh fair of the apprehension of these late friendly neighbours of ours, the forgers, some superstitiously observed that it certainly was not for nothing that such awful appearances had been seen in the morning. I ruminated on this, but, unread in astrology, could see no feasible connection between such events, any more than could my neighbours who made the observation.

* Several years after stating as above my observation of the meteors which I then saw, on the morning of the second Tuesday of November, 1798, I have been delighted to see some fine descriptions of the same phenomenon inserted in Maunder's "Scientific and Literary Treasury" under the title of "Falling Stars," principally as observed by Mr. R. C. Woods, at Richmond, Surrey, on the 12th and 13th November, 1838; and at the same time by Karl von Sitterow, in Germany, precisely forty years after I had witnessed them at Elliestoun, in Roxburghshire. May these not be fragments of some broken planet of the Asteroids still keeping their course around their primary, and with which our earth comes into proximity in that particular part of her orbit through which she passes on the days between the 10th and 14th November annually? And may these meteoric stones which occasionally come into the earth's attraction, and fall hissing, not be the smaller conglobations of the same material?

Yet ignorance is naturally superstitious—and indeed at that time I had very little understanding of most things any more than of the forgery, as on it I felt something like the old woman I have since heard of, who averred that "it was a crying shame to talk of hanging a boardly man for making siller, and it so scant." However, in despite of my sympathies, four or five more of the party were soon afterwards apprehended and committed for trial at Edinburgh. The fine-looking young man formerly mentioned as the accomplished poacher (George Gray) had drunk a phial of laudanum before he was conveyed from Jedburgh, handcuffed, in a chaise, and died about the time he reached Edinburgh. When afterwards two young women—the one the very pink-flower of my native village—whom he had seduced, came in consequence to a most tragical end, throwing their respective families into the bitterness of grief, and all around into the sadness of mourning, I began to conceive the enormity of such guilt, and the weakness of trusting to personal appearances, and verily drew from the whole catastrophe a moral lesson, which strongly impressed me with the propriety of good conduct. The fate of the beautiful young woman (May Wallace), who had been our door neighbour from my infancy, and by whom we used to compare, or rather contrast, every other beauty, affected me so particularly that the crime of seduction far surpassed in my mind even the guilt of the forgery, to which our sanguinary laws had awarded the penalty of death. Yet the heinousness of this soon also became clear to my understanding, and to both of these crimes I have felt a very particular aversion ever since. Two or three of these men were tried for passing forged notes. John Thomson was admitted evidence for the Crown, which, amidst all his usual boasted bravery of mind, he sneakingly accepted. George Elliot was convicted; but as being related to some of our squires here, the trial was so managed as to save his neck, he being taken at last by his advocate from below the statute, on the plea that the utterance was made in England while the trial had proceeded in Scotland. Sam Bell, an Englishman, was convicted and executed. He had been altogether a desperate and notorious character. All the rest escaped at the bar for the time. Several of them afterwards seemed to have reformed, and lived here in the neighbourhood till they died in their beds. Yet a degree of attaint seemed to have been left in the place, which showed itself some years afterwards in a lesser eruption. But John Thomson—although he then left this part, taking his old mother away to live in Leith Walk, where my father once casually visited the poor creature, and found her in the most abject state, a short while before her miserable end—still followed his evil propensities, being three or four times afterwards tried for his life, both in Scotland and England, always for the same crime, and always escaping by some irrelevancy of indictment or the death of principal witnesses, till at last we lost track of him. I have since heard a report that he ended his days in the hulks.

My father's visit to his mother was on this wise. Being in Edinburgh on some little business, he called on a late village neighbour (one of our blacksmith's sons), who had just previously fallen heir to an elder brother's effects of money, houses, and a lucrative building business in Edinburgh, and was then residing in his own grand house in independent or affluent circumstances. My father, conceiving him more dry in his hospitality than he could have supposed, wished to shift the scene; therefore requested, "Can ye, Robbie, direct me where I'll find auld Jean Harkness, John Thomson's mother, about Leith Walk? I canna leave Edinburgh without seeing auld Jean, poor creature." "I cannot direct ye, William, to where she lives, and would not advise you to look near her, as it is disgraceful to be inquiring after her since her son is so notorious." "Bless me, man, Robbie, the auld creature's the mair to be pitied—and have ye never really gane to see her, though ye're living here in a' fullness?—and for a' the years o' afternoons, and late winter nichts, ye sat at her fireside at Longnewton playing cards and reading newspapers wi' John her son an' the rest o' the idlers, when Jean washed the clouts, and dressed your sair leg, then rotting off ye? Now, I never sat in Jean's house, an' if she was never obliged to me I was never obliged to her in my life, yet she was a kindly neighbour, had seen better days, puir body, and cam' aye in to ask for our bairns, an' *her that's away*." "William, it requires people here in my circumstances to consider propriety, else we would soon lose our respectability." "Propriety—respectability—Robbie. I've often wished to be in better circumstances; but if warld's gear and windfa's like yours dry up the heart into that stately reserve, goodness keep me frae ever being curst wi' it. I'll go and seek and see auld Jean in Leith Wynd this afternoon, unless they have just sodgers placed wi' guns and swords to wear folk out frae seeing her. Lord have a care o' us! she's maybe starving for black want, poor auld soul—and her sinfu' son lying in the jail; and what's a' Edinburgh to her, or me either, if the heart's sair and the pouch empty?" So off he set, leaving Robbie to hug his soul in its own selfishness, and found out poor old Jean in the very straw of wretchedness.

I accidentally saw John Thomson in a farmer's house after his first release from jail, where he was boasting of how little ill he had done any one in his character of *king's evidence;* but as it was a year or more from the time I had last seen him, I had found some enlargement of mind, got some new perceptions, rather more understanding of character, some further extension of ideas, and instead of the man of worth and knowledge I had formerly in childish ignorance supposed him, I then conceived that he looked very blackguard-like.

Although at the time of their first apprehension my father seemed to feel deeply for the suspending fate of several of these young men, as sensible of their ever obliging kindliness as near neighbours, and of the affliction of some of their near relatives who should have been dependent on their honest exertions, yet he had been congratulating himself on having escaped from the village before I should have become contaminated by their example, for he had quietly perceived their conduct and been dreading bad consequences. As he told me afterwards, he had been afraid for me, from observing my eager and successful imitation of several of their idle indoor amusements, as well as of their field sports. A taste for shooting continued during all my youth as an occasional pastime. That of angling still continues, although from prudence I have greatly restrained from indulgence in even that, not having fished in all above three or four days a season for the last twenty years. But to cards, draught-board, and gambling of all kinds I took an early distaste, which has continued since. In truth, I would rather have cut wood or dug earth for pure exercise than have sat down to such mere trickster-like amusement. When, occasionally pressed to it, I have ever yielded for a game or two, I felt somehow as if my soul had evaporated, and the motion of life had been suspended, like a timepiece run down.

One of our blacksmith's apprentices about this time wrote doggerel poetry of the epistolary and satirical cast, just in our psalm metre. Though as old a chap as his master, he privately chose me for his confidant, and submitted his verses for my applause or occasional correction. I decided that his correspondent had more wildfire, while my friend had more of polished, sound sense. Though upon the whole all was mere ribaldry, yet I thought it good to be *home manufacture*, and began to attest a spirit of emulation, but found I could do nothing to any subject he proposed, and instead tried a ludicrous description of my own folly in having waded to the knees in new-fallen snow over half the estate attempting to fire at partridges grouped in coveys in every second field, my firelock ever flashing in the pan—when, after I came home fatigued, the blacksmith, who had lent me the fowling-piece, drew the shot, and showed me his own trick of having put the wadding in before the powder to hinder me (as he averred) doing mischief. This was the only case which this man of trick ever played upon me, and I felt somehow so tickled by the reflection on my own simplicity as to laugh the same as others. My consequent poem or reverie on the occasion delighted the whole group, when I was forthwith, from courtesy, constituted *Smithy* Laureate, and umpire infallible in judgment of all matters of rhyme! Though this fame reached not beyond our hamlet, neither was any butt of sack forthcoming, yet it was as interesting to me at the time as the present Laureate's fame is to him, for I have seen since that "the earth hath bubbles as the water has, and these are of them."

About this time, a young lad (John Anderson) I had formerly seen, a farmer's son, from some miles' distance, called into the smith's shop, and when he was asked whether he had seen any of Burns' poems, he said, "Oh, yes," and readily repeated, "Death and Dr. Hornbook." This was an electrifier. I felt something as I suppose people will feel when going crazy. I immediately made firm friends with the lad, accompanying him so far on his way home, when he informed me where he had seen the poems, that were still beyond my reach. John and I got exceedingly good friends, however, from a felt sympathy of tastes, and such youthful friendships are a perfect cordial in the cup of life. We arranged for future meetings, while he promised to prepare himself with future scraps from Burns at every opportunity he might have of seeing the poems, which he described to me as a great bookful. I seldom, however, saw him again for some year or two, and languished in mind for some of these new poetical treasures, which there still seemed no means of acquiring possession of.

Time, however, was moving; we were living on, and on, and thus passed through the winter. The following spring and summer were the wet ones of 1799, on which followed "the dear years"—ever to be remembered, by me at least.

CHAPTER XII.

AFTER a heavy winter of deep snow-storm, the spring months of 1799 arrived, but except in the name they bore little of character to distinguish them from January. The summer followed, cold, wet, and ungenial. This, I suppose, must have been general to a certain extent over Europe, since an actual scarcity approaching to famine followed. Corn bills, these late infernal contrivances, were then out of the question. Two days of that season I remember particularly: the 5th of April, for high wind and drifting snow, beat all I have ever since seen; and the 18th of July (St. Boswells Fair day) blew a tempest of heavy, cold rain from the north-east, such as occasionally, once in ten or twenty years, we may have in the months of November or December. Any crop that did grow was bleached in the straw to pale rottenness, and the summer atmosphere shed a sickly gloom over the soul, touching the nerves of life with a morbid melancholy, that Novemberish dankiness of feeling which excites a certain degree of nausea at existence.

As a family, we were scarcely yet so much reduced in circumstances as to feel the average weight of the approaching calamity, only some slight want of common necessaries; but I had not yet acquired the sagacity to calculate on such matters from appearances. And as to my father, it would have been hard to judge whether the philosophy of his mind gave more of colour to circumstances, or the circumstances of colour to his mind. But this I have perceived, that his natural disposition swayed him always rather to hope on the sunny side of every cloud of life, and often to hope even against hope. On looking to his face, I never found it without comfort, and was not come to sufficient experience ever to mistrust his opinion in general matters. On listening to his occasional dissertations with any neighbour on some such subject as the state of markets, I used to take great heart from his observations. "Oh, never fear; the Candlemas rents are to pay; they *must* sell their corn; the markets *will* come down if we can but put through till then; and the potatoes—'the enemy,' as the fat farmers call them—will be ready by-and-by; they are aye a first relief to poor folk now-a-days."

But, near the end of this sunless summer, a more disagreeable circumstance than even dear markets occurred to affect our family comfort. While my eldest sister (Agnes) made a careful and industrious housekeeper to us, the two younger, Betty and Ann, in the bloom of eighteen and twenty, were at service with a neighbouring farmer, a young man of five-and-twenty, who was generally esteemed as sober, judicious, and respectable as a master, as they both were in the condition of servants. He was the seventh of eight brothers, who, down to this time, had all been reputed the most respectable and correct living men in the country. But while at home he was accounted skilful and industrious as a farmer, he was induced to join the yeomanry cavalry of the time, and flashed out occasionally in the pride of helmet and plume. This appearance, set off with a cheerful disposition and fascinating manner, gave him a power for good or for evil which made him in a moral point of view as dangerous in the character of a friend as of an enemy. Thus it was that my second sister (Betty), though a young woman of most excellent mind and acute discernment, yet in the delusive dream of love and hope fell the victim to his false faith and powers of seduction. So soon as her situation became known, a kind of family consultation of his brothers was held on the subject of a proposed marriage, which was postponed at the time through heartless family pride; for this absurd mania pervades the weakness of human nature in all ranks of life, who will estimate, however mistakenly, even to a five pounds worth of family capital in property, money, interest, influence, even public credit. When she ascertained the proposed *delay* by the advice of *his council*, the misery of her state rushed back upon her mind, when she, poor creature, left his house; and, ashamed to come home and face her father, she wandered away without purpose, aim, or view, but only to escape in idea from the consciousness of her own reflection. Then began our week of intense grief and anxiety. "What has become of her? Has she gone *dimentit?** And what may be the consequence?" All former occurrences and all future

---

* She had wandered thirty miles on to Berwick-Spittal without any view or resolution further than to escape for the time being from the face of her friends and acquaintance, and there took lodging as a seabather, till her matronly landlady had suspected her state, and, gaining her confidence, advised her return to her father's house.

fears sank into insignificance, as "where the greater malady is fixed, the lesser is scarce felt." Our hearts were compressed to the point of bursting, with but one overbearing feeling which expressed itself tremulously. No track of her could be made out; and my father, shivering under fearful apprehensions, went and pressed the young man to satisfy him whether he knew of her absconding. He declared he did not, which was truth, though we durst not then believe him. After a week's restless days and sleepless nights, and when all surmise, supposition, and near private search was exhausted—for distant search or open alarm seemed of no use—we were glad to hear her open the door in the night, which was left purposely unbolted, and steal into bed beside her sister. My fathered whispered, "That's her," and at that blessed moment all the other evils of life appeared as light as gossamer: and had we had a fatted calf the heart was not a-wanting to have arisen and made a feast. In place of this, not a word was uttered till we all fell into a sound sleep, and rose in the morning refreshed. She was afterwards soothed with kindness, and we soon all recovered our wonted serenity of quiet family feeling—with hearts down, yet not miserable, and withal not ill prepared in spirit for submission to the will of Providence in the pinching famine then imperceptibly approaching us; for, though heart-hunger is bad enough in any situation, yet to be tumbled from a height of fulness down into the vale of penury and starvation all at once is certainly worse than to be stinted into it by degrees, as we then were.

The crop of that season was bleached by cold rains

to rottenness, and the crop of 1800, that next followed, was, from summer drought, nearly burnt up, light and scanty. Being then fourteen years of age, I felt some stirrings of desire to go out into the world, and endeavour to make myself useful to some person who might have bread to give for actual service. And had I then stood unrelated, an orphan in the world, I would likely have found my way, by some such proceeding as becoming a farmer's boy, or page, or shoeblack about some great house, or a gardener's apprentice, of which I had a fond notion. But as I stood connected with my father's poor family —two sisters at farmers' service, the unfortunate one at home with us under this clouded circumstance— my smallest occasional hint about out service naturally drew from my father some word or look of reflection savouring of doubt or disapprobation, which checked these emotions at their first rising. So I continued trifling on with him at my shoemaking, yet singing and *sauntering** occasionally, and musing between on ideas of various modes of pursuits, which were ever again abandoned on recurrence of the feeling of my immediate attachment to the family, from which I had never had one night's previous separation; while an inexplicable sympathy, in the midst of our saddening privations, suggested something like a necessity of my submitting along with them, and became a reason strong as fate for the abandonment of every selfish plan of movement so soon as thought on. Yet the pressure of this famine was sore on my youth, for our trade was nearly done up for the time, and, as in cities of the plague, so in this dearth sel-

* *Sauntering*—Straying listlessly.

fishness seized all. The bowels of compassion seemed greatly to dry up in the wealthy, while the bowels of the poor dried up for mere lack of material distention.

Though I was never the length of eating dove's dung, like the people of old, when besieged in Samaria, yet to be generally pinched of all matters in the consistence of human food for the space of two or three years—to be bleached skeleton-thin by a kind of protracted famine, wasting by daily degrees the blood from the young heart—was a sad concern, producing a feeling none can thoroughly comprehend from mere description, and few I wish may ever understand from sad experience, to go hungry to bed on a winter night, an unfortunate sister lying within hearing, with a leaching infant (a loved one) draining her hungry heart to the bottom of its deepest sigh; to dream of food—of boiled potatoes—three months before such potatoes could be seen in field-blossom, and even then few to bloom for us; to awake again and find "the soul is empty;" to look out from your cottage over the drifted snows or the cold, bare earth; to muse on what point you will move a two miles' distance in any direction, or to contrive what sort of eloquence you shall use to entreat credit for any description of human food at any named price; to set out to some distant cornmill, the proper country market for meal in those days, where likely you are at entrance told that all they lately had is sold off, or, which is the same thing in effect, denied credit for *half a stone* of meal, while you stand lank and heartless, with all the passions of the soul at bay, as in blank irresolution whether to attempt further progress on the road of life—at last, as if instinctively, to turn, heart-sick, slowly away from the most agreeable smell of the man's meal-mill; to sweat through the bleak winds towards the next likely place, at perhaps a circle distance of three more miles; and when, at last less or more successful, home through the woods and fields as the crow flies with her gathered grubs to her nest. Often have I then gone on these errands, exactly as thus related, taxing my ingenuity for some palpable pretence, which might be likely to have effect, though I never sought credit but with the full intention to pay the first possible opportunity, and generally with the green, youthful hope of future ability still fluttering alive in the bosom; but all at last would settle into the simple request—"Will ye trust us some meal, and I will pay you so soon as my father can get siller?" No distinction of kinds of meal was then made of choice. As my father was well-known to be an honest man, I was, for a first round, pretty successful; but then the blasting was so lasting, and the last year the worst, at least with us individually.

I never really used unfair stratagem but once, which I sometimes yet reflect on. Having somehow found a bad shilling (as John Thomson's counterfeit coinage was still maintaining a pretty general circulation) in a gloomy day of hungry necessity, I went to Longnewton to my old teacher, Walter Dun, who now kept a small village grocery and sold bread; sought a shilling's worth of bread, which receiving, I tied up in a towel, and when thus secured offered my shilling, which was, of course, rejected, when I could not help acknowledging that I really had some suspicions of it, but would bring a good one first opportunity, which I did. The old Walter is long gone. I still feel afraid he would see through the shift, though kind enough not to stun me by checking it; and this is a curious affection of the mind, which might puzzle a philosopher to account for satisfactorily.

No corn in those years was substantial; all meal black "mattened" and unhealthsome; nothing fresh and sound but the foreign white pease, the meal of which was yellow and solid as brass: it was five shillings per stone, and could seldom be got in our locality. Oatmeal fluctuated in price for two years between six and eight shillings a stone; but oatmeal we scarcely could see for months together, though it had formerly been our staple food when at an average price of one and sixpence per stone. Potatoes, when to be got at all, were at the rate of three-and-fourpence per bushel. And as for butcher meat, at about a shilling a pound, it became in our ideas classed with Ambrosia, of which we had somehow heard as food only for the gods.

In these times, when I set out, either with money or to try credit, to where we heard that meal was likely to be sold, the grand trial in such cases was to get home with my forage before I should have it devoured by the way; for I could have heartily snapt up a shilling's worth of raw meal on a mile's journey home! When I had got anything packed, in such case I had my hand in the bag first free opportunity, then after a mouthful would tie it strictly up, get it in my "oxter," determined to move manfully on, and withstand all further temptation of mouth-watering till I should reach such or such point of road; but this was a task which would have required the whole virtue of your most famous saints, even your blood-and-wound heroes. No wonder that it generally mastered mine. So at next opening of the "pock," I would keep its mouth only twisted round in my hand, so as I might pick out now and then, like a child greatly saving in idea, and yet unable to resist tasting his "fairings" of sweetmeats. As the thought of the impatience of those at home would again rush on my mind, I would tie up under a strongly-renewed determination, and set to running like a hare: all errands in those days were gone in half-running. In spring-time, when out on such excursions, I would have envied the wild birds and beasts—the very larks in air, who could at pleasure descend and fill themselves with worms. And often would I think if food could not be made of some sort of wood or other common product that had not been yet thought on—young elm-bark, or arnots;* and often would I chew beech, brier, and thorn buds, which tended only to excite a stronger appetite by giving the palate a recollection of its wants. Young nettles boiled were during all the spring quarter a special resource, and a very palatable dish they were when by any good luck salt could be got, for of all herbs else they were exceedingly fresh-tasted. But then salt was a luxury which it had become in my mind a sin to desire, as then taxed three or four hundred per cent. above natural value, to help in carrying on Mr. Pitt's wars with the French. On

* Earth-nuts, tubers of the *Bunium flexuosum*.

such journeys of forage, when I had come to a clear pool or spring well, I would have looked into it at my own face, and seriously said aloud to the reflection: "Keep up your heart, Jock Younger, my man; your face is honest yet, and there's better days afore ye." On which reflection would naturally have followed a castle in the air, at which sort of architecture I became as great in the ideal as Inigo Jones in the real, perhaps more fertile in my variations from the received five orders. I might have triple that number at the least—such variety in points of height, figure, and extension.

As I spent not a thought on what I found I had not the kind of genius to devise—how wealth or property might be acquired—I gave myself just at once a ready-made fortune, like an entailed duke or other gentleman, and I could be content with any size or form—from a snug little cottage (always, however, with a garden), and sixty pounds or so a year, with which I conceived I could do a good deal to comfort my friends and neighbours against future famines. Or I sometimes chose a fairy castle mansion, with extensive fields, rivers, and forests; or, by some strange, tumble-up-like enchantment, fell heir to an Indian fortune, with which I wrought miracles of blessing to an extensive range of district. And my taste was to do much with little show. I would have shed a whole primary of sunshine around my circled sphere; shot my rays in through the shadowed hovels of heartless poverty—the cold privations of human habitation; while gentlemen were riding past on blood horses, hunting, as occasion suggested, men or foxes to the death; and there I made all the little ragged children smile, like cherubs at a love feast, till in boundless joy the imaginary noise of their flightering mirth would awaken me from my reverie, when my home of penury and sister Betty's impatience would rush afresh on my mind like an electric shock, and set me again to running.

Young rooks in spring-time, procured from the nests by clambering the trees about Elliestoun House and Camiston, were often a feast; and in winter frozen turnips gathered on the cross-ways, as fallen from the farmers' carts, were made a notable supper repast when boiled and beaten up. I have often gathered these in the evenings, or by midnight moonlight, and then withered faggots from the snowy hedges or plantations, of which to kindle a fire and dress them, while all the rest of the happy world were sound asleep, except your toddy-noodled writers of gentle novels, who, busy over their "midnight oil," were describing the happy ignorance of the snoring *peasantry* without any real knowledge of such people's matters.

Harvest was a glorious time, as I could always cut corn for such sort of wages as were worth victual, and on cutting off two left-hand finger-nails at one whet, I could still glean from the stubble fields around wheat, barley, and pease, which, beaten out and boiled, was a dish for any such young lord of creation as myself, with teeth then so cutting sharp as to supersede the use of any millstone.

But all such resources would not, I believe, have held soul and body together throughout these years. had I not found frequent errands in to Elliestoun House, and become rather a favoured boy with the late Mrs. Tulloh and her excellent young family, from where I never came out fasting. Often have I there acted the simple young harper, and sung for my supper. And it was not till years afterwards I discovered that the old butler's care in closing the passage door, when I should commence my ditties to him and the servant girls, was often concerted by the young misses, that they might have the amusement of hearing me ring "through the wood, laddie," in perfect freedom. It was luckily against the laws of the house to leave, or receive returned, any of a mess of bread or meat presented to such as me; I consequently saved all I could for my poor sister at home, whom I always found awake and hungry at whatever late hour I arrived.

In this way we starved over the two years of general scarcity, and nearly two more of consequent entailed family poverty; but we were all hopeful candidates for long life and improved circumstances —my father in the high noon of life; my unfortunate sister yet young, a philosophical pupil in the school of sad experience, and the mother and nurse of an infant boy which she would not then have parted with (even to the care of the father) to have recovered even Eve's primitive innocence. Two of the three sisters were always out at service, earning "their sore-won penny fee," which, to their eternal honour, was never selfishly retained or expended foolishly, but always brought home, like Jennie's in the "Cottar's Saturday Night," "to help their parent dear," who was then in actual "hardships."

One particular hardship I recollect well. In the second year of this dearth my father was actually prosecuted for a small leather debt of four or five pounds by a merchant in Selkirk, who had never once previously charged him with the account, and before he could possibly overtake the sum, which might be a month or two, the lawyer had run him to two pounds of expenses. This became more fearful than the principal, and was at last raised by my two out-sisters bringing each a pound of their running wages at mid-term, when they got a leave to come to St. Boswells Fair, and which I saw paid to the heartless-looking lawyer in a tent on the sheep market, while not a shilling was left in the family of us, all present that day on St. Boswells Green. How hard was this earned? What necessary food might it have procured for us, the honest and hungry? And how abominably was it expended on a legal robber?

Few people were profiters by this dearth, except a miller here or there who dealt in corn and meal. My father remarked that Willie Hope, then the farmer of Temple lands here and "Clock-sorrow-mill," got a new coat on one of these years, for he had never met him out of the same old Sunday's snuff-brown one for thirty years previously—till then his cloth and colour never took a change; while Jennie, his wife, even brightened up considerably. Though Jennie long outlived Willie, they are both now "gone the way of all the earth," and I hope to a world where the pinch of famine shall never give an opportunity for the bettering of individual circumstances. Indeed, there was evidence amounting to certainty of Willie's ascent, as twenty years after his demise old Jennie averred that "on the very hour and minute that Willie Hope, her good-man, breathed his last breath, twa very decent men, who happened to be out to fodder the beasts, distinctly observed three figures pass the bright moon in full, fair flight." "Who could these be, Jennie?" "Aye, wha could they be but twae angels carrying Willie Hope's soul up to heaven?" "But souls cannot be seen with the naked eye, Jennie, woman." "Wie, what's souls but ghosts, an' ghosts are seen often enough, an' the twae whae saw them visibly wi' their een were never kenn'd for liers! Na, na; I ha'e nae reason to dispute them out o' that sicht; atweel ha'e I no."

CHAPTER XIII.

THROUGH the first of these years I had become wonderfully well used to even this state of life. And that a human being may become inured to hunger and slavery, and yet retain the social and moral virtues congenial to his natural disposition of mind, seems evident. Indeed, more particularly so in such circumstances than when by affluence and power he finds himself absolutely independent. "Jeshurun waxed fat and kicked." Yet as all extremes are dangerous, it is desirable that the general policy of society should, as much as possible, endeavour to prevent, or remedy, such extremes. "Give me neither poverty nor riches" should be a daily prayer from the heart of every son of earth and heir of immortality. It is one particular of what is implied in the general petition, "Lead us not into temptation." Extreme want may impel to desperate courses, and absolute power too often forgets its moral responsibility.

My mind was still occupied with boyish tastes and natural propensities; but now, as new ideas began to occur, I had some severe mental struggles between the propriety of certain pursuits and the desire of following them. I often reasoned with myself that it was unmanly to yield to vague desires which could end in nothing honourable or even beneficial, and on another view of the matter would consider it silly to stand starchly up, restraining from what was desirable, and not even accounted positive evil. To fishing and shooting, the renewed desire of taming birds and rabbits again returned; and at one time I got keen in the notion of snaring hares and partridges, supposing that in the event of success this would be a grand private resource for food. This last idea sanctioned the propriety to my own mind, in despite of game laws, which in this way I could evade, and which I was willing to consider a mere assumption of the all-grasping great. With whatever cunning I planted my snares, however, they were still more cunningly evaded; so that I succeeded in noosing only one poor hare, which I conceived to have had an awful struggle in her death, from her spurrings on the ground around the spot, while the wire had tightened her neck into a strictness little exceeding the diameter of her protruded and bursting eye. I carried her home under some qualms of disgustful reflection, new views rising on my imagination. There seemed a clandestine treachery in the pursuit; a sort of devilish insult on the peace and harmless quiet of nature; a hangman-like business altogether. Yes, a gun kills in an instant: but what feelings must this poor hare have had? I felt I was a wicked sinner. This, again, was as bad as the job of the pair of wood pigeons I had snared at their nest last summer in the fir tree, when I brought home the family, old and young together. Well, our little dusts with our neighbours are nothing to this business of casting out with ourself. In the first case, the blood is driven out into rapid circulation, and our life put into a foolish flurry till the flesh can hardly hold in the spirit; but in this latter case it is all dashed in on the heart, producing a suffocating sensation, something like what we may be supposed to feel under a sudden arrestment from the hand of the "last enemy." The remorse arising from culpable guilt must be dreadful, only that in many such cases the feelings may be less sensitive from heart-searedness.

I soon again subsided into quiet feeling, and resumed my usual amusive inquiry into all of animate and inanimate around me. I could not then tell how it was; but pleasures, and pains, and interests arose to me out of what my few associates often accounted the merest trifles. And although our sympathies ran often in counter parallels, with little affinity in regard to feeling, yet, from a childish dislike to oddity, and a fresh, youthful taste for sociability, I was often led to assimilate in cases of minor consequence, and sometimes even in opposition to my own convictions. As when looking at other people's works and arrangements, I conceived deficiencies on which I would calculate improvements to certain success; yet again as often doubted my own opinion, on reflection that people conversant with such things in the way of daily experience must certainly be better qualified to manage them than I could be, and therefore gave up my ideas as frequently as they were conceived. This, though prudent reasoning in a general way, was yet in many cases an error, as, on seeing more of the world, I have often since had reason to conclude. From this perhaps arose, or at least was confirmed, my succeeding habit of indecision through life, which now seems fixed as fate, and which has been the main disqualifying principle in my character as far as regards pursuit of worldly aggrandizement. As to what more particularly regards fixed opinion of moral principle, that I have never blinked nor sacrificed to the mammon of this world. In this way I then reasoned on such subjects as well as I can yet do. It surely becomes a created being to calculate upon the general goodness of God in providence, and the situation in which he finds himself placed. And as worldly circumstance seems merely fortuitous, a claim to such things as earth may produce can neither exalt, nor the want of such claim degrade, the human mind; therefore, whatever the present fashion of men's manners may be, creative intelligence must estimate us according to the use we make of that mind bestowed. And the exertion to retain, support, and exercise aright the mental faculties is certainly our proper part in life, in our longings and search after the highest gratifications of which our moral and intellectual nature is susceptible.

Even then, as yet through life, I felt very much interested in feeling through men's minds, where they might be at in regard to what I had begun to account the trammels of prejudice, or in ability to reason, arrange, and adduce for themselves. And whether it is that a considerable degree of intellect is exceedingly rare, or that the sympathies of the heart, in many instances, cause an unconscious adherence to friendly or family opinions, with a want of confidence to dispute and break through the long-settled habits of general custom, I could not then, nor can I yet, very well determine. I believed it might be from a combination of all these causes operating together, affected by present wants and immediate interests, with a desire of ease and personal gratification, that so determined the characters of mankind generally, producing all that variety of phase observable in the human mind when traced throughout society to any considerable degree of development.

My greatest-felt want then, next to a proper supply of daily bread, was a want of that (even common) education which I considered necessary to qualify me to arrange and express my ideas. This was a fettering of faculties quite puzzling, over which the thoughts of the mind effervesced to bursting. And at that age I had ideas equal to a long discourse on whatever subject presented itself to the mind, but the want of language equal to my taste of expression absolutely produced a stupid, if not often an absurd, appearance.

I used to think that it might be in the power of language, with time and opportunity, to express the many glorious thoughts of which the human soul is susceptible, as in holy moral musing it expands over the lights and shades on the face of nature; and then how deficient I must be in language, since my conceptions so far exceeded my power of expression. But I could find no supply for this deficiency. There was nothing of lexicon about our cottage except a tattered fragment of Cole's Dictionary, which in its prime had possibly belonged to my grand-uncle, a man of some education.

My father, indeed, had gleaned up some score or two of what I thought powerful words, which he applied much to my admiration, yet I could collect no string of them adequate to express my ideas. I was, in fact, in a felt want of something to gratify the mind's appetite; and except the few tragical ballads then afloat on the surface of village society, such as "Sir James the Rose," "Chevy Chase," "Child Maurice," "Catskin's Garland," "The Babes in the Wood," and the "Sleeping Beauty in the Wood," the "Gosport," and other tragedies of war, love, and murder, in addition to "Mother Bunch's Fairy Tales," interspersed with halfpenny ballads, or "garlands of six excellent new songs," I could find nothing of a metrical description till I again turned back to "The Psalms of David in Metre," to which the scripture paraphrases about that time made a delightful addition, and of which the versification felt so excessively sweet to my ear, forming such a symphony with the spirit of the text, as to express the sympathy of the soul under the impression of pure religious feeling.

Then the poetical grandeur of our fine old English translation of "The Book of Job," with several other particular passages of sacred scripture, cast such an indescribable halo of glory around my soul that I felt as if swimming in an atmosphere of inexpressible delight which I should never be able fully to enjoy or comprehend. And then the Proverbs of Solomon and the Ecclesiastes appeared as ladder-steps to the mind, lifting me above the mire of my native ignorance into a region of finer moral air and freer respiration.

About this time I accidentally got the loan of Thomson's "Seasons," to which I fell with avidity, but was at first nearly beaten, finding it neither prose nor rhyme, till at last, by resting at the lines, I found a harmony, and attending to the stops led me to the sense of such passages as lay within the reach of my comprehension. The simple parts of the rural imagery were charming, till by degrees about a third part of the whole opened up like a new sun risen on the horizon of my mental vision. And soon the solitary woods around responded to the hymn which crowns the "Seasons," as there, when alone, I sang it out in gusts of rapture.

From this time all subjects of amusement seemed in my view to sink into nothing as compared with poetry—that power of receiving the impressions of nature, or even fancy, on the soul, and of reflecting back their images in a mellowed light to the mind's eye of another; also of embodying and clothing gracefully the very phantoms of imagination, giving, as it were, an extension to our ideal bounds of creation. And although in the enthusiasm of the time I felt as if drawn by nature and tied by sympathy to consider poetry as the main flower of the heart, worthy of a life's care and culture, and from which a continual feast of soul was to be derived, sipped up out of life as the bee extracts honey from the blossom, yet as all of my acquaintance, old and young, around, even those considered the best informed, seemed so apathetic about that matter, esteeming the finest descriptions in the "Seasons" as at least frivolous and "of no use," I still had my qualms of doubt that my felt enthusiasm might proceed from some soft, unmanly feeling—some particular weakness in the constitution of mind, craving indulgence which it might be imprudent to foster or encourage. And as the language necessary to the expression of my ideas seemed so difficult of attainment in my case, I gave up thoughts of attempting to prosecute poetry as a study of acquirement, resolving only to love and prefer it as any fine thing of the kind might thereafter occasionally fall in my way. Thus I would then have neglected the taste for a time for months together, when again, under some sickening disgust at the paltry trifling and petty insignificance of every-day thought in common pursuits, I would have felt suddenly seized with a new fit of poetical love while some subject of fancy would have presented itself to the mind, and ideas arose and passed over it like spirits in a sunbeam; but the train of their succession was so light and fairy-footed that to catch and arrest them was an attempt to gather gossamer—since the very motion necessary to seize a pen would break the charm and dispel the visionary assemblage; and then in place of my fine field of ideas, which had arisen as if by enchantment—airy, light, and flickering like moonshine on streams—I would be left blank, as in a vacuum of mind, to beat about in vain for whatever stiff, cold sentence could be dragged forward with which to clothe a poor, deserted subject. Hence, a few written verses would turn out to appear so miserable an expression of the thoughts that suggested them, that, like a daub of a picture, they looked a mere caricature of their original idea.

As even my friend, the blacksmith's apprentice, seemed not to relish or understand the "Seasons," I had no participant in my admiration, and therefore, in social intercourse with my neighbours, I felt bound in to the mere twattle of daily trifle, without any stimulus to attempt ascent on the wing of imagination. Though as yet it was only green spots of the "Seasons" I could understand, I appreciated these at their full value, convinced that the poems would be a grand whole when I should acquire the power of comprehending them clearly, and therefore, ever as disheartened I had fallen off, I as often again took courage and returned vigorous to the study, read on again and again, screwing up the pegs of my understanding like fiddlestrings to the strained point of cracking. But, O gracious! what is the meaning of that hard word, like a locked box, in which the pearl of true sense must lie contained? The few left leaves of old *Cole* had not a twentieth part of the words I wanted, and then such short definitions as often to explain one hard word by another equally puzzling.

I would sometimes then begin to think—I wish I may not, after all, be a perfect simpleton, and not sensible of it myself, for I find I am not somehow like the general run of my neighbours in my tastes and notions; or will I just appear to them what they appear to me? But never mind; I feel I am not shabby in my intentions at any rate, and if I had the power I would put matters so right as to convince them all. And yet it is surely a simple thing to let that Andrew Smail bluster and threaten me at every turning, while sure in my own mind that I could blind up his eyes before he could bring up his lumpish neives* to their defence. But then, again, this ap-

* Fists.

peared like walking backward on the road of life. How could I get over that dislike to striking or hurting any one, when I saw such grief at casual distress, and such interest and trouble taken to cure the sick? This Andrew Smail was a farmer's boy from the next steading, a heavy sort of bullying chap, who had foughten Will. King, and many other redoubtable characters. He would *damn* the horses' souls; and when I observed that they had no soul of a kind to be damned, he replied that Will. Grierson damned the brown nag's soul on Saturday last, and, being a man, surely knew better than me. By a sacrifice of self-will I had managed to keep the peace with him for the preceding twelvemonth, although the while he would often disarrange my little garden or so in the rudest manner for the pure purpose of fretting me; and when I attempted a rescue of any trifle he would threaten fearfully. While at this odds one day some men standing by disputed his ability if I were willing, when he came forward and struck me slightly with his left hand, keeping the other in awful reserve for a dreadful blow. I instantly collared him with one hand, and with short strokes of the other literally sealed up his eyes in a twinkling, while in his astonishment he verily forgot all his boasted grand guards and principal hits; for except twisting his fingers in my long hair, he seemed incapable of working the smallest harm, and became quiet even to tears, henceforward submitting to my superiority, which my natural distaste to warfare ever afterwards prevented me from abusing.

In this mood I sallied out to the small burn, which, at that time, yet unrestrained like myself, chose its own vagrant way from Eiliestoun House to the Tweed, circling through the low rushy leas, forming dimple, pool, and ripple; and there I gumped out half a stone of speckled trouts, where my neighbours never suspected such a thing existed.

The poet is in error when he says—

> "The trout within yon wimplin' burn
> Glides swift, a silver dart;
> And safe beneath the shady thorn
> Defies the angler's art."

This the trout cannot do, for its clammy nose, and clear, round eye, are ever protruded on the alert for a fly or a worm, and well the angler knows where and how to drop the wormed hook into the pool before him. When a whale is not safe in the Polar Ocean, talk, forsooth, of a trout in a burn! Oh, dear shade of Burns! the poetical portion of your earthly feelings might have been too fine for an angler, as well as those of your grand successor, Byron; or they might not, for all the fascination of song; although I grant you that even I, when a hungry laddie, have often enough got into these fits of extreme sensibility, returning the small trout to the stream,

> "As piteous of his youth, and the short space
> He had enjoyed the vital light of heaven."

And, indeed, I have often felt the full force of Byron's satirical remark on anglers long before he wrote it; ay, and occasionally got into such qualms of reluctance that I would suspend my angling pursuits, and admire the trouts tumbling up in the streams, suppressing the desire to cast a hook amongst the freebooters. And the same sympathies have at times unfitted me for some necessary employment of life; yes, even to the length of requiring an effort of my strongest philosophy to bring me to prune a rose or pluck a flower! This was nursing the poetical temperament to an unnecessary tenderness. "No angler can be a good man," says Byron; yet I believe these sensitive gentlemen, the poets, could all eat lamb, veal, and oysters as heartily as trouts can snap up lovely, *innocent* flies, or gobble the small fry of their own species with all the mischievous appetite of a cannibal.* And, alas! the sensibilities of genius give no sufficient guarantee for that consistency of character which would justify us in bestowing the designation of "a good man" on any human being.

* From the stomach of a trout of about a pound weight, I have twice cut out six small trouts, pars, or smolts, averaging five inches long—the one first swallowed digested nearly to the bones; the last, whole and entire, still stuck in the gullet for lack of capacity in the stomach equal to the voracity of the creature's nature. One of these trouts took my imitation fly, over and above this gorged bellyful, by which it was caught; the other, the half of a small trout, with which a hook was baited.

CHAPTER XIV.

> "It's sair to think on friendship fled,
>   And live while hope decays;
> It's sair to seek amang the dead
>   The loves of early days."
>
> Miss JANNET RYLAND.

WHATEVER may be said in songs, I have often throughout life observed that when a lad of fourteen falls first in love it is not generally with an opening bud of his own age, but with a woman in the fragrance of full blossom. My first passion was about that age, and with a pretty, fair woman (Mary Scott), ten years older than myself at the least. Everybody knows the feeling of first love, surpassing all description, and for this very good reason in nature—every one feeling it in kind and degree, it comes under the class of instincts, where no description is requisite. She seemed in my view pretty, and pleasant, and wise, and more to be loved than any person I had seen—although I never thought her the least like an angel, as the very *exquisite* songs now have them; nor wished her in any respect otherwise than what she just exactly was—a kind, good heart, and sweet, social spirit, encased in a fine-skinned, neat form of flesh and blood, very much after the fashion of my fancy of female perfection: the identical creature I could have wished to have pressed to my bosom, in preference to all the winged angels of creation—a grand specimen of help-mate for man. I delighted to draw near her as much as possible, to hear her talk, and see her smile, which she could do sweetlier than any one else! But being in rather unfavourable circumstances for love-making, I had never the face to say I loved her. For besides my natural bashfulness, there was such a cast of the ridiculous about the idea of expressing love in my case, youth and circumstances considered, that it was lucky I had just sagacity enough not to despise prudence in the matter. I felt I must be considered a mere lad, and in a state of half starvation, with no near prospect of even clothes forthcoming to re-cover my fast-approaching raggedness; while she was plump, ripe, ready for marriage to-morrow, and likely already a-weary of "single blessedness," and must, of course, have faded while I should still be in the prime of life. However, I had the pleasure of gazing at her every opportunity, besides conversing with her in my dreams, and for a year or two afterwards, while she remained unmarried, she was still the favourite object in every picture of my imagination. From the appearance of her person, face, and features, she seemed to my fancy to occupy the place amongst the various colours and classes of women that the goldfinch does amongst birds. These ideas became so combined in my imagination that the sight of that pretty bird ever still brings the image of that sweet little woman full on my mind's eye.

> "Oh! that hallowed form is ne'er forgot,
>   Which first love trac'd;
> Still it lingering haunts the greenest spot
>   On memory's waste:

> 'Twas odour fled so soon as shed,
>   'Twas morning's wingéd dream,
> 'Twas a light that ne'er can shine again
>   On life's dull stream."

Oh! Tom Moore, that is the best verse you ever wrote, or perhaps anybody else. It is a fine growth of nature, a true expression of feeling, while many of your lyrics are mere prinklings of art.

This love concern, then, began to give poetry an additional interest. I could now feel, with a new relish, the charm of Thomson's episodes, Musidora bathing in the "Seasons," and Lavinia gleaning; could imagine the very shape of Palemon's hat, very different from anything of hat kind I had ever then seen—very low-crowned and broad-brimmed, raised in front, high above his brow, and flapped down behind over his coat-neck; but the coat had only indeed a lappet of neck, was single-breasted, snuff-coloured, and nearly half-bare worn. Lavinia had a fawn-coloured straw cap of her own making, with a check apron, something like my mother's, but folded round her waist, into which she gathered the detached wheat-heads. How I should have conceived the figure of these—hat, cap, and coat—I know not, having never seen any such in these days; black silk caps for women, and narrow-lipped, high-crowned hats for men, being in fashion all my youth hitherto, since some years previously they had supplanted the old flat blue wool Scotch Border bonnet.

My taste in songs changed then also from "a hunting we will go," and the old tragical ballad kind of "Chevychasery" hitherto in fashion, to the fine, simple pathos of the short ode. "A' the airts the wind can blaw," and "Their groves o' sweet myrtle," were then getting into the halfpenny collections; and these were a treasure for a young rustic who felt his heart flooded with a mixture of love and music as mollifying as milk and honey!—fine subsistence while other nutritive aliment, even blue-skimmed milk and pease bannocks, were un-come-at-able.

If love and music were not spiritual, and indestructible in their essence, but dependent on a bodily principle, they would, of course, have been starved out of me in these years, which they were not, but rooted, grew, and budded like intellectual evergreens, indigenous to my heart. Yes, love seems to be the main principle in life—the divinity of our nature—inextinguishable and inexhaustible, without which even matter would fritter and fall asunder. It seems to be the soul of life, the spirit, and the test of true religion. The more we love at home, the more we love also abroad. These glorious orbs that shine forth on our eye after the setting of our sun, our earth's door-neighbours in the vast creation, how I hail them as a portion of the works of our *general* Father "which art in heaven," no doubt replete with the same intelligent sympathies of homely love and kindling affections in the appointed kind and degree. Love seems to be the heavenly bond, the attractive influence, linking creation together. Gravitation is love, the divine essential principle, which conjoins to satisfaction the large and the small; from the orbs in heavenly space to the most minute atom in creation. Hence the breach, or the distortion, of this principle is sin, to the perversion and misery of the creature. And music is properly the voice, the harmony, and the expression of love.

> "And music is in all—from the high spheres
>   Down to the reeds that o'er the marshes bend:
> Those choir in concert to celestial ears,
>   These sing responsive to the wooing wind.
> The sympathy that swells the heart to tears
>   Of bliss or rapture may be trac'd to blend
> Itself with all existence, time, and space—
> 'Tis heaven's love, the source of heaven's grace."

But to descend from my lark-flights, I must tell you that all the people around this rural spot with whom I could possibly then become acquainted might consist of three or four dozen individuals, old and young together; and although every one had a particular character of his own, and they were very various in natural tastes, temper, and disposition, yet in the necessary plod of common life you could have made very little distinction, with less trouble than a close acquaintance.

I had now begun earnestly to take the measure of their minds according to my own notion, yet had very few good opportunities of seeing them in an excited state, as an occasional merry-making in my circumstances occurred but seldom.

We had, however, regularly once a year, on New Year's evening, a pretty full meeting in Eiliestoun House, where all around, who had any connection with the family, were invited, had a substantial dinner, and as much drink as to make us all sufficiently jovial without intoxication.

> "There was toasting and fiddling, and dancing and singing,
>   With old George* the butler, so brisk 'Highland-flinging;'
> All were lively and bright, from the laird to the *cadie*,
> And the cheerfullest face in the house had the lady!"

---

* Geordie Matthewson, a genuine old Highlander, who afterwards kept the steel-yard in the market place at Melrose. He was a great original, but rather too fond of *uisge beatha*.

To George the "Highland-fling" seemed natural—the dance of his native hills, his youth, and his pride. He did it, as he did all things else, most punctiliously, with all the scrape, prance, whirl, and evolution, to the very crack of his thumbs.

In "sang about" his was his favourite sentiment to his favourite air, "Highland Laddie," with all due precision of point, spirit, and emphasis. One stanza ran thus:—

> "A' the Figs 'ill gang to hell,
> Bonnie laddie, Highland laddie;
> Geordy, he'll be there himsel',
> My bonnie Highland laddie.
>
> "For Sathan sits in the black newk,
> Bonnie laddie, Highland laddie;
> Rivin' sticks to roast the Duke,
> My bonnie Highland laddie."

The *crouse* old hedger (Jamie Thomson), though in the *fidgets*, would formally resist all importunity to burst out with his favourite song until particularly requested by the lady herself, who prefaced her request by a winning speech, that, as he had sung it the first night of their annual merriment under the roof-tree, "The Prussian Drum" had ever since seemed to her an indispensable portion of that festive evening's hilarity; and, moreover, she considered it as his song most particularly, and almost exclusively so, as whoever had composed it must have had him in their eye to sing it, since nobody else could give it such expression. So, then, the "Prussian drum" was struck up in all the force of lungs with which he had made that hall resound annually for one thirty years of the world. That song was descriptive of the victories of Frederick of Prussia in the Protestant cause; but, like many such noisy effusions composed for the day and hour, it had not in the composition *poetry*, properly so called, sufficient to keep it afloat on the great tide of time, and therefore is not worth notification here, though I might recover it from memory.

About this time I was beginning to perceive that every one, however silly, had some particular point in his or her character which he or she considered a qualification or talent, and upon which each valued himself particularly. And, from observation since, I have been confirmed in this opinion of mankind generally. At that time, perceiving it in individual cases, I thought it proceeded from a narrowness of mind and confinement of ideas, which might have been expanded by education and general information, until, in highly cultivated minds, it would be altogether lost in a broad liberality of sentiment. Subsequent observation, however, has led me to a different conclusion, which is to consider it a general principle in our human nature, which, though in excess it may seem weakness, deserving the name of vanity, yet after all seems a constituent quality, perhaps, in the proper degree, requisite for keeping a person in sufficient conceit, or at least in charity with himself. However that may be, I have certainly seen it in all classes of people with whom I have come into communication, and it is also easily detected in the very finest of our various writers.

The restriction of this principle within due bounds, until it should scarcely be found to stir in the individual's own mind, and become imperceptible to the observation of others, would be an amazing improvement on the human character, and bring a person into assimilation with the feelings of the Christian apostle, who gave this injunction as a corrective of the propensity, "Let no man think more highly of himself than he ought to think."

And, what is the most remarkable trait in this disposition, a man seldom prides himself upon his best quality, but often upon something in which he is never likely to excel, or become even equal with the run of his neighbours. A fine singer is never so vain of his accomplishment as is one who has with much tasteless application just learned to bawl contention with "rude Boreas, blustering railer." Yes, I have seen a man, who was considered as wise in ordinary matters as most of his neighbours, value himself ostentatiously upon some supposed qualification, which in itself might be not only level to the most common capacity, but often trifling, and sometimes disgusting to ordinary sensibility; some, on the very absurd vulgarities of human action, esteeming themselves thereby grandly eccentric; even a heavy, lazy, lumpish lout attempting the easy jesture of youthful frolic, like an old horned ram at lamb's-play; and a young spectacled fop counterfeiting absence of mind as if he were a thinker. I have seen a sharp, small-eyed man valuing himself upon his property, his ridges, bonds, or money, to whom such things were as useless as the loose trundling-stones on his footpath, while his closed heart could not enjoy sixpence-worth of its comforts in his life, nor purchase a penny-worth of sorrow's tears to glisten over his coffin; another, in lavish and utter disregard of money and propriety, make himself ridiculous as well as bankrupt. One values himself on his exquisite taste in the cut and fashion of his clothes, and the very particular good figure he can make of himself in the vapour of his grand show-off; another on a slovenly manner, in studied imitation of the careless habits of some "learned Theban" he has read or heard of. An esquire boasts of his family, or lairdship, name, and supposed influence, and the awe with which he imagines he strikes all around him; while in fact the man is verily pitied or despised by the insulted community of his common neighbours, on whom he can make no impression further than to command a kind of shopkeeper respect for any trifle of ready money which he may have occasion necessarily to expend amongst them. I know a living, learned doctor who values himself so highly upon his "classical knowledge" that he assumes a tyrannical supremacy over myself and others, denying us the natural privilege of forming or expressing an opinion at all, even on matters with which we are from certain experience most intimately acquainted, and of which his Greeks and Latins were as stone blank ignorant as he is. By this folly he gets himself justly despised. I know another *very* clever man who values himself upon his taste in drumming *rub-a-dub-a-du* on the crown of his hat, the door, or the table, to the sad annoyance of a party, in accompaniment to one singing "Taste life's glad moments," &c. A late distinguished philosopher,* I am told, valued himself more on his knowledge of salmon

---

* Sir Humphrey Davy, who wrote "Salmonia; or, Days of Fly-fishing," about two years before his death.

and angling, on which he wrote a volume of something very like nonsense, than on all the rest of his valuable scientific discoveries; and what is equally strange is, that on account of his otherwise great name this production has gone through three or four editions—a sorry print proof of our general human weakness. We may see a fine woman value herself not only on her false curls, but on a certain grimace assumed to set off her repartees, which she supposes to be wit, yet which neutralizes the good effect of all the fine feminine qualities which, in the natural expression of her face, would have given her a winning appearance, and secured her many lovers.

I am even detecting myself at present as not a little vain in being enabled to note and express these trifling observations; and this is fortunate, as, should I follow the subject much further, I might be tempted to suspect some truth in Combe's description of Sir Humphry's cosmogony, that this globe was originally a fluid mass, a hot shower whirled off from the sun, I suppose, which, cooling down through the course of some few millions of centuries back, has lately become encrusted and habitable; that in place of man being created complete, and losing his first estate through disobedience, our progenitors were originally little better than apes, till, progressing onward, they walked away from their Monboddo tails, so that latterly the generations are looking more trim and wise like; and that henceforward, by paying proper attention to his rules of procreation, for breeding large brain-pans, instead of those old-fashioned austral skulls, people's wits will get room to ferment to a purification of principles, influencing mind and manner, which by some few myriads of ages hence will purify like strong old ale, and perhaps crystalize into a spiritual transparency, when, agreeably to the doctrine of the eternity of matter,

> "In our ashes live their wonted sires."

Musing on some such matters the other morning, while standing on the Tweed bank here looking over Dryburgh up to the Eildon Hills, I conceived some curious thoughts a little in analogy with this doctrine, which I endeavoured to embody in the following verses. Were it not in gratification of a certain propensity we have for rhyming occasionally I would prefer prose, as perhaps a better, as being a more fashionable, mode of expressing our ideas. Excuse the rhyme, therefore, here given under the name of

SOLITARY REFLECTIONS.

I am here like a visiting dream of the night,
   All unknowing alike as unknown;
I am here like a mote in a beam of the light
   For to-day, and to-morrow I'm gone.

And, oh! where did I sleep when these hills towering steep
   Rose in rocks o'er the wide waters blue?
Was my substance at rest in the bed of the deep,
   Or afloat in the air and the dew?

All at rest in the stone, or at rage in the storm,
   It hath pass'd through a long pristine hour,
Till call'd forth to assume this new change of form
   By the charm of a wonderful power!

And this power still remains, and for ever maintains
   Its original force, all divine!
Since this matter through the blood of a million's veins
   Hath enlapsed its way into mine.

And soon again reduc'd to that primitive state,
   Far below the realms of dreams,
Will this liquid that flows through the veins of my heart
   Give a voice in the ripple of streams.

Still renew'd and re-form'd in continual change
   Will this stream down through long ages run;
While each new-kindled soul it with life's frame supplies
   May think time only lately begun.

For, as thrown on a rock in the midst of the deep
   Of eternity's ocean sublime,
We live through our hour till the next swelling tide
   Sweeps us over that bourne called our Time.

Since Time is but a word to express our life's date,
   Or the date of a system or world;
While eternity's gulph is the where, under fate,
   All the rubbish of Time-things are hurl'd.

But here is yet a heart, a fond, keen-thinking part,
   That may never again meet decay,
Which we may, as inclin'd, call matter, soul, or mind,
   Or designate by what name we may.

Since all matter seems to live, to change, and to move
   Through ever-varying forms till refin'd;
Such progress may go on through cycles long to run
   Until all be resolv'd into Mind.

Then one essential soul may pervade the great whole
   Until space be o'erflowing with Spirit;
Of perception unconfin'd, in One Eternal Mind
   Each part shall the grand whole inherit.

In absence of a higher hope, the above might be a consummation to be wished, in proportion to our natural reluctance to quit this sentient existence—this state where the comfort of present life so greatly depends on the social compact, that to exist solely in the individual would be a neutrality more felt than would be a deprivation of half our human faculties.

By the way, Combe is an amazingly ingenious author, and, right or wrong—or, rather, right *and* wrong—takes up a striking position in the field of physiology, making a capital figure by his productions. His phrenological plans might very much conduce to the improvement of our race, could he continue to carry them out into general practice as easily as some of our half-deified generals can lead out a sixty thousand "flowers of chivalry" to dash out each others' brains on a sunny morning, in the "good old cause" of upholding the "good old systems." But he will find it not quite so easy to set a-going his vehicle on a new railroad to perfection as it is to feed on taxes, and lead the will by the old propensities. Steam and gas are more manageable. "It is amazing," says sister Nanny yesterday, "what wiles Diabolous used in old Bunyan's 'Holy War' to besiege and keep the town of Mansoul." "Yes," replies my wife, "he is spared of much trouble now-a-days, for I doubt we are all going his way of our own accord." "The world was never wickeder than now" has been the complaint in all ages, and any plan to make it less so is surely desirable.

Combe's grand theory would doubtless make beautiful practice, since the world, verily rectified by any fair-play method, might be much more comfortable to live in; but then I doubt whether he has calculated on the necessary means for carrying his scheme into fashion. He might first require an Act of Parliament to establish a standing order of college-taught phrenologists to take a physical and moral superintendence of that matter over all parishes; to examine the heads of young couples in regard to the order and propriety of pairing them, agreeably to a suitable conjunction of the developments requisite for proper breeding; also a law to prevent the *flat-sculls* from marrying, or otherwise attempting promiscuous propagation. A strong standing police force might be requisite to correct this, and let the scheme work orderly.

But even then, as present existence is, at the longest, so transitory and uncertain, his system at the best falls wofully short of satisfying the appetite of the human soul in its *individual* capacity, since every *single* soul pants after a continuance of personal existence. To have the full measure of man's capacity we must have an eternity of spiritual life, of which the happiest threescore and ten years here is a portion so comparatively inconsiderable as not to be worth contending for. This is a curtailment of our fondest hopes so disheartening that we are loath to give a free assent to it, and this although we could raise even weaker arguments in its favour than our present data will bear us fully out in.

The most that Combe's theory in his "Constitution of Man" can promise us is, some considerable improvement in this present life's condition, as the result of our attention to certain proprieties of life and conduct; and that more particularly to the future generations of our species than to our present drawers of breath, who feel we may die ere Saturday, or, at any rate, that "our make encloses the sure seeds of death." Now, though we would love to be assured of the coming generations being, by any means, much improved in the science or sound philosophy of life, yet this is but a stinted measure of consolation for the present generation, as well as of our sympathy for all who have passed through the ordeal of this life since the creation of man. And since even in our present life's very best condition,

> "The soul, uneasy, and confined at home,
> Rests and expatiates in a life to come,"

we naturally long for a further outcoming in the individual instance, and strain eagerly at even the idea of it.

Any one who can suggest any plan of present improvement has a claim to our respect and thanks, providing he can do so without infringing the charter on which we hold for a future resurrection to eternal life. But although in Combe's "Constitution of Man" there is much that is morally excellent and beautifully written, worthy to be acted upon—though gospel precepts are therein *acknowledged* and *approven*, and a *future state not denied*—yet, having in his system put man upon another footing in regard to his original creation, our scripture account of his *perfect* formation, his *fall*, and *redemption* is thereby set aside or tacitly denied, and consequently the New Testament doctrine of our resurrection to eternal life blown to the winds, for which deprivation of hope he has nothing to offer us instead, but an infinitely less reward, for even a far more troublesome exertion, than that plain, beautiful system of conduct which the scriptures have been pressing on our attention in the best form of word and doctrine. Now, though the doctrine of a resurrection to eternal life were even to turn out to have been a delusion, yet we cannot afford to lose the present comfort of believing it for any immediate compensation this world has to bestow. Nobody now will give us even Esau's mess of pottage for our glorious birthright, while the longings of the human soul, with nothing on earth adequate to its satisfaction, are in themselves indicative of its immortality.

Moreover, Combe's plan may not be workable, even if worth working, as in operation it might cause an extension of the common date of human life beyond the limits which he himself has prescribed as the proper order of Providence for giving place and room to the regular succession of generations; and if the world were made all so fine and so comfortable, our reluctance to leaving it would be proportionally increased, while leave at last we must in a heathenish uncertainity of any future light or life.

But be his views correct or not, of one thing we may remain convinced, that mankind will not trouble themselves about the adoption of it, because man as an animal will not forego his propensities easily for the benefit of future generations; since even in money-making, those who scrape and gather for future heirs have seldom that as their main view, but rather a hope that they may somehow be spared to live on—to shine, to enjoy, or require it themselves.

That procreation-preventive-police, too, might fail in strict duty, and voluntary example could not, I fear, carry his plan into general observance in the teeth of present reigning propensities; since nothing gives a more deplorable picture of human nature than this, that the experience of one generation gives no effective example to another. The father's experience, even his privations and misery from miscalculation and misconduct, though urged most seriously in example for the son's consideration, can scarcely be once thought of, far less counted upon by the son, until the young fool have gone the same round of aberration, and bent under the same pressure of consequences. Nay, even the same grey-haired human being, in the midst of all his mortifying compunctions, will, by almost no diversity of path or circumstance, *doit** into the same slough again ere ever the dust of the former mud be well brushed from his heels. This tendency to "following the bent of body or of mind" keeps the individual, even the family, nay, the world itself, in continued depression of life and spirits. From this has also arisen in ill-informed minds some false Turkish ideas of fatality. It appears that people have a desire to strain all points to suit their own immediate views, as well as to lighten their conscience of a moral culpability.

Phrenology is also tenaciously maintained, as well as denied, on the score of these opinions, more particularly than from attention to the proofs of its reality in the constitution of our nature. This is weak reasoning also, seeing that our nature and moral responsibility remain the same, whether we investigate the mechanism as conducive to the preponderance of affections, or refrain from so doing. And the denial that there is an existing second cause of the variety of character and affection in the constitution of the human economy is just on a par of weakness with the idea that any diversity of brain,

* Walk stupidly.

bump, or sensibility can go to destroy the great moral law of our general nature. No man unswayed by stupid prejudice (rather than stultified by preponderance of the affections of brain) can resist the impression that this diversity in the human character does actually exist; and he who, from application to study, can trace and investigate any of its nice varieties to demonstration, most certainly has a right to our attention and approbation, if not to our admiration.

The apostle Paul seems tacitly to have confessed the existence of some such principle, from the way he often mentions effects, such as in alluding to "the sin that doth most easily beset us," and defining the nature and effect of the fleshly resistance to the better will in his own person, as well as the graces of the Spirit qualified to overcome it, bringing all into obedience to the law of Christ, and powerful to the bringing down of every stronghold of iniquity, *et-cœtera.*

While, therefore, to deny the existence of that visible diversity in the seat of human sensibility, as an appointed means, conducive to a beautiful variety in the human character, is to deny much clear demonstration and all analogy; yet, on the other hand, to go the length of some in supposing it, when defined to a clear-acknowledged science, as supremely calculated to direct men in moulding the heads of their children, or in making a definite choice for their proper study and pursuit agreeably to the development of their natural taste and ability, and by such means to direct them and lead them in the paths of virtue, joy, and peace to the highest perfection of their intellectual nature, is, perhaps, in a fanciful anticipation, shooting beyond the mark, as it argues little wisdom or discernment to augur a coming hour of universal perfection on earth from *this* means; since nothing is more clear than that the earthly constitution of things will ever prevent the greater proportion of mortals from becoming sufficiently scientific to even get acquainted with that as a saving science; and that they would not be careful of it though they did is sufficiently demonstrable by the lives of many of the masters of science in the present day, who, while talking pompously of the "march of intellect," march their own minds out of much that is moral and intellectual.

Had this been the supreme method by which our Maker and Preserver meant men to be governed and directed to their chief good, so many ages of confusion, sin, and misery would not have been suffered to elapse without a *Spurzheim* or a *Combe* having been put forward with the comfortable saving science; or just to have made us all merely instinctive beings at once, like the other animals, would have answered the end of Combe's reformation as well, and much more easily.

Faith in Christ the Redeemer, which worketh by love, leading us to renounce the evil affections and gross lusts of the flesh, purifying the heart, and leaving it a clean residence for the Spirit of holiness, free to the incitements of a regenerated will, inclining to justice, benevolence, faith, hope, and charity, which is love, is the nearest and clearest way of arriving at the wished-for perfection of our nature, and the bliss which it is capable of enjoying;

and this by whatever inequalities our heads are distinguishable.

CHAPTER XV.

IN the narrative of a little life it may look incongruous thus to lay the two ends together, combining in the same short chapter the amusements of boyhood with the acquirements of age. But then, it may be recollected that between 1799, the time of which I write, and the present year, 1841, more progress has been made in arts and sciences than in at least all the preceding fifteen hundred years taken together. The effects have been astonishing!—the very elements brought into subserviency to grand human purposes, and more general knowledge—I would fain hope *moral* as well as physical—evolved and diffused amongst the mass of the human race. Nor is it strange that even I, existing in an agricultural district comparatively isolated from every grand source or mart of such movements, still, upon the same philosophical principle that a wag of your finger agitates the universe—even I, simple as I am, have not got through these forty years without feeling the influence of the grand motion, and I may be allowed to reason as well as another.

A wonderful change had then begun to take place in the world, the influence of which was extending into the very fibrous roots of society. As the light of science began to dawn on the public mind, and men to assert their natural rights of discussing and reasoning for themselves on religion and political economy, the oppressive Governments took alarm, and, in the hope of still suppressing knowledge and free discussion, drew their claws the tighter on society, as a cat does on a mouse that might show its supposed insolence in a struggle to escape.

The French Government had previous to this time become most insupportable to the people forming the body of the nation—having, even openly, freed the rich (their aristocracy) from all taxation whatever, and saddled the productive population with taxes for their own exclusive benefit, until its sinews began to crack beneath the weight of the burden —until at last, like a much-abused ass, it grew fractious, and kicked its heels in its master's face, even in the face of royalty itself. Driven to madness, it was not natural that the people should act with prudence or even common sagacity; hence the absurd and bloody scenes which followed, and hence, too, the opposition in all the old Governments, which then put forth their whole energies against liberality of sentiment, and drifted into war against the French people; out of which war arose Buonaparte, like a salamander out of the fire, whom it required the combined energy of old Europe to put down. The sequel of this war is now the subject of history, in which it is glossed up in various colours, according to the particular information and political spirit of the different writers.

Had I then begun and continued since to take notes, as often through life I have thought of doing, I might have arrested a variety of passing thoughts and useful observations, which would have afforded me amusement at least in reviewing the past colour of my mind under all sorts of excitations, hopes, and fears, with their consequent effects and sympathies, now fled on the wing of time, and vanished in the shades of the past, to be succeeded by others equally interesting in their hour, but which the worn sensibilities cannot so acutely feel and recall.

For previously to this time the rural life in Scotland had presented a more primitive appearance than it now does; nor had the smaller farming classes taken up any measured distance from their tradesmen neighbours. But now their wives, hitherto as plain as a barn door, under first low-taken leases and war-rising markets, began to look up to and imitate the style of small gentry. The tenant or his son began to ride a mad blood horse to market; probably dined at the Club, if the number of his farm acres would sanction his admittance amongst the more extensive holders (for they seemed as nice in their distinctions as much higher gentry); likely became a Yeomanry-Cavalry man, bold and terrible, to smite or terrify every poor, hungry tradesman neighbour who should give so much as a mousecheep about equitable rights in opposition to arbitrarily-assumed privilege. Hence, as they a-field became mighty, the mistress at home grew quite madamish; while a pianoforte and other *et ceteras* must be had for Miss the daughter. But as soon as their first leases expired their rents rose to a pitch above the average return of crops, and hence, after all their straining and worrying, and their ruining of classes below them, they generally broke down, under hypothec sequestration, to paupers, and, in some instances, to proprietors of the beggar's staff and wallet. In this case the legislative landlord had secured to himself a legal preference for his rents over the tenant's other debts, and this he generally made secure by previous private sequestration to the extent of all his claim; while the poor tradesman or small merchant neighbour must smart or pine under the loss of the heaviest bills they had been enabled to accredit.

I have through life seen the surrounding villages sadly swept by this "besom of destruction," while the landlord most unceremoniously pocketed the whole in a slump. Thus was the fool farmer's whole original capital generally drawn into the one vortex, the rich landlord's pocket.

Still, such is the predominance of clay over cotton, wood, or leather that a broken-down farmer was always better supplied, even in a pauper condition, than a reduced or superannuated tradesman or labourer. This provision for the pauper is in Scotland an assessment on the heritors of parishes, and allowed by law to be made by themselves and the kirk-sessions;* and for the purpose of keeping up the *respectability* of a dunghill rank, a broken farmer has been known to receive from this assessment as much as eight, ten, and twelve shillings a week; while a tradesman pauper, fallen into age, and ruined by the oppression of these very classes, with a body as large, and a soul often double the size, received eighteenpence! Yes, "these were the times, Mr Rigmarole," when

* This statement applies, of course, to a time antecedent to the passing of the present poor-law.

oligarchial absurdity rode rough-shod over the rights of common existence.

From the start of the war-cry against French Liberalism began our national consumption, Pitt's paper currency, his borrowing system, his most sublime hoax (as a blind to the national beast), the curious *sinking-fund*, with its bottom somewhere out below the bottomless pit. These things had then a strange effect upon common life, as well as a beautiful entail of debt on the productive portion of the community, which will be ever paying, and never paid, till the consummation of all things.

Meanwhile, under the power of science, steams, and gases, trade was becoming unprecedentedly productive of the necessaries and luxuries of life; hence of capital, which wealth, being abstracted by the aristocratic governing party, was lavished in hundreds of millions on wars and alliances to bear down liberality of sentiment, and keep the world arrested at the old dark-age point, that point supposed the best calculated to suit their own personal views and interests.

In this national struggle of production and consumption, my condition has, in common with that of millions, been exposed to the smothering pressure of its soul-corroding influence. Living in this corn district, where all things have in consequence been twisted into a form too unnaturally strained for the rational and lasting operation of the parts, I have seen new adventurers run on farming in the belief that, under landed-interest-supporting parliaments, oats would continue rising in price to the end of time! the consequence being that agricultural independence succumbed to landlords, and rents were promised by tenants above all calculations of faith or folly. And when Providence, over-ruling the discord, avarice, and presumption of man, determined that the poor, productive portion of the nation, though pinched for their sins of passive concession to tax-makers, should not yet all literally starve (though many did actually starve) under high markets, and that system of politics which landholder-legislators supposed barely proper to enable themselves to gain their point of exclusive ambition to swim in seas of luxury, and meet every pleasure-seeking absurdity of their general folly, such silly tenants have had since, in the bitterness of their disappointment, to appeal to their masters for reduction of claim in all the sweating eagerness of barest-faced beggary! The landowners themselves, who were all the while marked only by a more profligate expenditure than was necessary to general comfort, or at all consistent with the nature of things, must, of course, allow occasional reduction of rent, not in proportion as their own profusion had left them in non-ability, but in proportion to what their miscalculating dependents were at all able to advance. The honourable exceptions, though, of course, considerable, were yet inadequate to arrest or redeem the general tendency. Wages of labour never kept pace with a high-taxed price of victuals, but ran in a counter-parallel, so that the poor man's family bread of existence, dependent on his day's labour, made the necessary supply of food miserably limited. Such state of things, along with the "other ills that flesh is heir to," kept a country sutor in a queer condition.

Little as I was then acquainted with the different classes of mankind, I recollect I used to reason something in the following way:—Man is a wonderful creature, with all his powers and capabilities of soul and body! What, after all, is the origin of all things, or to what tendency? The world appeared to me as if sprung out of a mist, going on through a long disordered day, and perhaps destined again to settle in the shadows of thick darkness. Indeed, I sometimes became suspicious that the scripture itself, which gave an account of the grand phenomena, might be partly imaginary, like other poems, or perhaps a forgery—only that its tendency to correct wickedness and support virtue and rational propriety gave it a sanction in my mind which no distrust could thoroughly unsettle.

The state of affairs and parties around me seemed to arise out of certain combinations of particular circumstances. Every little hamlet had its affairs and parties, as well as the grandest state in Europe, and as seriously interesting, too. I found myself, with my father's family, in the lowest grade of society, on the extreme verge of exclusion; and yet I saw that the rich, too, had to struggle in the toils of life —had their gout in place of the poor man's rheumatism—though their struggle was for the most part only with the false ideal pride of place and pride of power; while that of the poor, the great mass of human beings, was, from the cradle to the grave, with poverty.

Here arose a calculation regarding the difference between the trouble arising from a bad principle in the mind, which might or should be discarded at first intrusion, and that arising from the stern call of nature to the necessary support of bare existence. For, oh! the longings of restricted satisfaction of natural appetence, the smart of the gastric juices on the dry grindings of the stomach, and the gall administered to the better feelings and finer sensibilities of the human heart, so often lacerated under the cruel lash of the arbitrary pride of poor-minded straddlers to petty domination. Still, I felt extremely loath to admit the idea that the world would be found to be generally as wicked and unfeeling as the sample I then had of it induced me to believe. I thought that, by concession on trifles of minor importance, a great proportion of the disagreeable amongst acquaintances and mankind generally might be entirely evaded or much soothed down. And I thought that to nurse this temperament might be a great part of the "whole duty of man;" and indeed a great variety of scripture texts which were often recurring to my memory seemed to sanction this idea. I therefore determined to foster the more milky sympathies of my natural disposition, and to adhere to the practice for the pleasure of my own mind at least, and this notwithstanding any opposition I might meet. I conceived also that it could take nothing from the real strength of my arm, under any possible occurrence which might lead to the actual necessity of resistance.

I reasoned on this point until I began to conceive that *true* humility of disposition was the most heroic virtue, which, instead of sinking an individual below the proper standard of manhood, had the effect of raising him infinitely above the level of even pointed insult. I tried it, and found it suit, and have never through life had occasion to swerve much from it. It has never prevented me from holding or maintaining my own opinion, but only regulated the manner of expressing or enforcing it. The only difficulty of maintaining this disposition lies in preserving the true criterion between points of principle and the casual occurrences of life, which latter, when divested of their imaginary interests and importance, are often mere trifles of inferior consequence. And, when points of principle come in the way, modest firmness has always secured to me, in maintaining my principles, general respect and exemption from insult.

Upon the whole, I began then rightly to regard my own mind as the only wealth of property I should ever possess in this world, and therefore I determined to take care of its health, whatever might be the servitude to which the attached body might be subjected. I conceived that the best friendship I was ever likely to have in life was to be on first-rate terms with my own mind, and therefore I resolved to be always watchful that no one principle of it should ever take advantage to abuse or betray another. The young mind is inventive. I often then used in imagination to play at life, and amuse myself by supposing myself in awkward situations and predicaments, and I would go through the whole like a drama, and find that I could always come off with my own approbation at least, however unreasonable the other party might be.

I have often since, however, found many people more unreasonable in life than I could then picture them to my imagination; yet, in general, kindliness of feeling honestly expressed to our neighbour will ever bring out the *best* principles of our frail human nature. And I have always felt it gratifying to the finest sensibilities of my soul to see the charities and sympathies of the human heart drawn out on the face into light and action, and to observe their effect upon society, like the play of light on leaf and stream, while the worse feelings are smothered in their growth, and are not allowed to distort the features of the "human face divine."

I had not before that time begun to ascertain the principle on which people so often act, or rather the no-principle (for the young and generous mind is loath to realize it.) I had still supposed that people in general must at the least be wishing to assimilate themselves to those principles which they severally conceived conducive to public good. Hence, partial evil, or individual selfishness, appeared to me as a consequence of ignorance, or to arise from the pressure of some hard necessity; as a thing, at least, of which the party would not approve in his own mind, or stoop to practise under more favourable circumstances. Nor could I then represent to myself the possibility of many having neither mind nor conscience in their moral character at all; yet the thought had fairly dawned on my imagination that the world was not half so good as I supposed it might and should be under even any circumstances; since I observed that even grown-up people were frequently deceitful, villainously selfish, and often absurdly ignorant of the simplest maxims of both moral and natural philosophy. But then I felt a fine elastic buoyancy in my own spirits, with a strong integrity of feeling, which threw my thoughts forward into future days, and led me to overlook, if not to despise, the trifling privations, or vexations, or false opinions of the then present. For a fifty or sixty years' life appeared like some very indefinite term, stretching away into almost interminable distance; and what might not one acquire and do in that time was the grand speculation.

I felt these stirrings of hope and joy often strengthen my heart when in the fields, and more particularly when alone in a wood on a winter day. There was always something in a winter day peculiarly grand to my imagination, while it appeared as if there were a temporary suspension in the progress of outward nature—as if all were on a pause, awaiting a new divine commission to proceed on the journey of general life. For even the leafless trees appeared to me as sensitive objects—stationary, calm, and contemplative, imbued with as much sagacious reflection as certain orders of living beings.

During all my youth I felt as if there was a spirit in everything, even in the calm of nature around me; and I have not yet, under all the "pitiless peltings" of fifty winter's storms, got quit of these same feelings, nor is it, I think, desirable that I should. Hence, I feel vexed to see these woods at Eiliestoun, where I then experienced such feelings, now being dug up by new proprietors, who seem to have more taste for Iago's injunction, "Put money in thy purse," than for all the sylvan beauty of creation.

All this while poetry kept its place as the darling jewel of my soul. It was to me what I suppose the miser's gold is to him—a private treasure of the heart. Though I could write verses at will, I never could please myself for want of words with which to clothe my ideas, and my verses looked so tame in comparison with such printed verses as I had occasionally met with that I used to destroy them almost as soon as composed, and yet could not forego the desire of again attempting to write more. The poet and the prophet had hitherto in idea appeared to me so closely affiliated that I could not properly separate them. This, I believe, came from early scripture reading; and the hope of meeting with a living poet appeared as improbable as that of finding the philosopher's stone; and, indeed, if I had come into possession of the latter I would have set about employing it in turning as much earth into gold as would have hired any living poet from any distance to come and live with me through life. I thought that, if such a being existed in this age, I would give all my chances in life to be stationed near him; for I supposed a poet to be one amongst the millions whose soul soared above the thick dross of common thought, and in whose bosom no deceit or evil passion could find entertainment—one who could see through the moral world at a glance, and laugh or weep over it agreeably to his state of momentary feeling. What a treasure, therefore, it would have been to me to have been his confidant, catching the ideas as they came glowing and warm from his imagination.

While under these feelings one winter evening, an old woman observed—"Dear me, ye're aye singin' sangs. I never hear ony o' ye sing 'The Oak Tree,' a fine sang, made by Andrew Scott when he was a sodger in the American war." "Who is Andrew Scott, Peggy?" inquired I. "Bless me! do ye no ken Andrew Scott o' Bowden, wha thrashes at Whinfield, barnman there this winter? He stops there a' the week, and gangs hame on Saturday nights. He has made mony a bonnie sang, and nice poems, too, and is a kindly, quiet man as ye ever saw—aye sae blythe and weel pleased. If ye wad gang up in the fore-supper-time, an' crack wi' him about poetry, his heart wad rise, for he'll ha'e naething to amuse him at nichts yonder but a book, for he's aye readin' or writin', or tweedlin' on the fiddle."

This conversation occurred early on a winter evening. So out I sallied, and flew like a meteor over a mile of ground to Whinfield, dropt in to the farmer's kitchen, and found Andrew Scott, my friend to be, sitting on a form seat, tailoring his old grey coat, which had got very poetically out at the elbows. Though I felt abashed to tell my errand in the hearing of the rest of the inmates, yet at one glance I saw he was just the very thing for me—a tight, handy-like man, of middle age and stature, with a face kind and inviting. I must, of course, break the suspense, and tell my errand, which was done in simple enough terms. I said I was very fond of poetry, and that I had learned that he wrote poems and songs occasionally, and had come to request him to let me hear something of the kind. He seemed to measure the stripling before him as exactly as could perhaps be done with a look, and then very invitingly asked if I ever tried to write verses myself. I said I had, but could never please myself so well as to think any of them worth preservation; yet from the request I had made to him, it would be but fair to repeat to him from memory some sample of my first productions, which I did. This happened to be a story in the "Chevy-Chase" measure, at which, when I had done, he smiled kindly—for he never laughed loud—saying that it was not bad for a first attempt, and that he hoped I would continue to nurse the feeling for poetry, as, though he had scribbled much, but had never shone in print as an author, he had found it an amusement more congenial to his best feelings than the every-day talk of common life. He told me also that when a soldier in the American war, and a prisoner in Long Island, he had written more than would have made a sizeable volume, but that his officer had borrowed his book of manuscript, and lost it on the passage home. But now, he said, Burns had come on the carpet, and spoilt the market for common Scotch poetry. These two events, he added, had disconcerted him in his poetics till very lately, when he had again begun to preserve the manuscripts of his casual effusions, having been encouraged to this by Mr. Balfour, his parish minister, whose approval of some of his late pieces had gratified him much. Nothing of his American poetry had been preserved except two songs, which had lain in his memory. These were "The Oak Tree" and "Betsy Rosoe," the latter a rather tragic love affair between one of his comrades and an American girl. But his latest production, of a few days old, which he first read over to me, was on the "Emigration of the Larks," and was founded on a rustic report that these birds had been seen that season to assemble in large flocks and leave the country, it was feared for ever. Andrew had a better idea, and had celebrated the matter very much to my taste. I then considered him to be likely the best of all unprinted poets, and I daresay my praise and observations, simple as they must have been, even gave him encouragement, since a very few years afterwards he published, by subscription, a very neat volume of poems, which, though not of a high-flaming cast, did nevertheless express much of the native manners of common country life, impressed with the ingenuous simplicity of his own mind.

He was of a truly religious cast of mind, and his conversation was far superior to his poetry. He was cool, and reflective, and patient under his general lot through life, which was in the humblest walk of day labour, bordering on poverty. He delighted in the employment of dressing hedges, though for the most part engaged as a flail barn-man or thrasher of corn.

On the occasion of publishing the first edition of his poems in Edinburgh, he had fallen into acquaintance with individuals among the eminent characters of the age. Mr. Watson, one of the few most justly-famed artists of the day, who had taken a fancy for Andrew more as a man than as a poet, gave him an excellent portrait of himself in a present, which was at the time estimated to be worth thirty guineas. This painting, like everything else, had a history of its own, too. It stood some years in Mr. Watson's famed exhibition, and at last was packed and sent to Andrew at Bowden, but was miscarried, and lost for ten or twelve years, when it again dropt back on Mr. Watson, who again sent it out to Andrew; and it now remains with his son, Mr. John Scott, schoolmaster in Bowden.

I felt a pleasure in the friendship of this man, which was uninterrupted to the days of his old age, and to his death. Every meeting with him was not so much like a feast of soul as a cheering refreshment of heart to us both. We never thought of requiring any stimulus to excite us to spend the hours agreeably; nor, I daresay, did we drink five shillings, all put together, through a forty years' acquaintanceship, yet we continued to grow to each other the more interesting to the last.

I saw him in all the variations of his circumstances, better and worse occasionally; and under some severe trials and bereavements he showed a notable example of how the Christian faith, as an active principle, is calculated to support the well-informed and humble mind. I visited him once in his last illness, when he conversed the same as ever, and showed the most sensible resignation to the event, which he calmly told me he felt approaching. He spoke of our favourite subject, "Poetry," with the same cheerful relish as ever, and desired me to read him some of my latest scraps, with which he seemed much pleased. He expressed himself glad to inform me that one of his sons, David, then in the Isle of Man, had sent him some newspapers with some of his pieces of poetry, which were highly finished, "quite classic," and far beyond his own stretch of pinion.

On the 26th of May, 1840, I was invited to attend the deposition of his remains in the "narrow house," under the shadow of a favourite great plane-tree, at the south-west corner of Bowden Parish Church. I came home as quietly reflective as the nature of such events is calculated to make us; and in such cases a feeling of desertedness pervades the heart (and this altogether apart from worldly considerations), as if some particular prop were gone, the bare idea of which had helped to steady our slippery footing on the verge of this life.

Andrew had republished his poems several times, with considerable additions of new matter; but he seemed a little behind his day to get even his due quantum of fame, as the new-school English poetry had begun to supersede the Scotch dialect, in which none could come after Burns (our northern star) to shine equally bright. Even superior ability, suppose such possible, could not now have gained equal celebrity. There can be but one Shakspeare and one Burns.

Only one ballad of Andrew's seemed ever to get very popular, having found its way into some collections, and even the theatre itself. This was "Simon and Jannet," written on the occasion when the beacons were accidentally lighted on all the hills around, and gave a false alarm that Buonaparte had landed for invasion in January, 1804.

Out of many of Andrew's anecdotes I can at present recollect two, which may be worthy of relating. They had, in his regiment in America, a Jamie somebody, a very short, squat fellow, who was quite below standard pitch, but was kept as wrestling bully of the regiment. Running short of vegetables, they had eyed a Yankee field of turnips, and stolen out occasionally in small night parties, at all risk of punishment, to supply their wants in spite of laws civil or regimental. The farmer, a six feet fellow, had been on the watch, determined to make a capture, and have an example made of the culprit. He let the party get loaded before he sallied out on them; but so soon as he was perceived they all slipped their loads and ran, except Jamie, who had not observed the surprise until he was seized, when he slid his load, and very handily grappled the tall farmer round the middle, and laid him on his back, kneeing him down, and threatening him in broad Scotch until he became quietly submissive, and durst not follow him. Jamie then coolly resumed his load, and waddled home with it. The farmer came next day with a complaint to the colonel, who drew up his men to let him pick out the defaulter for exemplary punishment. When he walked along the line he recognized his moonlight customer; but pretending not to observe him he gave up the charge, and only confessed to the colonel privately that he was ashamed to own in public that he had been floored and mastered by a man of such diminutive stature, little more than half his own height, and that he was perfectly satisfied with his own good fortune in having fallen in with the dwarf of the English, and not some of the big fellows, who would probably have crushed him to death. The colonel was, of course, too much amused to keep the secret.

The other anecdote was this. While a prisoner in America, lying long confined in some wooden shed barracks, their men got low-spirited, dull, and heartless, in consequence of which disease broke out among them. Andrew, for want of other recreation, chose some pieces of wood, and with a pocket-knife, his only tool, formed a fiddle, and in a few days had her ready for the strings. These at last he contrived to procure, and got her strung and tuned up, when she sounded remarkably well, everything considered. The dance was immediately commenced, and instead of their former listlessness and low gambling, here was a new incitement to life and healthful exercise. In the course of a few weeks their barrack sheds were half stripped of fir-deal for fiddle bellies, and ere long a number, something like fifteen or five-and-twenty, were all screeding on together—spirit and life everywhere. The Yankees without, entering also into the spirit of the thing, became more and more friendly, and brought them all the necessaries they wanted.

Long after I first knew Andrew he wrote "An Address to the Fiddle," a very pretty Scotch poem, of which I shall here give a few stanzas:—

> "Wi' cunning art and knack o' lear
> Hath science op'd her bosom bare,
> In catgut, hollow wood, and hair;
> Wha ance wad thoucht
> The soul o' music lurking there
> Should thence be broucht?
>
> "When Boreas bauld, wi' surly breeze,
> Blew through amang the rocking trees;
> When sair he did thy branches teaze,
> Thou little thoucht
> In thy auld age some fool to please
> By art thus wroucht.
>
> "When ye the juice o' earth did tipple,
> Ye didna ken but sile o' kipple,*

---

* "The sill of the couple" is the piece of timber on which the rafter rests, in the roof of a house.

Or stock to some auld wife's lint ripple,
    Might be your fate,
Or else condemn'd to hang a faple
    Some dowie gate.

"Now bless your fate, your station's snug,
  Sentenc'd to mony a blythsome hug;
  Wi' your but-end up to my lug
    Ye may be canty;
  Sae let me gi'e your strings a tug
    Whene'er I want ye."

CHAPTER XVI.

Though "These are foolish things to all the wise,
Yet "I love wisdom more than she loves me;
My tendency is to philosophise
On most things, from a tyrant to a tree."
Don Juan; canto 6, stanza 63.

TO return to the point I left in my simple narrative, though I had now seen a living poet, and one likely to be a new friend, yet it was not till some years afterwards that we fell into frequent communication. During this time I was again left to my serious reasoning, to settle in my mind various phenomena both in the natural and the moral world. My perceptions of individual character were, on account of being limited, perhaps the more acute. This is reasoning upon the principle that the more concentrated the powers the more powerful and irresistible their force. Brain and gunpowder may be thus compared: the force of their action is greater under certain confined limits than when diffused loosely over a more extended surface.

I was, in fact, a stranger to any proper notion of the great world, and knew only a few human beings around me—although my ideas were a little more extended than those of the old woman who, for the first time, had strayed from her natal village to the top of a neighbouring hill, and came home fatigued with admiration that the world was a thousand times larger than she ever had suspected.

I was indeed then frequently running into musings regarding the nature of things, of rather too scientific a kind for my means of solution. As for instance, how did a tree grow? Were the leaves simply for ornament, or were they also subservient to the growth of the tree by somehow taking up sap?—for I had a notion of a plentiful sun-heated sap being necessary in all vegetative productions, though not the most distant conception of gases. But a grand puzzler further presented itself. I could count the age of growing fir trees by the branches, and any tree cut across by the liths of growth; but then how did the year's progress go on? Was last summer's growth added to the body of the tree around the heart, or around the outside of the wood immediately below the bark? If by the heart, there must then be an inconceivable amount of force in operation to extend out the whole body of the tree till even the dried bark on the outside should burst; and, on the other hand, if on the outside, why should there be so much sap in general circulation throughout the whole wood? In such case I thought it should sooner become more dry and consolidated than we ever find it. In the absence of all information, I settled on the latter idea of adding the year's growth to the outside.

Several individuals, who seemed to be winking-wise on most subjects, even religious controversialists, would tell me that I was a fool to trouble myself "about such nonsense things, which were of no consequence, and profitless." I saw this was very true in regard to themselves, who could remain content with dark ignorance about whatever was not material meat and drink; but then so could not I, as such subjects were ever, in spite of myself, recurring to my imagination, and pressed for solution, right or wrong.

The idea also of how stones which were dug from a depth came to be polished was another phenomenon which puzzled me; for I had a notion that they had not at the creation been made by the fingers of divinity just in the shapes in which I found them; and how such a mixture of kinds and colours should be got amongst clay on the edge of a precipice, or at the dug-depth of a draw-well, was very perplexing. But I had by this time somehow got the notion of the Newtonian system of the earth's diurnal whirl in my head, to which I added the workings of Noah's flood, washing up all the surface to a great depth, breaking up rocks, levelling former heights, and filling former hollows, on a tremendously grand scale, as our rivulets are seen to do on a smaller one when highly flooded. This seemed to solve the matter, and the idea occupied my mind in a kind of floating way without any attempt at going deeper into the question, until within a very few years back, when the study of geology became popular, even amongst common tradesmen; and this has already, on the inductive principle, tended to clear up these matters.

My friend, William Kemp, of Galashiels, has lately conceived, and now plainly demonstrated, that the terraces on the Eildon Hills, and all the hills around of corresponding levels, have been formed by the action of former seas subsiding at distant intervals of time, while the island was in the process of being thrown up by volcanic agency from below water. These terraces have become more particularly worn and marked by the frequent concussions and general friction of glaciers or icebergs, many of which must have got enclosed amongst the towering rocks, which still, though greatly worn down, form the peaks of our mountains, and hence, resting in the hollows, have in time thawed and melted as the lower levels became gradually dry. From the earthy matter and loose stones, as broken off, and taken up by these, and held amongst their grounded ice for the time being, are the depositions of these moraine ridges and beautiful little hillocks, which here and there diversify and adorn the bosoms of our valleys: hence also the travelled boulder stones, left dispersed in blocks here and there on the general surface, with a vast deal more of particular phenomena.

This is a very different account of the matter from the description of our darling bard, when in the glow of poetic fancy he imagined

"The hillocks dropt in Nature's careless haste,"

just as if the mother lady had been on a morning's excursion with a lapful of hills to sow about like pearls over earth's fair bosom for our admiration.

Another idea is here very striking. When we think upon our past great men, our geniuses of a very few years back, looking with a sort of veneration and solemn awe to old baronial castles, with their keeps and towers, the abodes of feudal barbarism, and turreted abbeys, the nursing boxes of superstition and low roguery, built in the sacred name of religion; and when we hear them speak of "the good old times" as of some blessed era or golden age, vanished soon after the beginning of Time; and then think that now, only some ten or twenty years later, we grasp a larger idea, and behold all these, which in their conceptions constituted grandeur, greatness, and power, as the mere bagatelle ruins of yesterday, founded in lawless oppression and enthusiastic ignorance, flourishing their short hour, and at length swept off by the better information and just indignation of a more common-sense generation; their appropriated sites and ruins grasped up, of course, and taken in possession by the land-worms —our all over-reaching and self-constituted aristocracy; and all this while the neighbouring hills have resumed their annual verdure through immemorial time, far out beyond the date of ephemeral man, the insect of yesterday, we behold an interesting monument of the divine eternal Being, and the principles upon which He proceeds in preparing fitting habitations for His various offspring.

For instance, Sir Walter Scott sat in the midst of this district to a good old age, and devoted a mind of considerable ability to the building for himself a monumental house and a name out of materials ferreted from amongst the dirty rubbish of a few very late ages—three-fourths of the whole, of course, a mere low bagatelle of literary flummery. It would have confounded his poor idea of greatness to have been told that William Kemp, the cooper (now gasmaker) of Galashiels, one of his door-neighbours amongst the multitude of those whom he considered, and wished to hold designated, as a low, degraded, "plebeian rabble," should, from the ingenuity of a truly noble mind, be in the act of appropriating to himself an eternal monument, not of stone hewn from the Sprouston new sandstone, and cut into monkish figures, but of all the "everlasting hills" around, with their peaked turrets and green terraces, which cannot now fail to be here associated with the name of Kemp until the island itself may be again changed by some grand new combustion of nature, and the mountains again riven by future earthquakes or submerged in ocean; or, if the earth be still in the process of gradual consolidation, till the moist become more dry, the heavier portions deposited and crystalized (as is not more unlikely than many other phenomena), then the name Kemp may become associated with the name Agassiz, since, though not the first conceiver of the general idea, yet certainly he has the credit of being the first observer of it in our district.

But to return again to the first year of the present century, in which I found myself a lad running fifteen, hungry for the food of both body and mind, while the means of supply for both were extremely limited, little more falling to the share of the poor Scotch "plebeian" than would keep soul and body superficially linked together, none of that scientific knowledge which now pervades all classes being then ever perceived, except perhaps in the dreams of philosophers.

Gas, steam, and galvanism then were, in regard to the public, the same as hidden qualities in nature, their powers or application not being then understood, not even their existence ascertained. No Humphry Davy or James Watt had yet come forward with their sublime discoveries to illume our world and improve the general condition of human life. And amongst the classes with which I fell to be associated the very idea that such qualities existed in nature would have been thought not only ridiculous, but a most irreligious presumption, not to be named or tolerated without an attached stigma of impious profanity.

The liability of the mind to superstition, and its influence on the mind, is a strange phenomenon in the constitution of our human nature, more difficult to be analyzed than gas. For, seeing enough of it in individuals who are generally esteemed wise and religious, I was frequently then touched with it, and remained sometimes for days and weeks together under its influence. And hence occasional qualms of suspicion, that it might possibly be presumptuous in me, and, perhaps, in the nature of things unwarrantable, to attempt to pry into and investigate the secret workings of divine power in nature, which would have been but a poor attempt, after all, without the means of improving upon any idea, however simple, that might differ from the commonly received opinion on anything. The effect of this superstition on my mind was something not unlike that of suspicion in animals, only that the animal suspicion seems the more reasonable use of faculty, as it arises in an animal from the fear that a man may catch, strike, or kill it; while a man is superstitious from a false idea that divinity may harm him—a far more unreasonable notion than that of the animal, which is simply a cautiousness acquired by something akin to experience. These occasional fits, however, never lasted long, as a little reasonable reflection always led me clear out again.

About that age particularly there was a certain freshness in the feelings, which, in despite of the world's wants and pinchings, used to give me a heart's relish of existence. I enjoyed all I saw, and cared not who held the world's woods and fields in fief or entail, or enjoyed the exclusive privilege of calling them their own. All I wished of them was the pleasure of looking on them, while no lord-proprietor, I thought, could possess or enjoy them in my style. Though on the haughs and braes of Ayle water I knew not the proprietors, yet I used to think —What ciphers they must be never to be seen near their inheritance; where could they find such pleasure on earth as to walk on their own land and fish in Ayle water? I pitied them sincerely, whilst yet, comparatively speaking, I had seen nothing of the romantically beautiful in either bank, lake, or stream, for I had not then got well acquainted even with the Tweed, nor ever heard of Highland scenery. But it is all the same on what scale we look at nature, since a world in miniature is as interesting as one of the full size; and there is enough on any acre of surface, even moorland, to keep a philosopher busy and in admiration through his day and hour. I am told that the German philosophers now find such delight in the minute that a whole water-fly is far too extensive a subject for an individual, the construction of a limb or a single eye being considered sufficient labour for a life-time. An imaginative mind is as good, at any rate, as a magnifying glass, as Ebenezer Elliott has lately illustrated in his most admirable poem on the "Wonders of the Lane." That poem is all so rich that I cannot select a single quotation.

I was lately, however, talking of myself, when a poor, ragged, half-starved lad, sincerely pitying even the rich proprietors of hills and valleys for their apathy. Now, it is clear that there is nothing of which any man knows less than by whom he may be either pitied or despised. How little, for instance, does often the sagacious teacher comprehend that the simple, musing boy may be mentally busy in taking a pretty exact measure of his master's mind and disposition. Aye, we talk of mind, but what is mind?—that wondrous power so superior to all known gas. Electric fluid is materially heavy, coarse, and combustible in comparison; so capable of motion and extension that the light loses it on journeys; that it can at will confine itself within a needle's eye, or swell abroad and fill all space; now nestling with the sparrow in the thatch, and anon playing in the sunshine of other systems, or musing on the frozen poles of planets belonging to other suns, flaming in regions far beyond the range of our best telescopes.

By-the-bye, I would give all I am worth in the world to have a bodily eye-peep through one of these great forty-feeters at some of our own sun's planets flashing through the blue, with their natural offspring, the Misses Moons, around them. But I suppose this ardent spirit must await in patience until it has "shuffled off this mortal coil" before these heavenly fields shall be laid open to its admiration.

> Oh! may we entertain a hope of grace
> That spirits of the sav'd be free to roam
> Abroad amongst celestial orbs of bliss,
> Even to expatiate in a boundless home;
> With still expanding powers to admire and trace
> The wonders of eternity to come!
> But let us fold imagination's wings,
> There's interest enough in nearer things.

CHAPTER XVII.

THERE is a great body of phenomena in the human mind and feelings of which I am not certain if they have ever been rightly investigated or noted in any kind of writing. And yet I cannot pretend to be the individual able to note and express these in such a style as would be generally understood, and consequently render them useful as landmarks in the ocean of life. There is one of these more easily to be observed than accounted for, which is this:—When a poor family have lived in a country hamlet or single cottage for a few years, they grow so attached to the spot that they become, as it were, indigenous to it, and the more deserted and miserable the situation is, the more closely do they seem to cling to it, till hardly any poverty will ferret them out. They become somehow like cattle in a burning byre or stable, that will not budge for smoke and flame till driven forth by human force. In fact, nothing but the hounds of rigorous oppression can hunt them from the locality.

Although we had felt nothing but general poverty, and often bitter want, in this hamlet cottage for four years, it was yet a saddening tale to be told us that the landlord wanted the house for another tenant. The family sorrow, though great on this account, was, however, not half so much as the pride of the mind which was hurt at what we thought might be the reason. Fifty suppositions were by us suggested over the evening fire, or at least the place where the evening fire should have been, none of which could possibly be conclusive, as we had no certain data whereon to build a feasible reason, till at last our little invidious neighbour, the joiner—a mere miniature skeleton of the creature man, in mind and body both—set our solicitude at rest by hinting that the laird had got notice of my sister and me hurting the fences by gathering faggots about the hedges and plantations. Here, again, the sins of our poverty stared the face of our conscience out of countenance, on the only point of offence in which we could never have thought of pleading wholly innocent, but only the use and wont of the whole hamlet, as well as of all the neighbouring ones; for the truth was, that it had always remained an undecided point whether the laird was hostile to the faggot-gathering invasion of his property or not. He had certainly seen us all occasionally, without even a reprimand; and on such occasions, in the country, silence is always understood as half a grant. Besides, there was continually in these then rising plantations as much brushwood rotting down amongst the sodden grass as would have boiled all the potatoes and other victual that the poor cottars for a mile around had got to boil. But, be this as it might, we had to look out for a new dwelling place.

It was comparatively nothing for the brothers Jacob and Esau to part encampments and take up new ground for their flocks and herds to the eastward or westward in a fertile district of country, being lairds wherever they went, and slack in hand; but it was very different for a family who could not find sixpence to buy the day's provision to set out to seek a new habitation amongst our impoverished villages. My father must look out, however; which he did, and he succeeded at length in renting a single end apartment of a cottage in this village of Lessudden (St. Boswells) from an old widow who kept her three orphan grandchildren. The same day, calling at a village shop, which was also a public-house and bakehouse, the landlord (James Dickson, a free, good-hearted soul) gave him the promise of a cart-load or two of long broom in gift for the rooting up to begin with for summer fuel. This broom grew on the East Haugh, that field on which the south or west end of Merton Bridge is now placed. So, on a fine May day he and I came down to hoe it up, and hearing that it lay on Tweedside I brought down my rowan tree sapling fishing-rod, and had a spell at the trouting, wading middle deep in what is now dyked up into a cauld pool (or dub) for Merton Mill, where I caught a large strap of large trouts, to my father's great admiration. I found then that the Tweed trouts were more capricious and shy in their rising than the Ayle-water ones, yet they were generally much larger, and required only greater patience and attention to entice them.

It brought me in mind of Thomson's hymn on the "Seasons," where he speaks of the Almighty bounty spreading a common feast for all that lives. No famine now, thought I, for the summer at least, and so, in strict adherence to that poet's advice,

I returned all the smaller captives to the stream. One, however, I had hurriedly strapped on the osier twig among the large trouts, and on calling at the village on our way home a stout-looking man, very starch and precise in his manner, began admiring my success, and after fingering them over picked out the small one, and told me it was a *smout* (smolt) or young salmon; that he was water-bailiff, and must report me, being sworn to it; and that the fine for such trespass was £10 with expenses, or some months' imprisonment, only that the gentlemen *justices* had a power to modify it. This gave my father and me no heart-relief whatever, as we knew that we could just as easily pay ten thousand pounds as ten shillings, having as little means with which to pay the one sum as the other; so we drew home, vexing ourselves sufficiently on the subject. In a week or two, however, we were relieved by learning that water-bailiff Balmer had given information of the offence to the authorities, but had stated it as the unconscious act of one not likely to transgress again, and that therefore no prosecution was to proceed on the matter. I felt more thankful to all parties than there was likely any occasion for, had I then understood what I afterwards came to perceive very clearly. There might, in fact, have been a better reason for my undergoing no prosecution than either justice of peace clemency or my own comparative innocence— from the general knowledge, namely, that a justice clerk possesses of his district individually as to who has money and who has none. Just two classes are pretty free from being much troubled with law: these are the extremities of society, the very rich and the very poor. A duke or other aristocrat is protected by his influence and power of patronage, mail proof against all the tiger-claws of justice: indeed, he is the hereditary maker of what is called country justice. A country cobbler, or other penniless sinner, is, like other lean animals, useless as a prey, not worth baiting a legal trap for.

Well, the term day came, when our furniture was laid on a cart, and we trudged by the side of it down to St. Boswells Green—I, with my poor sister's son on my back, a fine child two and a half years old. The first person we met as we approached the inn at the Green was James Ross, the innkeeper's second son. "You're welcome here," says Jamie, holding out his hand to me, when my heart flew to him— something in the same way of feeling, I suppose, though in very different circumstances, that Jonathan's did to David while he spoke with King Saul, his father; for the heart beats much the same, I believe, when it gets full room for fair-play, be it in the breast of a king's son or that of a cobbler. As I saw at the time, and found afterwards, Jamie had all the generosity of good sense and good feeling, though he was in the main as poorly circumstanced as myself. Besides, I had accidentally met with him some time before about our blacksmith's shop, and found him possessed of intelligence far beyond my own degree; nor could I then conceive how he had come by it. But the fact was, he had seen more of life than I had about his father's inn, was a year or so older than myself, and had read a good deal from the St. Boswells Library, which had been founded some three years previously by Captain Erskine, the late Sir David of Dryburgh Abbey, then a young man, son of David Earl of Buchan. That same Sir David was a good-hearted creature, and as generous as charity herself.

Settling down here, where there was no opposition to our shoemaking but a poor, handless *guff* of a fellow, half knave, half fool, who soon left, we began to get work enough to keep us very busy, and the prospects of life brightened upon us daily. My father wrought very diligently, and began to find hopes of redeeming himself by degrees, paying off such trifling debts as he had found credit enough to contract in the four past starvation years, and to live in the meantime in comparative plenty. Two of my three sisters were always out at service, and being able servants got the best wages going, which they never individually saved or wholly expended on behalf of themselves, but threw all into the family stock at term days to clear up matters and keep the whole family comfortable. Finding it necessary, I began to sit more steadily at work, and curtailed my fishing to good days for the fly only, such as the first and second days after a spring or summer flood: in the meantime, cultivating the closest acquaintance with James Ross and John Anderson (son of the farmer at Hiltonshill). "Three merry boys, I trow, were we," without ever tasting "the barley bree." And what is perhaps rather uncommon, we all felt that real generosity of regard for each other in such a manner that, without at all thinking on the Christian injunction, we "each esteemed his neighbour as better than himself," really and truly "preferring one another in love" as well as in courtesy.

We had little reading the first summer, as I was required to work now more closely, and they were engaged in various kinds of labour about their fathers' farms. We could only meet occasionally on evenings, or on Sunday afternoons take a walk about Tweedside, which was to each a kind of social feast of soul. Although they had the use of their fathers' shares of the subscription library, and so could read for their own part, they durst not risk the five shilling penalty of lending a volume, and as I could by no possible means purchase a share at fourteen shillings, I had to depend on other sources of amusement. My fishing excursions became also interrupted from an illness taken in the beginning of the autumn, some sort of slow fever, which left a continued stitch in the side that greatly prevented exertion. My friends and neighbours believed me in consumption, the prevalent disease of that time; but I had hope myself, which, I think, arose from a vigorous, keen relish of life, and a conviction that my lungs were still in good order. Dr. Oliver made me keep an open blister on my side for some months till the stitch left me, and I got well. Fishing, which was blamed as the cause, was forbidden, and from inability indeed prevented. The most congenial amusement in its stead that next offered, though very foolish, was adopted, and afterwards carried to a ridiculous excess. This was the snaring and taming of birds.

Willie Ovens, the village cooper, bred canaries, for which I had at first no love, from their loud, yelping song; but I bought from him, for fifteen-pence, a hen goldfinch in an old cage. That bird could not and would not sing, however; so I must snare for myself. I therefore set to work and made a trap-cage, and soon became successful in trapping all favourite kinds—goldfinches, bullfinches, &c. The bullfinch was at that time only a new-come stranger to our young plantations about Tweedside, and, from its soft notes, its beauty, and its tame simplicity of disposition, was a great favourite. I sometimes had above a dozen together, and hence arose the necessity of making cages of various descriptions to fit the windows, and an entail of expense for wood and wire, as well as canary and hempseeds, then double their present price, which was hardly consistent with my circumstances. I had to do extra jobs of cobbling to raise every sixpence necessary for such ends. All the while I was aiming to secure an indefinite assortment of the very best birds, with the view of cheering our workshop, and to have the matter set upon the best basis for what I conceived proper enjoyment.

But in following this bent I fell into a more keen relish for the mere amusement of catching them on mornings in the fields and gardens, and I soon became favourite enough to have a roving commission in half the village gardens and orchards, a matter of no small preferment indeed. But this became an ungratifiable passion, after what might properly be called an aimless object, and one in which I ran to such excess for ten succeeding years, or more, that it consumed most of the spare time and means which should have been occupied more properly in making attainments even more in accordance with my native taste.

I often yet wonder on recollection at my father's patience in allowing me to block up the very light of our workshop window with birds' cages. But, perhaps, he feared that the prohibition of this might drive me into still worse pursuits, for he could not miss to perceive the ardour with which I then entered into the heart of all I set about.

In following this pursuit, I was, however, not without many a qualm of conscience from the thought of depriving the bird of its native liberty and the common rights of its nature; but I quieted my mind with the reflection that it was from a pure love to the creature I engaged in it, which I meant to make so very comfortable in other respects, in the character of my own dear companion. I knew this reasoning was false in the main; but it is astonishing upon what untenable grounds the mind will found a plea to sanction a favourite passion, the propriety of which becomes, as it were, established from daily custom, and the example of others who account themselves people of taste.

I would on occasions, however, get very thoughtful on the subject, and reason myself into the resolution of giving up the amusement; but then, here was a stock on hand, which it always puzzled me how to dispose of properly. Some might not be able after confinement to shift for themselves in the fields, and to sell them with the cages, or present them to acquaintances, was not, in a moral point of view, any mending of the matter. And these paltry arguments (such as Washington would probably make to himself in excuse for retaining his household slaves after he had gained the liberty of a country) generally suspended the decision until the virtuous feeling wore off, and thus the folly was from time to time continued until some years afterwards, when the more serious concerns of every-day life made me forego the paltry trifling.

Perhaps no language could convey a proper idea of a boy's love for a bird. He would often wish to gratify the bird with its liberty, but then this is parting with it never to see it again, even in the air; so he holds it, as the American still holds his slave, though from better feelings and on better terms than the slaveholder, and its captivity is confirmed. Besides this bird folly, other notions were also daily intervening to fill up every spare crevice of the mind in the absence of some better aim, which would also have been far more congenial to the native taste.

The want of proper occupation is certainly half the cause of all the mischief arising from misdirected energies, which thus fall to be expended on unworthy objects, and from this, perhaps, spring two-thirds of all the evil under the sun. An entail of family poverty is often the cause of this in the humbler conditions of life, where thousands of the most finely-constructed human minds are left to expend their buoyant native force on the most unworthy objects; and in place of expatiating amongst the rolling spheres with the spirit of Sir Isaac Newton, or amongst the pistons and spindles of Watt and Arkwright, are left to sink and grovel in the mires of mental pollution.

Governments have hitherto determined that what they call "the people" (esteeming themselves the gods) should have no equal rights in legislation, and that what they are pleased to term ignorance, and want of landed property, form a disqualification. Suppose this assumption valid in equity—which it is not—are those who find themselves born rich enough, and suppose themselves therefore wise enough, to govern for others, excusable in acts of general legislation calculated to condemn the landless millions of their fellow-men to a servile condition, from which it is impossible to rise into what the more fortunate, in their selfishness, may be pleased to term a *qualified* state of rationality?

Were the bodies of men only thus subjected to a life of moil for the benefit of tyrants, it would be the less matter; but that a human soul should be thus doomed to remain in uncultivated degradation throughout the term of its earthly probation, and returned to its Maker, not only like an unimproven talent, but an abused gift, is a saddening consideration. This effect of partial legislation is a general departure from the chief end of man, and is calculated to make every thinking being to sit down and imitate the ancient prophet of Israel in writing Lamentations. It is not, "How are the mighty fallen?" but, How are the millions kept low, degraded in ignorance, and lost for lack of knowledge?

> Oh! how is the glory of man debas'd?
> While the heavens are concern'd in his fate!
> The mass is sunk low that a few may be rais'd
> To prance in the madness of State!

Christianity is the only principle hitherto promulgated which is calculated to reform the world, individually and generally; yet its influence has, properly speaking, been hitherto much confined to the first or individual case. The single Christian may take up his cross, and wade through the guilty world, finding plenty of exercise for his unappreciated virtue of humility on his humble way to heaven. But the broad principle of Christianity, which is calculated to renovate the general state of human society, has as yet had little fair-play amongst the worldly great, who constitute themselves the exclusive lawgivers and the leaders of general society. Even those who adopt it as their national creed never seem to make even a rational attempt to carry out its moral principles; and when the sun shall arise on the first fair morning of an earthly millennium is a question yet as much in abeyance as ever.

CHAPTER XVIII.

ANOTHER equally foolish passion, which had hitherto been partially suppressed, was beginning to take a fixed possession of my fancy. This was for the old affair, the gun, which was now employed with the intention principally of shooting small birds for the feathers for fish fly-dressing, though this was only a part of the business, as, in fact, it was impossible to restrain it to less than direct poaching, as our gentry term every intromission with their *legal* encroachments on the natural rights of the general species. This was vigorously set about, since whatever started or flew across within range of my borrowed fowling-piece shared equal fate—the hare tumbled heels up, the partridge down. As the less noise a poacher makes the better, and as powder and shot was to me a matter of considerable consequence, I blew very little away at risk—indeed, hardly ever fired without a confidence approaching to a certainty of aim and distance; and there is not a field or wood, bank, glen, or hedge around the parish but has echoed to the crack of some morning, evening, or midnight poaching adventure of mine. Ross and Anderson both tried the gun occasionally; but Anderson was far too hurried and reckless, and Ross too apathetic: hence both got disheartened from a want of success, and turned to other amusements. It had been better for me if I had been less successful, since I lost much time that might have been more profitably improved, either in the way of work or in the acquirement of some useful knowledge. The only information I got by these starts of poaching and bird-catching was a further insight into the habits of the animated creation—the birds and beasts of our own locality—in which knowledge there is at least a pleasure to the mind even now, when all desire of killing them is fled, with the other follies of early years.

Ere I had long followed these practices, I could have known every bird, fowl, or other creature by its song or call of friendship, of love, or alarm—from the cheep of a tomtit to the call of the curlew, or screech of the heron high in air—and could detect every new-comer to the district.

I then believed, on seeing any bird in air, that I knew to where it was certainly bound, and on what particular errand of love, friendship, or forage—as, for instance, the heron from his high roost, on a skirting knoll in the Merton woods, taking his afternoon aërial journey westward to his evening fishing excursion in the Lang Moss, or Cauldshiels Loch, in Selkirkshire. The same with the four-footed tribes. None of their motions ever puzzled me so much to account for as the wayward vagaries of a leveret on an early summer morning. Its friskings, saunterings, and round-aboutings seemed like some possession of what, in more superstitious days, was accounted witchcraft; but wearying to make out its meaning at the time, I set it down to the old proverb, "The madness of a March hare," and bagged it for dinner. There is a cause for everything under the sun, as well as above it, if we could only contrive to discern it; so this young hare's frolic I afterwards conceived to arise from the first impression of the genial influence on its natural constitution, before even the creature's instinct had given it a decided feeling of what it would be at.

The pheasant had been then only newly introduced into some gentlemen's preserves, such as Lord Somerville's, at The Pavillion, above Melrose; Lord Hume's, at The Hirsel, &c. The first cock pheasant that had been ever seen about St. Boswells had been hunted for a month, and fired at by all the poachers in our parish. It was a single bird, and rather shy. Surprising me in its flight direct over-head one morning, it dropped at my foot exactly at the dropping well. I skinned and stuffed it.

The starling, which had been plentiful in olden times, had entirely forsaken our district before my life-time. They returned here again in 1826, and have since nested and bred with us as plentifully as sparrows. I tamed one of the first nest I saw. This was in 1828, and it is still alive and healthful at fifteen years old.

The brown squirrel was not known here until introduced a few years ago, but is now numerous, despite all means adopted for their destruction.

I think I have shot every kind of bird and beast of the district here excepting a fox, a badger, and an otter, a kingfisher, and a wild-goose, of which in all my rambles I never once got a chance; indeed, the wild-goose could not be said to belong to our locality. It had formerly occasionally frequented our meadows and outfield moorlands by way of baiting on journeys when the country around was in an undrained and half-cultivated state, but it was never even then stationary; while in my time it was seldom seen except forming figures in a cross-country flight in air.

Since first feeling delighted with the sweet lark-like song of the water-ouzel, which few people observe, and having seen its active habits of diving and fishing for its food of fly-maggots and fish-roe at the bottom of the river stream, I have sometimes, even in the bustle of middle life, wished for leisure to write out a minute description of the kinds, characters, nature, and habits of all the creatures, bird and beast, inhabiting, or casually frequenting, our locality in Roxburgh and Berwickshires. The other year, after seeing Mr. White's most delightful "Natural History of Selbourne," I could not help feeling sorry that I had not preceded him in some attempt of the kind. I could delight to follow him up still, but the cares of the world seem thickening on my downhill of life. The hourly attention to the necessary labour for daily bread will not permit a gratification in anything like mere amusement.

But at this time, when in the middle of my gun and bird-catching folly, something like a new enchantment intervened to divide and engage my attention. I had gone up to our annual St. Boswell's Fair, very unlike my goings any year since, for then it was with no other business on hand than just to amuse myself and look about me. I had saved some eighteenpence with which to hold my fair, and had proceeded but a short way into the market, when I perceived a man laying out a few books on a stand. Curiosity led me to take a look at them, when among the first that took my eye was a coarse, sewed-up copy of Burns' "Poems." I inquired the price. "Sixteenpence," says the proprietor of the stall. I immediately down with my dust, and, pocketing the volume, turned homeward. Just to have a quiet peep I retired into the heart of a straggling blackberry bush outside our shop window, and there commenced a new course of heart and nerve-shaking raptures. It was a keen-fixed-glance sort of reading, at wherever I happened to open, interrupted only with alternate bursts of irrepressible laughter or tears, agreeably with circumstance of text or feeling. No such day of keen soul-felt enjoyment through life have I experienced since. A certain of kind of delirium pervaded my mind. The fair was neglected: its distant hum sounded like a water-fall, but it was unheeded. What I had formerly only partially heard of Burns had given me but little idea of this grand opening up. A kind of pleasure was produced, such as is produced by an interesting dream. In fact, I was ere evening as drunk with poetic rapture as any rustic in the fair likely was with love and whisky.

These poems brought not so much the idea of a new creation into my mind, as a new illustration of that world I had seen. Here I perceived many of the scenes of outward nature as if set in a more rainbow point of view. Common-sense seemed also to have taken up a proper position, while superstition and hypocrisy were turned out in nudity to be ashamed of the light, or to clothe themselves in fig leaves or fustian in the best way they could. At the same time the light of that rational piety, which is ever the concomitant of true religion, shone out through the openings of some mists that had formerly obscured it to me. The very clouds of heaven, as well as the human face, seemed to me to change much of their former aspect; so much of charm does the imagination, when partly excited and partly corrected, throw over the face of things generally. The poems appeared to me as having given our old-fashioned every-day life a new clearing up, a general repair. The springs of motion seemed to have acquired some new impulse: all moved briskly to my view, like the wheels of a new-cleaned timepiece. I felt, at least, my own mind strengthened up to the assurance of occupying a grander position on the theatre of life than I formerly durst have supposed myself entitled to assume.

Independent ideas which I had formerly conceived myself as naturally entitled to maintain as even my richer neighbours, but which, from the silly habits of life, I had hitherto feared to assert, hardly even to cherish in private thought, seemed now confirmed under the sanction of a higher authority of mind than any I had previously met with, or even supposed to exist. The servilely-acknowledged dignitaries of the day and hour seemed to sink into petty insignificance, and my formerly-repressed idea that the mind alone made the man was now positively established. I began also to conceive the moral mind and genius of Scotland to be more obliged to Burns than to all her other authors taken together; and I remain yet much of the same opinion, and this notwithstanding all the aspersions alleged against his personal character, which, in a moral and religious point of view, have been sanctimoniously or invidiously urged against him by the ignorant, who did not understand him. Although it would be with difficulty I could justify or excuse the same alleged personal aberrations in myself, or rather, I mean, copy the errors of his life into mine, yet I can as well excuse them in the character of poor Burns as in that of David and Solomon. They were all three mortal men, and alike liable to casual aberrations, excess, and error; while these kings of Israel gave way under more vague temptations, and perhaps less strong excitements to passion, than even did Burns. Neither in those days had they whisky-toddy, or their family's bread to make by looking after illicit distilleries, to lay them under extra temptations to intemperance, to lead them into rest-disturbing debts, or stimulate them to impropriety.

Though Burns has been sometimes quoted to sanction irregularity of conduct, yet are his writings, upon the whole, more free of anything approaching to any species of infidelity than most free writings of his or perhaps of any other age, and there is also less of self-seeking or time-serving fust about them. He seemed to have discovered the true link of sympathy between his own soul and the souls of others, and the sublime art of passing that fine subtle influence, like electric fluid, through every sensitive nerve of feeling with which he could possibly come in contact.

Whatever were his individual failings or follies, they were his own; he never gloried in them nor taught them to others; and who of his depreciators can tell the influence of temptation upon a mind like his, or the bitterness or holy seriousness of such a man's repentance of error? I can only aver this, that no one could ever study Burns more eagerly than I have done, and that with very little exception I have always found my heart the better for this study. He came always out from my refining pot, in which I tried him, purer gold; in truth, I soon came the length of being enabled to repeat all his poems and songs, every line, from memory, without any intentional effort to commit them. Many think they act in a very Christian manner when they teach or preach servility in place of humility. Burns taught me to respect myself, and in addition all human worth, under whatever garb I should meet with it. He confirmed my former suspicion that the world was made for me as well as for Cæsar; and I am yet convinced that there is no lesson of which the human race still stands more in need than this, which I do not understand to be taught in colleges any more than in kirks.

I had formerly reasoned out in my own mind many of the ideas which I then found illustrated in Burns; but had previously no proper standard for reference either amongst the dead or the living: hence, Burns became to me like a modernized prophet or a pocket oracle.

In this I am not adverting to the beauty of his

poetry, which is above encomium, but only to his principles, for he has hardly emitted a stanza in which some principle of his mind is not impressed upon his reader: hence the intrinsic value of his poetry. Burns does not seek, like some authors of even great celebrity, to amuse you for his own pride and interest, and to put you at his feet all the while. He takes you out with himself, arm in arm, as his equal, while he shows you all the way along how to think, to act, and to endure—what to be amused with, what to love and revere, what to hate, to scorn, and to despise. Though I admire all his poems, excepting just a few, which have been carelessly written from the impulse of hurried feelings, or under particular excitements in jovial moments (his publishers having drained his manuscripts to the dregs), yet over the whole the "Mouse," "Daisy," and "Winter Night," as well as those even more famed, such as the "Cottar's Saturday Night," have ever been my first favourites of all human compositions. These stand on a level, at least, with the chief flowers of all authorship—the lasting pictures of all future times, or at least till the language shall be lost. They are poems of which the reader will judge for himself without appeal; while the quibbling critic will be held in no higher estimation than a restless house mouse which cannot resist a desire to nibble at leaves.

As to the lyrics of Burns, they are just gems and flowers of nature's own garden, the most delightful, like the ladies themselves, of whom they speak, and so to be loved, and who also thoroughly inspired them.

CHAPTER XIX.

BUT leaving our old friend Burns for the present, we may revert to some occurrences of the same season in which I first met with his poems. This was in 1803, the autumn of which season brought to us a new experience of life, as the militia had, for some years previous to this, been a nursery for the regular army, the constant supply of which was draining off numbers of our youth as food for the French wars all over the world. This was, no doubt, against their wills, so much so that high bounties of fifty and sixty pounds were often given for a substitute in cases where the unlucky youth balloted felt an aversion to the slavery, or the *service*, as it was genteelly called, and who in any possible way could command the means of thus redeeming his liberty. I was just then turned 18 years of age, and, of course, taken into the leet for the ballot. I saw no means of redeeming myself should I be drafted; and to go to be a soldier in earnest, to fight in these wars, to be cuffed about the world under a *cat-o'-nine-tails*, or to go and be hanged, was to me a matter of almost equal choice.

But the actual threatened invasion of Buonaparte

caused still more extensive measures to be adopted for the defence of our *gentry's* precious island. Hence, a general volunteer force was raised all over Britain, which included the flower of the youth of the whole kingdom. This I joined amongst above a score of our parish lads, not so much out of any felt loyalty, or in the passive way of being neighbour-like, as to save myself in the event of my being drafted as a regular militiaman. And it was lucky I did so, as, in a short time afterwards, I was actually drawn in the ballot (the summons still lies past me here), but excused on account of being found an effective volunteer, serving in the ranks of the Roxburghshire second battalion, No. 44, head-quartered at Kelso. Well, here we were!—all drums, guns, bullets, bayonets, and bravery. Songs were even composed on the occasion. The priest, our chaplain, had one to the air of our adopted march, "The Garb of Old Gaul." We were all individually served in the ranks with a copy of it to excite our desperate daring.

It spoke something about

"On the mountains of Cheviot now present to our eyes,
The deeds of our forefathers we fondly recognise."

"Blast the recognition," whispered I, for I had now seen Burns, and must despise such stuff in the shape of song. So I wrote a kind of tarantara myself, which pleased my cronies, Ross, Anderson, and Co., much better than the other. Indeed, they pronounced mine superlative; but I luckily had a higher style of taste than of composition, so I saved myself the future blush of seeing it in print, like that of the warlike priest's, from the *Mail* office. And he has not been a flourishing bard after all, as his name and fame have alike perished from memory. But how much and how many of the more substantial are since vanished from the face of the earth! What a poor, faded figure we would now muster in the Square of Kelso Market Place! Instead of the five hundred then in the blossom of existence, could we now muster fifty as a remnant of grey-headed survivors? I doubt it. Where are all our heroes, from Sir John Buchanan Riddel, then of Riddel, Bart., our Lieutenant-Colonel commanding (a gallant, proud-looking aristocrat he then was surely), down to the tinsmith's apprentice (then a tiny-looking lad), who luckily won the head prize for ball-shooting from the whole corps by the first two bullets he had ever fired in his born days? So much for the chance of hitting Buonaparte should he have then come in person, which I actually had some hopes of either the young tinsmith or myself doing, for I was then becoming a pinner as a marksman with the soldier's musket, eventually gaining some nineteen raffles in the course of the ten years during which I continued volunteer and local militiaman together. For as the local militia came to supply the force on the volunteers being broken up, I was obliged again to join that corps, like most of my poor neighbours, to save myself from what I abominated, the regular militia, as, in case the man who was next balloted in my stead had failed, fallen, or enlisted to the regular line, I should have been called up in his place, or was always liable to be drafted again. Our drilling was then carried on by two or three neighbouring parishes meeting weekly or so on some central field, where we would march, counter-march, attack, charge, retreat, retire, and defend the day long, and then be summoned to head-quarters in Kelso for a fortnight or three weeks' general drill in the "fall." The first few months of our soldiership we were very hard drilled, and more particularly so on account of the winter quarter setting in with exceedingly raw and foggy weather, and continuing much the same all the winter, which was thought very favourable for Buonaparte possibly stealing a march on our Channel fleet, with his tremendous armament of flat-bottomed transport boats stationed at Boulogne, Brest, &c. In consequence of this, beacons were erected on all the hills around to give signal should the French force get out of harbour, escape our fleet, or attempt to effect a landing; and we volunteers were harangued on our dismissal from head-quarters to keep every man his arms in order, and be in readiness for the first flash of the telegraphs to rally at head-quarters on the instant.

The three winter months had been nearly got through, having passed drearily in point of weather, and every day bringing alarming news of the force and views of the French under the king of tyrants—when, on the 31st of January following, about ten at night, I had dropped work for the day, and run up to Willie Ovens, the cooper, to see after the health of his favourite canary bird, about which I was driving a bargain, when casting, according to custom, a jealous eye to the south, I saw a red meteor-like light in the distance, which appeared to me rather of a dubious character, as, seen through the mist, it might be a beacon light, though as much like Mars in a haze, being apparently quite above the verge of the horizon. I called Willie Ovens out to see, when we agreed that though it was in the line of the Dunion it was too high in air, and could not be a signal light, more particularly so as the rest were still in darkness. But while we stood thus conjecturing, up blazed Penielheugh, when—hulloo!—up I started to the Brae-heads, and there were Hume Castle with all the other signal hills on flame. Here was the signal summoning every man to his musket, and all the village was soon astir, something between a hum and an uproar. There were sad and hurried partings, as Byron has somewhere since described, "such as draw the blood from out young hearts;" for we then had all our sweethearts as well as had his heroes at *Brussels* on the eve of that finishing kick-up at Waterloo, which gave Wellington his pension and secured his country's slavery. We had besides fathers, mothers, sisters, and friends; but had not withal yet got our coarse regimental red coats, white breeks with black legs, like Highland sheep; and so, of course, we marched as we were, in our own various-coloured raggery. We of the village were soon collected, ready, and off ten miles to Kelso. The waning moon then arose, and, wading through the dank east of night, gave us some small countenance on the occasion. What that man of the moon must have seen first and last, if his spectacles be good! Jamie Ross and I got some half a mile in advance of our party, when he gave me a treat of a lecture regarding the nature of our ancient national bravery in the times of the Border wars, when the mounded encampments on our way were first thrown up. He seemed enthusiastic about these stirring deeds of other years from the days of Ossian's ghost downwards; while I took another view of the matter, and reasoned down his inspirations by asking him what the servile creatures who had borne the burden and heat of these former days had verily foughten for but to rivet the chains of their own feudal slaveries, and finished by picturing him and myself lying shot, or half-shot, in some ditch on the east coast some day or two hence, and that by some swallow-tailed French tailor, who, poor soul! was in all likelihood dragged or driven on in his side of the matter, or no matter, as much against his real will and better sense as I then was. All this, too, I pointed out to Jamie, was to happen in the bloom of our opening life, which our Maker must certainly have intended for a better purpose. "And in defence, after all," I asked, "of what?—of our gentry, their estates, and their coercive and game laws both by land and water?—for never a thing of our own, Jamie, have we to defend; not a poor dog, which, if we had, would be taxed above our means, nor a cat of our own, nor a peck of meal, nor indeed aught in the island but the *dudds** on our backs, which the devil a Frenchman would take the trouble of stripping us for. Frenchmen would be as polite and honourable to even our fathers and sisters as are their present masters, our 'gentlemen farmers' and landlords, to whom they are the every-day slaves, in the name of 'humble servants.' The names they give things do not alter the nature of them, Jamie.

"Would our self-constituted governing landed

* Ragged clothes.

gentry do anything in the way of legislation, or otherwise, to ease or ameliorate the condition of our working classes, or indeed cease from their plans of taxing us to the bare nakedness of everlasting starvation for their exclusive benefit, and then laughing at our well-bredness, as the brute planters in the West Indies do at their black slaves, who, after all, have uncultivated souls triple the size of their own at least? There might then be something in the colour of reason, or rationality, or sympathy in this mad-dog prank of you and me running out in a night like this to risk being shot in the defence of their lands, castles, cattle, and grown carcases, for we have at least as much brotherhood with that man o' the moon, who lives in his moon castle unapproachable by us, as with these our door-neighbour lordlings. And if it were not for this fiendish scramble about the division of the earth, and the fruits of other people's industry, amongst a few of these all-grasping and overbearing robbers of our general species (since they produce nothing themselves from their birth to their rot but war and waste to others), and their gross, shameless effrontery in their plunder of its natural inhabitants, we should live at a comparative quiet everywhere; and it would never once enter into the imagination of a French tailor to come here with a gun and bayonet to invade me, a Scotch sutor, and deprive me of my brose and bannocks, any more than it would enter into my brain to wade across the Channel to kick him from his cross-legged position on his shop-board, or rob him of his apple-tart dinner, far less to disguise the 'human form divine'—(such beautiful divinity we make of it!)—

in a blasted red tax-bought coat, in which disguise to blow out the brains of the man we have no dislike to!"

Jamie hummered some sort of assent to the truth of this harangue; but Jamie's bravery was like that of many folks—just a kind of cock-bird passion of the animal spirits that would answer in kind any crouse craw, from whatever distance it could be heard—a kind of warm animal instinct that reason had no ready art of cooling. So, though he could give no cut-down answer to my reasoning, he still paddled on with an intention, like mad King Lear, to "kill, kill, kill" all the French he might meet; while I kept pace with him, more from having got into the training of so marching than for any stomach I felt for this martial glory.

On our arrival at Kelso Bridge we found our point of road so highly palisaded, as if in defence against the French, that we despaired of being able to scale it, and likely would have stuck on any night but that. This was caused by a late alteration of the road. So in default of scaling tackle up we climbed, by finger and toe, till on the main top, on a slippery position, a sharp-pointed stake took a very French-guard-like hold of my corduroy breechings, and in my hurried descent tore me up in a most unpolite manner. "So the campaign is fairly commenced, Jamie," says I; "I am down and half-stript already." Jamie was alert at the rescue, but all our skill could not make any, even temporary, repair of this indecent breach, for lack of pins and strings. So in we must march through the Kelso causeway to join the assembling force in the Cross Keys big ball-room—

my shirt all the while doing, of its own free-will, the kindly office of a Highlandman's kilt very sympathetically. No matter for the colour of kilts in such a night as this, and such a ball-room surely! It might beat that at Brussels, I suppose, for mud, crowd, noise, and confusion. We must all be in ball-rooms, it seems, on the eve of any great dust.

By one in the morning we were all in to answer roll-call from all the country around. Just two individuals of five hundred were a-missing. It being resolved to dismiss us to billets, with the injunction to be ready to start at tuck of drum, your late brother, Adam, and I found ourselves very snugly feather-bedded in a middle flat of Mr. Swan's, Horse Market, where in half an hour I was out in dreams after my own fancy. A four hours' nap had brought us to near the break of morning, when my still dreaming imagination seemed to suggest some sound like the rub-a-dub of a drum, and I was thus sliding into a new campaign at once, when Adam, springing over bed, threw up the window, and thus awoke me to hear a drum in reality. For an instant, between sleep and wake, I discovered myself in a very nightmare-like condition of feeling, much the same as if I had been already drawn up like a ninny before Buonaparte's Lancers. "Confound their wars," muttered I; while Adam, reconnoitering half out at the window, aroused me by a most unholy volley of country oaths, fired off at old Pirly Walker, the town crier, who was still roul-roul-rouling, to warn the civilians of some new shop sale of cheap goods, to be given away on the following day for a great deal less than nothing. "You old mad idiot," blattered

Adam, "you are rousing the whole world about your ears; but just wait another minute till I come out, and if I don't give you a drumming" (and he seemed in a hurry to put his threat in execution.) "Come to bed, man," says I, "till fair daylight, and let old Mr Pirly go about his lawful vocation. Are ye not thankful that it's not the drum to rouse us to march to the east coast, and face the squads of that restless ruffian? Old Pirly, honest creature, has been to bed early, with his instructions for his morning's work in his mind, nor has he known a single thing about us and *our* drum orders." So Pirly and Adam both settled down to silence, and we lay and conjectured about the issue of affairs till broad daylight, when out we got at last to a morning's parade, when, to all the returns of all the couriers, from all points of coast and compass, no satisfactory answer could then, nor has yet, to this day, been given why, how, where, or wherefore, these beacons were kindled all over the south of Scotland.

I felt very happy, however, that it was a false alarm, having never any appetite even to hear of wars, and far less to mingle in the blood and dirt of them. Kelso streets made a fine show, however, on that first of February, 1804; for here were fathers, mothers, wives, sisters, sweethearts altogether, flocking in from twenty circular miles around; and you might have seen in reality "seven women taking hold of one man" in the heart-swell of friendship, some in a *cackle* of joy for the feeling of present security, and all for heart-gladness that the parting, perhaps for ever, was yet thrown into the idea of an indefinite distance of time.

I may further observe on this matter that, although, as before mentioned, I continued for ten years a volunteer and local militiaman, very like a soldier in earnest, I actually felt more in the character of something like an impressed hangman. They then talked of glory (never was a word so affronted), and boasted much of our native land, of Scotland in particular (being on the north side of the Border), and of *honour* (there's another decent-looking word pressed into the ranks like a blackguard) in defending our "thistle" against invasion, &c. Whilst inwardly I thought, blast their thistles: I have not a thistle, nor a spot to raise one on earth's surface; they grow on great men's grounds to shelter great men's game, who are all so selfish as to challenge my setting a foot on an entailed field of it. Shakespeare's Faery had liberty to fetch its Queen Mab at request a humble-bee's honey-bag from the top of a thistle (I had then read the "Midsummer Night's Dream.") Such liberty had not I. The very Buonapartean creation of *noblesse* could not, as conquerors, have been more unmannerly and tyrannical masters to such as me. Defend their property, forsooth, that they may continue to enjoy, by the power that property gives them, the exclusive Government means of coercing me into starvation; and for this purpose voluntarily forego all the comforts of simple existence, expend the trifling remnants of native ease, body, blood, and life, in acknowledgment and defence of their usurped privilege to deny me the common rights of common existence. In these great struggles for national or tyrannical supremacy, it is nothing thought of, the slaughter of thousands of rank and file, to fill up the trenches with human flesh, so that the ambitious prince or other leader may pass over. But the thought is rather a serious one to the individual who is dragged from his home, the bosom of his family and friends, and all the sweet, peaceful sympathies of existence, to be shot or bayoneted for the animal pleasure, amusement, mistake, or ambition of those rulers, who on these accounts will not let society rest in peace; and who, if they do succeed in their views of aggrandizement, never allow us or ours to participate in their advantages of war plunder. In short, a young man, whose philosophy of mind could calculate on the right his Maker has given him to the comforts of existence, and had as poor an opinion of Buonaparte, Georges the Third and Fourth, their House of Lords, their Wellingtons, and all the pack of them, as I have had, would very unwillingly condescend to be shot to oblige such as them. I do not believe that nations would ever think of going to war were it not for the political machinations of their Governments. Although I then trudged occasionally for ten years about the fields around the district here, until in the eye of heaven I verily thought shame of such worse than idle conduct, exercising in the character of a volunteer soldier, facing east and west as ordered, yet all the while I had an utter aversion to all things military. Their technicalities of drill-jargon were an unqualified abomination to my natural ear, and the prim, starch-up gait of a drill-sergeant, even in his civil conversation, is scarcely yet endurable. However amiable in his civil capacity a man may be, I cannot help hating man as a soldier. But it is not easy to account, even to ourselves, for our antipathies. I have a natural distaste for all things military, even to the extent of disliking military music, drums, and whistles, and, above all, red coats and lipless hats, with sow bristle tufts. What brutes we allow our oppressors to make of us, and what an awful idea does it present to the moral mind, these throat-cutting habits, on a national scale, in by-past unnecessary wars and devastations. The consideration that

> "Millions have in battle died
> That villains great on blood might dine,
> And millions more have hungry sigh'd
> That *legal* knaves might swim in wine!
> Was earth, for this, plac'd in the solemn void?
> Were men created to be thus destroyed?"

How many bones lie bleaching on foreign fields, of those who were "welcomed to their gory bed" and "covered with glory," as the French regarded it, while those friends they ought to have been left to labour to support are now corn-billed into starvation at home. Confound their "glory!" such as it is; but it is heaven-confounded without any of my imprecations. I have always had a notion of letting these ambitious rascals seek their glory for themselves. Who, even according to their own professional creed, is to answer in judgment for their premature self-destruction and damnable abuse of the Almighty's rational creatures, or those who should have been rational, but for their prevention? The major wickedness is certainly more particularly on the side of the great in power, while the silly folly is ours. They call us names which signify something less than asses, and so, in this sense of the matter, we certainly are, since they use us worse than such beasts of burden, and we keep ourselves in a lower scale of degradation than that creature; for how often have I admired the noble spirit, the remains of that glorious wild-mountain independence, still unbeaten out of the ten thousandth generation of that excellent animal the ass. I have seen a mad, lordly-spirited gipsy lad basting the hide of the overladen creature, which would not gratify that absurd lord of creation by doing his dirty work upon such terms. Though the poor Israelitish-looking animal could not shake off his panniers, he yet showed the sturdiness of his spirit and the grandeur of his nature by refusing to budge a single foot. I wish human beings could be so wise as to imitate that worthy, and, therefore, much man-despised, animal, more particularly in the sturdy qualities of its disposition rather than in its proverbial spirit of stupidity and patient endurance.

Before being done with my soldiering, however, I recollect I was very desirous of the downfall of that most insolent of all upsetting scoundrels, Buonaparte, who had the consummate impudence to set himself up as the stationary pivot, upon which was to turn the affairs of the universe—the one only "ME," and to look upon men generally as no mere man has a right to look upon meré maggots. This he ought not to have done, although those of the powers he was fighting against might be as bad as he or I have supposed them.

I was at that time only suspecting the false principles of tyrannical domination. Had I been as well convinced of the thing then as I am now, I would sooner have been dragged out and shot on a dung-hill than have gone a-volunteering on any side of such disputes, which was only a building up of the kingdom of Satan, and a furtherance of his government in this world.

CHAPTER XX.

I forgot to observe in last chapter that at the previous Whitsunday we had shifted into the old village farm-house then belonging to Mrs. Kyle, beside the old school-house, my father having taken a five years' lease of the old steading, and, to lighten the rent, fitted up the old barn, stable, and byre for dwelling-houses with *claut and clay* chimneys and partitions—he and I having become, from experience, first-rate hands at that *claut and clay* work. We got old Janet Allan, with her widowed brother Robin's daughters, to rent the one, Christy Donald another, and poor old Johnie Young, then turned pack-pedlar, the third. My father sat like a little landlord amidst so many sub-tenants. Then James Inglis, who had been late forester at Greenwells and Eildon Hall, under Governor Elliot, at the sale of that estate, came down the next Whitsunday term, and took Mrs. Cochrane's big orchard and garden, separated from our *kail-yard* simply by a gooseberry hedge.

James had a large family of young people—two sons, the oldest and the youngest, Adam and John, then weavers, as well as strong spademen in their father's garden. John was about my age, Adam a few years older. John was of a forward, off-hand, rather reckless disposition, but completely bridled in by the vigorous moral and religious discipline of the family; and he was, besides, happily under the jurisdiction of Adam, the elder, having been his bound apprentice. Adam was, according to our old saying, not the man to creel eggs with. He was, however, through life a person who could measure his means to his end, and live upon his own product, the best of any man I have ever known. Before we had fallen into proper acquaintance, I had, on a summer day, about cherry-ripe time, given a very unconscious offence to old James, who had perceived me throw, as he supposed, a stone over into his cherry-tree for no other end that he could conceive than to knock down some fruit to be gathered up at conveniency. He immediately told in the family what he had perceived, and assured them that that young shoemaker was a very dangerous-looking door-neighbour to a fruit garden, by whom they should certainly be much troubled in the fruit season during all time coming, unless he should just on this first appearance of offence be vigorously checked, so as to deter him from ever again giving even an anxious look over the hedge. "Don't go in a passion, father," says Adam, "an' in before his father—that is making enemies at once; but leave him to my management; I'll speak to him the first time he comes out." This was accordingly done in a very civil way, and much to my astonishment, as I had forgotten the simple circumstance, till all at once recollecting—"Oh! yes," says I, "some birds alighted in your cherry-tree, which from a flirt of a wing I suspected to be either *goldspinks* or *whinlinties*; but, as they were silent, I lifted a little loose clay and threw to raise them so that I might see, or hear by their voice, which they were." "And could you have known by their voice?" says Adam. "Of course," says I; "it is easy from a little acquaintance with birds to know every one in air either by its voice or manner of flight." Adam, who was fond of all kinds of observation, though then little of a naturalist, told me some time afterwards that he took a good feeling for me from that moment, which soon settled into a lasting friendship; the reflection of which burns like a light in our old cooling bosoms to this hour, though the wide Atlantic rolls between us.

Some few days after this occurrence, meeting me on the street, he asked me into his shop, where he had some curiosities of his own hand-manufacture, one of which was a reel in a glass. I, by chance, lifted from his loom-window a loose leaf, which, seeing to be written, I laid down again. "Read it if you can," says Adam, "but the writ is bad." When I glanced it over, I found it home-manufactured love-verses, very like gooseberry wine, in which the foreign spirits are nowise fiercely predominant. "The ideas are an age before the versification," says I, "and both as old as the pastoral songs in black print, or of those days that *Raeburn* (our squire) speaks of 'when people would have hanged themselves for love, and drowned themselves for love'—not the least like the present, when he avers 'you will not find ten pounds worth of love in all the parish.'" "Do you think you could improve the rhyme?" says Adam. "I think I could, by writing it all new over," I replied. "Take it with you, and try," says he. I gave him in my new edition in the evening, when he confessed the first to be his own attempt, but thought mine better rhymed, and more expressive of his whole idea—just what he wished to be at. I stood henceforward of considerable poetical repute in his estimation; so companions we became more and more close daily, till, by-and-by, he learned me to take snuff like himself, and here our minds became daily more and more congenial.

So now, amongst a circle of new acquaintances, what with talking and reasoning about life, religion, principle, and poetry, I was kept busy and amused, besides feeling a still growing desire after fishing, fowling, birding, &c., all over and above the work which my father laid to my hand, so absolutely necessary to be accomplished daily or nightly. What a hurry of life! And often have one or other of these lads sat beside me till I should work up my task, sometimes an hour beyond midnight. Twelve at least of every twenty-four hours were then required to be devoted to the necessary work for bread: hence the struggle in the youthful mind between virtue and necessity on the one hand, and those other vague wanderings of the juvenile fancy on the other, into which entered so much of what may be supposed to constitute the soul, that, if the soul be not spiritually re-furnished daily, one might suppose it would have been exhausted by the age of majority, since the tides of every flow of spirits, and the consequent ebbs of exhaustion, were very considerable. At this time my mind seemed in a hurry to live, grasping at all things at once, and amassing little. I would have wished to note down a hundred ideas as they rushed through the mind, but had not patience to catch or select even one of a thousand, since it seemed such a trouble to wait and note them down, from the want of capability to arrange the expression to my taste. Adam, on the contrary, was a cool philosopher, without any of my out-door follies. He regulated his time to purpose, wrought his hours, lectured his brother John and me occasionally, and went through the week like an eight-day clock. He had only one shortcoming, and that was a lack of method in arranging his expression in the communication of his best ideas, otherwise Chalmers could not have beat him at preaching. In many cases I had to read out his explanations as if he had been conversing by signs; but from the context I generally understood what he wished to convey. And as to confidence, in our long friendship I always have wished that I could come up to the standard of his good opinion. I soon came to be his man of business general, his clerk in all his affairs of consequence, and, of course, confidant in his life's transactions. We could have told each other what neither of us could tell any third person. Though we were soon afterwards, and have been always since, removed to different villages, yet every occasional meeting was always with a rising of the heart and spirits; and the comfort of virtuous conduct, amidst all our world's difficulties, was always the main point on which we congratulated each other. The

Inglises soon after this first acquaintance, lost their father by an accidental death, when Adam became head of the family, remained unmarried, and kept his old mother till her death in a very advanced age, five years ago; when, his trade being here completely done up, he went out to Upper Canada with his only remaining sister, Mary, and her grandchild, there to join his brother John and sister Ann, who had been there for several years thriving with a large family. They now all live at *Greenwells*, by Guelph, John's property, which he purchased in a wild state, and named after *Greenwells* here, where he had been bred up from a child. John's family are nearly all married and settled around him—very excellent stock from which to propagate a rising colony, and make future justices of the peace for the district. John is now the oldest justice in Guelph.

While my circle of acquaintance was thus extending, the world appeared as if opening up and widening around me; besides, I had now the opportunity of feeling the strength of other minds, and could weigh myself against my acquaintances individually. And here I began to perceive more clearly that the diversity of mind in regard to ability, aptitude, taste, temper, and capability was minute and endless in its varieties of kind and degree. I began to entertain an opinion of what the experience of life has since confirmed me in, that there is more diversity in the human mind than in all the other works of nature, animate and inanimate, taken together, with all the machinery of all the sciences to boot; and, therefore, to suppose that the individual, if any such could exist, who should become master of all the arts and sciences of past discovery or invention, should next attend to the science of the human mind, he would be entering upon a field of investigation that he should not be able to get through in an eternity. Tables of logarithms and British finance that appear so complicated are but child's study to the more complex machinery of the human mind—its tendencies, capabilities, and so on—a very few only of the more common traits of character having yet been understood and defined. There is a grand development yet forthcoming. These ideas were then, however, only in the process of opening up amongst my door-neighbour communications, which might be said to be a correspondence of mutual inquiry, as we were severally all alike desirous of gaining information on every subject that seemed to lie in our way. Our inquiries, or rather reasonings, were more generally a kind of household philosophy than of a scientific character, having chiefly regard to mind and characteristic, the nature of the affections, the causes of their leanings, twistings, and general workings, with the effects and consequences, particular and general. Besides, Adam and John Inglis would teach me arithmetic, which they had both learned at school; but the lessons were always delayed till more leisure; hence the first lesson is not taken yet, nor ever will. I recommended to them English grammar, as a branch of education for which I conceived a keener taste. We were all to set about these things, this last in particular; yet none of us has ever set about either to this day and hour. We were past our school time, and the rule-part of the matter appeared like a drudgery to the mind, so all settled down to Adam and John taking delight in a little occasional reading, and me in writing from the ear rude imitations of Burns, copies of which Adam stored up at the time, but which, unluckily for the lyrical world, are long since lost.

James Ross and John Anderson were still my chiefs of the lyrical taste, and we sang like larks; besides, Jamie read me some three or four plays while at my work in winter evenings. In this way twelve months slid on, the most amusing and pleasurable that perhaps I may have had since. All that time I found myself, in one way and another, as busy as a bee in a box; but as is ever the fate pendent over all sublunary existence, where there is no permanent abiding, my circle of agreeable acquaintance was soon to be broken up. John Anderson, scorning his apparent poor means of getting forward in the world either as a small drudgling farmer, like his father, or as a baker, to which business he had served an apprenticeship, took the West Indies in his head, where he thought he should either make a small fortune, with which he should be enabled in a few years to come home and marry *the gentle* Annie Gray, or perish in the attempt, which last he eventually did. He left this the following spring, and landed at Kingston, Jamaica, in July, where he struggled on for several years, wrote his father and me frequently, lost his health by yellow fever, went to the island of Cuba to recruit, there commenced land surveyor, and soon afterwards was understood to have died, not having been more heard of. James Ross, losing heart from the state of his father's family circumstances at the time, and the want of proper occupation at home, engaged to go with a passing drove of black cattle to England; and on leaving them pushed forward to London, where he continued for a few years doing very well as a steady journeyman baker, till, in the heat of an impress of seamen, he was carried aboard the tender, and in a few days thereafter was returned on the ship's roll *a-missing*, and was never more heard of. I have often thought that as he was an excellent swimmer he had likely attempted to swim ashore in the night, and perished in the attempt.

These two had scarcely left us till I got another new companion, for whom, although I felt a great regard, yet no new friendship has ever through life made up to my feelings the loss of any former one. Still, all these bereavements must be submitted to by minds even the most sensitive and devotedly affectionate. This new acquaintance was David Ovens, the orphan son of a Dr. Ovens, who had been bred in our village, and was then the ward of his uncle, Thomas Ovens, who lived next door to us, having come to reside with his uncle, who rented David's patrimonial inheritance.

David was with me on a fine summer evening when I killed my first *clean* salmon with the small trout fly. The salmon nipt down my fly in the *Broom-ends* strong stream about sunset, and the full moon was high and bright before I could land him safely. Great and glorious as we both were on the occasion, we resolved to be honest; so, wading across the water, we went up to George Sanderson, then the fisherman at Kipperhall, and showed our fish caught with the trout fly, expecting that he would generously let us have it to carry home at something like half-price, which we had boldly resolved to muster. But George was a shabby fellow; he demanded the full price, a sum so far above our joint means that we were obliged to forego the satisfaction of our prize, and suffer a severe reprimand, amounting as nearly to a full prohibition for the future as the strict law of the case could warrant him to threaten. So we had to re-wade the water, and be content to go home as we were, reconciling ourselves as far as possible with reflections on the straightforwardness of our conduct, and at the same time finding excuse to appropriate without appeal all we might so catch in the moonlight of the future. And as individuals were then casually employed by the tacksmen of the waters to fish for the one-half of what they could kill, and we having thus found out the gentle trick of the trout fly on the fine single gut, then only newly introduced to the country here, that very week, in the pure summer water, we took the liberty of repaying ourselves in full weight and measure. Years previous to this I had been famed in a local circle for fly-dressing; had dressed a "Nancy Dawson" for old John Wight of Crago'er, a fly as long as his fore-finger, dressed upon fifteen horsehairs for his cold winter weather slaughter; had in consequence gained credit with him; and had been frequently down along with Will. Balmour fishing for old John, then himself unable to handle the rod from old age, on which occasions he allowed half of what we would catch. I therefore had killed several salmon with the regular salmon fly; but this trout fly used for salmon in the fine, clear summer water was a new discovery. After this David and I resumed correspondence with old Wight, gratifying and amusing him with the fine gut and the trout fly, which, conceiving to be such inadequate means for the great purpose, he viewed as something in the character of magic. This, together with a drop of whisky in a bottle, gave us not only a roving commission, but made us always the most desirable guests imaginable. There were no gentlemen fishers in those days as now to come three hundred miles in cold spring snows, lodging at the inns here around us at some pound a day, besides both treating and paying the tacksmen at a high rate, something like another pound, for *the favour* of a liberty to starve and fatigue themselves on the cold water. One might have proved them mad before a jury of Athenians. It was years after this ere Scrope* came round and succeeded old John Wight and Geordie Sanderson, by trebling the rents of the Mertoun waters, commencing what we may call the gentle epidemical mania for salmon fishing, which has had the effect of these great lordly pikes driving us smaller fry out of the water.

* William Scrope, a famous sportsman as well as writer on field-sports. He rented Lord Somerville's water, with his charming seat of The Pavilion, near Melrose, between fifty and sixty years ago. He had previously had a lease of the Mertoun water. He published in 1842 a splendid two-guinea illustrated volume, entitled "Days and Nights Angling on the Tweed." Another work of his, which appeared in 1838,—"The Art of Deer Stalking,"—adorned with fine plates after the Landseers, is now very scarce, and brings five or six guineas in the market.

CHAPTER XXI.

IN last chapter I have been again getting a little a-head of my regular narrative, as the anecdote last related occurred some year or two after our first intimacy, about which time, in the spring of 1805, my father, then about 58 years of age, took it in his head to make a second marriage. His ostensible reason was that his family were now getting so far up that they would most probably soon all marry, and that he would be left in his old age perhaps lonely and comfortless. This was one of those subterfuges by which people generally excuse all those proceedings, which they themselves secretly suspect to look a little foolish, and, in the act of justification before others, generally mislead or deceive even themselves. Besides, having so good and kindly a heart himself, he could not possibly conceive but that any one he should hold so dear as the woman of his imagination, converted into his wife, would, without mistake, feel the same affection for his children as he should ever do himself. In short, he had plenty of natural philosophy, though he could not bring it to bear on both sides of this delicate question, where his general feelings were so decidedly interested.

In such second marriages there may be much that

is imprudent, and yet hard to censure; for, though the first duty in such cases may appear simply plain, there is often a complication of lurking sympathies, influenced by constitutional propensities, giving natural enough reasons for a decision, which, though not on the most proper side of the matter, is yet in itself not contrary to the written commandment of positive duty.

My three sisters, however, took the matter very much to heart, while I did so only so far as it ran in pure sympathy with them; for, in fact, I had not then, any more than now, thought much about self, except as I stood in relation to my friends, or those I particularly regarded. My father's "flame" was Jean Troup, an Aberdeenshire woman, of about forty, who had come in her youth a servant in Mr. Tulloh's family, when he bought the estate of Eilistoun, some twenty years previously. My father had conceived her to be a paragon of good sound sense and quiet honest industry of disposition, and consequently an agreeable companion, and a likely good housewife; or, at least, he had found himself willing to take chance of her being all such. He had very fondly even taken lessons in the Aberdeenshire dialect, which those bred in that country seem incapable of ever giving up for life. This my sisters had for some time observed, and seemed by their looks to disrelish very much. But they were prudent girls, and never said anything to grieve or affront their father, although they had much to do to conceal the tears in all their eyes on the day of his marriage. On the first declaration to us of his serious intention, which was made to the demand of my second sister, then his housekeeper, we were all made aware of the necessity of looking out for a new family arrangement.

My father simply thought we could just look to his house as our home the same as usual; but so, alas! felt not we. God bless the fond old heart! We saw the matter with different eyes. So, some weeks before the Whitsunday term, the intended marriage day, my out-service sisters came by appointment, when we all together walked down to the haugh by Tweedside, and there held a consultation on our family affairs, when it was agreed that their running half-year's wages should be clubbed for the purpose of purchasing some household furniture; and as such articles were then at the very highest known price, for what we might fall short of value, it was thought credit would perhaps be allowed for six more months till their summer's wages might be earned, which would fully clear up all scores. It was further agreed that I should be constituted goodman of the house, and I was deputed to purchase some respectable-looking second-hand cot-house beds, which they could already furnish with blankets, ticks, &c.,* and a few such other household utensils as might be necessary. It was also stipulated that whoever of us should marry should leave the house without further claim to any of this mutual furniture,

---

* One chief family duty that occupied the attention of a country housewife of those days was the growing of lint and the provision of wool, and, setting the family example herself of sitting late and rising early, to card, spin, boil, bleach, and get up a provision of necessary bed clothes for the daughters of the family (enough to furnish each two beds was considered the necessary quantity), which was called such a one's "providing." This practice is now greatly superseded by our manufactories producing such necessaries at a cheaper rate than they could be provided on the old fashion.

and that the last who might remain single should consequently retain all; while we resolved that none of us should ever say a word to vex our father, but only signify our plan to him, as being in all our opinions the most prudent and eligible. (I believe our mother's spirit was present with us that day.)

In pursuance of this commission I went and purchased the necessary articles from a Mr. Bain, then steward at Mertoun, who was leaving the place; and thus were we furnished, although I have forgotten how the full sum was raised, since he was paid ready money. The next immediate point of my attention was clothes, with which I might appear decent at the marriage, as till now I had never received any direct wages, and was not worth sixpence on earth, and from use and wont had been generally held low in the wardrobe department, never able to cut a much better figure than Paddy O'Rafferty, poor fellow, who comes over annually a-harvesting. I must, however, look out in earnest, and somehow or other take the world by surprise. In my first bold stroke to seek credit I was successful beyond calculation, as on my first application Mr. French, our village haberdasher,* gave me the outfit of a whole suit till I should be able to pay for them. I kept very low, however, so that the whole should look only respectable—not *a la mode*, but all a-piece. I have forgotten whether the colour was blue or grey; no matter now. I was certainly a very spruce youth, with my three pound sterling suit on my back, though I knew there should be a sweat for the getting it paid. And so there

* Mr Thomas French, a most intelligent and worthy man, and one of the founders of the St Boswell's Library.

certainly was on the following harvest field, where I gained it by the sheer tug of muscle and sinew in a month's hourly unequal contention against two of the merest boors ever graced with our biped form.

No matter, I was in the meantime bright at the wedding, except being beaten at the "broose," where, after running away from my main antagonist, I took some sudden silly qualm of foolish feeling in entering the village, and, like a simpleton, let him come up and pass me. However, the marriage feast was got over by ten at night, when we, the offspring of the first family nest, fled out to seek some roost amongst our acquaintances.

I had much to do to get a cottage shelter, all being let at that season; but at last I succeeded in getting the proprietor's consent to the vacant end of old Tibby and Christy Douglas's house, apportioned off by itself, with its own door. This was, of course, at risk of being *witched*, as they were accounted the weird sisters, and set (with all their bristle) against this proceeding; and you know that their landlord, David Kyle of Fens,* held them in dread on this account. He thought me mad to venture, till I convinced him that I had a sovereign counter charm, which kept us all *cantrip*-proof. The old goose of a Scotch laird and church elder, who could believe in the bane, could not possibly dispute the antidote. The poor creatures, Tibby and Christy, were indeed as cankered and *ettere*† as nettles, though silly, and

* Father of Thomas Kyle of Greenwells, near Eildonhall, who used to brag that he was the possessor of a Rubens, worth a great many thousand pounds. He was one of the first who rode "tandem" on Tweedside.

† Virulent, from Anglo-Saxon "ætter," poison, venom; "attry" (Chaucer), poisonous.

more particularly so from having found the world hard to live in; and having got a partial share of their own will from the still lingering superstitions of the age, they, agreeably to the old saying, "got mair for their *ill* than for their good," since many durst not cross them, nor refuse them little favours, such as, from their general ignorance and accustomed success, they had got into a habit of asking very unceremoniously. Their title to witchcraft did not rest upon the principle of the good old Mause in the "Gentle Shepherd," who felt herself accounted a witch by the more vulgar of her neighbours,

> "Because by education she was taught
> To speak and act aboon their common thought."

On the contrary, old Tibby and Christy were ignorant below all common thought. However, by a little kindly attention I contrived to keep them sweet, while I lived three years with only a partition wall between us. Sister Betty kept my little house, and was always busy spinning, sewing, or such like, to produce some necessary comfort. Here I sat at the one window, looking out to the sweet south, and daily working journeyman for my father, having no particular charge but a dozen of the laird's (Kyle's) orchard trees beside the door, which stood then much exposed, though the best bearers in the village. Your good old father, being then well-liked, used often to rent their crop at risk, and the "hempies"* would not rob from him as they would from a laird. And I was, then, since you had left us, his secretary-elect; while he, good old soul! had

---
* Mischievous boys.

some notion of my becoming his son-in-law, though he did not live to see this occur.

In this small circle of acquaintance, and in the way already described, some eighteen months passed on, with little variation of circumstances nor anything of occurrence worth remark, except the awful thunderstorm on the 9th of August, 1806. This event, so terrifically grand, was much to my taste at the time, as no crash of elements I had ever previously seen or have since witnessed has been in any way the least comparable. Indeed, I cannot conceive that all the thunder-storms I have here seen throughout fifty years, crushed together, would make such another five hours' growl, roar, and rattle, with gush and swash of water.

The storm first came about midday, darkening on from the south, where "heaven's artillery" had already broken out in full play. The thickening was not like that of a simple gathering thunder-cloud, but of the whole atmosphere in agitation congregating and condensing before the storm's advance. This was in copper-coloured masses, throughout which was seen the electric light hissing and flickering as it wove and threaded the still darkening clouds, which, ever blackening more and more, soon enveloped all to the horizon around. The zigzagged lightning then became truly awful in its waving, striping, and spangling these mourning curtains of the shrouded heavens. And now the hiss of transient gusts of wind gave a feeling as if they were the messengers of some last-day tidings, and the unintermitting growl of the distant thunder seemed like the voice of a dire-approaching vengeance on an errand of extermination. The thunder neared and neared till the incessant howl, roar, and rattle of the peals became continuedly intermixed and astounding. The rain gushed, not in a regular shower of drops, but in a hush, like an universal waterfall. The fray of the elements was so near to the earth, and the crash and roar followed the bolts so instantaneously, that we found we were now enclosed in the middle of it; while the rain rebounded as if enraged at being so dashed on the ground, till the fire and water appeared as if in maddened contention. Every living creature seemed to have retired to its own seclusion. While my sister and I stood in the doorway of our little cottage witnessing the scene, one bolt of the thousand around, with its attendant rattle of noise, burst immediately before us, leaving a smell of sulphur that gave a feeling of suffocation. "I am hurt," said she, and, retiring, lay down on her bed. She felt powerless, as if benumbed. I told her she was not struck with it, but only a little confused by the disturbance of the air in the sudden passing of the bolt. She soon recovered so far as to recollect that our shirting web was being neglected at Tweedside, where it had been laid down for bleaching. Bad as things looked, I felt a little glad of this reasonable excuse for getting out just to feel the weight of the rain and see the doings abroad. The feeling was like as if one was being bored down and pressed into the earth. Still, I made way a quarter of a mile down to the Tweed, where I would have arrived too late to save our treasure had not some of our neighbours in a similar predicament been long before me, and already got all rightly secured above high-water mark. The Tweed was only yet fast swelling, while the surface was half-covered with floating wrecks of paling railings and other woodwork, swept from the burn courses above.

But what astonished me to almost utter confounding was to see a villager (Alexander Adamson) standing in an eddy of the gullet-ford* to his middle waist, labouring with a long cleek to drag out whatever wreck came within his reach. So, thinks I, will the greedy ones of the earth be employed on the morning of the day of judgment,—those who can relish only one idea, and that a selfish one. On wading homeward up the roadway, now flowing like a river, the thunder was dreadfully grand! Some balls of fire shot across my vision, sweeping the ground between me and the height, much resembling a man's head with the hair on fire. It might have given the idea of red-hot cannon shot had the thing not been projected before at the defence of Gibraltar. Getting into the spirit of the matter, I began to lose fear, and examined the roots of the hedges on both sides to trace the tracks of the bolts through, but could ascertain no singed mark of their course. After again looking in on my sister, I hurried to the west burn, where down the hollow dell rushed the flood, some thirty feet deep; the confined force of the current wearing and tearing up all down to the solid rock, which, with the travelling boulders dashing at turns

---

* At the Gullet at Dryburgh Townfoot, the Tweed formerly used to rush with irresistible impetuosity, from the dangerous ford above, into a deep pool below, the width of the river being contracted to some half-dozen yards. Many a poor fellow has been drowned there.

against the jutting banks, gave the slope above the agitation of an earthquake. I never felt in such a position in life as I did while standing half-way down the bank, within some twenty feet of the top flood of that burn. The continued burst and roar of the thunders above, with the shake of the earth from the noise and dash of the water below, gave me a sensation of that loneliness which an isolated individual might feel amidst "the wreck of matter and the crash of worlds."

This storm pelted just five hours in passing us, directly from south to north; went off over Mid and East-Lothian about nightfall, and out to the north seaward. It had struck on to our coast, I would suppose, about Liverpool, and had, I understood, commenced in some far southern latitude, I have no doubt, near the line. It covered some fifty or sixty miles in breadth, though the main middle force of it might not extend above ten or twelve. We were here in about the middle of it. On the subsiding of the flooding the burn courses around us presented a wonderful alteration. The Tweed was not swelled in proportion; but these small tributaries had cleared their courses of stone, earth, and gravel, and carried all into the Tweed till she was cut half across with a deposition of the *debris*. About a quarter of an acre was gained on the Tweed, and high mounded in at our Lessudden west burn foot to mid river, where I measured it ten feet above the surface of the low water; and it lay there till the tremendous high flooding of the Tweed on the 7th of September the following year, 1807, which carried it off, sweeping all down to the present level.

To give an idea of the burn current, I may mention that one boulder stone, which had long lain upon the burn-bank, above the old bridge, at the back of St. Boswell's Green inn, was carried amongst others into the middle of the Tweed: that stone was estimated at above two tons weight. The Bowden and Newtown Burn was so large, and the rise and gush so sudden, that Andrew Mather's carts at Bowden Mill, standing loaded with meal, were swept down, and the wheels and bodies of the carts carried on the flood over above the old bridge at Newtown Mill, where a new-built kiln-house and granary were at the same time swept away to the bare foundation rock; while the freestone rock down that burn's broad course to the Tweed was laid bare to glitter in the sun.

Although the lightning had struck the ground in many places around us, and several persons were less or more hurt, yet no human lives were lost in our neighbourhood. One shepherd boy about Muirhouse-law, who had drawn to the shelter of an old thorn, was struck on the side, and the wound burnt in to the intestines. Dr. Oliver, who dressed it, told me that this wound was caused by the attraction of a particular metal button. The boy, however, recovered. Though this thunder-storm might have made but a sort of every-day appearance in some sultry latitudes, yet fifty generations may pass through life without witnessing anything so terrifically sublime in our sober climate.

CHAPTER XXII.

I WONDER what can tempt me to go on scribbling here, since I am suspicious of having become silly, in continuing to note recollections so trivial and common-place in themselves that possibly no individual of the passing generations would think them worth telling over, far less worth reading; for every one who has lived fifty years must have had a life of as considerable interest as mine, but generally of more adventure. Still, as the same stamp of circumstances may not make the same striking impression on the wax of all minds, and the incidents having been interesting to myself at the time of their occurrence, and clinging to memory as still bearing on my present life's fortune, it is as well to occupy any vacant hour in thus embodying them, as expressive of the philosophy of common life, as to spend that hour in the same noteless way in which we are too apt to let pass a considerable proportion of the hours which make up the few years of our pilgrimage through what we call *time*, yet which, more properly speaking, is a portion of that eternity, of which we can gather as little knowledge comparatively as an insect can do of the general history of its summer day of social existence. And what, after all, is all that which most men do through life, even the most virtuous, but just spend one day after another in labouring for, or otherwise striving to procure, the food which must pass through their digestive organs before the next sun-down, and talk over the silly outline of the running hour's news, to be daily effaced by that of the succeeding to-morrow, till from age, disease, or other casualty they are pulled down to their grave, "and the place which once knew them knows them no more for ever?" A new face has taken their place to run through the same silly track of life, and at the end of a few years all the world have forgotten, not only that they were perhaps influential in their day, but that they ever existed. Many of my youthful compeers of whom I am writing are forgotten by all but myself. I shall soon now, of course, be forgotten in turn; and were it not for some principles which a notification of the growth of mind may tend to explain—as that mind comes in contact with the raw materials of creation—and this narrative for the amusement of at least a few other minds, it might not be worth even the simple trouble of noting a single trifle of that which, as a whole, has made up the sum total of the interest of these fifty past years. Besides, in another point of view, I cannot see that my life, ephemeral as it has been in regard to its relation with the general universe, has been of one whit less consequence in point of social interest than that of any, or of all, of the past popes of Rome, or of the last sevenscore and ten kings, emperors, and warriors who have cut most petty figures on this our paltry planet. Yet, were there any standing still in life, I believe I should have stuck fast at the beginning of this chapter; but man's existence being held on the natural conditions of progression, we may as well get onward, with what wind and tide we can have for the whistling, and make the most of our poor life's cargo.

So here, arrived at the age of twenty-one, some new scenery lay before me to be opened up, with its variety of phenomena, then strikingly new. And here it came upon me, as came that knowledge of good and evil which flashed out upon our first parents on their eating of the forbidden fruit. We were comfortably enough situated in one main respect—three of a family proper, sister Betty, George Knox (her boy), and myself. But to keep house over our heads, and find a daily supply of food, fuel, and clothing, I must out hands. I found it no easy matter to keep myself fixed to the irksome, sedentary, journeyman task necessary to earn the average sum of eighteenpence a day; and I often fell short of this, though the only source of supply for the whole family expenditure—to keep to the task or suffer want to-morrow. Food was then at the extreme height of French war prices—all markets high, and coal in our district between 35s and 40s per ton: as the poorest man has ever to go to the dearest market, I then paid 40s.

Country shoemaking was then a worse craft than it is even now, and still it is the poorest of all *country* trades. A country tailor is much better either as master or journeyman—the wages better, or as good, a trifling outfit, and no risks in outlay. A weaver was then an excellent trade, with no risk, though entirely done up now. A joiner has also comparatively less risk in outlay, and better wages—a shoemaker's outlay on materials being over two-thirds of the whole value. A blacksmith may be considered the best *country* trade, the more particularly as the work required cannot be postponed, and the exertion requisite keeps the workman from flagging while his body is at all capable of the necessary energy; therefore, his day cannot so readily pass without his having earned a day's wage.*

If a man come to find that he has begun an unproductive trade, it may be asked, Why should he continue at it? This is answered by another interrogation, How shall he get out of it? Like one who finds he has got into a bad boat in the middle of a current, he must just oar or paddle on the best way he can, to prevent drowning, till he get ashore.

* In this, however, as in most other country occupations, I have remarked that an ordinary workman who has a ready use of his hands, and can execute his work just passably well, will make more wages than one who happens to be very ingenious, as in this last case the individual is so ready to follow his own nice taste, putting more work on the article than the price considered common will remunerate him for. I was once comparing some article of work done by a blacksmith with a thing of the same kind done by Rob. Wight. We were remarking its faults, observing how little pains had been taken on it, when I observed that the man said it would not pay, with the work I wanted. "He could not do it," says Rob.; "he works *for money*." "So do you," says I. "No," says he, "I have never yet wrought for money. In doing a job I never spare contrivance and labour, and would re-work it ten times over rather than not be perfectly pleased with it myself, though my employer were an idiot. The remuneration is quite a secondary consideration with me, and must be so with every good workman." A conscientious and tasty workman has much credit for his work, of course, whatever line he follows; while his less sterling neighbour beats him at picking up the coin.

I wanted the requisite school education to enable me to set out for anything like even a clerkship of any kind, and could enter into no new apprenticeship to any other trade from the want of present means, together with the way I stood relatively circumstanced. From the necessity, therefore, to earn family bread by any such means as were already in my power, I must continue to nibble on at the craft I had learned, however scanty the earnings; and just endeavour to live within the mark, however difficult the economy necessary. Clothes must be kept on the back of some kind or other, though clothes like those worn by the run of lads who were my contemporaries were hardly to be come at. But the concern in this was the less felt from my having hitherto been held so low in this respect, so that from use and wont I had become passive in the matter. And what very luckily made me still more careless was that I could perceive that my favourite part of the fair creation did not hold the male dress in such estimation as their lovers were ready to suppose. The darlings were more taken up with the adorning of themselves, and a bonnie lass with a new ribbon could hardly settle to perceive whether her lover's coat was a fine blue or a coarse grey, whether he walked out on Sundays in peacock pride, or was negligent, from being engrossed in admiration of her own pretty person. So busy watching the eye the fair could perceive little else, and I knew they despised nothing so much as the beau lost in the fulness of himself. The well-dressed fellow also loved one nothing the worse for being modestly inferior to himself in the sleek of plumage. My poverty did not therefore perplex me much on this account, particularly as I really felt rather a disgust at nicety and finery, and saw no free use one could get of himself primped up in clothes he was ever in terror of staining. I then tried to give expression to my feelings on the subject in the following lines:—

> I cannot plume the wings of idle show
> To pride in what from senseless pride doth flow,
> To look on gaudry with admiring eyes,
> Nor once perceive in what true greatness lies;
> Enough to keep the person cloth'd and clean,
> Nor prink in frippery o'er the summer green.
>
> I'll leave such fool-vain baubles all behind,
> And try to dress the beauties of the mind;
> Learn to be wise, or nurse the gentle art,
> To pour in song the swellings of my heart—
> Song, likest heaven of all I see on earth,
> Save friendship's balm on wounds of suffering worth.
>
> Oh! had I power to regulate all below,
> No fruit from root of bitterness should grow,
> No tear but that of joy from living eye should flow.

This last wish, and the power to exercise it, do not very often unite in the same individual; therefore, although I have had little power of wiping tears since, I may yet stand very much on a level with the run of my neighbours in regard to this virtue. I have wiped all I could.

I was much in this spirit, however, when an occurrence took place which led me into another scene, and gave a somewhat new colour, if not a new direction, to my whole life's circumstances. My eldest sister, Agnes, the best woman, taken altogether, I have ever been acquainted with, was engaged servant to old David Kyle, then of Hiltonshill. He and his old lady were, in their way of life, people of the primitive Scotch school, had no family, and had grown into age together, still adhering to their ancient habits of life, which began to look a little odd to the more modern generation rising around them; in fact, he was a hale old man, walking steadily his way up to fourscore. This sagacious couple had kept an old woman as their servant for upwards of forty years, till they had grown all old together, so that when the big old mistress fell on the floor, the big, old, unwieldy maid fell also in her attempts to help her up; while the old man had to call in the aid of his farmer to get all again on end, and correctly reseated in the elbow chairs. It was of absolute necessity, therefore, that they had to resolve on hiring some able-bodied person to take charge of all parties, and for this purpose they had fixed on my sister as a steady, active woman, and in the prime of life. On her first entrance on this service, she found it to be a rather alarming undertaking. The old house was full of old dirt of half a century's accumulation, with myriads of live-stock of the most disgusting names and qualities. On this discovery she came down and consulted with my other sister what was to be done, since, as the old people were considered rather remarkable for their penurious dispositions, little hope could be entertained of their condescension on any plan of a general renovation, and nothing less could be effectual. They resolved, however, to go out together and make a fair trial, which, after a proper representation of the case, was happily acceded to. To work they both set, bought and sewed up new flannels for the old couple, boiled and scoured up all body and bed clothes worth preservation, kindled a good fire, and had all the old stuffs burnt, and had the house thoroughly cleaned and whitewashed from floor to roof-tree. This was a species of new comfort, which so decidedly pleased as to open the hearts of the old people, and excite a latent desire to increase their daily comforts in regard to their whole mode of life. And so they well might, as the skin had been actually eaten from their backs, and hence the sense of comfort. And now that they were once all cleared up, it was just a possible case for one active woman to keep them all right daily, and Agnes was just the woman who could actually do so; in truth, she had a natural taste and sympathy, as well as curiosity, for the eccentricities of old people and children, and at all times of her life would have foregone much personal ease or comfort for the accommodation or gratification of others. Her occasional severe headaches were, however, against her in this service, as the old lady was apt to sleep all day in her arm chair, and keep awake all night, and had no sense of sympathy or reluctance in calling Nanny up on the most frivolous supposition of some want, even to ask what was the clock. Half a year of this had so far exhausted her wonderful patience that she had determined to forego all the other advantages of this otherwise easy service, and rather again endure the severe daily labour of a farmer's kitchen. But on a hint of this the idea was not brookable to the old people. They consulted their *heir-apparent*, as well as some other friends, who proposed the settlement of some annuity in her favour if she would at once condescend on living with them for life. This at first sounded something like nonsense in her idea of the matter, more particularly as she was already convinced that this heir-apparent had a considerable spice of both knave and fool in his composition.* He was a cousin's son of the old gentleman's, and already proprietor of Fens, the Langlands, and other considerable village property, and was now likely to fall soon into the inheritance of this old Hilton's effects, then worth about ten thousand pounds. But having on his majority succeeded to his mother's estate, he had (his father being a silly man) already begun horse-racing and a number of other follies, which were likely soon to run his horse from under him, and leave him on his feet, as it eventually did. However, the idea once suggested, the old gentleman got upon the scent of following it out in verity, and for this purpose sent for David Ovens, who, he had heard, was willing to sell a house and fruit garden in the village. He proposed to purchase these, and infief her in them. David would have sold them and Kyle have bought them for three hundred and thirty pounds; but, on finding that David was not yet *major* for a year to come, Kyle declined the bargain as unsafe, and resolved at once to give Nanny the money named, that she might either buy the same thing afterwards, or lay the principal out at interest, which would be to her equivalent to a yearly wage for life, and this on her signing a deed of agreement to continue their servant for their life, which, as he described it, could not be for many years; and then, as she was thus perhaps missing

* See Note on page 250.

her market for a chance of marriage, this would either be a future dowry to her or a moderate source of livelihood. He sent her down to consult her friends in the case, and I fell to be the chief adviser. I at once agreed that if she was willing to undertake the trouble of the service—which, taken all in all, I could not see to be worse than the current run of service generally—it would be a godsend for her—quite a fortune, and I had no moral question as to its being very honestly come by. A deed to the effect was then ordered, and written out by a Jedburgh lawyer, and three hundred and thirty pounds of the money paid over to her on the legal signing of it.

But here the old hag, *Envy*, who had hitherto been slumbering in regard to our poor family, opened her ferret eyes on the matter, and assuming the ghostly appearance of a certain wealthy villager, so plied and pestered "the heir-apparent" that the blockhead, and worse, as he certainly was, and still is, was advised to raise a prosecution against her on the plea that she had cozened the old laird out of the money. A charge to this effect was then served on her, which was answered before the Sheriff with a presentation of the deed and a statement from the old gentleman himself, besides a private intimation to Tom Kyle that he (old Hilton) had some other friends nearly as closely related to himself as a cousin's son, and could at any time, by a deed of settlement, leave his property to whoever he pleased. Thus was his insolence checked for the time, and the matter silenced, till after old Hilton's death, which occurred within the year afterwards, and about a year prior to the demise of his old lady. This inconsistent young laird would confess to some of his more rational friends that he considered the transaction fair and just, and in accordance with his own original proposition; but immediately again, when the envious party got him lectured on the folly of *missing* that money, while he was wealthy enough to law us all to the door, "bring down our pride," as they termed it, and make us succumb to his will, he would bluster about the village, and his lawyers needed but a hint to proceed with any plea by which they could strip him of money. Hence, the prosecution was again begun by an application to the Sheriff, of which my sister was never informed until an interlocutor was passed ordering her to consign (or lodge) the money in the Sheriff-Clerk's office, Jedburgh, until the prosecutor should raise a process of reduction of the deed, and see the issue. I advised her that lodging the money on this order was just "putting butter in the black dog's hause"—she would never see it again; and conceived that they might as well have given an order for me to lodge the coat from my back, or the hammer and awls by which I earned my daily bread. Her non-compliance was, of course, considered a resistance of legal authority; and hence a "charge," and "hornings," and at last a "caption," with a postchaise, a messenger, with Tom Kyle, the goose himself, arrived at Hiltonshill, where she was still in the old lady's service, to carry her off to jail. A lad in the village gave me the hint of what was going on; but just barely in time, as before I got out to the top of St. Boswells Green the carriage was coming down from Hiltonshill, about half a mile in advance of me. I took to my heels, and running on overtook them on the steep ascent of Lilliard's Edge, when, very unexpectedly to them (who were purposely stealing a march on me), I looked into the carriage and bid her take care of herself amongst such company, make no concession to them, even in word, nor touch a pen to sign any paper, however they might threaten or entreat, but trust to me, telling her I should be in Jedburgh as soon as they. She brightened up at this, and assured me that I might have confidence in her observing my instructions. So off they set at the top of the hill, whip and spur, down to Teviot Bridge; while, loosely clad, I ran on foot, never losing twenty yards of them. On the next long rise of the old hill-road I pushed past, and went over the hill, leaving them quite behind, and waited in Jedburgh some twenty minutes before they arrived. Though carriages did not run on those rough steep roads as they run now, yet I had run eight miles in little more than an hour. What will youth and vigour, under a certain degree of agitation, not effect? On landing at the inn-yard, the big fellow of a messenger attacked me on the wisdom of my sister signing a paper, advising us to just submit the matter to Mr. Kyle, who would certainly "as a gentleman return her most part or all of the money, only he was not to be beat at the law with such as us, for the very name of the thing; and certainly a man of his means had it in his power to ruin us at law whether we had a right plea or a wrong." I observed that it certainly was a very genteel sort of legal threat, but that I was so far from possessing any such gentlemanly feelings that I must in all civility despise the proposition, as well as the projectors of it. I observed, also, that the money was more a secondary consideration with my sister and me than with Kyle: he had wealth and property, and could dispense with character; but my sister's character and mine was the only piece of possession that we could not possibly afford to lose, and this not so much as it might be seen in the eye of the world, as it was perceived by the eye of our own mind. She could part with the money perfectly well, to be sure, and be as rich as she was when she entered on that service; but the giving it away upon these terms would be equal to a concession that she had not come by it honestly; and this would be throwing away a character along with it, of as much value to her as Tom Kyle's was to him, with all his wealth and possessions to boot. I observed further, that as things then stood she could not part with the one without losing also the other; therefore, if they meant to incarcerate her upon that "caption," following upon her disobedience to the Sheriff's interlocutor (whether that interlocutor was given legally or not—which was, and still is, a question with me), why, we must just submit in the meantime, and I must try to get some information on the next legal mode of proceeding.

Kyle and the messenger looked at each other in such a way as to convince me that Kyle at least did not somehow or other comprehend his own position. He looked for the law from the messenger, while the messenger looked to him for direction in a matter of which he was not very certain whether he was acting in warrant of a full and proper authority. Though there certainly was a "caption" in hand, yet I had suspicion that there was a shuffling in the matter. Indeed, I really then conceived that the warrant was given more out of courtesy to him as a rising young gentleman, than anything else, with some sort of understanding that he would not verily execute it, but only use it as a means to frighten my sister into submission to his will in the matter. If this was the case they had mistaken their man, for he could not comprehend a position so delicate, nor understand to act his part in it; therefore, the messenger took the nearest alternative, and ordered her incarceration, perceiving that the young laird wanted decision, and knowing that he was able enough to stand the consequences, be what they might. So in effect my sister was given in charge to Baubie, the jailor's wife, and a fine hospitable woman Baubie was, as I discovered in the first hour of my sister's imprisonment, while I stopped to arrange her jail terms, and also to transcribe a copy of the "caption," that I might have all the papers down to the moment to submit to some person from whom I must seek advice. I left my sister to sleep in the same room with her mistress, the jailor, in whose eyes she had at once found favour, and returned home late and at leisure. How I slept I cannot now recollect; but, at any rate, I rose early on the morning, and set out on a new path, down the Merse to Antonshill, where I had heard of a gentleman lawyer, Mr. Dickson, who was noted for giving good legal advice to the poor and oppressed. I found Mr. Dickson at home, and soon told him my errand, while he began making a couple of strong large new quill pens. I eyed them as a pair of good legal cannons, with which perhaps to level the jail and free my sister. Mr. Dickson was a good man; he heard me to an end of my story, then glanced over all the papers, then observed that this Tom Kyle must be a goat of a fellow, but I had got him in a net at last, and hoped I would manage him. I asked him if the Sheriff was correct in having given an interlocutor on Kyle's application without informing us, so that he might have had an opportunity of considering the statements on both sides of the matter. He observed—"You are too poor people, my lad, to contend with the powers that be. It is not a simple matter for shoemakers to meddle with Sheriffs, do what they like. Were you ever in Edinburgh?" "No, sir." "Then you likely have no acquaintance with any Edinburgh lawyer?" "No, sir." "You will be acquainted with some gentleman near your own place who could recommend you to a man of business in Edinburgh." "Yes, sir; I know one right gentleman's family in our parish, Mr. Tulloh of Eiliestoun, who is friendly to us; but I would prefer a letter from you to an honest lawyer of your acquaintance." "Well, then, you shall have it, and you must start to-morrow. People do their own business better themselves personally than by any writing. Deliver the letter I shall give you to John Orr, Shakspeare's Square, with your own hand, and all these papers; and be sure to tell him the tale over in the same way you have told it to me, and he will get a suspension, and have your sister liberated in a few days hence." So, thanking him heartily, home I returned "like five ell of wind," got a sleep, and took the road early on the morning. To Edinburgh was a pretty day's walk, thirty-six miles—no stage-coaching in those days. The poor Jedburgh fly or diligence (or "the roaring Dilly," as they called her in a song of those days), to hold a pair of passengers, had the old road by Lauder to herself. I was not fly furniture; so I trudged it before nightfall; took a spare room from widow Mac-something in some street at seven shillings for the week; called on John Orr next morning, who gave me all possible encouragement; and then set out to see the town, devoting a day or two to stroll about and see it all. I took a pleasure in losing myself, and again getting out to main streets without asking my whereabouts. I felt quite amused with this new theatre of life, and the gallery of the theatre, which I twice attended at nights. However, as the impatience of my friends at home ran in my mind, I could not stop to make remarks on Edinburgh at this turn, and having then hardly a town's acquaintance I had the less enticement; so home again I trudged, and visited my sister next day, giving her all the encouragement I could afford her. I never in my life observed her express impatience but that day, not that she felt uncomfortable, but from the idea of a jail. She was, however, liberated on a writ of suspension a few days afterwards, and the plea proceeded till she had gained the bill of suspension, with costs. She was then understood to have a right to damages, which plea I would have foregone to have let the matter now rest; but our lawyer had raised the action before we could say Jack Robinson, and laid the damages at £70, to which Kyle might have even then submitted, had not his evil angel, or rather his lawyer, insisted on raising his formerly threatened action of reduction of the deed. And this was done on the plea that the late old Hilton was from age and natural infirmity of mind unqualified to enter into any such dispositional transaction. Our plea for these damages was sustained by the Lord Ordinary, but was left to lie over till the issue of this process of reduction, which would determine the case fully. In the following winter, a Mr. Leslie, a friend to the late Mrs. Tulloh of Eiliestoun (an excellent lady), had come from Aberdeenshire to Edinburgh to direct a serious lawsuit of his own. On his visit to Eiliestoun, Mrs. Tulloh sent for my sister and me to come up together and give him a history of our case, so that we might get his advice, and interest him in our behalf. I told him all the story over, down to its state at the moment, when he broke out in a rhapsody against our agent:—" John Orr is the greatest rascal in Edinburgh or in Europe, and will, of course, rob and ruin you, as he has very nearly done myself. It was on account of his mismanagement of my plea that I had to come to Edinburgh and employ another agent, and I mean now to trust none of them entirely, but await the issue of my plea in Edinburgh for the session, and direct it personally. Therefore I can attend to yours at the same time, so you must come immediately in to Edinburgh. Let me see you in by Monday evening, or Tuesday at farthest, and I will introduce you to my new agent, who is not only an honour to his profession, but an honour to human nature." I ventured to remonstrate just a little by observing that John Orr, Esq., had appeared to me a very respectable-looking man, as so certainly was

Mr. Dickson of Antonshill, by whom I had been recommended to him. "He, be d——d, looks well enough, but there is not a greater bleck under the sun! You must not bring favourable impressions against certain proofs. The short and the long is, I shall expect to see you at my lodgings on Tuesday first at farthest, and have you set all right for certain victory over that idiot laird, your bad neighbour. I see through the fellow; his pleas are beginning to multiply in the Court already; no good sign of him."

Here, amongst good friends, so much more powerful and influential than myself, and pressing me to my good out of the most disinterested kindness, I felt I could not advance anything further in defence of my deep impressions of John Orr's integrity as an agent, and I was too poor and dependent to start out from the trammels of such kindness and set up as my own master. I therefore agreed that I should endeavour to see him in Edinburgh by the time appointed, whatever weather might blow. So in pursuance of this I set out on a winter Sabbath night about six o'clock, under the sparkling star-light, hard frost, with a crisping snow-storm lying on the ground, and walked to Lauder (twelve miles) to my supper; there waited till the farmers' carts began to pass after midnight on their way to Dalkeith meal market, and joined one of them, which was a lucky circumstance, as otherwise I should have been beaten by a raging snowdrift on Soutra Hill. I reached Edinburgh, however, early in the day, secured lodging, then called on my good friend, Squire Leslie, who presented me to his agent, John Craw, in the evening. We found John a *gaucy* fellow, of the middle age, up eight stairs in the Parliament Square, and I gave him the history of my affair, as directed to do by my friend, who vented another full volley of his rage against my old agent, John Orr, as the most consummate rascal in Britain's isle. "You must go to him to-morrow morning," says he, "and bring all your papers from him, with a copy of his charge for odds and ends against your sister, but which you must not pay him until we submit his bill to Mr. Craw here, to see that he do not be over-reaching you, which he shall not be allowed to do." How or where I slept I recollect not; but I would rather have chosen to have met the French at Dunbar next morning, on another "false alarm," than to have gone to John Orr on such an errand, and under these particular restrictions. Still, I found I must go, and so I went. I found him the same plain, civil man I had formerly considered him. "Strange," thinks I, "that this man must be such a rogue; for I still like his face very well. However, tell my errand I must." Mr Orr looked a little astonished, though no ways confused; only requested to know the real meaning of the matter. I gave him a slight sketch of my situation, and general obligations to my gentle friends of Eiliestoun, whose opinions in this matter I found I could not thwart with propriety, and that the gentleman, their friend, who had interested himself so in this matter, was going to do some great kindness in attending to the direction of this affair himself, being stationed in Edinburgh for the session at least, and wished to have the full direction of the agency in the matter; in short, that though I had no reason to be ill pleased with him, Mr. Orr—quite the contrary—

and at the same time under due obligation to his friend of Antonshill, yet I felt myself impelled to please these other friends in this alteration. He replied that he wished us success in it, and hoped I might be correct in the confidence I was placing in this new friend and his agent. I got his bill of charge against my sister, of I think some seven guineas (he had been paid the awarded expenses by Kyle), showed it in the evening as desired to Mr. Leslie, who submitted it to Mr. Craw, who recommended me to pay it off-hand, which I went next day and did, parting with John Orr very reluctantly, and with a feeling nearly allied to shame. However, I daresay he saw my confusion, and understood and excused it. When I called next evening on Mr. Craw to arrange matters for the time to come, Mr. Leslie and he were at cards and negus. I was half distracted with toothache, so they recommended me some cold glasses, as I had to go some distance to my lodging; and while this was in discussion, Mr. Leslie asked me at what number John Orr lived. "At so and so," says I, "in Shakespeare's Square." "O lord! that's not my John Orr at all," says he. "That may be a decent man, for anything I know." "And I believe he is," says I, "as firmly as I believe that I myself am a born idiot. He was recommended to me by the very best man in our south country, or in all broad Scotland besides, and I have every reason to believe is likely the most able and honest lawyer in Edinburgh. But since it is now done, let me not think of it again. I would soon grow down to skin and bone on the thought, or maybe go mad. The thought is to my soul like this toothache to my head." So to lodging and bed I went, reflecting sufficiently on the folly as well as the providences of the past, and deeply harassed in thought by straining my mind's eye to see into the thickening mists of the future.

I may here observe, passingly, that when I first walked through the streets of Edinburgh the town did not startle me with the wonder that even might have been supposed, or with any such new great ideas as I myself might have suspected. The only things that confused me were seeing every door a shop—where do they all get customers? But then I soon concluded that so much went out to the country far and near, besides what was required by the down-close congregated masses, which reflections settled that point. But as I had come in on a law errand, I was led to observe what appeared the most astonishing phenomenon ever I could have conceived—the W.S.'s on the brass door-plates, of which I had seen scores before I understood their meaning. If there are, I thought, so many of one class of lawyers, what must be the mass of the whole body, and how supported at the rate such lodgings would bespeak? And then, on my necessary calls, to find them sitting with bands of clerks dressed like gentlemen, and old John Craw, up eight stairs in the Parliament Square, drinking his wine with his clients, and then supposing the quantity of "old red" it would require, along with all other *et-ceteras* of house-keeping, to have brought John to the pitch of Shakespeare's fat knight, and to keep him at it, and the immense numbers in town who uphold at the same rate. I became confounded to think how that even turning and factoring over the whole capital of Scotland annually, and picking all the per centages, with even the loose shiverings of capital, that could possibly be got detached from the general mass for their share— these would still in my computation do nothing to support the whole tribe. "Now," thinks I (for what will untutored lads not think?) "I have read of terrible banditti-nests of robbers, inhabiting caves here and there; how they would harass and spoil a district before they were ferreted out, broken up, and got all hanged. But what were all the bands of robbers taken collectively over Europe, even as far back as the history-books go—all the plunder they could ravage and collect—compared to this? The whole," thinks I, "taken together, since Noah's flood, would not support the law in Edinburgh for one winter! And what is the actual value they are giving, or pretending to give, for this spoil? *Justice*, of course; yet that is a question which it might puzzle the wisdom of the General Assembly to answer. I wish that the great blessed spirit of justice may have any acknowledged acquaintance with the matter." Another question arose out of this, "Is such a law establishment any sure sign of our national love of justice?" But I now recollect I got drowsy to bed before I had solved this point, and when half asleep I was trying it on comparison with other things—as, for instance, was our great Church Establishment also any sure sign of our great national religion? But here I found myself "the further in the deeper," and, while in a state of uncertainty whether thinking or dreaming, I ended the matter thus—that with all our great establishments of law and gospel, our parish schools, *et-cetera*, we must surely be the best-informed and wisest nation on the face of the earth; and when even I, simple and unlettered as I must consider myself, saw so much cheatery, deceit, selfishness, duplicity, and barefaced roguery on the one hand, and so much general ignorance of very common things on the other, what a batch must mankind be upon the whole? I carried this idea so far, that if it had not been from the force of habit and mere fatigue I durst not that night have fallen asleep in such a world. I thought if the thing were possible that if I might be transplanted out into some other respectably inhabited planet, I would be black ashamed to acknowledge where I had come from.

On late inquiry, I have learned that the flood of law which then threatened to overwhelm and ruin the island is now greatly subsided. My law informant gives me to understand that the highest judicial court in the country (the Court of Session) is now little more to appearance than an old-fashioned District Justice Court; and the reason he assigns is this—that the public have got up to them, that poor men cannot enter a plea there, the expense being so enormous, and the wealthy having been once in, and milled through, retire with empty pockets, and, like a man escaping drowning, will never again trust the current; or, to change the simile, those who will at all dance there must pay the piper—the one having money must do it whether loser or winner; or, in short, the two cats in the fable will not now employ Mr. Justice Monkey to divide their second cargo of stolen cheese.

CHAPTER XXIII.

ABOUT the commencement of this law-plea some silly occurrences took place which gave me sufficient uneasiness; one of these may be worth mention. Prior to this time David Ovens and I had a roving commission with the licensed Tom Kyle, Esq., in regard to the gun. In fact, we often went out all three together under this unmentioned understanding, that when bird or hare dropt from his own shot they were his, of course; when from mine they were his of courtesy—so much has a sutor to concede to a squire for a liberty to live. I have been occasionally hurried out for him with his own dog and gun, especially when Miss Birkwhistle or so-so were to come and dine, on which occasions I seldom failed to furnish largely. I believe the lady used to jilt him in regard to promised visits; no matter, he could always dine himself with an appetite: he was especially good at a goose eating, carrying more off than he could bear home. The hooded crow could have traced him on a winter morning from the inn to Fens. But his goose anecdotes are far below par, except when Mr. Kinghorne* has the relating of them. Well, so soon as this law-

---

* Mr. Alexander Kinghorne, parish schoolmaster of Bowden, afterwards tenant of Crossflat, near St. Boswell's, and latterly Colonial Surveyor in New South Wales, where his only surviving son now resides, a territorial magnate.

suit commenced I was done up as a poacher, as he would have felt gratified in getting me into a scrape.

One winter day, while David Ovens was sitting beside me at my work, in dropped James Thomson, the joiner, with a gun in his hand, requesting me to come out and shoot a hare for him which was seated on the fallow in Kyle's little croft-park below our gardens. "I dare not shoot now, James; I'm afraid of Kyle." "She is sitting so low," says James, "I am sure to miss her, which would be a pity. You could do it easily; just slip on my coat and hat, and if Kyle's uncles see you from Weirgate House they will suppose it to be me, and say nothing about it." I could not then resist him; for though he was fond of a dyke-side shot, I knew him to want confidence in himself; so without more ceremony I exchanged coats, took his gun, and round to the under hedge, over which I picked up a view of my Lady Mawkin sitting musing in her form, and very uncourteously, to be sure, fired in her looking face, when up she buffed, and began forming circles in the field. I perceived she was blinded, and motioned James and David to come down upon her. When they did so she found her way through to my side of the hedge. While cowering down I gave her another shot, and in seizing her she screamed fit to raise the whole village. Our motions, however, had alarmed the Kyles in Weirgate—old Mungo, and Johnnie, and Tom Brown together—and they were out to see the last act of the performance. Seeing my predicament, I signalled James and David to come down to me, when, to mystify the matter, I led them out over the fields away from the village, then we parted and came home separate ways. I soon learned that all was up with me—that I should be prosecuted, as sure as a gun. The fine would be heavy, as the Justices were then just voracious. What was to be done? The change of coat was no blind to people who were half blind already, both bodily and mentally. All three would swear to me, and all were too much of an animal nature to be by any means bamboozled or decoyed from the right scent. Sir John Buchanan Riddell was the chief of the Justice Court for the district, and very imperious. He knew me well as a volunteer, and, besides, I had been then lately asking his advice about some point in my lawsuit, in which, though I had found him more ignorant than myself, I felt aware that I could little afford to lose a particle of character, or favour, if such a thing as favour was ever to be found amongst the surrounding squires, whose word might weigh against a character; since our main plea was making a noise in the neighbourhood, and every one was taking a side just as people stood affected to the parties, or were otherwise influenced or interested. I never, in fact, had found myself in such an awkward predicament. What was to be done? was the grand question. I rummaged every corner and cranny of my own mind, and set my invention on the stretch without the effect of devising any plan of extrication. Next day I became quite fidgety—could not sit to work, and had been out vexing and consulting with David Ovens to no purpose. Kyle had been up in the village, quite elated with having me hooked, and certain of victory; in fact, as elated as an Indian who has got the enemy of his tribe under the torture.

When I came in, my sister Ann, then at home, was sitting spinning. "What are you going to do," asked she, "about that business?" "Oh! go and be fined, Ann, of ten pounds, at least, much against my will, to be sure; it's a bad business." "Could James Thomson not take the blame?" said she; "maybe they would not prosecute him." Here was a woman's wit at her hand, without an effort to fetch it. So, glad of the hint, I took not time to stay and tell her how much I despised my own insignificance, but bolted out again to Ovens, got him up with me to James Thomson, and proposed the matter. "Oh!" says James, "I don't think Kyle would prosecute me; but yet there is no saying." "Oh! James, my good chap, the thing must be done in a far grander style than you are yet supposing. You will go down to Fens just instantly, and tell Kyle that you have heard they are going to prosecute Younger, and that all his three uncles are clear on witnessing against him; but that you have heard that Younger is quite tickled about the business, going to let his uncles all swear as witnesses against him, and then bring in Ovens and others for clear proof that you shot that hare, of whose murder you will say that you cannot in conscience clear yourself; and then hang upon this point, that Younger is quite full in thinking how he shall have you all disgraced and laughed at. Now, James, mind your cue in this, and if any trouble or expense should occur to your account on the matter I will take it in hand before David Ovens here, who will be my cautioner, to pay it all." James set out immediately, caught the old laird, as Tom was not at home, stuffed him with this story, which was poured into Tom's ear so soon as he arrived, when up he came, post-haste, to the village, and questioned James all about the matter. "And was it you, James, that shot that hare?" "Oh!" says James, "the hare, sir, was really shot by my own gun from this shoulder of my own coat here, and Younger, I understand, is quite bright about getting us all befooled together." "Oh, d—— him!" says Tom Kyle; "we shall disappoint him; I wish Paton be not gone; he was to be informer; but I shall see." He soon returned and told James that all was snug yet, that Paton was just putting on his Sunday's coat to go to Melrose, but he had stopped him; "so for your life, James, say not another word about the matter in case Younger should take it in his head to inform on you, and play the very devil after all." So all was hushed as cosh as midnight, and the real trick was never divulged so long as Kyle had it in his power to hurt honest James Thomson. My poaching was, of course, stopped for the time, and in a great measure for ever after, as I have always found plenty of employment, and more sources of amusement otherwise, than I could find opportunity to follow, down to the present hour.

The necessary attention to my sister's lawsuit through the tedium of all its windings gave, upon the whole, a new turn to my life's general interests, whether a favourable direction or not can hardly now be properly estimated. Though it gave me an opportunity of seeing a little deeper into life than I might otherwise have done, yet it occupied the particular attention of the very five years of my life which of all other years were the most likely for me to have made some small shift on my seat, and it ended at last in leaving me still glued down to the cobbler stool for life. To be sure, there was a great deal of fresh air inhaled on the foot journeys necessary in running after it. I once added the miles of journeys together, till I made upwards of seven hundred which I had walked on one pair of shoe soles after it. It wore off more pairs after that, as it lasted five years, just the time that Tom Kyle's fortune lasted him; for I believe that his lawyers might have had it called, re-called, and hammered at until this blessed hour had his means lasted; but so soon as they had got the goose plucked bare they must look out for quill feathers elsewhere. In the days of his glory he had some fifteen pleas all in the Court of Session at once, or at least in one court and other. That with my sister was, I believe, the oldest of the number, and cost him of itself some five hundred pounds of expenses, over and above ultimate defeat. But about the time of its commencement the interest in it ran high in the neighbourhood, the more so on account of the influence he possessed from his wealth. Many took his part publicly who would privately acknowledge him to be little else than a born idiot, and indeed a fellow who has got some thirty thousand pounds which his good neighbours think he has every chance to throw away around him has a great claim on their sincere friendship for the time being; and here Kyle's interest in the public ran five hundred and fifty per cent. a-head of my sister's and mine.

That plea was scarcely well started until very few of my neighbour villagers durst enter my door till after nightfall, in case that, being seen, they should lose favour for such employment as Kyle might occasionally have to give in their particular lines of occupation. Hence, from being previously nobody, I became, through my daring obstinacy in this plea, notorious as being verily somebody; and hence, also, I got a special lesson of how little friendship is proof against even the distant idea of the most paltry self-interest. Ovens and Adam Inglis were still, however, my daily associates, standing out in relief beyond the pale of Kyle's feud or favour, both in mind and circumstances, until Ovens and I, unfortunately for him at least, had a separating difference, arising out of a piece of the most childish trifling imaginable. Dr. "Zea Bermudez," an older schoolfellow of his, who had been born and bred the son of a surgeon, and a portioner in the village, just then arrived home from where he had been out in some sort of service as a surgeon in the navy, and cut an excessively grand figure, quite alarming to David's taste for the sublime; and here to come home on half-pay, and find his old neighbour, David, the smart college youth, daily associating with such *low-bred*, vulgar people as John Younger and John Inglis, mere mechanics, was a most disgusting affair—indeed, a most unpardonable breach of the propriety of true college breeding. David, who might feel duly ashamed of this, could yet not break off all at once, and perhaps did not wish it; but a circumstance soon occurred which made the reasons for so doing perfectly conclusive. Our hero had brought home with him some manuscript songs of the love cast, the composition of a fine young sea poet, some midshipman of the name of Tyrrel. These David showed me as a great treasure, and as they were much of the olden style, such as were fashionable in days when fair maidens were much shyer than they have been of late years, the writer complaining of the cold indifference of his water nymph, I was daring enough to write pretty soft, yielding answers to them in the character of the adorable fair one, and submitted these to David for his criticism, which came in a folio sheet, rather terse, tart, and severe, and altogether too brackish for the sweetness of the subject. Taking all in good part, however, I went into the humour of reviewing the reviewer with interest, taking a full-sweep latitude of freedom, without reserve or submission, which had the effect of rather irritating, partly from my unsubmissive freedom of opinion, and particularly from his felt pressure of defeat on the subject. It was audacious in me, to be sure, who had never been at college, nor read Anacreon in the original, to set up for myself to judge on the nature or propriety of the expressions of love or song; but so was the state of the matter. While he (or I should say *they*) praised up Horace as "the master of melody and prince of poets," I advanced Burns as the standard of song, sentiment, and measure, and also assumed that I had as good a right to write songs as either, when David at last became aristocratic, and assumed the supremacy of dictator in the matter—being, indeed, rather imperatively abusive. I then took the liberty of throwing in my gage of defiance, telling him that I might have had some respect for his own judgment or feelings on such subject, however lame they might have been, while I felt none for the assumption of that dictation to which I was convinced he had submitted, the more particularly from being aware that neither he nor his prompter had as much natural taste or acquired knowledge on that subject as to enable them to distinguish one musical sentiment or sound from another, while I was independently sensible that I had a natural ear, at least, and some power of expressing myself, besides the idea that a tom cat and a nightingale have both alike a liberty to make love in their own language. All the while I felt no personal irritation, considering the whole thing like child's play, or like two advocates pleading the different sides of a case, and yet good friends over their bottle. But so felt not David, for he gave me up in a sort of gentlemanly pet, apparently consigning himself to the guidance of his great, grand literary friend, who then led him out as a visitor to his mightiness, the redoubtable Tom Kyle, Esq. of Fens, Hiltonshill, Langlands, and other village property.

> The rich goes to dine in the lighted hall,
> While the poor stays without and starves;
> It would puzzle the wisest heads to tell
> What both of the two deserves.
> Shakespeare says whipping, the priest says hell,
> While there's nought left for me to propose,
> But accept what is given us by Wellington and Peel,
> Cat-o'-nine-tails, and corn-bill'd brose.

"Save us from our friends!" is sometimes a necessary petition in a poor man's prayer; and that "persecution drives a wise man mad" holds good in more senses than one, for my sister had no sooner got this money, and we had got enemies on account of it, than those who openly took our part became to us doubly dear, and thus the more easily succeeded in borrowing a greater part of the cash. The three farmers, brothers (the Knoxes), who held excellent leases of the then Eiliestoun farms of Mainhill, Charlesfield, and Thornilaw, and were at that time accounted amongst the most sagacious and able men around us, and who, except for the disagreeable affair relative to my other sister with one of them, some seven or eight years previously, had, in all other respects, been all good friends with my father and all of us, and were now seemingly sincere well-wishers, taking our part firmly in this matter; and besides that my father had been accustomed to respect them from their father's days, and not wishing to deposit the money in the bank for fear of some arrestments which had been hinted at, we all agreed in feeling rather gratified in being enabled to return favour for friendship, and oblige these three brothers by lending them fifty pounds a-piece on their mutual bill. My suspicions in this case were only like a kind of instinct, and hardly strong enough to prevent myself from acceding to their wishes, far less to convince my father or my sister, who was the real proprietor. Had any of us happened to have mooted objections firmly we might have kept safe; but, in fact, we acted in this as in most family matters from sympathy rather than from worldly prudence. Whether one or other, or all, of these men had afterwards deceived us by letting the transaction be known for a cunning purpose, I could never make out; but not very long after, in the course of Kyle's prosecution, the money was arrested in their hands, which disenabled my sister to lift it from them until the lawsuit should be finished, which was some five years afterwards, in which time they became gradually poor, and their credit justly doubted. They were, to say the least, now a down-coming family, such as wise people generally escape from as fast as they can. But this was a point of wisdom which had never found its way as a maxim into our poor family; indeed, none of us seemed capable of ever learning it, even with a life's experience. There is such a thing as family weaknesses even on points of the most common prudence. These people were, however, *friends* to us at the time; and having got into intimacy with Kyle, from his driving bargains to purchase up the leases of their farms, as he was beginning to get something like stark mad on a foolish notion of farming to a boundless extent, I had hopes of their being thus influential in advising him to drop his lawsuit with us; for, though I had seen no cause to doubt its final issue in our favour, yet I was convinced that under his sanction the lawyers could branch it out like a growing tree till the groaning of its extended limbs might keep us awake throughout the storms of as many winters as Kyle might live on, and his means last. I therefore secretly wished that he might have been persuaded to give it up, either through wisdom or lenity, or from any principle or cause whatever. I then was in love with peace, as much for the sake of peace as for the purpose of escaping the trouble and inevitable expense of a prolonged litigatory warfare; and could peace have been purchased with all we possessed, without the loss of character, I would willingly then have bought it at the price, really regarding money in an inferior degree to what I conceived to be the true integrity of life, the principle of which I felt then becoming so strong in me that all else seemed merely adventitious. In fact, this principle was something like a growing oak, rooting the firmer in proportion to the force of the storms that pressed it from above; and every discovery of the deceit and duplicity of others made me, first a little heart-sick, and then the more resolute in mind to bear up against the hateful declensions, as if, in the eye of Heaven, the general character of our whole species had depended on myself individually. This may perhaps be considered a too indelicate declaration of feeling, and yet I do not see why in truth it should not be made. As one cannot urge one's pacific plans on an enemy without giving him advantages which one cannot consistently concede, the prosecution proceeded, and some other petty persecutions, suffered for conscience' sake, were then also set afoot on the part of my *great* opponent. Your good old father was then turned from that house of Kyle's, in which you were all born, and which he had rented for forty years previously, for honestly stating his opinion to him when asked, and that as a well-wisher, saying that he considered he was wrong in his prosecution, or rather persecution, of the Youngers. He got another house for an equal rent, however; but our vexation proceeded from Kyle and his friends showing their teeth in such an insolent, ignorant, and disgusting manner, such as his often riding along the village with a servant behind him, calling aloud to his favourites that the shoemaker's awls should be all sold by auction next week.

However much I despised this treatment I yet felt the matter upon the whole disagreeable, and at last got tired for the time of the locality. One evening, at a social party meeting of about a score of the volunteers of the neighbouring parish of Bowden, with most of whom I had now got intimately acquainted, I was pressed to go to their village and set up shoemaking. One of their number, then present, offering to let me a house, and all the rest volunteering to patronise and support me, I consented, and took the Campknow Cottage, and so removed thither at the next Whitsunday of 1809, taking along with me my home sister, and my young nephew, George Knox, then a most engaging boy, beloved by ourselves and everybody. One extra motive in removing there was that, as they had an excellent teacher in Bowden, I had a wish to have that boy some decent education, feeling so vexed at having missed it myself. In this new situation I felt considerable relief; for, though our lawsuit was proceeding, it was now fallen into the settled state of other lasting lawsuits, and my new neighbours were entirely passive, being quite unconcerned in that matter.

I soon found plenty of employment in my shoe line, although no way particularly from those of the party who had given me the greatest encouragement, some of whom got shoes from me, which are not paid to this day. I began, however, on the determination to recommend myself by the superior substantiality of my work, as laying a good foundation of character for business in the time then to come, and being unable to keep up to my employers with my own hands I engaged a stout country-bred lad, who, I found, could work substantially, for a journeyman; and, as I thus required the very best materials of leather, &c., which was then, in the time of that devastating French war, a most expensive article, and comparatively ill-tanned generally, I found it impossible, with the credit necessary to be given in the business, to make a day and way living. I had but little credit with the curriers, of whom there were then scarcely any choice, being but few in our neighbourhood. I had, besides, resolved not, even with my sister's consent, to take of her money for any purpose but the necessary expenses incurred in attention to the plea itself. So expensive were the materials that in working out orders I was often glad, with not a halfpenny of profit to myself, if there was only no positive loss incurred on the most valuable of those shoes then wrought by my journeyman; in fact, I had the journeyman solely for the purpose of keeping forward with my general customer orders, depending for wages on those only wrought by my own hands. Added to this, I caught a most severe cold in the month of July, from a combination of circumstances—hard over-work and want of due rest before the St. Boswell's Fair, and on the fair evening, being kept up all night by a neighbour happening to fall from a cart of hay, which caused his death, starting out on the morning on foot to Edinburgh on some law-plea necessity, and being so unavoidably trashed late and soon before I got home again on foot. So hoarse was I on arriving home that I could not speak above breath high, and no wonder, as with all this fatigue I had only slept as many hours as amounted to one ordinary night's rest throughout the whole week. I had an intimate acquaintance along with me out through this journey, who had business in Edinburgh, and took the opportunity of accompanying me. On our walk home I stood him out in the feet, for roads were then comparatively bad for long journeys compared to what they are now, but he over-matched me for bodily constitution. I thought to work and sweat out the cold by degrees; but it beat me up, till at last I was laid bedfast. I became very ill indeed ere I thought of calling a doctor, which was done at last, when it might be said to be within a day of the nick of time. Pulmonary consumption was then the generally prevalent disease; so common that I could always have numbered some dozen laid down to die in my known circle of a few miles around, and these generally the finest-looking young people of both sexes. I was by all friends and acquaintances numbered in that list. The doctor was not at first very sure of me; however, to relieve the fever he took blood freely, when I sunk down strictly bedfast for some weeks, until by his good attention and my sister's particular nursing care, I came out of it, just like one awaking on a summer morning from the most restless and disturbed dreams. And, indeed, for the time that the fever lasted I had most perilous dreams. I was continually running with the boy, my nephew, over dangerous places, and amongst all the fields I knew, hiding him and myself from a bull that presented himself, watching me at every turn or hedge corner. I could always have escaped from him for my own part, as I thought, but the boy was the concern. I have sat behind a low hedge for an imagined long space of time, something like a summer afternoon, keeping little George down and quiet, watching that bull grazing a ridge-breadth or two in the field on the opposite side, while the brute was continually keeping an upturned eye to my point of observation, as if cunningly sensible that we were there, and on my least stir in attempt to creep away he would gove up his head and prick his ears in the startling act to pursue me, when down I would again cower, squat in the ditch, and press the boy in to me to hide the closer. I can at will conjure up the particular eye and horns of that fever-bull to this hour; he was of the Highland breed, of a reddish-black colour.

On coming out of this fever entirely free of cold or uneasiness, for the first few days I felt the most pleasant sensations over my whole body that I have ever experienced in life, and a soft kind of holy calm of soul was produced, filling me with love, and hope, and happiness, approaching to bliss itself. I would give all the kingdoms of a thousand planets to inherit such bodily and mental feelings for ever; yet I was then, and hitherto had been from earliest youth, rather religiously disposed upon the whole, could have grasped all animated nature in the arms of benevolence, had love even to a toad, because I saw it had a sense to fear and to feel, and to enjoy in quiet, and was the handiwork of God, the author of myself, and all of great or small, even the stars in space, which I had long apprehended and now clearly perceived to be worlds. In regard to this class of feelings I have stood much the same ever since, except that from the tug, tear, and wear-out amidst the selfishness of life, one is apt to lose much of respect and native veneration for man generally, and I feel that a part also of the enthusiasm which then gave a higher colour to life has evanished along with some of the keener sympathies of youthful existence. But what need I say, since upon closer examination I perceive that it is only the cunning selfishness of men that I hate, being in the main as socially disposed as ever, and now I love many new faces as well as the old ones, my grandchildren also as well as, or perhaps better than, I even loved my own, their fathers and mothers; and my poor, fading, half-blind Nan is as dear to me this day as when we first nestled in together. In proportion as we dislike the evil dispositions of men, do we venerate the good; and I hope that the love of God and His creatures will abide with me, as an influencing spiritual grace, to the end; it gives such comfortable feelings, and is nearly all that appears now left me amidst the approaching cold privations of advanced life and fading energies.

CHAPTER XXIV.

IN process of recovering from this illness, it was some months before I gathered strength sufficient for my usual employment; but, secured from actual present want, I took the matter as easy as possible, finding pleasure in conscious existence and the dream of future prospects. I had also some visiting companions, in whose company I delighted, with a true taste of the pleasure of their temperate sociality. Besides, the prospects of the past, the present, and the future were all seemingly on the dawn of opening up before me.

The past took the form of an ideal prospect as well as the rest, the pleasure of which seemed to lie in books, which I determined to get hold of by every means in my power. The present lay in the enjoyment of social intercourse with my favourite companions, amongst whom, from his poetical tastes, I very naturally preferred old Andrew Scott, and also James M'Donald as much from his partiality for me as for his very amusing powers of perception and description of living character. James was very little older than myself. We enjoyed each other's most perfect confidence; and he could note and relate with the most graphic minuteness what came under his observation. Hence, we regarded each other with more than common friendship. My future prospects were made up of rainbow hopes of I knew not what, of which, however, a book I then got hold of seemed to give me an astonishing presentiment. This was Ferguson's "Young Ladies' and Gentlemen's Astronomy," on which I sported my mind, and in which in delighted imagination I flew through the heavens. I have since wondered that in then opening up these paths through the milky way I should have sailed in imagination out beyond the rules there laid down nearly as far as Mr. Nichol has since done by the combination of that faculty of the mind and the aid of the best telescopic observation.

I then supposed systems beyond systems in ever rising infinitude of variety, with new creations going on daily and progressively, and which I believed the human mind qualified to comprehend, in idea at least, from its felt wonderful powers of comprehension, expansion, and condensation; its elasticity, and faculty of combination; its individuality and divisability—in fact, a spark of divinity in some grand link of connection with the eternal mind. I supposed that if we were not bound down to grapple with each other about silly pride and interest, as well as the real or supposed means of obtaining life's comforts, daily bread, and so on (and this not so much from the circumstance of God's dispensations in universal providence, as from mismanagement amongst ourselves, in our wranglings about principles of civil government), we might severally find plenty of time and opportunity to inquire and expatiate freely throughout our generations. We might thus also arrive at much more useful and pleasant knowledge than is generally conceived to lie within the verge of our human speculation. Be this as it may, we had in the meantime, in that village, a medley variety of character, from the statedly cautious, church-plodding son of wisdom, to the "born idiot," as our then worthy priest (Mr. Balfour) emphatically designated one of our most *knowing*, money-scraping, bargain-making, corn and cattle-dealing farmers, who was at the same time generally regarded as more worldly-wise than the current run of his neighbours. That village was then reckoned rather remarkable for the number of deranged or silly characters—somewhat eccentric, from something that appeared like a general individuality in their manners and way of life; and the remark was current about St. Boswell's here that Bowden was a hundred years behind the other surrounding villages. I used to combat this foolish assertion as made in the vanity of ignorance, and could always name about a dozen of men in Bowden whom I would venture to match against any dozen from any neighbouring village in point of general knowledge or other ability, as well as respectability of general character. And, besides that, Bowden could produce a greater number of what might be accounted good scholars than perhaps any Border village of equal population. Indeed, Bowden was rather remarkable for this, having for some time previously, as well as then and since, enjoyed the very particular blessing of a succession of very successful teachers in the office of the parish schoolmaster, and this I have always considered as a far greater benefit bestowed on a parish, both in a moral and religious point of view, than even a great gun of a parish priest.

By the way, a parish priest who is very diligent and serious in his calling may be a very useful member of society, not alone for his public teaching, and his presiding over and dispensing the ordinances of religion, but also as a superior example in the eyes of his flock for direction and encouragement in the sphere of moral and religious duties, public and private. But the salaries of the clergy being comparatively liberal and fixed, and the duties left so much to their own discretion, we have had frequent and flagrant instances of woeful derelictions even in stipulated duty; and, besides, these salaries being paid in grain, or its annual value, these priests are generally influential, or desirous of being so, on the most illiberal side of State politics, as well as in all other matters by means of which the proprietors of the land are ever extending their encroachments on the commons of life—distressing, harassing, oppressing, and coercing the labouring and productive poor. Hence, the priest's influence on society is lost for good; he is either feared through mean selfishness, which shapes itself into hypocrisy, or adhered to through bigotry and superstition, and in stronger minds disrespected and disregarded, or privately hated and despised. Hence, also, many of our peasantry, whose minds are well enough able to entertain philosophical truths or ideas, but from want of the means and opportunity fall short of acquiring the power to reason, calculate, and elucidate with the necessary propriety, are left in a mist, or dilemma, in their ineffectual endeavours to reason between profession and conduct, till, aweary of the harassment of their own vague thoughts, they at last settle down into cold indifference and scepticism, and in many cases sink into openly confessed infidelity.

Much enthusiasm, having the appearance of warm religion, may be kept alive in a country or a district by clerical agitation and occasional dissents, where matters of faith and notions of Church government are made the subjects of bandied debate; but these are generally wild astray from the true knowledge of gospel truth, or the feelings of a heart actuated by the spirit of a true religious charity.

Be this as it may, the able, diligent, and conscientious teacher of youth may justly be considered as the most valuable public character in any community, under whose tuition and direction the yet flexible spirit of the young is to commence a course of mental and moral training for present life and immortality.

Impressed with some floating ideas like these at the time, as well as feeling what an inconvenience I laboured under, from inability to express myself to my taste either in conversation or in writing, and seeing the clever boy, George Knox, getting on so charmingly at school, it gave me a strong desire to have him made such a scholar as I conceived might give him a far higher relish of existence, as well as enable him to make his living by it in some much easier way than now plainly appeared to be my own fixed lot in life. Of course, it gave me great pleasure when Mr. Lowrie one evening requested my company for the purpose of proposing to begin the boy in Latin, as he was forming a small Latin class at the time, and wished to have him to commence as leader in it, which he averred his talent and temper exactly fitted him to become. I then freely told Mr. Lowrie what had been the cogitations of my own mind on that subject, as well as my circumstances in life, both present and probable; that though I despaired of being able to carry him through to be what might be termed a "scholar," even with the good-will of his aunt (my sister), should her law-plea result so favourably as to leave her a small reversion of money, yet, as it was only the extras of school fees that were required, with some Latin books, which in the meantime we would struggle to get up somehow, the thing might be proper enough; since by the age he should be stout enough to be apprenticed to any craft or other business, he would be, at the least, a master of Latin grammar. This Latin grammar, I considered, would go far to give him the etymology of words and language, which was all the part of scholar-craft after which I felt any very particular personal desire. This I supposed from having found in Bailey's Dictionary (into which I had now broken freely, as into a quarry, to dig out the materials of a language for myself), how our adopted English words germinated from their roots in the Greek, Latin, French, &c. I believed also that a perfect knowledge of the Latin grammar would tend almost wholly to supersede this; and thought that, with a ready-made language stored in his brain, a fellow might start on the world as a well-equipped sportsman takes the field, forest, or flood, with all open before him.

Well, with my sister's consent, the matter was

settled, and George got on with his Latin, whilst I got on with my shoe-making and mending the best way I could. This craft of mine was the most unproductive and vexatious business after all, a constant botheration, what with pleasing my customers and looking after my journeymen, who often would not, or could not, attend to matters so pointedly as was found absolutely necessary. This, through life since, has entailed a world of hourly care and extra labour on myself, with a super-sufficiency of daily vexation. If I had my life to begin again just now, I would rather at once commence henchman to the gipsy kingfisher in the most troubled waters above ground than be a village shoemaker on the most promising conditions ever brought within the vision of a poor son of the craft.

I had not then, however, formed these views, but was fondly nursing what I conceived a proper degree of taste for moral responsibility, more so then, to tell the truth, than, after fifty years' disgust with this way of life, I can possibly feel now.

I soon began to find that unless the shoes were made most substantially good, one could have no peace or credit with his customers, and then this very ill assorted with their idea of the price, as the common market price of a very inferior article was often brought into comparison, while there was no reasonable comparison at all in the case. And besides, there is not a more false idea prevalent than that country people are more easily pleased with such articles as shoes than are the inhabitants of town and city. In a large town, the prevailing fashion of the hour, however absurd that fashion may be, rules the general taste; while in the country districts every customer pesters the tradesman with his own peculiar notion or conceit, to the embitterment of his life and patience, whatever may be the extent of his ingenuity.

Another evil in the matter is this, that in a country village situation a journeyman shoemaker is his master's master, pay him as he will, since he cannot easily find a man to suit his purpose when he wants him, while he who is titled the master is in fact a servant of servants all the days of his life.

But the worst feature of our craft, over-topping all our other troubles, is our liability to be taken in by bad-paying patrons, since we must, in a general way, take such customers as offer to employ us; and though we may refuse to work to a known bad hand, yet we feel that we somehow or other must credit our neighbours less or more, and trust servants, labourers, and other tradespeople till term days of payments. We are thus often given the slip where we least suspect it—aye, and frequently, through by-way means, we are robbed by those who carry their head quite cock-nose above common suspicion. Indeed, where I have ever had suspicion, I have, in three instances of four, found myself too correct eventually throughout the last thirty years. And all this over and above the being obliged to sit on a low stool, in a puddle of sweat, throughout the long summer day and half through the long winter night, with feet often as cold as the philosopher's stone, which I believe, after all, to be my own iron-blue lapstone, which was, forty years ago, brought in a present to me, as taken out of the Tweed from the back of Benrig cauld dyke by George Sanderson, then fisherman and ferry boatman at the then Kipper Ha' of Mertoun.

However, while in Bowden then, I was only necessarily beginning the experiments of which these are now known results. So on I grubbled there for another year and a half, with very little occasional out-of-door amusement, and sufficient harassment, mixed up with very trifling amusement within doors. The chief drawback in my character all the while—can you believe it?—was a too scrupulous conscientiousness of feeling, which, the more I perceived the want of it in others, the more deeply struck its roots into my own mind. I then felt somehow as if I was privately accountable for the defaults of all mankind, and that I must maintain and uphold some certain preservative quantity or quality of virtuous disposition, as if the earth's respectability in the eye of heaven depended upon my inconsiderable Self individually—inconsiderable, indeed, as how could this disposition be maintained or expressed, but in a charity very inconsistent with my leather-aproned condition, in the off-sides of society, where we are tortured into the selfishness of general life, even in self-defence?

And this condition of affairs existed, though all the while the Church-going formal duties of religion were being carried on with all the stated forms of punctual observance, both in the Parish Church and in two separate forms of Dissent beside us. But I had by this time got deep into the confidence of several of the most noted observers of character, two or three of them free-thinking, or rather free-acting, practitioners on the passions of life; and the history of their intrigues and immersements in the under-currents of society gave me a very curious, and often a very sorry, picture of my brothers and sisters of mankind—of several, at least, of whom the outward walk and conversation in the world gave the superficial observer but a very faint idea.

All the while Kyle's law-plea was progressing, very *legally*, of course. His agent had led him on at last to raise a process of reduction of the deed on which David of Hilton had consigned the money to my sister; and Kyle was allowed a proof of his assumption of the deceased old man's superannuacy, or rather of his natural imbecility.

For the convenience of all parties, Mr. Bruce of Langlee was commissioned by the Court of Session to take the proof at Melrose, where they had three full days' examination of the matter of five-and-twenty witnesses on Kyle's side, and fifteen as exculpatories on ours.

Having to direct John Craw, my sister's agent, through all this examination of witnesses, I set myself to do so very dexterously, and certainly it was done so between us. Here I found old Mr. Bruce, the impartial gentleman, civil to the extent of well-expressed kindness, and our John Craw a wise examinator, as he proved himself on the first day; when he found that they so drained down their own witnesses to the very dregs of frivolity as to render their evidence sufficiently over-strained and despicable. John therefore almost altogether declined cross-examination of them, reserving himself to establish only a few essential points by our own cited evidence.

Kyle's agent[*] might have exhausted his whole stock of wit on me in the course of these three days, and left himself bankrupt for life, had I not saved him by simply cutting the thread of it on the morning of the second day, as one might snuff out a candle. He looked as simple afterwards as the genius of an empty cannon might be supposed to look out on a cocked pistol.

Kyle, being comparatively rich, and quite a goose, had plenty of witnesses brought forward, who, not now afraid of the dead gentleman they were come to prove mad, any more than of my poor self just placed before them, would willingly have favoured the living representative of property, but he and they all lacked tact to manage the matter with the necessary discretion.

Once, in the anxiety of his own ill-conditioned mind, he broke through the rule of form, throwing himself, without even preface, on the courtesy of the Court, and asked a witness the following question:— "James, eh, James, what would you have thought of old Hilton if he had been a poor working man like yourself, James, ye ken?" "I wad ha'e thought him a very silly man," said James, who, being delivered of this heavy thought, looked extremely wise. "Take that down," says Kyle to the clerk. The clerk looked knowingly to Mr. Bruce for assent or instruction, whilst I interrupted him with a request, in my most polite terms, that I might also be allowed the privilege of asking the witness a single question,

---

[*] William Somerville.

which, though perhaps not exactly to the main point, might set the preceding question in its proper light. With permission I then asked the witness—"Now, James, on your oath here, speak the truth of your mind, as you would in your own sawpit. What would you think of the present Thomas Kyle there standing if he were as poor a man as yourself? Would you think him nearly half as wise a man as you thought old David of Hiltonshill?" James hesitated; then looked a little bitter to me; then gave a side look to the Judge; and then came to a fixed gape of irresolution! Kyle looked more like a male sheep than a lion-lord of field and forest. His agent seemed to have got into immediate possession of more faces than one; at least he had a curious one for me, and another for the Court in general. John Craw sat looking at some papers, wise and at his ease, like Falstaff in his inn; while the Commissioner very properly took us all up out of the awkward predicament by seriously declaring that he could not further condescend on allowing these frivolous and irrelevant questions, on either side, to go into proof, and that he was even afraid of a reprimand from the Court for frivolities already admitted. I then perceived that I had likely done ill by running the thing so far into the ridiculous, and thus preventing their folly from getting its full sweep. However, there was still left sufficient of that leaven in the whole mass to show the nature of the accumulated evidence. In short, old David Kyle of Hiltonshill was made out a much wiser personage than anybody throughout the course of his life-time had ever happened to perceive, and I would advise any one who may wish to bring a friend, dead or alive, into notice, and get him up a character, to be at the expense of a couple of hundred pounds to prove him mad by five-and-twenty picked witnesses.

Out of many answers to curious questions asked in the course of this proof, I may mention one which is worth remembrance. Old David Kyle, the gentleman to be proven silly, happened to have been an elder in the Parish Church of St. Boswell's under four different ministers; and Mr. Scade, the then incumbent, was specially interrogated regarding his capabilities, when, as a crowning question, he was asked, "Did you consider the late David Kyle a man possessed of all his faculties?" "I did not consider Mr. Kyle as a man in the full possession of all the faculties which God intended for human nature; but I always considered him a man well qualified to act his part in life and in religion."

Well, the plea was proceeding on beautifully, like all other very grand law-pleas, down through its splendid course of five years—the fine image of a ship down the tide of time—and this in all the regularity of charges, hornings, captions, incarcerations, appeals, repeals, replies, duplies, treplies, suspensions, condenscendences, reductions, allegations, proofs, counter-proofs, interlocutors, judgments, expenses, and damages! Parties were often much in distress and anxiety, like other passengers in a storm. But the landing amongst the breakers, with the personal escapes from the wreck of canvas and cargo, which the "sharks" must prey on, of course, may be mentioned in proper time and place in some future chapter.

Meantime, as two years make a considerable change in human life in regard to friends, acquaintances, and circumstances, as well as the feelings of our own mind, I had begun to perceive that I might as well have commenced shoe-making for myself in St. Boswell's here, which I believed to be, in most respects, after all, rather preferable to Bowden. In spite of my philosophy, I still was retaining a hankering desire after an occasional out-start to the trouting, for which St. Boswell's lay so convenient on the grand river, and I felt that whatever my necessity for constant work might continue to be, there still might be some favourable leisure hours out of the many twenty-fours of the long twelvemonths which might be spared for such congenial amusement as angling, which I found I could improve to purpose; and besides, I was still followed out from the river sides to Bowden for fly-dressing by all my fishing acquaintances, so that in a short time I found I would be obliged to do a great deal in the line gratis, unless I should make it a proper stated branch of my business for daily bread through life, as it eventually has been down to the present hour. I had several other reasons for cherishing a preference to St. Boswell's, such as my father's desire that I should be near him, for our mutual convenience, of course, as well as occasional assistance in daily occurring cases of less or more consequence.

But as there is always some main idea lurking, or moling, or nestling about the bottom of our soul, forming a quiet point of concentration for the swarm of vague desires, these out-aërial affections that are so ready to alight everywhere on their attractions, like fluttering butterflies on flowers, so these other reasons were at best only as auxiliaries in sanction of the main argument, which, being heavier, lay deeper, and more shadowed in the mind.

This main weighty idea, then, was still a reasonable one, a desire of marriage, forsooth!—since, as I had formed such a taste for the right rational enjoyment of myself, I felt as if it would be gratifying to have more of self to enjoy. I conceived a wife to be a more real, substantial, and positive addition to a man, as a man, than all other possible acquisitions that he is capable of making on this side of time taken together. "*And they twain shall be one flesh.*" What a delightfully grand addition to a man's *corpus*, besides the idea of double souls winging space together, and listening to the harmony of the spheres.

Here I had grown up slowly since first recollection, like the oak from the acorn, to a middle stature, and this by imperceptible degrees; but here, by splicing a wife alongside myself, I might, in an instant, make a most convenient addition, equal to another five-and-twenty years' growth. Could anything be imagined so personally delightful, not to speak of the extra degrees of delight by being mutual? Oh! nothing on earth. And then another convenience was, I had one ready courted, or rather never courted; for the beauty of the matter was this, that whatever faults or failings she might have as a daughter of Eve, she was just wise enough to require no regular course of courtship, with its foolish accompaniments of worthless praise and protestations, such as it might be as amusing to teach a tame magpie, as to pour into the ear of the rational being whom we wish to make a proper part of ourself for the term of our existence.

Your father had then died in the month of April of that year, 1811, and your sister was left alone in his rented cottage-room at St. Boswell's, with all her brothers scattered abroad amongst the French wars over the world; so that all that was a-wanting with her and myself was the appointment of the day of our union, and to manage that ceremony in as homely, cheap, and quiet a manner as possible.

Her house was already furnished with most of the few necessaries that people in our condition at the time required, and therefore I could leave my sister in my rented cottage at Bowden, with all the necessaries of furnishing that had been mutually ours, where she could still, for a time at least, keep our nephew conveniently at school, as he was getting on delightfully with his Latin and other branches.

When I married and left Bowden I had been two years and three months in it, in which time, according to my strictly-kept books, after deducting my expense of materials—leather, hemp, and rosin—journeyman's wages, &c., I found I had just earned at the rate of 1s 6d a day, or £28 a year, with which to keep house and *haddin'*; and £14 10s of this is never paid me to this day, nor ever will!

There was a country business for you!—this, too, while victual was very high under French war prices. I can at present recollect the exact price of only one article of provision, which I then bought from a neighbour, a strong bacon ham, for which I paid him one shilling per lb. By-the-by, I trusted him also seven and sixpence over and above the price of the ham, which is also unforthcoming till the general restitution of all things! Is the world worse now than it was then? No, nor likely ever to be!

CHAPTER XXV.

A PIECE of autobiography, without something like exploit, intrigue, or loose living of one kind or other, may be considered dry and unfashionable—too tame even for ancient martyrs and "defenders of the faith" such as Daniel Defoe, John Bunyan, and Henry the Eighth, and may lead to a suspicion that the writer is either suppressing the darker shades of his character, or else has lived a life so tame and unimpassioned as to be unworthy of being recounted. But there is one thing worthy of remark, that a life of comparative continence by no means implies a feebleness of desire for the objects of sense, for one may easily ascertain from observation that there is often more loose living amongst people of merely medium propensities than individuals who might have the excuse of stronger passions to plead for their usual casual aberrations, or even for any career of vice. This matter depends not so much on the waywardness of passion, as on the moral virtue of the mind, exciting to nobler feelings, feelings that can only be gratified in the exercise of restraining the less virtuous inclinations. This is more a matter of balance of passion and principle than of the peculiar strength of either. In every lewd or wayward act we may plead the strength of temptation—the irresistible force of desire. But if the sense of duty amount to a very high and vigorous moral feeling, the bodily desires will eventually succumb, and sink into due subserviency. If a man have real virtue in his breast it will never rest so sound asleep that the pleadings of passion will fail to awaken it. Hence, every sensual act implies no particular strength in the passion that impels to it, but rather a culpable weakness or declension of the moral principle. Thirst is a strong natural desire, and yet in its extreme intensity, if a man of sound mind were convinced that a drink of cold water would cause immediate internal inflammation, he would resist the desire from the fear of severe pain and sudden death. But the same individual, under the impulse of other desires, might commit a lewd act, not because the passion in this case was stronger in his constitution than his former fever thirst, but because the moral principle in his mind was weaker than his love of present gratification. That virtue in the human mind which is founded on a love of God and goodness is calculated to resist every temptation to flagrant acts of vice, and there certainly is a virtue which is sufficient to withstand the very strongest temptation, and excite to the most noble and sympathetic affections, and this may be defined to be an intuitive and fixed sense in the soul of the love of God, or of that of Christ, as the best friend of man, and the *perfect* pattern of rectitude.

But the grand climacteric in every human life has perhaps never been plainly stated in any kind of biography. Whether this is omitted from a due delicacy of taste, or from a false idea of giving offence, I am not aware: it may likely be from a mixture of both feelings; yet it is most certainly a grand omission, as it involves more of real interest and principle than all the rest of life taken together. What consequences to the individual and to society at large are involved in that one major passion of the heart, the workings of which are generally two-thirds screened or darkly hid from the view of others, often concealed from the main object of its excitement, as well as huddled up from even our own scrutiny.

Songs say much of love's *darts* and *flames*, and such passions are often hinted at in sermons; but they seldom or never bring into view the contentions between desire and duty in the mind and feelings, nor depict the evolutions of those affections which are brought into motion between the strainings of desire and the resistance of the moral principle.

Nothing is more true, however, than that every one has his day and hour of something like trial between the stronger desires of nature and the virtuous sensibilities of the soul, and that much of the pains or pleasures of the future of his life depends upon the early issues of this warfare.

In the ascendency of the master passions, it is saddening to think of the wreck of the individual's own virtue, the loss of the native integrity of soul, of the approbation of conscience, and also of the true social feeling of meeting every human face with a smile of sweet sympathy and gladness; besides lying under the sad sense that even a single human nerve has lost its music-tone on our account, and may lie unstrung for ever, while the fiend-fierce feeling, like an evil genie, riots in the virtue-deserted mansion of the soul, perhaps there reigns imperious, impelling to further misrule, still urging to grosser gratification, till the milder spirits of the heart, the more angelic affections of the soul, are fled, or perhaps, like the fallen enemy of our nature, become at last demonish. Still, bad as this is, it is trifling in comparison with the evil wrought on the object of its excitement. Led from the paths of prudence, the soul stained or thoroughly polluted, many a lovely face in the bloom of life becomes clouded, and the smile of innocence is left flickering amidst the shadows of grief. Even hope sickens, in searching its dreary way to light, through the blighted objects of reflection, till the beam of life sinks at last into the sadness of settled sorrow.

Many date much misery of life from early marriages. I date more misery and mischief, both to individuals and to society generally, from the preventions of marriage at that season of life when nature dictates such union as proper for all parties, their health of body and mind.

Those interested in the evils inflicted on the community by restrictive acts of party legislation, such as our accursed present corn-laws, argue against the natural increase of population, and urge also the propriety of upholding a bloody war system, with all such destructive and starvation means of counteracting the native energies and current flow of human progression—a most preposterous way of going to work certainly, worthy only of the combined brains of a tyrannical aristocracy, and an enslaved and submissive community, to raise corn markets, and consequently the rents of their lands, by cutting the throats, or otherwise consuming the lives, of the eaters. Hence, also, amongst their nefarious schemes for marring the general beauty of creation, have most honest pathways into life even been attempted to be barred by Acts of Parliament. This renders it most difficult indeed for well-intentioned people to enter the marriage state comfortably, or to enjoy life in many other respects agreeably with the wise ordinances of God. And all this wreck and ruin is caused simply to gratify the mistaken avarice of a comparatively very few families—a set as unproductive as slug snails, and, viewed in a proper light, mere incumbrances on a general community.

I wish that part of ontology which is more particularly applicable to political government were at least evolved, elucidated, and reduced to a common every-day science, that something a little more rational might thereby be infused into the constitution of governing parties. But this lies yet in the distance, some ages perhaps before us. Phrenology offers to come in aid of it, but that is utopian, even though the principle were correct, for how shall such fashions be got instituted in the teeth of brutal reigning propensities?

I had, however, previously determined to be led more by the feelings of nature than by the dogmas of starch prudentialists, ignorant speculators, and silly projectors; and having managed to escape "the illicit rove," I found it congenial to my taste to take unto myself a wife—determined, in at least this agreeable point, to "obey the ordinances of God," and taking my further chance of the world, since I could not re-order it; for I never had got scared from the common proprieties of nature and life by the ideas of such as seemed to choose celibacy from what they called motives of prudence. Several individuals I knew would not marry because they saw the world was hard to live in, and because gipsy potters and tinkers bred great families in cart encampments behind hedges, which would soon, if they went on, and continued to increase, like the eastern locust, eat up every green thing! "Well," says I, "marry yourself, and raise what you account a right race of moral plodders on the turnpikes of life, to overbalance the tinkers, and keep God's world somewhat respectable!" But, no. "Would they beget children to live and starve in a land of tinkers and State pensioners? No." Others had such respect for the fair part of the creation that they would not wed unless they could previously acquire the means to furnish a parlour somewhat in style, and keep their wife in it, with a bell to ring on her servant girl. These, and fifty such excuses, were common, while I knew excellent young women longing to wed them on any plain, honest conditions, rather than linger on in "single blessedness." But, no; Mr. Wiseman had determined to have his affairs at such and such a point first, which, under the most favourable circumstances, might happen when he would be after fifty, and I have found him at ten years above that still only busy furnishing his parlour; the looking-glass already cracked in two halves from top to bottom, with its frame fagging, and one of the large sea shells that lie on the corners of the mantelpiece already cracked and spider-webbed; while the good woman, his ancient "flame," had sunk into old mopping maidenhood, or otherwise found means to escape from the dulness of "the solitary's lot," with some chap who would never on earth dream of parlour comforts, and the two comfortable enough in their way, with their young *Jocks* and *Jennys*. For the elegances of life, though good in their way, when they come of accord, are yet greatly ideal as a means of happiness, not at all essential to the true enjoyment of life in the main. Though nobody would like better to sit in a comfortable, warm parlour in a winter evening than I would do, there to muse on all I've felt and all I've seen, yet as this falls to the lot of only a few, why should I desire it?

I am convinced, however, that women in general are more generous in their natural disposition than men, and will for love submit to circumstances of fortune and adversity with more ingenuousness of mind and cheerfulness of heart. If nobody were to marry but such as have fine-furnished parlours, what kind of a world would the angelics have to look down on here? "The abomination of desolation," as a scripture prophet might have emphatically termed such things. No, no; God's world must and will be kept up and going on in spite of fools and tyrants, work what legislative mischief and present discomfort they may, in their evil days and miserable generations. Yes, yes; the day of retribution is at hand for all and sundry, as time stands only in the relative position of an idea in regard to an eventual renovation.

Throughout my long courtship—if courtship it could be called—which was more a kind of mutual attraction, akin to that which is now known by the name of animal magnetism, there was in it very little of that raging, panting, frenzy kind of love-extraordinary—neither darts, flames, nor other warpings of taste and fancy—such as we read of in songs and novels.

It was just a case of here was the young woman left alone since her father's demise, with nothing either romantically enticing, nor anything to forbid our union. We knew it would be quite agreeable to those of her brothers who had strayed abroad, and whom we had no certainty of ever seeing return again; and we were certain it would have been agreeable to those over whom the grave had closed. And as to wealth and marriage settlements, about which lovers of this world more than lovers of each other will often differ and part, we were, by God's blessing, not troubled with either, though neither destitute of the present means of life, nor hopeless of the future. Her father had left her by regular will the best part of what he should die possessed of, which might be to the value of thirty pounds. We were both able and willing to work for bread, and take mutual chance of the world; and, in short, to seek that enjoyment in each other's bosoms which we individually thought it might be difficult to find elsewhere. These thoughts might not then present themselves at all in the regular succession in which they are here related; but there is no better way of detailing the one feeling which inclined us to nestle in together.

w

I was then as a volunteer called away to quarters in Kelso for three weeks; but before daybreak on the morning of my departure I rapped up John Scott,* then schoolmaster and session-clerk, who spoke over the window, when I desired him to proclaim me for marriage before my return. He observed that he need hardly ask to whom, only that for form's sake he ought to have security for both parties. "Dare you dispute me," said I, "in security for myself? and I ask *you* to stand in security for finding me a bride." He said he would then match me to his own mind. "Well, as I have a friend here who has joined me this morning, and who is to be my 'best man,' you will, I hope, be second best, and make one at my marriage when I return three weeks hence. There will be few guests, and, as you were a very particular friend of her father's, you will stand in his place, and do the form of consigning the lassie over to my care and keeping." He promised he would be very happy to do what he believed her father would have been so very well pleased to have done himself.

I was then poetical enough in my feelings and disposition; but I had drunk too deep in the real philosophy of life to be carried away with fanciful imaginings or fairy scenery. Besides, I had dated so much misery in common life as proceeding from slights in love and courtship that I heartily disliked the rascally and thoughtless actors in these little tragedies.

It would be tedious to define how it came to pass that, in my young man days, while a heart-feeling admirer of almost every good girl of my acquaintance (though never a professed lover, so far as to

---

* Son of Andrew Scott, the poet.

give or receive even the idea of a slight), I often came to be the confidant of those who had been courted, sometimes ill-used, and basely deserted. Several histories of love affairs and blighted affections I have had opened up to me through bursts of tears, with a detail of the sorrows, hopes, and fears of the victims. The misery in such cases was, that the abuse of their kind affections only tended to strengthen their regard for the unworthy object. The divulgence of such cases to me by the fair mourners was sometimes induced by a vain idea that I might, as a companion, sound the lover in regard to his real feelings, or have influence in recommending them to his affections, who had "stole their poor heart away," as the old song has it, and escaped with the booty. In such cases I always saw that the attempt was nonsense, for where the rover had thus left a sweet, sensitive girl, it was invariably in cases where I conceived it impossible thus to recall him, and where often indeed it would have been a sin to have advised him back if even possible, he by his conduct proving himself incapable of appreciating such a blessing as the love of such a girl would have conferred on a proper object for life. In most cases it was no present comfort to tell the fond, fair mourner so, as nothing but time could cool down the fever, or a new lover displace the idea of the old by exciting a new passion. I therefore used to promise to do my best, advising them in the meantime to keep up heart, with a proper respect for themselves, and to take a serious thought whether it was then prudent to admit him again into their good graces, believing that the fellow who could thus basely sport with their affections was altogether unworthy of them, and that by perseverance in prudent conduct they might soon make a conquest worth a dozen such as he. I used also to lecture them on the folly of that romantic bravery in their sex, which makes them often incline to the brisk, pert, wild young bucks, who value themselves on qualities of which they ought to be ashamed, while the bashful, sensitive, ten-times better young man would be scorned off; some of the latter of whom I had known who, from the mild goodness of their disposition, had forgiven the flirtation, and taken up Jenny to dry her tears, to comfort and guide her, or be guided by her, through the brambly mazes of life, even after mad Tom, her foolish passion, courting her like a fury, had broken off at a tangent, like one of Job's wild mountain asses.

Some thirteen years ago, when in Edinburgh on business, sauntering down the Cowgate, a woman with a child in her arm seized my hand, saying: "Is that really you?" "Dear sake, Jeanie, how are ye here?" "This is my uncle's house, but come in to my ain." "An' is this your ain house, Jeanie?—an' this your ain bairn?" "Yes, an' this is mine, too," says she, sleeking down the head of a running child, "and the oldest is down in the school, a seven-year-old laddie." "Jeanie, I think I heard o' your being married several years since, and where's your husband?" "He's west at a job o' wark near Glasgow; I'm sorry he's no at hame; he wad ha'e liket to have seen you." "I should have liket to have seen him, too, Jeanie, for your sake; but, Jeanie, woman, what kind o' man have ye gotten? Is he half as good as

Geordie T——, that ye nearly lost your wits about lang syne?" "Oh, man, aye; I see the world in a different light now, though I couldna take patience to believe you that cauld starry night out on Tweed braeheads, in the bield o' Paton's corn-stack, when ye advised me, an' I couldna be advised, to vex mysel' nae mair about Geordie T——. But mony ane forbye me gangs delirious i' their first-love fever." "Yes, Jeanie, Geordie was a wild chap; ye would hear o' his end?" "Yes, an' I was sorry to hear o't: he got a braw wife, as he thought, an' I've been often sorry thinking o' her, too; for I daresay she had trouble enough in her short married life. But he would dance and sing the soul out o' her, too, the same way as he confused my young senses till I really didna ken mysel'. But it's a great blessing in this life that Providence often stretches a hand o' care to us poor creatures, when we're sae far misled as even to forget oursel's." "Yes, Jeanie, that should employ the lasting gratitude o' our hearts to think that there's aye ae poorfu' Ane to care for us; and it should make every mother particularly anxious to instil a proper idea of it into the souls o' her little dears, alang wi' the milk wi' which she fosters up their bits o' sweet bodies, till their bonnie clear een just glance wi' the spirit o' love, honour, an' human charity. Oh! Jeanie, woman, I've been perfectly ashamed o' my sex, that we should sae aften be seeking to gratify our ain selfish passions by attempting to mislead the kindliest affections o' yours, while we ha'e the maist solemn calls o' nature, an' reason, an' scripture, an' honour, an' manhood, an' a' thegether, calling us to respect and protect your honour, as the maist precious blessing in this world, that wad be a brute wilderness without ye. But gi'e my compliments to your ain gudeman, and tell him that, as your early friend, I'm glad to hear that ye're so weel pleased wi' him, although he and I may never meet to shake hands in this life. But keep faith and heart, Jeanie, through a' trials to come: the langest term draws to an end: there's a blessed hour on the wing approaching, when God's grace will be the universal hymn, an' the cares, an' the troubles, an' the trials, an' the friendships o' this life will be reflected on by happy meeting of friends, through the last shining tears of love and rapture."

But amidst even the sublimity of our reflections, we must not lose the thread of our narrative, however slight a thread that may be—whether of the gold twist, silk, cotton, lint, wool, or hair of human thought—still it is a thread of life, holding together a train of circumstances and ideas as real, and, viewed in a proper light, more interesting to man, *as man*, as is the life of these lords of hills and valleys, or even still more mighty foot-kickers of kingdoms, your sojourners in palaces, who have no time, in the course of their fateful hurry from their ivory cradles to their mahogany coffin shells, to look down and pass a heart-improving thought on the circumstances of their poor fellow travellers over life's commons, or the soil that was such prior to the date of its appropriation by lordly banditti,—these harassing and distressing bad neighbours of ours, who dust and din us with the *dirl* of their equipage to distressful confusion on our passage over this highway of time to that bourne where all plump down level, to await, as in a mesmeric sleep, the second grand scene of the human drama, where, for aught known to the contrary, the heel of the present cobbler may be made a gag to the mouth of the late chatting Prime Minister of green bags and budgets—these vile imitators of that fellow who once carried the purse amongst a very respectable little company of our earth's poor world-worn reformers.

Meanwhile I look back to the morning of the 9th of August, 1811, when I arose at Bowden, no more there to live a single person, and stitched up a fellow to a shoe I had made on the previous day, to form my wedding pair, with which I walked down to St. Boswell's here, meeting my bride, with a very few friends, where the priest paid us the respect of attending in our cottage, and joining us by one of the most beautiful sacramental sort of ceremonies that can be heard in the whole range of human composition.

Two things have been very peculiarly gratifying to me through life—to see loving couples linked together in honest wedlock, and little children drink milk; and these pleasures are particularly heightened when they happen to be sensible, cheerful-looking young people, and curly-haired children. So, of course, my own marriage was a treat which I have not lost the relish of to this day and hour.

CHAPTER XXVI.

THE first month of marriage is verily a lovely and loving affair—the summer blossom month in a man's life, come the autumn fruit as it may. Nothing here below the moon falls so short in idea of the reality as the picture of marriage in the imagination of the bachelor, when occasionally amongst his most genuine calculations of cool prudence such "a change comes o'er the spirit of his dream!" No, this is so like the joining of the soul and the body that there seems to be no proper comprehension of it until the junction is effected.

He must be a very coarse sort of a once married man who, ever in after life, no matter to what age he live, cannot warm his cold heart in a winter night with a casual reflection on the first month of his marriage—I might say his *first* marriage; but this might appear an invidious distinction, though I have no doubt whatever that a second marriage may often be as agreeable as a first, since so much depends on circumstances. But the fellow who cannot, particularly with the casual assistance of a single bottle of good evening ale, warm his old heart of seventy with the thought of his marriage week five-and-fifty years ago, is not a right old chap. I should even want faith to credit him a pair of winter shoes, however cold-like he might look amongst the frozen dews.

'Tis pity that first month of marriage does not last the long life throughout; and yet, in such case, what would become of its natural effects? when such are to be palpably forthcoming, and constitute "life's cares," which "are comforts," as we all know as well as did the grand gloomy bard of starlight and solemn shadow.

At anyrate, we may say of marriage what Mr. Macbone* said when rallied upon the inutility of his profession: "Oh! man, there's shinteel manners, an' mony muckle mair grand tings to be learnt at a dansin'-skule, forby the bare dansin'." The woman of our heart, however, never in any month of her life looks exactly so well, either before or after, in the eyes of her husband as in the first month of her marriage, when he finds he is succeeding in polishing off the maiden shyness from his fair bride, and letting the *native* modesty shine out unsophisticated, in its own fine-tinted colours, to adorn and set out her other housewife virtues, and form, as it were, the rose-knot in her dress cap.

Well, it is needless to attempt an illustration of a honeymoon, which shines with a milder light than any other moon throughout a long lifetime. He who has had his honeymoon knows it already, and he who has not can make little of the matter from any possible description "in prose or numerous verse," and this from the want of anything to give him com-

* A Highland dancing master of the old school, to whom many hundreds of the Tweedside beaus and belles of the first decade of the century owed their callisthenic skill and grace.

parison by. Almost every one come the length of eighteen or twenty understands something about that "draught of heavenly pleasure, below the milk-white thorn that scents the evening gale." But heavenly fine as that is, and finely as it is described in living language by my grand countryman, Burns, it still can give "the youthful, loving, modest pair" but little comparative notion of the dear associable interests which crowd themselves together into the first month of marriage.

But I wish I were out of this particular piece of description—it is too frill-fine a theme for my handling, so unlike any other of the common occurrences, hardships, necessities, flittings, and fightings of this journey of mine through sixty years; and too long thinking upon it at a time is a disqualifying exercise of the mind, very ready to bring a poor fellow into some ideal sort of Mark Antony situation, losing a present world for an imaginary honeymoon. It is lucky that few of us have his sort of world to lose, and that not so much for himself, as for the world so to be lost, and left to be brutalized. Indeed, if I had stood in his shoes at the time, I should likely have lost the world, with my share of the benefit of moon and stars to the bargain, as I cannot see how it would have been possible to resist that splendid madam, unless he had just happened to have been nicely married a neat fortnight previously to seeing her; and then, of course, all the eyes, diamonds, ruffs, fans, and furs-below of Egypt, with the ambitions, victories, and triumphs of Rome, could not have drawn his affections from home. No, he had too much of heart in him to have left a lovely bride within the first fortnight of their wedded love. Yet this is indeed what history, in accordance with the brute spirit of those times, accounts his fault or failing, a love affair through and through—itself a long honeymoon—for which he lost a Roman world, like a true man. Indeed, I admire that Mark Antony for this as a far grander character than any of his compeers. Their Roman kind of virtue was far too rugged and stern for my taste; like a death's-head, rough and shaggy with iron-wire hair.

And then that still more upsetting fellow of recent date, that Buonaparte, though I did not dislike to hear of him kicking a pack of saucy kings about, yet the yetlen-hearted* ruffian seemed to have none of the softer sensibilities of the true manly character, or the common meltings of human affection, in his cast-metal nature, and was so magnificently mad, *outré*, and insolent as to suppose the whole wide world, land and water, man and beast, made and spread out thick over the broad surface for the abuse or gratification of his personal strutting consequentiality.

I have never seen a figure on earth that I liked as ill to see as that of Buonaparte set up here and there in all metals, and in clay, stone, and stucco, all in the same starch-up, arm a-kimbo, quite disgusting position, expressive of nothing so much as of main bad taste both in the man and the model-maker. Those on chimney-pieces, set amidst crockery and curiosities, look wretchedly bad, corroding the sympathy of all around them, and spoiling the soft sweetness of a fireside. And that large one I saw lately, on a private pleasure plat at Stratford-on-Avon, gave me

* Cast iron.

a distaste to the present England, even if there had been nothing else in it to have excited such a feeling—a stiff, perch-up, full-sized image of Buonaparte, as if disdaining to stand on above one foot on the surface of the centre of England, next door to Shakespeare's tomb!—taste as bad as the devil's horns prominent in a landscape.

But what have we here to do with the worshippers of the images of dead ruffians, set up in wood, clay, or cast iron here and there? Let us rather talk of native savagery, or hut homeliness and private virtues. These are still to be found here, there, and everywhere, though hardly now in such plenty as State tax-eaters and Irish beggars.

Here, however, came the household virtues to be arranged with me in a family capacity, and put upon a new footing of practical improvement. Family living was the first concernment, and hence the possible means of product calculated and balanced to a practical strain of nerve and muscular capability. I felt strong in personal qualification for any work in my line of business, to the full extent of the current or casual demand of the day and hour in my neighbourhood, and set to work with the firm resolve of "Go to; the world shall go worse than the eye of history hath hitherto seen it, if, with the blessing of health, I do not make bread and support existence, and, moreover, find some small means to serve a poor neighbour in necessity."

In the truth of life I then felt a greater desire to imitate the good Samaritan, even in the dark, than to get forward and shine in parties of fashionable village merchants and tradesmen. There was a something in the idea and exercise of this which took my taste, while the other appeared quite a silly, sickening, gossiping kind of concern. Those in these adventitious circumstances I often indeed regarded in private idea as the butterflies of the current sunny hour, of no conversation worth attention, and whose dress and intrinsic virtue would prove very insufficient against any slight blast of adversity, and altogether unequal to the regular wintry storms of life.

At the distance of thirty years, I have seen the proof of this simple philosophy of my youth. Only two or three of the extra cunning and super-fortunate of the fashionable of that day now survive to eat solid bread in age, and are now shrinking at last, with myself, to nameless and inglorious graves.

If a man had the spirit of revenge in his brain or bosom, this is the very world calculated to afford its gratification, could he only have the patience to wait and look on. He need not whet the weapon, or procure a cudgel, to avenge himself: he has only to wait a little, and be too sure of having more satisfaction than the very devil in his nature could desire. The psalmist bears us out in this philosophy—"Fret not thyself because of evil doers, neither be thou envious," &c. But I had then fixed my maxim without even the prudence of attention to the inspirations of antiquity. The fact is patent to the common observation of all who will only look about a little. My youngest sister, Ann, had ascertained the fact very early in life, from personal experience, before the time of which I speak, once observing, in a family consultation we held under some oppression or other, "I'm aye in terror when anybody attempts to hurt me either in person, family, or character." "Why should you be so afraid of that, Ann?" says I; "they cannot so seriously hurt you if you take care of yourself, and beware of doing what they might justly blame you for." "Myself!" says she; "it's not myself I'm thinking about; but I've observed, since ever I can recollect, that everybody who ever attempted to vex or hurt me in any shape has invariably got enough of the same kind, or far worse, to vex or hurt themselves, till I have had ten times more revenge than ever I wished, and then my main vexation is their mistake in thinking that I'm glorying in their misfortune." "O dear, Ann, those who keep themselves busy in trying to vex others, and who in return get so much to vex themselves, are not so tidily minded as to conceive, or ever care about, what you are thinking." "Aye, but it often takes far mair nice management and caution to convince them of that than would keep my own mind correct for a twelvemonth." "Ann, ye're a genius after a'; that's just half o' the philosophy of life that ye need to carry you through *hale-scart* to eighty. The other requisite half is just a single step of the mind farther up the ladder of observation, and that step ye should endeavour to gain, without losing foot-grip of the one you now stand on. It is this—not to vex yourself about these things at all, for I'm convinced that there are few of our acquaintances who seem to be troubled about these matters of mind. I often wonder whether any of them ever think on them at all in the way you and I are doing just now. We may suppose it likely that they should, and yet I can never get so far into the matter as to form even a faith that they really do. The fact I believe to be this, that it is from perceptive feeling that the impression of these points is made on our mind; therefore, those who do not feel in the way we are talking of have no perception of them, and those who do stand in the exact position of ourselves, and cannot, under any circumstances, glory in the misfortunes of others. But, Ann, you always remind me of the hypochondriac who wept to see the ducks going barefoot in winter."

It is a curiously-constructed world this, upon the whole; for here is the creature, in all his or her variety of constitution and character, and here is the world, so adapted to the application of all these powers, a broad field for the exercise of all these principles and propensities, with an endless variety of mind and matter, calculated to excite, amuse, and outlast the penetration and research of all ages; yet if the existence of this human mind is destined to be eternal, and in its present state of individual capacity to outlast the present combination of the material embodiment, the goal may ultimately be so neared as to bring us within the perspective view of intellectual perfection. No wonder that the Christian creed is precious to the soul of the human being—that the doctrine which adds immortality to the gift of common life should be held pre-eminent. A pity it is that its professors did not better understand its precepts, and form their morality of life upon them, that we might have the credit of beginning our eternal being more respectably.

In previously stating my feelings with regard to a

disinclination of joining in parties of our fashionable villagers, I should at the same time have given that cream of our class their due credit, by observing that these worthies of that day seldom showed the least disposition of drawing me into any participation in their socialities. The leather apron of such a "lean, unwashed artificer" was too dark-soiled for their tastes, and their conversation was generally too light for mine; and hence we remained alike gratified in different sections of our general circle, and on the best terms imaginable, being at the most convenient distance for such degree of friendship as could best subsist in all seasons, alike unaffected by the heats and colds of our summer and winter feelings. Several of these, however, very frequently, or nearly all of them occasionally, would come strolling in to my stall, which literally then "served me for parlour, and kitchen, and hall." This was in their hours of relaxation from their lighter occupations (vacant hours indeed, in as far as mind was concerned!) always sure of finding the poor cobbler at his everlasting task of fitting in new *understandings* to old skulls of upper-leathers of the liege subjects of one or other of the late Georges—I forget just now whether "third" or "fourth" reigned at the time; no matter which, since they were both as *kingly* as other potentates of their evil day and generation, and served their full time to wear out the *soles* of their under *subjects*, like all other superlative upper-leathers.

To state this matter more plainly, I should say that amongst these people then around me there were a very few, a mere sprinkling, or five per centage, of those that we designate by the title of "nabbery," or small would-be gentry; or, more properly speaking still, only apers of such. These I was sensible of looking upon me as a person infinitely below their nose—poor, of no studied etiquette or "genteel education," having no standing in any respect, although perhaps admitted to be of some tact and skill as a poor cobbler and fish fly-dresser, yet as nothing worthy the notice of their *better class*, which floated over the surface of our common society, like blue scum on ditch water.

Meanwhile, I was occasionally pondering in idea on what Providence had verily intended in their creation, as I could not conceive even a midge fly to be made in vain; or at least conceiving them as those who would "strut their short hour on the stage" and leave no shadow of memory behind, not even what I am here writing of them; whilst, not to blink the truth, some unaccountable, indistinct impression had taken its place in my mind, that I might be remembered for some time after I had in bodily shape passed away, though for what I could in no wise determine, even in imagination. In fact, this was something in the character of a dream, a vision of the soul, to which no substance seemed attachable, nothing even positively desirable—something indistinct, implying a kind of indefinable presentiment. The more particularly was this so, that I was in other respects then further from the thoughts of any attempt at an endeavour to prosecute any work, either of soul or substance, than I had even been sometimes formerly. When in the casual flush of some fine fit of poetical feeling, I had occasional dreams of being, some time or other, able to embody the splendid visions of imagination, and show them to the mind's eye of others, I gave the vague, indistinct idea no settled credit in my inmost mind, but yet could not help occasionally playing with it in imagination, as a gentle intrusive vision of fancy or a dream of love; and indeed, like a changing skylight, it would bear no palpable form, and did not arise from any idea of ever producing, or being able to produce, any work of art or poetry, or anything that might possibly confer a degree of celebrity. And then I found myself fixed to the cobbler's stool for life, where my daily shoe-work, however excellently managed, was of the most perishable character, trodden into the dust of forgetfulness within the twelvemonths. Well, no matter, here was I then, a very poor candidate indeed for the fame of leaving the impression of my thoughts upon a few of the next generation, without even the idea of supposing how it might be effected; nor had I then either time or patience to form any plan for the purpose, far less to act upon it. The passing day required always the full exertion of every faculty for making bread to carry me and mine through itself, and every approaching morning brought in its new bill of necessity for renewed hand labour and care. Still, that idea kept alive, and is hardly extinguished yet, fluttering here and there from time to time, like a wild bird in a forest, amongst all the thoughts, hopes, fears, cares, and even despairs of my mind.

About the time of which I am writing, however, I began to take considerable enlargement in my views of human life, and all affairs connected with my relation to it, and particularly in computations of the propriety or impropriety of various human labour—of its direction to the useful or to the unnecessary, its utility or inutility. In fact, I then naturally became an utilitarian in the principle of mind and practice, while yet unacquainted with the present word by which I am now expressing it, distinguishing it then by the designation of the *useful* or the *useless*. Hence, something like a warfare of mind took place between the propriety of following this principle steadily in everyday practice, and the more congenial desires of formerly-indulged habits. The desire for outfield recreation in the shape of field sports was as strong as ever—occasional shooting or fishing. The restraint, therefore, was something like the necessity of tying up an active, brawny limb, so as successfully to imitate a lame beggar.*

---

* This has frequently been done by daring, dissolute, and idle vagrants. A curious instance of the detection of this occurred with the wonderful footman of the late Lord Cranstoun of Crailing—a person altogether remarkable in his day for athletic feats, particularly running, which, in those times of running footmen, was his profession. He had never met with any one the least like a match; but one day when he had set out on a hurried message, he was hailed by a sturdy, leg-lame beggar lolling by the way-side with his *innamorata*. The time of the day was first civilly inquired, and then the request was made, if the footman would oblige by taking silver for a guinea—which, being agreed to, the beggar told out the change into the hand of our runner, who in frolic skipped a little along, telling the couple that he would call at the spot and produce his guinea on his return from Edinburgh. Our beggar, limping, followed a little with bold and reasonable remonstrance, to no effect, which the other continued, by word, caper, and gesture, to mock at, when the beggar's lady called aloud, "Cut your hough-strings and run, man." This being no sooner said than done, a race in ettle earnest commenced, which would certainly have ended catastrophically had our

From reasoning and restraint, however, I succeeded amazingly, even to my wife's admiration and almost uneasiness, as, in place of the frugal character of the matrimonial lectures so common in family cases, she would occasionally observe—"Ye never go out to catch us a wheen trouts now. I thought, when we married, I would aye be sure of a fry o' fresh trouts twice a week, through the summer at least, and now we hardly ever see such a thing." "It's better to hear ye saying this than bantering me wi' the auld proverb of *losing my bread seeking my kitchen*. But when ye get very ill for the want of trouts, I'll be glad of your order in excuse to myself for taking a start out to fetch you in a strap of them, and in the meantime I'll shoot ye twa-three fine half-grown rabbits to-morrow morning before ye ken where your head lies. I'll slip the key below the door, and be out by the *screich* o' day, and we shall have a fresh stew for dinner." This was another point of out-door indulgence (for I cannot be brought to call it an indiscretion) in an autumn morning about sunrise, which, besides the pleasure of the out-air exercise, in a life of sedentary confinement, would also repay the time, particularly when it could be followed without risk of restraint or prosecution, as, though our old village squire, then Walter Scott of Raeburn, was in nowise proverbial for allowing liberties, yet being no lover of such sport himself, and disliking the increase

---

now hard-run footman not taken just timeous refuge in the first gentleman's house they reached, and made another person go out and deliver the follower his own, with some additional shilling, and a high, swelling compliment in pacification, of having beat the best runner in the south of Scotland.

of the rabbits about his haughland fields, it required only to do him the "justice of peace" honour, not of asking his liberty, for that would not do, but ouly to shy him a little, as if afraid of giving offence, in which case he would never resent the crack of a morning or evening shot, even in the very vicinity of his beautifully-situated Tweedside old mansion-house.

The famine of my former years, and the fearful aspect of poverty which they still represented to my imagination, often then excited occasional stirrings of desire to better my circumstances before any unforeseen scarcity, or the wants and frailties of age, might overtake myself or relatives. But day-labour in my profession was felt inadequate, even with the closest application, to produce more than an existing supply for the wants of the day, and that even with difficulty. And although, by observing the manners of the money-grasping race I could perceive that very little mind, and less genius, were requisite to success in that pursuit than seems generally supposed, while sensibility of mind seemed inimical to it, I could never get myself wedged within the compass of the necessary rules. The greedy, over-reaching appearance on the one hand, and the gripping, holding, straining sense of security on the other, excited a kind of mental nausea; and the force necessary to keep the mind at the requisite pitch gave a more acute sense of pain than the wealth of the planet could give pleasure. So every attempt I made at even giving thought to the subject gave way to the next qualm of sympathy that shot across my imagination, without waiting the assistance of the next generous sentiment produced on ordinary reflection.

A neighbour of mine has often told me that I was "a *ninny*," else I might have enriched myself by a different application of faculties. "I might have been grubbing on like you still," says he, "had I not set myself out to market determined to do business in earnest; and the market is the place to know a man's *real abilities*. Be sure you make your bargain well, and then pull them up—bargain's bargain! —*a-aha*. I will defy any man, no matter who he is, to *do* me! Keep your eyes open." His meaning might more properly be rendered—that he would *do* any honest simpleton he might meet with in a low bargain; and here lay his pride of manhood, tugging and fighting his way through thick and thin in a *tag-rag* and *tear-him* manner. On weighing this individual's intellect to a scruple, I found that it might not be very deep to "delve a yard below his mine, and blow him to the moon," and that I required no new qualification for such a way of fortune-scraping, but rather to be divested of some faculties of soul which I already possessed—to wit, all those sensibilities of mind which sickened at the idea of indulging in a *cow-couping* propensity. I found I might submit to dig dung for eighteen-pence a day, but could not condescend to be told by a poor hind or cottar that I had got a ruinous advantage of him in a bargain, and with a brassy face retort "bargain's bargain." I could as soon have condescended to wear a slave's collar.

Upon a general view, however, I have found that to maintain an ordinary good keeping with the world depends greatly upon the sacrifice which the generous mind must always pay to the self-interest of the gripping and the needy. This being conceded on my part, in the shape of a given advantage, has kept me on friendly terms for at least present transactions, although such way of keeping the world in cue has held me to this hour on the brink of poverty.

I have sometimes, however, thought I was wrong in submitting so passively to my fate of low-life poverty, bordering on want, and supposed there might be honest means within my reach of bettering my state and circumstances, and sometimes since have even made attempts at plans of a rather speculative kind to improve my fortune a little; but the ability to execute such generally depended upon hopes and promises of help, in the shape of money advance from others, friends or acquaintances who had given me encouragement, but who always withdrew at the crisis, upon some excuse of disapprobation of my plan or opinion. On such occasions I used to return from within sight of the very harvest of my hope, and sober down into the calm reflections of that philosophy which never scorns the humblest seat, even in the sheds of poverty. On the first check of disappointment I used to feel considerable disgust, and would run into such reflections as the following:—I dislike the low trickery of life and its day-tale trifling. I could well retire to some lone wood or cottage window, where I might see the clouds of heaven pass by careering, or slowly sailing on the wind; mark the sunbeam checkering their skirts, or the lightning bursting from their bosom; observe the course of animal economy, the loves and habits of the forest tribes, of footed or of feathered life. I love acquaintance with the trees and rocks, or anything that is silent, or speaks truth—the simple truth of nature and of feeling, just as the mind imagines or conceives. But to be lodged amidst the tide and whirl of selfish loves and passions, and bursts of noisy mirth excited by idea of what is neither natural nor rational, destroys the proper relish of existence.

CHAPTER XXVII.

I HAVE been the more particular in these last chapters, because it is about this age when the mind bursts out into a more full development, and when the earlier opinions of youth are either relinquished or more definitely confirmed. A world of new ideas is also often engendered, or a crush and concentration of more solid impressions received. Hence the mind feels strengthened, and we are enabled to converse with outward nature a little more discursively. In short, we begin to feel our manhood of mind; while the consequent ability, as well as the necessity, to exercise it, is sure enough to increase.

Fixed in this position, with a family forthcoming, the world had already shown me the nature of the responsibility of such condition—the necessity of care for one's household—and this without even considering the propriety of the apostolic injunction regarding the matter. I had determined to seek the comfort of life in obedience to the mere rationality of the consideration, as well as "for the glorious privilege of *feeling* independent." Hourly attention to work had the effect, as it generally has, of bringing in more customers. So I laboured on diligently at what appeared to be the immediate, every-day, indispensable necessity, vigorously suppressing what, in the world's language, is called the more vague or natural wanderings of the mind, until the very poetry of thought was smothered up in a cold obstruction in the quiet nooks and crannies of the brain, like a live *gleed** in ashes, and could only glimmer forth occasionally, like a glow-worm from its clod, in a kind of gliding, shadowy ghosthood.

To suppress the native tendency of taste in such cases is a greater effort than one-half the world is aware of. The greatest labours of life are not always seen in the greatest productions of human genius. It was easier for Milton to write "Paradise Lost" than from any worldly necessity to have resisted the agreeable labour. Had Homer and he had their eyesight, and been fixed to the necessity of cutting bread out of leather and prunella, we should likely have wanted our two principal epics. The labours of Hercules were child's play at club and shintie compared with the labour of suppressing the major passion, or of diverting the main current-flow and tendency of thought in the human soul. Let that be as it may, I know I had then much of native poetic desire to combat with and to overcome. Overcome it was, however, in a great degree, and from a moral necessity, but never extinguished. It is a quick spark of life-flame from the divine bosom of everlastingness, which, however circumstantially obliged to glide its quiet way through the trumpery

---

* An expiring ember.

of that portion of eternity called "our Time," will still exist and burn on, unquenchable for ever.

And here comes another spark of everlasting human soul-fire, newly emitted, newly arrived! On the 7th of June, 1812, I had the pleasure of receiving my first-born, my Barbara, a sweet-faced little infant from her earliest exposure to this our atmosphere. How I blessed her in my soul, and how well I have ever since thought her worthy of blessing, I need not here attempt to express in the language I am at present master of. Many think it manly to pretend caring nothing for looking at infants till they begin to prattle. I hate alike that apathy and the puerile pretence of it. An infant's face has ever been to me the loveliest image in creation, as there we have nature herself in her finest display of earthly combinations—all young and sweet, in unaffected interest—bud of promise, opening to loveliness, like a rose born to the morning—a blossom yet unstained, uncropt—virgin gold yet unalloyed, or at least unpolluted, by any vile stamp of earthly monopoly, Cæsar, rex, or dunderhead.

We talk much of original sin, and consequent perversion of the human will, as of a standard stumbling block in the path of life. Its existence may be undeniable in argument—as, for instance, "who can bring a clean thing out of an unclean?—not one." But even in this view we have got grace to restoration; so, under the influence of that grace, let the human couple nurse and cultivate proper affections themselves, and in place of bull-beating and pelting the devil into their children, on the supposition or pretence of beating him out, teach, lead, and train them with gentleness and affection to feelings and deeds of kindness, faith, hope, and love, and we shall soon have a better race from which to construct a better world. Instead of fox-hunting, man-hunting dukes and squires, who would also hunt cobblers if cobblers could run fast enough, we should then have *men* who were rational, more like Christian evangelists, leaders of the people, not apt to cut each others' throats, like Waterloo fighters or jungle savages, but to lead in the ways of rationality to righteous conduct, equity, brotherly-kindness, all-embracing charity, and soul-brightening hope and joy, till this earth, this seedling-bed of eternal being, should itself become a field of Paradise, a heaven in epitome.

This would be the way to commence the religion of God and Christ in the world, which has never been fairly commenced yet, notwithstanding all the fuss that has been made about it. At present, amidst all our talk and contention about points of faith and doctrine, kirks and creeds, we seem merely taken up about indefinable forms, and shadows of something which we imagine to be real only in the distance. Hence we get into the habit of looking at religion as if it were something distinctly apart from the other concerns of our common life—as some necessary affliction of the natural passions and feelings, to be statedly and voluntarily undergone in a kind of penance of soul for the supposed aberrations and tergiversations of the other free actions of life; while we should rather consider religion as that which constitutes the main ground and end of our existence—as the special preserving virtue of life, "the salt of the earth," which warms and actuates the whole constitution of our general and individual nature—a felt and stated devotion of the heart's affections and life to God our maker, and His service here, with a disposition of will, and confidential trust of, and agreement with, His eternal purpose in provision for us here and hereafter.

Our village at that time showed, as I believe most pleasantly-situated villages do at all times, a certain phenomenon, which is perhaps one of the greatest deceptions of phantasmagoria on this our earth—something like the vision of the rainbow in the boy's eye when he supposes the golden spoon at the end of it. Lessudden, as seen from the high roads around, looked most pleasantly situated on the gently-sloping upland, facing the sweet south so wooingly. Though standing comparatively high and open, it was flanked in on all sides, at respectful distance, by still higher, and here and there undulating, ridges of hill and dale, crag and tail. The scattered cottages, seen through a fairy paradise of orchard blossom, seemed like the bowers of the happy, where it appeared impossible for a passenger to conceive any lurking canker of discomfort, misery being out of the question. It was one of those spots upon which a heavy, weary, way-worn heart might incline to settle down for rest and repose; and as the blackbird might be seen at all seasons winging its way through the open spaces to the thickets of winter shelter, or summer shade and blossom, the appearance of the place gave the idea of comfort and heart's ease. It seemed the very spot of earth where the plant so named must have sprung indigenous to the soil. And yet, after all, this highway view was only a mere outline of our real ground scenery, as what may be called the chief pleasurable point and characteristic of our situation was the *Braeheads*, or north facing bank of the Tweed, which could not be seen, to be conceived what it really was, from any of our surrounding roads. This point, in two minutes' walk from his door, brought any villager into a broad field view of the most picturesque scenery to be seen on the whole course of the river.

You might, here and there, in the many lovely windings of that fine stream, from Peebles to Berwick, find a tuft or two of the more romantic than perhaps could meet the eye from any given point of our *Braeheads* view; but from no spot on the whole sweep of the river could you find such a concentration of all that forms the beautiful or interesting in landscape thrown on your eye into one broad sheet of the picturesque in nature. From any of the surrounding heights you could at once perceive that our village site was the breast-bone of the bosom of the main vale of that majestic lady river.

Though Roxburgh Castle, or Floors, near Kelso, have a splendid command of view over a most fertile district of the vale of the Tweed, yet from *Lessudden Bankhead* you have a view around, and to the north particularly, with Dryburgh, like the map of Elysium at your feet, embosomed in the centre of the most beautiful and protecting hill and high range, from which scene a painter might prefer to take sketches when wishing to represent an oriental paradise.

And yet a paradise this was not in reality, as a kind of Buonapartean cancer was preying in this very breast of the vale, eating much of the best of their spirit out of the inhabitants. The possessors of these gardens, as well as the poorer cottagers in general, felt very little of that heart's ease, the symbolical plant which we have pre-supposed to be there growing spontaneously. The fatal apple had, alas! been tasted, and our garden-innocence was gone. The canker had eaten into the core, and the milk of human kindness had become curdled and soured. Like filthy creatures sliming into holes and crevices, evil spirits had entered there in the shapes of hate, envy, malice, pride, and, over all, oppression, with its misery-making concomitants, heart-burnings, false seemings, and lurking desires of revenge. The devil's horns, however, were nowhere perceptible in the landscape, nor a cloven foot-mark on the soil, except those of a cow or sheep. Indeed, that particular kind of superstition had gone by, in the wake of the palmy old Abbey days, of supposing that we saw these horns or long cloven foot-marks.

But I suppose that wholesale and retail dealer in wickedness keeps as much as possible in his invisible coat, wherever he finds he is succeeding by more sly, mercantile methods in his mischief-making capacity. We had our sly dealers of those days in the characters of even most honourable professions; and even horns were occasionally imagined to be observed by sharp, prying eyes on some of the highest-tossed heads of our community. But that, of course, might be mere suspicion, these matters being often better left unascertained by clear proof.

Besides, our village had then got into almost mere animal prose both in thought and expression, not a seraph note or a spiritual whisper to be heard in the vicinity—not a poetical inspiration to breathe life into the mass of organic matter forming the body corporate.

Be this as it might, here was our village, with all its visible and invisible country-village concomitants and appurtenances. Among the most prominent of these was our Parish Church of St. Boswell's, placed, as of old, on the extreme east corner point of the parish, in view of the Tweed, with its weak-sounding bell, keyed on C sharp, and venerable churchyard, the green bed of our village ancestors, where the gleanings of our generations are gathered in. Our first public character, our parish priest, is there, alive beside the dead, set down in the manse, with glebe and stipend; for, even as moral remembrancer and tongue of the dead, he must still live his day and hour, and keep his clay from withering in drought, while he keeps us in weekly recollection of our dust and our duty—though, in truth, we are not apt to forget the dust part of our being, as we seldom get out of it. Our late incumbent, who had just previously to this time left us, had been of no great note or far-fame in his profession, but was rather remarkable for his eccentricity of figure both of body and mind. A man of short stature, say five feet nothing, yet, being Dutch built, he required (and indeed the greatness of his soul demanded) the common six-feet quantity of merchants' cloth to thatch him; and he had, of course, the whole manse, glebe, salary, *et ceteras* of his situation, the same as any giant in the Establishment. He had been bred for the English Church originally—a scholar, of course, broad and deep, for he was ever going to the root with new renderings of the original text in Greek and Hebrew, to the wonder or amusement, if not to the information, of his audience. He was held conceited and peremptory, but every man has a right to be so, particularly every man below the height of five feet nothing. Upon the whole, Mr. Scade was a moral, as well as a natural, curiosity—of a rather poetical taste, however (not talent), for which I liked him, in spite of all his other comparative insignificance, throughout the seven or eight years I heard him weekly. He was quite a little Alexander Pope in his way, particularly in didactic conceit. Of the *Moderate* school, at least not what is here called the *Evangelical*, in his religious persuasion, he was as nearly as may be free of fatalism; at least, he threw no spark of light on those grand questions of questions—*Free-will and Necessity*. After spinning out the thread of his day and hour, and lifting his fated number of annual stipends, he left this world and these questions as he found them, much as we shall all do, waiting a grand eventual solution. In fact, these matters seem to every one of us to be just much as we may for the time think them; since we can change our opinions of them every day, while the facts in nature and fate remain unalterable.

He went the way of all the earth, however, to a certainty; and we got another in his place—namely, Peter Craw, who stood half a foot higher in the pulpit; at least he did not require the little stool from which Mr. Scade was said once to have slid down out of sight in the enclosure, which proved a kind of accidental full period to a scripture quotation,

"A little while I am with you, and again, a little while, and I am not with you," when down he slid!

Mr. Craw might be said, however, to fill his shoes pretty fully. "New besoms sweep clean," and therefore, of course, after the old paralytic, hackneyed John Scade, the more fresh Peter Craw made, for a while, rather what may, on a small scale, be called a figure.

He was our parish priest at the time of which I speak, in all the consequential fistle of a new umbrella, reasoning powerfully every Sabbath against "the enemies of our faith," &c., till Andrew Crammond observed to me one day on coming home from church, "I'm afraid our priest will reason me into infidelity, for he quotes stronger arguments from the infidel writers than he seems well qualified to refute; and if it were not for the saving clause of our general ignorance, I would fear he might infidelize the kirk."

The only other remarkable traits of his clerical character were, that he had a particular knack of enticing the heritors to do what he wished, and had the full modicum of priestly goodness to the poor, a first Christian virtue, as our priesthood goes now-a-days; but above all was his devotion to that very particular High Church text, "Obedience to the powers that be": that he dwelt on down through his twenty years' incumbency to an alarming extent, never neglecting to touch it in his skirtings round every knotty nook and fretted corner of all his built-up sermons. But in one sermon, written expressly to the point, he was fearful with it, every now and then horse-rattling us into obedience to Pitt, Castlereagh, and Peel Government as "ordained of God." But at last, when, in the ordination of God, the Reform Bill was carried under the Grey Government, and we, in spite of his pulpit eloquence, had got the Whigs voted into office, I observed that he then would not, in his own proper person, show us example by giving the obedience of his faith, goodwill, and vote in support of the powers which had then come to be, the Whigs in office. When I asked him to sign our parish sheet of a county petition for the West India slave emancipation, he shuffled me off by saying, with a rather starch-up look, that he would "not petition *the present Government* for anything." Here I found what I considered as good as a tacit acknowledgment of more gods than one, even an extra three in one, duly acknowledged—Peel, Pock-pudding, and Mammon—a true Tory-triumvirate. Here was hero-worship still, and anew proving that it is every dog to his master all the world over. His old text was blown up, however, for his day at least. There was no more lecturing on obedience to the powers that had then come to be, but a clean trick at another point of life's trade compass; for, in fact, he was quite a parish *Peel*—the same small, sly, chicaning mind. He then bought a genteel cottage house, with a little field, and a large acre-garden attached, lying down into the centre of the village, which front garden ground he built up into a row of street cottages, now called the Crescent, and took the advantage of selling these for Tory votes in that party's great Carlton Club struggle of buying up qualifications to over-balance the Liberal majorities. By this he was understood to have cleared the cottage and portion of land and garden still remaining attached to it, which may now be worth some £600. But he died suddenly, the only victim of the Asiatic cholera, then travelling the country, that occurred in our parish, and one of the only three who seemed to show a great presentiment of alarm regarding it. This settles the clerical part of our relation for two incumbencies, down through a period of some thirty years or thereby.

But to return back to the point of the first years of this Rev. Peter Craw's start with us, our next first public character, who stood out as prominent as a parish steeple, was a character so strange that neither Shakespeare nor perhaps any novelist that I have read—Sir Walter Scott, his own cousin, included—ever depicted anything the least like to it. I will leave him to a separate chapter, and in the meantime only touch him gently in points where he may be found necessarily connected with this present history of my own life and village circumstances; it would, indeed, be improper to give a detailed description in this autobiographical narrative of any individual character, further than may fall out in the illustration of particular circumstances relative to my own affairs.

Well, here stood, or rather sat, I, in this St. Boswell's, at that time, and long since, in the extended and elevated position of son, brother, husband, father, uncle, debtor, creditor, sutor, cobbler, and fish flydresser, to which I then added fishing bootmaker to whomsoever would employ me—a most responsible situation truly. Notwithstanding all this, I could not yet fully master former desires for out-airings, in the shape of a casual early morning shot by Tweedside at rabbits, or at birds for trout-fly feathers, nor a cast of the fly on a very particularly fine fishing day, besides something in the character of occasional romantic scene-haunting, around every fairy nook, peak, or corner in the vicinity, from the tops of Eildon and the Bell-race down to the salmon rock-lair at the bottom of the Hare-crag pool. I felt it not at all easy or agreeable to sink the sentient soul betwixt the soles of a stinking shoe for the term of even this little life-time; for I considered that though (as our priests averred) the next stage of eternal existence might give the confined virtuous plodders in this world a free scope from the walled imprisonment of earthly clay to enjoy the flowers of Paradise, yet I felt that my whole present constitution of soul, as well as my bodily senses, were adapted to the enjoyment of the morning's freshness, and the free, skylark songs of this present planetary life, its spring and autumn mornings—a voluntary constrainment from the pleasurable enjoyment of which I could not possibly be persuaded to consider a virtue. It might have been all well enough to conceive this very comfortable doctrine of future releasement, in cases where distress of body or incarcerations for breach of game-law legalities might confine us in damp cells or hovels of starvation, while the framers of these partial laws enjoyed the free moorland twelfth-of-August airs, with their meat-bag and bottle bearers, Joe Manton's, and fifteen guinea pointers. But let those who can try, to convince me of the religion of monkish voluntary seclusion as a means to an end of gaining heaven. No, no; he who rejects the present free gifts of life—sun, moon, and star influences, the open breeze of hill, flood, or forest, with woodland airs, and the music of moving waters—may be regarded as throwing all these gifts of supreme goodness back in their Author's face, unappreciated and unenjoyed, like a petted urchin refusing the refreshing and delightful enjoyment of them. With what face, I wonder, can he pray for or expect any other gift of future heaven pressed upon him, or propose to himself the probability of his enjoyment of such to satisfaction, supposing his precious little naked soul really ushered in, liked a winged finch, amongst the bowers on the banks of the river of life and the everlastingly enchanting songs of the birds of a heavenly paradise.

Here, however, I found life a pretty even-handed struggle. Leather on credit was highly charged, and the three or four months' bills were ever recurring, often before the stuff was wrought up, while it had to be given out in shoe credit for a twelvemonth. Besides, a journeyman was indispensable to the carrying on of daily business, and I found too surely that one who could and would interest himself necessarily was very difficult, or almost impossible, to be had. Even such as could be tutored to be at best only partially useful were sufficiently upsetting and hard to satisfy with terms of wages and victuals in any way at all consistent with the general products of the business.

In short, to serve my customers and myself mutually and any way agreeably required " double, double toil and trouble"—constant, daily, late-and-early, vigorous attention and exertion, and to live within the measure of the gains actually realized was the grand criterion of the whole matter.

The workman or labourer who must keep a family upon a specific day's wage may know every day or week where he is at in regard to his finances, and regulate his supply in some degree conformably, and he soon ascertains when in the least degree he overgoes his means; nor can he, to any extent, find credit to get far wrong, though he were even so inclined. But the tradesman who must provide the materials on which he works or speculates, such as a country shoemaker, whose outlay for these materials is a full average of two-thirds of the whole product, while the positive gains amount to only the most scanty means of possible subsistence, is in a condition of ceaseless uncertainty. This, together with his constant and inevitable risk of losses, renders him the most liable of all beings to overstep the prudence necessary to correct expenditure, and this is increased to the full extent, where the calls of the poor man's family for even the most common necessaries of life far exceed his stinted means in the measure of production. This no journeyman I have ever had could clearly comprehend, or seemed at all willing to consider. It was just what he could for the time wrest for his own hand. When I found one, therefore, at all qualified to suit me, he must eventually be paid over and above his strict value for my purpose. Besides, as is generally necessary in country situations, he must be boarded in his master's house, while he is not contented with the same stinted mode of daily living, either in kind or quantity of victual, as that which the family finds it necessary to be satisfied with; and this has a tendency to increase the general expenditure on the whole daily provision beyond the exact measure and means to which the family, if alone, might otherwise agree to stand restricted. All the journeymen I have had for thirty years have, in these respects, been much the same, by whatever difference in point of ability or character they were otherwise distinguishable. This did not perhaps so much arise out of the men's particular unreasonableness, as just from the general state of human nature brought into these particular narrow circumstances.

How often then, and since, have I felt vexed to find myself so bustled about the necessities of jobs in my own line, and other concernments of this paltry life's business, so frequently unproductive of the necessary return, and not seldom fallen into for the service or gratification of others more than for necessary profit to myself, to see times and seasons slipping past without ability to enjoy life calmly, advantageously, or reflectively, while many of the more independent or lucky of my neighbours were going comparatively idle, sauntering and trifling away the hours which would have been so precious to me, and employed after the way of my own heart, without any power of mind to enjoy life more rationally than a quadruped, either to conceive philosophically or describe what came under their eye, who were as stupid as owls, and who would have believed me mad had I talked to them of any idea beyond their silly taste or power of comprehension.

How often through life since have I been tempted to murmur on the reflection that I have never been able to get into circumstances where I could have the free scope of my own uninterrupted thoughts—

"these thoughts that wander through eternity"—but have been bound to sit in my little shop, amidst the mere casual din of half-idiot ignorance, to listen with patience, if not with seeming respect, to the small tittle-tattle of insignificant life, or the discordant noises which break the soft-imagined hum of nature in her musing solitude in house, field, or forest, the continual dupe of my own heart's sympathies, amidst the oft-repeated recitals of the rogueries, the robberies, the low-minded duplicities of the disingenuous amongst the common herd of my brethren of men; amidst all these disagreeables bound to labour late and early for the mere purpose of pleasing those so often unworthy of the sacrifice, as well as the attempt at supplying my family with the bread of landlord-taxed corn.

Yet now, after all, why repine for this? while in the bustle of life around I perceive the lords of hills and valleys, the heirs of hereditary entails, the tax-devourers of the life's blood and sweat of the working portion of the species, senseless of the import of more necessary occupation, galloping over all the comforts of rational existence, casting their proprietory eyes over their woods, streams, meads, groves, and hills of earth's surface ere they tumble in, bloated corpses, amidst the dark family vaults of stately rest, and leave what they call theirs to others.

CHAPTER XXVIII.

IT is curious to trace causes and consequences throughout a life-time. From a certain cause at one time this village seemed on the eve of coming into the list of deserted villages; and again, after having stood an aristocratic siege of some forty years, it was renewed and rebuilt under a further pressure and new phasis of the same cause by which it had been laid into the very throat of danger of desolation. The first cause was the then so common appetite of a big house to eat up all the neighbouring little ones, till in many cases considerable country villages had vanished from the surface, leaving only the neighbouring mansion, or villa, to mark out their ancient situation. The renovating cause, again, arose lately from the tendency of that "ruin's sweeping besom" to produce more the liberal sentiments, whence sprung the Reform Bill, to counteract the effects of which the same amassing spirit of the old party had to encourage a division of property for the purpose of overbalancing the Liberal majorities, and by arousing their own energies to this with vigour our village has again of late been greatly restored. Five or six years previously to our coming into it, however—just about the commencement of the French war, and the more improved system of husbandry—it stood a risk of ruin as great as ever it had done in the old English wars, when it was twice burnt down.

A Mr. Boswells, an Edinburgh lawyer, came at that time to the village for a country residence, and bought a cottage house, "a cottage of gentility," the only slated one then in the village, except the squire's mansion. This cottage stood out respectably on the height of the slope, some ninety or a hundred yards above the main village line, pleasantly situated, alike for view, convenience, and seclusion. He then set to work to purchase all around it, to form his garden and "double coach-house." In this he broke the main centre of the village, as Buonaparte used to break up the enemy's lines in war. Fourteen cottage hearthstones were removed by the hands of James Wyness, his gardener, and a garden with a high wall was built up around to occupy their place.

This had a threatening appearance, and might have led to sad consequences if the man had not, very providentially perhaps, been stinted in his means of further ruinous progress, for whenever in those days we saw a nabob pitch his country house at the skirt of a village, we considered it much the same as seeing a pair of large pikes find their way into a river pool, where the trouts, the aboriginals, would get into such a flurry of fright as to run down the open throats of the great intruders for mere shelter from their own terrors.

From some very good cause, however—some deficiency of *fin*, I suppose—this gentleman got extended little further in his day, and his very respectable family became dispersed into other situations. His place was then bought up by our more stationary squire of Raeburn, who not only delighted in it for the remainder of his days, but then began keenly to buy up all the rest of the village as any portion of it came near to the verge of the market, till, in about twelve or fifteen years, he had acquired one-half of the whole village and much of the lands around it.

Very luckily, however, Providence is often conservative in such cases. This squire was not in ability to buy the village at double and treble value, and then sweep it off into the desired level of wood and lawn, with a winding coach drive out through the site of it, as I was led to suppose had once been projected. No; he was under the necessity of letting the cottages for rent, and to produce this found it requisite to keep them a little in repair. Hence, cobblers, weavers, tailors, and other villagers were obliged to apply to him in all submission, that they might rent a cottage on his own proposed terms, and in this position I was placed at the time of which I am writing. I then rented the former gardener's cottage-house off him for four pounds some odds of yearly rent, which cottage had been so exceedingly damp when I entered it at the preceding Whitsunday term that the foot sank over the shoe-sole on the spot where our wooden box-beds behoved to be set up. I obtained a visitation of the squire in person on this point, which he made light of, saying, "Oh! you can just knock down four wooden pins in the ground floor there, and set your bed-feet on them; then it will do as nice as anything." I observed that the two very respectable tenants who had previously occupied it had both died of consumption on beds set on the same spot, and alleged the damp as the sufficient cause. "Oh! very true," says he; "but the pins will save all." So, finding it impossible to drive him off his pins, I could only bring him to an agreement to stooth the bed-length of the damp back wall, where the water was trickling down in droppings, for which stoothing I engaged to pay him full five per cent. in advance of rent; while he should allow me to drain the cottage all around the inside of the walls, and out to the street. This, in the way kings are said to do many things, he graciously permitted, and it cost me an extra thirty shillings of men's wages, besides a week's work of my own hands and a fortnight's stoppage of ordinary occupation. In this house, then, tolerably dry below, yet often so scanty in the thatch above that a flock of pigeons might have alighted on my garret floor, I sat for fourteen years, as busy as a bee, really and truly gaining family bread in despite of all back draught or hindrance, such as "the devil, the world, and the flesh," proving the full force of Burns's emphatic consideration of

> "Manhood's active might,
> Man then is useful to his kind,
> Supported is his right."

I found mine *thus* supported. But fourteen years, as a portion of a life-time, is easily named, though it is not so easy to relate or explain from recollection all the little interests, incidents, cares, anxieties, and casualties, with the hopes and fears, real or imaginary, that contrive to crowd themselves into such a term, in reality a great portion of an individual life-time. Since such might weary the hand to note from memory, and fatigue the ear to listen to, a few only of such points as may tend to throw a light on the general current of the interests of these years shall be here mentioned.

Kyle's lawsuit with my sister had now come to a final issue by a full judgment of the Court of Session in her favour, with expenses of suit, after a five years' summering and wintering of the matter; and he, falling a prey amongst a full pack of his creditors, was unable to resume it upon any new pretence. John Craw's last bill of expenses, laid against Kyle on the *action of reduction*, was £84. With this bill he first formally charged my sister, writing me that we must first immediately pay him that sum, while he would in the meantime be prosecuting Kyle for it on our account, as well as for the former damages, laid at £75, which damages must now, of consequence, be awarded by the Court on the issue of the main plea. I wrote him that as my sister's money was still under the unlifted arrestments, the holders were taking advantage of that, the more particularly as they were getting into fading circumstances; and as Kyle, like a run wild beast, was nearly down, and on the verge of falling to be torn up, he must now stick in on his agent for the expenses before any failure should be announced, as being by far the readiest way that he could finger the sum. This he knew as well as I did, but then I believed that he thought to strike at both sides, right and left, and beat out a double sum, which he could afterwards manage with his legal discretion. "You are out, old John," thinks I; "I can see the cloven foot as well as feel more knowing than you are likely to suspect of a simple country lad." I had not subjected my mother wit to the tedium of a protracted plea for nothing. John, however, could not contrive to hide from me that he had recovered his expenses on the very first application to Kyle's agent, and began to proceed with his motion for £75 of damages on the former plea of oppression and wrongous imprisonment, which had formerly been sustained by the Lord Ordinary, and only lay over till the issue of the then entered action of reduction, which was to determine it. "Now," thinks I, "old John, I must have a settlement with you, and get clear out of the mire of this troublesome anxiety." So off again I set on foot to Edinburgh, which thirty-seven miles on old-fashioned, rough roads was, even in good weather, a sufficient day's walk. I called on John, up eight stairs, next morning, where we had some pleasurable congratulations of each other, and on my proposal of a settlement up to the time being, John produced his *private* bill against my sister for such odds and ends of expenses as he said he could not lay in along with that charged against Kyle, which, in its own magnitude, he had had, he said, enough to do to pass with the auditor.

This private account was monstrous, though I have now forgotten the specific sum—something, I think, above three-fourths of his other figure; but remarkably neatly struck at some fifty shillings above the sums he had recollected of having receipted me as advancements throughout the course of the long plea. On receiving that account, I told him that I held receipts for £22 more than he had there given me credit for on his bill. This he startled at, and requested to see them, which I freely ventured, knowing that he durst not barefacedly abuse that confidence, with the £75 of forthcoming damages still hanging suspended before the vision of his mind's eye. Of course, not being able to deny it, he handed me back the receipts, wondering how he had neglected to give me credit in his books for these two remittances of £10 and £12. I made out a strong case of necessity for having the odd money for the payment I must make to Mr Aitkin, of the West Port, in the leather line, which he declined, first passively, then firmly; only in the end agreeing to give me credit on the account for it until we should see how the damages were recovered. While this was proceeding, his clerk came to his hand, motioning that he had made some neglect, and took the account to his own desk, adding some few pounds more to it in the name of something else, so the actual balance struck at last was £17 due me.

With this I left Mr. John Craw, resolved to get out of his further legal paws as soon as possible, having now begun to suspect that if John should succeed in getting hold of the damages I should likely find it impossible to draw any share of the money from him, as he would have some account foisted up, in the name of prosecutions for the recovery, equal to the whole sum, and likely that £17 over and above; or, what was even more dangerous still, there was then such a crackling noise of Kyle's actual breaking up, like river ice on a spring flood, that in case of the loss of these "damages" in that way, old John, having set his mind on the £75, might rake me up for even as much in the shape of expenses on a blank prosecution as a final clincher.

"Well," thinks I, "such money is not at all likely to find its way into my sister's pocket or mine on any account whatever, so it matters not to us a straw whether John Craw or Kyle's creditors get hold of that £75. I therefore agreed with William Aitkin, currier, West Port, that I should, as a payment of leather to him, draw a bill for £17 on John Craw, Esq., W.S., which he should present for John's acceptance so soon as I should be understood to have left Edinburgh, and in a day or two he informed me of John's acceptance of it, though very hesitatingly. I then wrote Mr. Craw that as Kyle was in a general break-up state, we should refrain from prosecuting the action of damages until I should gain some closer information of his affairs, and on no account whatever to proceed with such action until I should see it prudent to give him further orders. At this he was so dorted* that when William Aitkin produced the bill for payment he refused it, and would not come forth till prosecution had been gone through against him, up to the point of the arrival of the messenger to carry him to jail, when he pulled out a drawer, and paid the amount down before the messenger, plack and farthing.

Here ended my sister's long lawsuit, and my acquaintance with Tom Kyle, once Esq., and John Craw, W.S., up eight stairs, Parliament Square, Edinburgh.

I then felt like a Tweed salmon that had run hooked for a long spell, and at last got the tackle

* Thrown into the sulks. "E'en's ye like, Meg Dorts!" is a common exclamation, when a young woman gets sulky, or refuses to do something.

broke, with the stream on his nose, and the waters of a thousand clear fountains collected around him. How happy must a fish feel in such circumstances, as is often indicated by his bold dash out of the water, as much as to say, "I'll live and sport and play yet, in spite of you land-lubbers all, and the devil shall take your feather fly before I again be the ninny to look at such a cheat. I'll starve first!"

"No, no," thinks I; "no law after this for life, except irresistibly netted into it, and forced to repel in the shape of self-defence, and not even that if there's a broken mesh by which to escape out through."

However, I had by this time got some country credit in the way of managing such matters, while my wealthy opponent had lost all fame, along with all fortune. As for the commonest sense, he never was even suspected of the loss of that, having never seemed to possess it. I accordingly came to be consulted in some common country cases of quarrel, plea, or outcast, and in several instances since have succeeded wonderfully in a kind of under-current management of my neighbours through small law creeks and expensive squabblings. I always, however, began by retreating my clients, wherever I found they could be got back from the trap-mouth with any degree of safety and by any kind of least expensive honourable compromise of matters. And when they had got past the *Rubicon*, and were in for a fair barley-milling through any of our courts, then my business was to guide them artfully by the steps such as old Bunyan's "Christian" needed to observe as he waded "The Slough of Despond."

To lead a human animal through a law-plea with the skin safe on his back, and his claws left uncut, is a very dexterous performance in such cases, little short of Packman Wyllie's* mastership at the draught-board, as it beats even getting him out at an angle before he is souce over head and ears in for it. One plain instance is as good for example as a volume of *hum-ha* description of such cases; therefore, I will just relate the first in turn, and be done with such dry matters.

* The celebrated "Herd Laddie," in his time the best draught or "dambrod" player in the world.

CHAPTER XXIX.

A THRIVING weaver in our village, who went under the cognomen of "The Manufacturer," having fallen to a considerable clag of an Indian fortune, through his first wife and her children, whereby he had enough to keep him alive without further exertion for bread, got entangled under a prosecution for aiding and advising, as art and part, a tailor lad, who had been working some days in his house, to break into his neighbour's apple garden. The black charge libelled stated the case as clear as daylight, the act being done in broad sunshine. while the garden family were supposed to be all absent working in the harvest field. The proprietor's son, however, unexpectedly sallying out, caught the lad in the act of handing his hat full of apples through the hedge that separated their gardens into the hands of this "manufacturer," who was then followed into his own house with the booty. He had not even the presence of mind to throw it from him, or hold it out again to the lad; and several people, diverted in passing, witnessed the affair. He was legally held as principal offender, the lad, with some others like himself, being cited as witnesses against the accused as having been advised by him to the deed. And as the offence was alleged to be aggravated on his part by its having been understood to have been his usual practice throughout a course of years, the prosecution was held to stand strong against him. This man, like several other villagers, had been in the habit of coming into my shop occasionally to while away an hour, and also frequently to get me to write letters for him on any particular business. But now, after these summons, he would come and sit beside me the whole day, one day after another, in such a lag of spirits that it became pitiful and irksome to see him.

The libel appeared invulnerable and unanswerable, and when I asked him what sort of defence he thought of making, he said, "None; what defence can I make?" "It implies," says I, "a heavy fine, and even insinuates something further in the shape of banishment; but I daresay, knowing you have money, a fine will be their main mark." "It's not the fine," says he, "that vexes me, could I only get that paid privately and be done with it; but the loss of character, and the stigma attached to my name for life." "Well," says I, "what does Spence,* your friend, the lawyer, advise you?" "Oh! he says that nothing can be done now, as the prosecution is at the instance of the fiscal, while the proprietors, father and son, whom I had got soothed up on their own account, are both now cited as evidence against me. Mr. Kinghorne,† who assisted me in arranging terms of agreement with them—which arrangement now makes the worst feature in the affair—is also

* Mr. David Spence, writer, Melrose.
† Mr. Alexander Kinghorne, Crossflat, near St. Boswells.

summoned as a witness. In short, from the strength of the evidence altogether, and our inability to produce anything of an exculpatory nature, he says I am in for it, heels over head, and can only appeal to the leniency of the Court." "The leniency of mad dogs," says I, "is as rational to calculate on, and more chance with them, too, as you could then get a stick used, which is prohibited in Justice Courts." Nothing more could be thought of it, till within two nights of the Court-day morning, when a door-neighbour merchant's boy came in to me, desiring me to come over and speak with his father. On going into his room, "Come away," says he; "here's our friend "The Manufacturer" and me resolving to have a bottle of warm porter, and we think we would be nothing the worse o' you to take a share o't, and help us to

"'Forget our woes and cares,
And mind our griefs no more.'

But afore we begin to drink an' get fu', let us just take a bit look an' see if you an' I can possibly discern ony speck o' licht ava out through this black clud that's hangin' o'er our neighbour's brow, like a Quaker's hat, till I canna brook to see his face below the dark shadow o't." "Come, John," says I, "take a good drink, man, and cheer up; dinna look sae half-hanged-like at ony rate; ye're no killed yet; it's an age till Saturday. There'll may be a yirthquake come ere then, or the world itsel' may gang a-fire, and level matters a'thegither; and the oily Judges o' the yirth 'ill make a fat fry, to keep up the combustion on us puir, thin-chaftit skeletons, tax-drained dry till we'll hardly burn ava. We'll soon be that rarified and spiritualized, wi' ae Act o' Parliament after another,* that we'll can come through the general conflagration like scouthered salamanders, very little the lichter in respect to material diminution." "Come, come, man, gi'e o'er your mad flichts," says the merchant, "and let us set in soberly, and see if we canna contrive some kind o' scheme in regard to our friend's bad business: here's to ye. It's an unco idea to see a man standing judged and condemned, an' able to say neither 'buff nor stye'† in his ain defence. E'en Gilderoy an' Macpherson rantit at the gallows foot! Ye've had a sort ado amang lawyers an' papers an' sic-like lately; can ye no write up some rigmarole o' some sort o' stuff or other for him in the shape o' self-defence, if it should be even the greatest havers under the cluds. Onything 'll be better than to just stand wi' a shut mouth, waiting 'justice o' peace' condemnation, like a dumb animal." "Od, man, I can see nae licht out through the subjec'; not a single hair to make a tether o'. I've thought o't several times, but John has just got himsel' woven into the meshes o' law, like a fish into a cairn net, as if he had done it on purpose, till the never a hole's left big enough to draw him out through at. A gun bullet beats a' for pushin' through these things, legal net-works, prison doors, and sic-like. It's sae round and smooth, and hasna knees an' elbows, joints an' feet, like a gomeril falla, to prevent its free passage out through a'thegither." "Come," says he, "try novelty wi' them; I've seen ye dab at poetry; wad something o' that kind no be better than naething,

---

* Our gentry's infernal Corn-Law was then in Parliamentary projection, whereby the millions were kept hungry till its repeal.

† "Oxhide nor hogskin"—proverbial for "neither one thing nor another."

even something like the dyin' speech o' Johnnie Armstrong? Johnnie wadna ha'e been famous till now gin it hadna been his bold, dyin' speech, threatenin' future vengeance in the King's teeth, wi' the rape drawn o'er his head—which vengeance was even perpetrated by his son lang after, when he brunt down the Canongate o' Edinburgh. Od, man, try to make up some sort o' story for John, either to speechify or read o'er in reply to that ugly black libel." "My good neighbour, ye see these flichts o' free thought will not do in what's termed our Justice Courts. Law papers and poetry are as unlike ane another as a mole's like a lark, though they both fend upon ae fare. The 'moudie' is aye riddlin' below grund, grubbin' an' huntin' worms i' the dark everlastingly; while the laverock picks what offers on the surface, an' then, towerin' into the blue of heaven, showers a flood of music superior to onything I have ever yet sensibly heard in the spheres. But, John, after consideration of that black libel, I see only just ae thing micht be done, and, though it winna save ye, yet it's aye something in the way o' showing fence, ye understand; far better than nae resistance at a', which would just be taken for a blank confession now, as the matter can be so clearly proven by half a dozen of these witnesses that they have already cited. A blank denial will do at no rate, and ye know it would be perfectly ridiculous to plead what would be a very natural plea of a lad to his father, 'use and wont,' which, though it would be the truest plea in this case, would be a very unjust one, while it would exasperate beyond all imagination of bounds. Well, as you have no real plea, the next best face you can put upon the matter, by the way of saying something in defence, is to find some plausible objections to the fiscal's general and particular allegations. He states in the libel that he was impelled to the prosecution, through the instigation of some of the respectable of your near neighbours. Now, if you will go up to-morrow to Spence, your chief man of business, and request him to write out for you on the top of a sheet of paper (for it will do better in his hand-writing than mine) something to this purpose—

'We, the inhabitants of the village of St. Boswell's, near neighbours of J—— T——, have long known him to have been an industrious, peaceable, quiet, and obliging good neighbour, and have never known anything of a flagrant nature to his character, &c.'

Spence knows what to say better than we can tell him; only warn him against anything too strongly favourable—I mean that he must not make you out a very particular saint. It must be as shortly expressed as possible; and bring it in the evening, and I'll try to get it signed. It may do good for you without the risk of doing ill." So, without proposing anything further, home I went, and spread a sheet of paper on my knee-board, determined to blot it in some attempt at a defence for the poor culprit, thinking that if I should not succeed somewhat to my own satisfaction nobody should hear of it.

"There are two ways, now," thinks I, "of telling the same story, all the world over; and if I can only invert these main points of charge as having proceeded from a different motive, I may at least interest the feelings or confuse the judgment of these same judges, which will be two-thirds of a good point gained, at anyrate." So to work I went to make the main motives appear point blank the reverse to those alleged in the libel. I despised style, and chiefly aimed at simple, modest effect, and got all my most formidable points surmounted, and mountains of difficulty levelled, before I was well aware of having got into the heart of my story. I next just supposed myself the judge, who should previously know nothing of the matter; then read, as if hearing, over for the first time, the black libel charge; then the simple, and apparently unvarnished, answer; when, believing I had hit it, I turned into bed for the night. Next day I wrote out a clean copy in a plain school-boy hand, that it should not be spoilt in the reading. And John, arriving in the evening with Spence's copy of certificate of general character, I marched through the village, enlisting all such characters as I supposed the Justices might possibly know by name, and approve of as conscientious individuals; represented the matter to them as such a pity that a neighbour should be so broken down with a kind of combination against him for such a trifle of malversation; that if he had really and truly aided and encouraged the lad in such an action, which was a highly disputable case, he would now be cured of ever committing or countenancing such like again; asking who had not inadvertently, from our old grand-lady-mother downwards, some time or other, in the course of a life-time, done some small thing or other, and often in the apple line particularly, that the law and one's neighbours might make a noise about, and which we ourselves might seriously regret; that, in short, those who would not sign this merely general character might likely be suspected as the persons who had given the information to the fiscal. The idea of this last imputation drew them to the pen at once, till I got all I asked to sign it, including the very proprietor of the garden, who yielded to my very eager solicitation from the more humane feelings of his nature, contrary, as he said, to the strict justice of his mind. There were forty-two signatures in all. "I've the number of the 'Highland Watch,'" thinks I, "the 42d Regiment of Foot, who are said to beat anything at fair fighting. It's a good omen; I'll not alter the number by increasing it even by one."

Next morning blew a snow-storm that prevented the Justices assembling to hold a court; so our neighbour gave in his signed certificate of public character to the fiscal, who, on sight of the forty-two, promised to withdraw his prosecution before next court day, if at all possible, which gave great relief for a week or two, until the citations were again served for the next monthly court, when again his pains returned. At last the day arrived, when I added just a further observation or two to my original paper of defence, in the same way as we might add a codicil to a will, and resolved to go, *incog.*, and witness the effect. I gave him my last verbal instructions by the way—thus, "When you are called up, and this libel is read out against you, you will next be asked for your confession or denial. Then observe to them that as you are not accustomed to address gentlemen in the way of a speech, you had taken the precaution to have written out what you had got to say, which you trust may throw some more clear light on the matter; and if it have the desired effect, and you happen to get clear off, make no demur about payment of the clerk's already incurred expenses, which will be but comparatively trifling; pass that point over lightly, as if you did not stand up about trifles. But on the other side, if, disregarding your statement, they proceed to a long leash of proof, and have you condemned, then throw down a shilling on the table, and tell them that you suspend the case to a Court of Law, and you may do this the more firmly, as I am now convinced that in a Court of Law you could baffle them, with about as little expense as they are at present warranted to affix as a fine in the Justice Courts, the extent of which I understand to be forty pounds. In this case it would then throw the matter out of present agitation in our locality, you could take your breath more freely, and at the worst you would not in the end perhaps be over half the money in expense that you averred your willingness to throw in the merchant's fire the other night when your horrors were at their height, supposing that hundred pounds would set that matter altogether to quiet rest. Now, mind your cue on these points." And he did so remarkably well, as it turned out to be settled on the point of my first proposition, where he happened to have the least to do; for when the Court was set, and he was called—the room being crowded to excess with persons in a state of almost breathless curiosity—and the black libel read over by the clerk, accusing him of having advised, aided, abetted, and assisted the lad in the case, and advised others in similar cases, which could be proved by present witnesses, to the commission of such a flagrant theft and breach of the peace, and that good cause could not be shown why a very heavy judgment of fine, imprisonment, or worse should not be passed upon him, and being asked what he had to say in answer to this charge, he did exactly as I had advised him, to the very letter indeed. My paper was then handed to the clerk, and read distinctly aloud, to my private satisfaction. Standing in the throng of the crowded room, I was then observing the effect upon faces. The same faces which had been rounded into something approaching to a smile of gratification when the case of charge was being maintained were now gradually lengthening into oval as the clerk read on in the defence; and exactly the reverse in others, just as they happened to be affected to the individual, or felt facts or arguments agreeable to their natural propensities. This reversal of various countenances I took as an excellent sign; and by the tone of the clerk's voice, which was getting more animated as he went on, and by one of the leading Justices giving a "hem," in the way of clearing his throat, I premised that their minds were gradually falling into the wake of my sail. His defence ran in these words:—

"Honourable Gentlemen,—Though innocent of the charge here libelled against me, yet from a complication of circumstances, mostly simple in themselves, I believe I shall feel as much difficulty in the attempt to clear myself before your honours as though I really were guilty as alleged. It seems to me, from the beginning of this affair to the present moment, as if some evil genius had tortured his invention to work me a mischief, being led into a connection with the matter in not only a simple manner, but in even an attempt to prevent in another the crime laid to my own charge. I beg leave to make to your honours a short, unvarnished statement of the affair. T—— T——, apprentice to W—— H——, tailor in St Boswell's, being working in my house one day in harvest last, amidst other boyish talk, observed, in a forward and thoughtless-like manner, that, as John Paton's family were all out in the harvest field, he believed there could be little danger in his slipping into their garden and taking a few apples. I conceived, from the open manner in which he communicated his intention, that he was not serious; at least, that he had no design of putting his proposal into immediate execution; and hastily (I believe rather too inattentively) replied simply that Paton would 'dress' him properly if he did. I took no further thought of what had passed, until a short time afterwards, missing him out of the house, it struck me that perhaps he really might have gone into the garden. I then immediately went out at the back-door into my own garden, which is separated from John Paton's by only an open old hedge, when the first object that caught my eye was the lad running to the hedge with his hat in his hand full of apples, pursued by the junior John Paton, who, following hard, seemed in a high passion. The lad's awkward predicament first engaged my attention, when I hastily met him and relieved him of the hat, while he made his way through the hedge. John Paton immediately blamed me as an accomplice, from the circumstance of my seeming to take the lad's part, and from an instantaneous conviction that John must verily, and very naturally, think so, I, for the moment, really felt uneasy. Amidst a storm of threatenings he vowed to have me made an example of. Though I did not in the main regard this threat, I was yet sorry he should go away in the presence of some people then gathering around us without being convinced of the real nature of the affair, and of my innocence, which, however, he did. Shortly afterwards I called upon Mr. Kinghorne, and communicated the matter to him, when he advised me that rather than let it get abroad into the mouths of the country, and be transformed into a hundred different shapes, it would, he thought, be much better to endeavour to come to an agreement with John Paton on any, or the easiest, terms possible. I therefore requested Mr. Kinghorne to accompany me to Mr. French's house in the evening, where we sent for both John Paton and his father, when I proposed to pay for any damage he could say the lad had done. This he genteelly declined to accept, saying that the damage was quite an immaterial consideration, only he felt exasperated that I should have been guilty of aiding the lad in such a design, which he was so clearly positive I had done. I desired that, though I had failed to convince him of the innocence of my movements, yet I hoped he would suppress the whole matter, as my ill-wishers (as every person had some) would doubtless put the matter in the very worst light, to my disadvantage. To this he acceded, and we have since been on the same door-neighbour terms as we ever formerly were accustomed to be. The matter, however, got noised abroad, and my enemies, whoever they are, have used it in even a worse way than I then feared, combining a number of trifling words and little incidents whereof to form the present charge. And whether by the instigation of those enemies, or simply from the idea of clearing himself in the public eye, the lad T——, who, I understand, is also cited here as a kind of 'king's evidence' against me, has been publicly averring that I advised him to the act, and aided him therein. From similar reports which I daily hear, though not here worth mention, I am thoroughly convinced that the mass of such proof as here cited, along with Mr. Kinghorne, to prove my anxiety for that prior agreement with Paton, will, in all probability, tend to make me *appear* really guilty as libelled. As it is a concern hateful to think on, it is, of course, my eager wish to put it to immediate silence. I therefore humbly pray that the honourable gentlemen on the bench, after having attentively considered the above plain, honest statement, will proceed to do so immediately, without any tedious arraignment of useless proof, or putting themselves to any further unnecessary delay whatever. I shall trouble your honours with only one brief argument in my own favour, which is this:— Had I ever, at any time, designed to have taken fruit from John Paton's garden, I certainly could have had numberless opportunities of so doing, without even the knowledge, far less the aid, of any person, and it is not at all likely that I should have employed a garrulous boy as an accomplice, where so much attention to secrecy would have been necessary.

"I am, with due respect to the honourable Justices present, their most obedient, humble servant,

(Signed)   "J—— T——.

"*January*, 1815.

"*P.S.*—The honourable Justices will perceive by the date that the preceding was prepared for last month's Court-day, when, in consequence of a certificate which was presented to Mr. David Sinclair, the procurator-fiscal, from the inhabitants of St. Boswell's, my near neighbours, disclaiming their having desired this prosecution, as the libel falsely sets forth, and desiring him to drop the process, I was verbally assured by him that the matter was put to rest. Since that time, however, though it has been renewed, contrary to my expectation, it has assumed for me a more favourable appearance, since it is now in my power, should the lad T—— persist in his intention of clearing himself, to my prejudice, to refute his evidence in the clearest manner.

(Signed)   "J—— T——.

"*February*, 1815."

The letter of character formerly lodged with the fiscal was then called for by the Justices, and read over, with the names of the subscribers to it. Here the No. 42 were again, as usual, successful. And then the leading Justice took speech in hand, addressing the panel to this purpose—that, when he saw a man of his sedate and respectable appearance stand up under such an imputation, he felt really vexed and sorry, as, he believed, did all his friends on the bench present; and he must say he was in proportion as glad to have heard him clear himself, by means the most simple and efficacious; that whether Mr. T—— himself, or some friend for him, had drawn up that paper he did not know or inquire, but it did him and the writer alike credit. It was not done by a lawyer—of that he was certain—but so much the better: it was like a child's tale, bearing the marks of ingenuous simplicity and truth. For, suppose the libel were all proven as alleged and drawn up, still the plain statement in that explanation, as showing the misconceptions, from the appearance of the actions, put it out of their power to prove or suppose guilt; that he had sat in one Court or other for about forty years, and he must say that he had never heard a defence conducted in that manner, nor with that particular effect. And then they had it backed up by a certificate of general good character, signed by a most respectable number of this man's nearest neighbours. (No number like 42, thinks I again: it must beat all, sure enough. I'll have my trout-fishing wheel exactly 42 yards length next summer, and clear out the water.) He knew all or most of the names, all respectable villagers, mostly heads of families. He must now ask the fiscal how he came to persist in this prosecution after having, a month ago, received that attestation of the major and most respectable portion of the villagers of St. Boswell's disclaiming their connection with that information or approval of the prosecution? Mr. Sinclair said that he was most respectably instructed to do so in his official capacity. The Justice did not doubt that; but he must know by whom, the more particularly now, as it would leave perhaps some of the signers of that certificate under some undue suspicion, as out of that list it could not be easy to suppose who of Mr. T——'s "near neighbours" it might possibly be else. Mr. Sinclair still seemed very unwilling to state names as his informants, till by severe remonstrance, and even some little threatening, he felt impelled to it, when at last he said, "If I must tell, I must. It was the Justice of the Peace for their own parish." The Justices nodded assent, and made no further remarks, while Mr. T—— was set clear at the bar.

Here again, thought I, everybody is getting righted, whilst I have no doubt that I have, very unwittingly, been getting myself into a new trouble. The Justice of Peace for our parish, who, it seems, has urged that prosecution—for the love of justice!—may yet perhaps be partly influenced by another feeling instigating him in the case. The cause of this prosecution may be in J—— T—— and his brother A—— confronting and pulling him up at every public sale of small properties in and about the village, always aiming to purchase and secure a house for themselves, or some spot of property on which to rear one, even at a high contended price, thus raising the price of each to him, who, it seems, *will* have them all. At that late sale of Miss Mercer's of five or six separate patches of village properties by public roup, I noted that the squire had better have bribed these two brothers, at a hundred pounds a-piece, to have lain a-bed all that day; and he would have been a saver of a hundred and one upon the purchase of the whole day's sale. This is vexing to a man of might. Lords and lions are much the same in one respect— they don't like lesser animals to cross their path. Should this interference of mine, then, in favour of this man, reach his ear—as, from village clatter, of course, it must—I fear that, being my landlord, I may be driven to seek shelter in some other village, as I see no cottage at all likely to be let in St. Boswell's of which he is not become the proprietor. Well, I cannot help it now, and indeed it is recreant to think that I would if I could. Yes, I'll still follow the bent of my inclination, come what may; so, should I see a man drowning, I'll try to help him out, though all the world should cry, Let him go; he is a devil. These thoughts were privately traversing my mind as a party of us were leaving the Courtroom, and retiring to seek a necessary refreshment of John Merton's ale at the Fox Inn* before we should walk home together.

In the evening we landed in at our door-neighbour merchant's public, where our friend "The Manufacturer" figured as quite another man than he had been in the morning, now as bright as a new-lighted lantern. And indeed his causes of brightening were increasing in all points of his particular interests, as, besides getting out of this scrape, he was also getting matters righted in another grand concern in which he had been for some time engaged. One of these was this: he, and Spence, his lawyer and banker, had advanced the needful to carry Willie Herring, then farmer of Fens, through with his farming improvements, under a high rent, by which he had been sinking, and now they were getting matters brought to an issue, by which themselves, at least, were coming to be well paid. As for Herring, of course, he

---

* Johnnie Merton was long famous for his pies and porter. His threepenny mutton pies were delicious.

was got into salt, and had no escape from being picked to the bones by somebody. My neighbour, the merchant, was also now going to recover some £40 of a debt, which he had been on the point of losing should Willie Herring have been left to fall under the risk of his extra improvements in husbandry and the aristocratic law of hypothec. Here had been a complication of risks all getting righted. I had also made a few pairs of shoes for Herring and his family under the verbal order of "The Manufacturer," and about this time I had been almost daily or weekly writing letters, &c., for him to Spence and others relative to Herring's and others' affairs. Therefore, while over our refreshing cup of ale that evening "all was going merry as a marriage bell," our landlady, the mistress of the house, observed—"You are all getting very right but poor John Younger; he is to be the only sufferer here. I can see he will lose his house through his interference, which has set you all right to-day, and I do not see another lodging for him in the village. We shall likewise lose a good neighbour." "We'll surely get a house for John Younger some way or other," said "The Manufacturer;" "by the course of nature old Tommie Sibbald can hardly be supposed to see Whitsunday; his house will be in the market to sell, or to let at least, and Raeburn will give bigger prices than he has thought of yet if I don't get a house for John Younger by hook or by crook, in one shape or another." His son-in-law, who was seated next me, gave me an elbow touch, and whispered, "My good-father* may likely forget what he is saying, but we

---

* "Good-father," Scotch for father-in-law.

cannot easily a' forget." "I'm obliged by your good intentions, Andrew," said I; "but it is something like the old story of crying *fyshoo* to an egg; much will come and go before Whitsunday. I shan't die in the meantime under the terror of probabilities, which are trifling in comparison with the main business of life."

Well, we retreated all to our own firesides, went on with our usual exercitations, of the doggerel daytale of common existence, till in a week or so came Candlemas day, the 2d of February, the squire's rent day, when his agent came to draw his rents and arrange the terms of sitting and flitting amongst his cottars for the ensuing year, when I found myself turned out of the list of his small tenants, and must, of course, look out for a shelter elsewhere.

The "Manufacturer," now so entirely relieved from all awkward and spirit-cramping circumstances, had got bright upon outward airings, and now, daring to go even within sight of the Tweed, free of the nervous terrors which he formerly said had alarmed him on casually seeing the river, so tempting for a perplexed fellow in which to cool and end his hot-burning cares, had forgotten to pay a visit to my old stall for some ten days or a fortnight. At last, one evening, while I was sitting tugging and drawing before the candle, in he dropt, quite lively, with his hat set half an inch higher on his brow than he had worn it the previous month. "How are ye the night, John Younger?" said he. "Oh! much as usual, John," replied I; "you're well, I hope?" "I'm in my ordinary way," said he. "What's the news o' the day, man?" I asked. "Oh! naething extraordinary that I hear o'," rejoined John. "Well, John, no news is good news," I observed, "and I cannot tell how much I am obliged to the wise inventors of these old proverbs; they are so useful in our Scotch conversations." "I'm aye due you for thae shoon yet," he next remarked; "I must have ye paid now. What's the price o' them?" "Just the old price, John," I informed him. "What's that?" he queried. "Ten shillings," I answered: "they're just like penny pies; they may alter a little yearly in shape or fashion, agreeably to the market; but they're aye the auld penny." "But ye're surely dearer than ye used to be? I never paid ye ten shillings before!" "Ye certainly never paid me less, John, since we were first acquainted, nor anybody else, for the same sort of plain, good shoes." "But ye're dearer than other shoemakers; for I see bigger shoes brought from a' the towns around us for 9s or 9s 6d at most, and I really grudge to pay mair than value." "Those who want them cheaper, John, will just have to go to these sale towns and buy them; for my customers look for good shoes, in which they can walk a twelvemonth every day at least, and the best of all work and material is required to produce shoes of that description. Give them worse even at a cheaper rate, and I would soon lose their favour and custom; therefore I may work my heart out before I can make a penny above the strictest point of day and way. I shall not leave a fortune of five pounds to my heirs at the end of a forty years' life's lease on my present terms; therefore to reduce the price is out of the question with me." "Well, John Younger, I may pay ye the ten shillings this time; but it will really be the last time ever I'll pay as much for a pair of shoes, I must just tell ye plainly." "Well, John, ye can take ye're will about the next pair you may need; but I'll not abate sixpence on the price of these to secure your custom to the end of our life-time." So he told down the ten shillings, which I lifted, and went on with my work. He sat silent for some minutes, and then resumed thus:— "By-the-bye, John Younger, I'm perhaps rather hard on ye, a' things considered; for, to-be-sure, I've been often very muckle obliged to ye—very often, very muckle. I should not have said so much about an odd sixpence on the price of these shoes after a'; for ye make them aye good, and I daresay ye might have won the price of several pairs in the time I have taken ye up from your work ae way and another." "But I suppose ye'll no need to take me up much mair now, John, for ye seem to have got yourself tolerably well righted. Ye have got Willie Herring's affairs drawn into a focus, rather profitable for Spence and you than otherwise; and you're getting our neighbour the merchant his forty pounds from the funds. As ye have taken Herring's affairs fully in tow, will there be any chance of my getting payment amang ye for the shoes that ye once advised me that there was no risk in making for him and his family?" "'Deed, I cannot say that I see ony way that ye're to get payment, as he has no power of anything himsel'; and before Spence get our affairs wi' Herring settled up, I fear it will be a' poison that'll be o'er the plug* wi' him." "Well, John,

* A pin screwed into the wooden quaich or bicker out of which our forefathers quaffed their liquor, to mark the exact nett depth to which the vessel should be filled, and which a niggardly host or hostess would not exceed.

I'm certainly nothing obliged to you for that loss, at anyrate; for I suppose it would be more trouble than a' the money's worth to swear you in as cautioner —which could be done, as I would really not have made them but for your voluntary assurance of safety, amounting in effect to your order. However, I think I'll just do best to try and put up with the losses I have had, and beware of getting into new ones. This I can do upon your present example of drawing in, and taking care of new scrapes for the future. I shall not, however, attempt to do business exactly upon your present plan of throwing yourself out of obligation by making a sham pretence of supposing yourself over-charged a sixpence on your yearly pair of shoes. You might have saved yourself the degradation of that barefaced quibble as a means of escapement from your imaginary obligations to me, as I should never have put you to the necessity of any acknowledgment whatever." He sat for a minute or two as if recovering his sensibility from a slight shock of electricity; then opening his mouth again to speak: "John Younger, I never thought you had been the man you are!" says he, with a look of consciousness of my having caught him in the quick of the very idea on which he was studiously acting. "And what have you always taken me for?" says I—"for a mere automaton, as a horse in a mill could hardly be supposed to have moved so long round and round to the crack of a clown-driver's whip without some sort of supposition of what he might be grinding. Could you, for years past, suppose it possible for me to write letters for you on various intricate points of business, when you often even failed in language to explain to me what in the world you wished to be at. How, then, could you suppose that I had not perception to see through yourself, as well as your concernments? John, I have long known the character and tendency of your mind and disposition, better perhaps than you have known it yourself; and, to convince you, I'll just now explain where you are at present. You feel you have got out of your late troubles, and all seems laid to rest, and you are now determined to take exceeding good care of yourself for the future. This is all, so far, very well. But then you further think that I will be considering you so much in my obligation as to bind you to a late voluntary offer of somehow endeavouring to find me a house to live in should I be thrown out on your account. Now, when I actually am so thrown out, and after at least a week's consideration, you have fallen upon this little *very cunning* plan of finding fault with the price of these shoes, by way of getting as plausible a break-off with me as possible. Now, John, in place of contriving thus to get even below yourself, which is an ugly depth surely, you had nothing to contrive in regard to me but to have withheld yourself, and withdrawn your visits to me, as you have been doing on a small scale of late, which I could always have dispensed with, as I have a hundred and fifty sources of amusement without talking with anybody. However, you have, in this instance, shown yourself little worse than I always have suspected of you. Man, you are dull in learning that 'honesty is the best policy.' To be sure, a man is not blamable for the weakness of his mind, though he certainly is for the immorality of it. John, you may go rest in perfect security of any further claim of obligation I hold on you; and, if you still should ever want any help in which I can assist you *honestly*, I shall still be willing to do it on the principle on which I have done *all* hitherto, merely to gratify my own disposition, without any hope or prospect of anything, even gratitude, in return." We parted thus, so and so, and have seldom met since.

CHAPTER XXX.

NOTWITHSTANDING the diversity of the human character, we are apt, in calculating on our own feelings in particular cases, to suppose much the same of all others generally, and are often thus led to err, and to vex ourselves in vain, by feeling for others in a manner in which they are unable to feel for themselves. This is what we may call the acute sympathy of human feeling. In the last related case I could not help being more vexed for J—— T—— than I am convinced he was for both himself and me taken together. But there is something so woeful in perceiving, in such casual cases, the insensibility of a human mind, not to call it, what it perhaps more properly is, the *depravity*, that the degree of indignation which it very naturally excites is overmastered by the reflection on the poverty of the mind in which such sentiments can find nourishment to the maintenance of their existence. But, feel as I might, there seemed to be no proper case made out upon which anybody could ground a feeling for me; and yet I felt puzzled, as much perhaps as Burns's field mouse when she was turned out of her winter nest by the plough in cold November.

Our village cottages were at the time so fully occupied that no house of any description was left in it to rent, except those belonging to the Squire, which comprised about one-half of the whole. It appeared very inconvenient for me to leave the village, in consideration of the state of my small business and other affairs at the time, although I could easily have overcome the feeling of any particular local attachment, as well as the chagrin natural to being so forced out. But in walking out one evening in the drift of a snow-storm, I came in contact with William Hunter, then proprietor of some separate houses in the village, who happened to mention the subject, when he immediately proposed to sell me a little old bad cottage-house of his, that stood wedged in crosswise, with its gable-end to the street, and a stripe of garden running up to the north. The old, ill-thatched rickle of a house itself was of little other value than for the spot of ground on which it stood; but to get hold of a spot of ground on which to form a footing for self-defence against what might have been not improperly termed the rural invasion of aristocracy, had become with me a matter of nearest interest. I thought I might extend that old *cruive* of a *houselet* back lengthwise by an addition at the back-end, repairing up at the same time, or rebuilding anew, the old to suit my purpose tolerably well; and by borrowing the money to do the whole, I should still be within my means of a rent supposed to be somewhere about six or seven pounds a year. Well, after I had run over all these considerations in my mind, in less time than I can here note the recollection, I requested Will. to state what he asked for it, privately resolving to be at the end of my solicitude by striking a bargain at once. "Come in to Will. Thomson's, at the Green here," says he, "and we will try to drive a bargain." "Well," says I, "do not name the business in Thomson's before any person who may happen to be there, and after a glass I'll accompany you on your way home to Longnewton, and agree, if you are at all reasonable with the price." On going in, however, here sat half-a-dozen villagers, who handed us each a glass of whisky before we had even got seated. Will. swallowed his at a gulp, and with his returning breath says, "Come, sit down, Younger, and let us try a bargain about that house; I wish to sell it off, as it does not lie in with my other property." So, the subject thus started, they all got vociferous in the clamour for a bargain off *loof*.* I immediately then perceived that I must strike the iron hot, since it might not be so easily bought on the Monday following, as the Squire would likely by that time have got note of the intention, and come between me and it. "Now, not to make a tedious long *haigle* about the business, Will.," says I, "where lies your figure at the lowest point?" "Well," says he, "property is higher now than when Sandy Adamson bid me thirty-nine pounds for it, when I would not lower it a single shilling below fifty, nor ever will." "Well," thinks I, "even ten pounds above the true value in buying a house once in a life-time is a consideration I shall soon get over, in comparison with the vexatious botheration my father and myself have been so often in, fitting up other people's old houses, and

* Off-hand, immediately.

being obliged to leave them so often and so soon again." Still, I made it seem that I hesitated a little, because I knew he was a kind of cow-dealer, and might be ready to start back should I seem to strike him too eagerly. However, they all insisted that I should close with him, while I consented somewhat hesitatingly. David Ross, the baker, Will.'s nephew, —who, by-the-bye, was as much my friend at heart as he was his uncle's—pulled out a shilling with which he insisted that I should *arle* the bargain. I then laid down the premises at length, by stating that he should produce titles so good as to give me indisputable possession, and that by the Saturday of next week, which day he would come down in the morning, and we should go up to Melrose together, and have the matter legally confirmed, and that punctuality in this should stand a term of our present bargain. This agreed, we drank *helter-skelter*, till Will., the old laird, got mortal *fou*, and I was saluted as laird out and out, and so we parted.

Next day, Andrew Crammond, mason, in our village, looked into my shop, and, in speaking over the premises of our bargain, observed that I could not get the paltry house enlarged, from a circumstance of which I had not been aware—namely, that one-half of the stripe of garden did not belong to Hunter, but to another person, who had formerly left the country, and that it lay claimed only by such or such people as next nearest heirs to the departed, but without any title on which to sell it; that this unfortunately formed the middle half of the whole of what I had supposed the garden I was purchasing, lying close to the north gable-end; that the cottage could not therefore be made up to suit me at all, being in its present state only half-size, with no room either way to get it extended a single inch; and that, nearly related as he stood to Will. Hunter, he could not hesitate in stating what he saw quite clearly, that Will. had taken me in by a misstatement of facts generally, and particularly of what Sandy Adamson had once bid him for it. I then went and asked Adamson about the matter, when he told me that as the thing lay on with his premises he had once bid Will. Hunter £29 for it, on which occasion they tampered and parted about a pound, as Hunter would not break it from £30. I then found I was completely taken in, though, in my anxiety, I would not have regarded the money, but that the subject, bounded as it was, was completely unfit for my purpose.

Hunter did not come down, however, for some eight days beyond his stipulated time to go to Melrose, agreeably to our appointment. In the interim, I went one evening up to Longnewton to state all my disappointments to him, when I found him quite in an uncompromising mood, saying that if I had not known the exact bounds and relations of the premises I should previously have informed myself, and that I must abide by it now, as "bargain was bargain," &c.

I found no more reason or consideration from him than might have been expected from an idiot, while old Henry Cochrane, late farmer of Merrick, reduced to day labour, and sitting by the evening fire, as being Will. Hunter's lodger, tauntingly observed to me that he made many a bad bargain in his life-time, but had never flinched from one. "You never had the common-sense to flinch, Henry," says I; "I can get better examples than you anywhere." So, just stating that I would not now take the subject unless compelled, I left them quietly.

On a morning shortly after, Hunter called in, asking me to go to Melrose and have the writings examined, and the deed of conveyance ordered, when I remonstrated again with him to no purpose, but declined to budge a foot. Off he set by himself, and paid two separate lawyers five shillings a-piece for advice as to whether he could draw me up, when they both agreed in opinion that, everything considered, he could not bind me to implement a bargain so loosely entered into, and so slightly confirmed at the time.

Meanwhile, learning that the house I was still living in was not yet let, I formed a curious notion of going to see the Squire, in which case I might either have matters better explained or get more fun out of it. When announced to him as on business, I was admitted to an audience, when the first offset was: "Well, John, I hear you have made yourself a laird in the village." "I can hardly say so yet, sir," said I, "although I have the thing in that position that I can either be a laird to-morrow night or not, just as I find it will best suit me. I have still a power of rejection of agreement with Will. Hunter, and finding I am buying at a present disadvantage I would rather desire to continue to be your tenant as I now am than be a poor laird for myself. I have just come to say that if you are agreeable to let me remain in my present *sheddin'* on reasonable terms I will let Will. Hunter keep his old premises, and have no more to do with them. If not, I shall not now be obliged to leave the village, at any rate. And moreover, Mr. Scott, I cannot discover what fault you can possibly find with me as a tenant. I'm sure I take daily care to give offence to no man knowingly, and wish to do all the civility I can to every one: why, then, should you have any dislike to me?" "Bless me, John, I don't dislike you; only I sometimes think that you trouble yourself too much with people who would not give the toss-up of a straw to serve you in turn." "Faith, it's true; you have hit it, sir. But then I can never stop to measure matters so neatly and knowingly; and indeed, if we were to regulate our charity by the exact points of measure for measure, doing no good but for seen good again, we should be no better than black savages who eat one another, and kirks and Christianity might be given up amongst us. But to come to the point at once, sir. I rather suspect that you are particularly alluding to my taking some thankless trouble in endeavouring to get J—— T—— off *hale scart* from that apple-garden concern. Now, before you think further on it, please, sir, just allow me to tell you my reasons for meddling with that affair. In the first place, here was the man got into a very stupid scrape —a low, dirty business, of course—and there he came in, and sat beside me at my work for days and weeks together, without being able even to converse, till I began to dread that he was growing so nervous as to perhaps lose his senses; and I got *wae* for him, and French, ye ken, who is a very good sort of neighbour, got sorry for him too; and then there was another sma' consideration—two of my wife's brothers had been weaver apprentices with John, and there had always been a sort of good, plain, open understanding kept up between their families; and so I thought that if he even had been dipping just a little into that stupid apple-tart concern, he had, for some months past, been paying penalty enough for it in the coin of heart's vexation. And ye ken, sir, ane canna bide to see a poor, vexed, repentant mortal broken down a'thegether, if there's a possibility to help him ava." "Faith, that's verra true," said he; "I met him in the baker's house one day, where I dropt in for change of a note, and I says, 'John, what ails ye? ye're looking verra ill.' He hummered and said something, I forgot what. 'You should take care of yourself, John,' says I, 'and take some walks out about, and see the hunt sometimes.' I was sorry for him; he looked as if he was gain' *dementit*. 'Cheer up,' says I, 'John, man, and dinna let yoursel' a' down to staps that gate.' It's surely verra right to help ilk ither a' we can when we see our neighbours in sic *deleeries*." "Ye've just hit my notion o' the matter, sir, and what I did in the way of help for J—— T—— was nae mair than what I think ony neighbour should be aye ready to do for another, whatever thanks he may chance to get." "Well," says he, "ye may, if ye like, just continue in your house as ye have been." "Thank you, sir," says I, "and I hope we're going to have better weather now for our out and in-door work; that is, both my work and your pleasure, shoemaking and fox-hunting. That grey horse of yours is still keeping up in fine condition I see, sir, in despite of your hard exercise." "Oh! bless ye, sir, he's in grand spirits; if he did not go over Eildon Hills the other day in such a style, nobody ever saw the like! We started on the clints of the mid hill, when foxy took out in fine style over Bowden Moor, west by Cauldshiels Loch, and doubled down by the Shirra's at Abbotsford. I saw where he was to come, and did not need to follow round, but cantered down and keppit him at *Johnnie Martin's tub* on his way back to the *Gateheugh*. They were nearly a' thrown out but Mr. Baillie an' myself, with Andrew Lumsden and half of the hounds, when we got over everything like fleein' birds, down to Old Melrose, where, just as we were on his brush, he took the water, and got into the *Gateheugh grey rock*. Here Mr. Baillie says to me, 'Od, Raeburn,' says he, 'you're as knowing an old jockey as ever; you know how to ride, and when to save your horse. I never saw that nag in better order, now when the season's well-nigh over.'" "You have had more experience than a score of these gentle young bucks, sir," says I; "it would be well for them if they only had the sense to take example; but they'll ride down a deal of hunder pounders before they arrive at your knowledge of field matters. I'm glad, however, that foxy got into the *grey rock;* he'll serve you another day, when I hope to see you come fleein' home through the village with the white tuft o' his auld grey brush waving at your saddle bow." What a rogue I then was in saying this, as I always feel pleased in seeing foxy give his pursuers the jilt, keeping up his credit, as in the old fables.

However, little do we ever know what is for the best. I had reason afterwards to rue at not having taken Hunter's old house at any price, as then I could have got up the money I intended to pay it with, which belonged to my sister, from Andrew Knox, tenant of Mainhill, and his brother John of Charlesfield, which, not thus requiring it at the time, lay still some years till they failed, and it was mostly lost.

But we would require to live ten life-times over to get ourselves properly summered and wintered into the saving knowledge requisite to surmount, with any chance of success, the casual obstructions to a poor man's pilgrimage through this world on his way to the next. Yet we are always getting on in some fashion, through the windings of this life's chase, long or short, the hunters and the hunted, like the old rock fox, and the Squire's old grey hunter, who, with himself, have all alike long ago run to earth, and got numbered amongst "the flowers o' the forest," who "are a' wed away."

Thus again settled, I stuck down to my stool and awls, as fixed as rosin, and now more easily restraining all desire of outfield recreations, such as fishing and shooting, yet still reputed and employed as chief amongst our local fishers and fly-dressers, in the way of directing and advising, according to circumstances. In this I felt a pleasure, just in proportion to the gratification of others, for I have yet had no pleasure in life equal to that of pleasing others rationally. Some may urge that the above-named pursuits are not *rational*, but that is a question in ethics not to be solved rashly. Yet, in such sort of agreeable exercise of the ingenuous mind, we feel often sad disappointments, such as to throw us into frequent low spirits, when we perceive that, notwithstanding all our professional adherence to proper rules of life and conduct, even Christian rules forsooth, let the pretence be what it will, the moving influence actually stimulating all action is too generally low, grubbing, and selfish in the extreme.

What a deplorable view of this life does it present to the sentient mind to perceive clearly that from potentates, prime ministers, and priests, up or down to cadgers and cobblers, all are professing a religion, as they term or suppose something in its name, that they do not seem to comprehend, hardly in the meantime practising the precepts of wild heathen virtue, far less the charities of life, as a duty for Christ's sake, if opposed to their desires of in-bred selfishness. Upon an inquisitive review, indeed, we perceive that most men are still acting in open accordance with all the past history of the human race, the leading features of which seem to have been the conceits of ignorance, superstition, and fanaticism, generally expressed in the hypocritical cant-phrase and professed opinion of the running day and hour; while their gods of the earth, these incarnations of the vilest human lusts, are claiming the idolatry of the heart and the daily practice of the life. Any advance from this to more elevated thought or moral action I have conceived to be a wonderful move in the scale of improvement, and have ever since been aiming at it, because, if there is any virtue at all in the constitution of our human nature, it is a pity to let it lie inactive through life, and remain a dead principle in a world where there is so much occasion for its active operation.

CHAPTER XXXI.

My friend, David Ovens, on the occasion of his pet parting with me, had got on with Tom Kyle in one of his mad speculations, by commencing wood-merchants, in partnership forsooth. They set up a woodyard at Hiltonshill, and made a roaring business of it. David considered himself secure, having the retail and book-keeping departments of the business in his own hand. Nor did he take account of the possibility of his co-partner buying and selling great lots of timber in name of the firm, leading him into immense liabilities, and in the end leaving him, as he did, mulct of half his original patrimonial inheritance. Calculating on the remaining half, David again joined in partnership with another adventurer in the wood-merchant line. They went to the north country, bought and felled some Scotch forest about Beauly, and floated the wood down the river there, in which way he floated away his last acre of separate lands left him by both mother and father. This loss of his *all* might have even been foregone or got over had he not still stood bound for some of Kyle's other concerns to an enormous amount, over-reaching all his means, and totally overwhelming to him. So, swept from the north, where he had been some year or more sojourning, down he fled here, as a temporary retreat before the sough of ruin's brandished besom.

I had heard he was in the village, and had seen him passing, though I knew not the extent of his misfortunes, when one day, standing on the river bank looking over to the water, I saw him coming along, and knew he must pass me or move off at a tangent. "I shall put his pride to the test," thinks I; so kept my station till he came forward. "Well, how are ye, David?" "Thank you, quite well." "Are ye come to have a plunge in on these fish?" I asked. "The water looks well," says he; "I should like to have a trial, but all my feathers and stuffs have gone to wreck since I left; I have nothing now to dress a fly with." "You shall have anything I have, David, on condition that you will come in with me and choose for yourself, as you used to do long ago, before that silly estrangement." "It was silly, I daresay," says David, "for I never had any dislike to you." "Well, no more of it," says I; "I only wish I could get out a-fishing along with you, as we used to go together formerly; so come in with me and let us be good boys again." So in he came, and had a review of my stuffs, from which he picked the necessaries, when I proposed to go to Eiliestoun in the evening in order to get a further supply of turkey feathers. He offered to accompany me. We accordingly went, and got a fresh stock of fine grey spreckles and white-tops. In coming home over St. Boswell's Green he remarked that he felt thirsty, and not a little hungry, and, as his uncle's sober family might be turned into bed, he would have us just call at the inn and have bread and ale. "No, David," says I, "my Nan will be wearying for us, so rather come on with me; I have a fine tail-piece of a kippered salmon, and we shall take in some ale from French's," in the discussion of which we renewed all our former friendly intimacy. In the course of conversation we came to touch on his late pursuits, when I remarked that I hoped he had been more fortunate in trade in his late engagements than he had formerly been with Kyle; for that nothing had vexed me all these years of our foolish estrangement but that I was thereby prevented from keeping him in alarm of these deceptive fellows, these fashionable vagabonds. Bursting into tears from a filled heart, he exclaimed, "I wish I had kept friendly with you. I have found very little true friendship since I left you; and I need not hesitate in telling you now that I am entirely ruined, and into liabilities far beyond my means." The words ran cold over my nerves, and we sat silent together for some time. At last I said, "David, don't let down your heart altogether; you are yet in young age, with superior abilities, and now with some dear-enough-bought experience. You are fit for many things—as, for instance, a head clerkship, or some such situation—for bread; while of personal look and figure, you have sufficient to entitle you to respectable prospects, even in case of marriage. Your easy trust and simplicity of character seem your only failing. That is certainly correctible by the application of the first three rules of arithmetic, not by that ungenerous maxim of 'taking every man for a rogue until you have proven him honest'—no, David, I would rather be cheated out of my skin than wear that disposition as a garment through life—but by just exercising the prudent every-day caution necessary in our general transactions with all mankind, combined with a little firmness of action and decision in cases of slight suspicions, at the same time guarding against the intrusion of ungenerous prejudices. Get down to our friend, John Haliburton, on the Mertoun water, in the meantime, where you can get your pleasurable satisfaction of salmon fishing by saving him of a hired fisher till the time that Scrope comes down, in which case you will have your sport, and your victuals to bargain." He agreed to this plan, and succeeded in getting a full swing season of salmon fishing and hard feeding, the heavier work part of which very much improved his muscular powers, as well as broke him in to a better use of his hands, in case he might find it necessary to follow some useful occupation. He was just getting into the regular russet look and manner of a true-bred, every-day fisherman, when, like a hunted creature, he was again traced to his resting-place, and beaten out of cover by the precursors of the pack-hunt of Kyle's creditors.

He bolted north in the first instance, where he managed to recover as much money as to pay his passage out to Canada. Landing at Montreal, he found his uncle, with whom he had previously been boarded, and who had brought him up from a boy. This uncle was then on his own farm of Cot, St. Paul, close beside Montreal, and this was a fair retreat till he should consider how to arrange for some new start in the world. David considered this lodging the more peculiarly favourable, as he had previously advanced his uncle money to a considerable extent on his original setting out with his family to America. He had afterwards remitted him more in the shape of loan—to the amount of some £300 at least in all. I may as well just here gratify myself by tracing my poor friend and youthful companion to the end of his life's journey, in a few more paragraphs, before taking a sorrowful farewell of his memory altogether.

He stopped there with his uncle's family till the Canadian winter had set in, when one day he had somehow found it necessary to explain his state and circumstances. On learning how he stood, his uncle, to use his own terms in writing home, flew in a passion, and swore him out of the house.

I afterwards heard that he thereupon went, as on a casual visit, to the house of another Scotch settler some miles distant, had dinner, and stayed till tea, when the mistress, thinking it was drawing late enough, and David still not proposing to move, took occasion to observe that she had hopes he was meaning to stop for the night, as it was now late to return home, when, with the salt water rushing to his eyes, he told them he had no home to go to. Being kindly people, they kept him till he, for a second time, found some employment in Montreal in the line of a clerk, where he stopped for some time, and then somehow got a recommendation to go up as a teacher to Hamilton, then to Cobourg, where he succeeded tolerably well, and wrote his uncle William here and me frequently, through the course of some fifteen years that he remained settled there.

At last a disease of a dyspeptic nature, by which he had long been troubled, became so insupportable from his in-door occupation that he was obliged to give up the office of teacher, and take to the open air, in which he always felt complete relief. He wrote me to inquire what interest he might here realize on sinking £500 at his age of 48, which sum he had saved by strict economy, and the advance in value on some village property in the rising town of Cobourg. Satisfied in this, and in a plan I proposed for the disposition of his capital and for his occupation here at home, which would afford sufficient for a livelihood in his *very* moderate manner of life, he arranged to leave Canada and return here, when, to his utter confusion, the bankers with whom he had there deposited his collected money failed and shut shop, leaving poor David again not worth a cent.

This stroke was the more decisive, as, from the state of his health, he found it impossible again to resume his former employment; while the most vexing point in the whole affair was this, that, while he was delaying giving his uncle or me here due intimation of this, he had been writing to another villager, in whom he had the infatuation still to be putting some silly confidence, to try whether he could possibly find for him, from his step-mother's family in Berwick, an address of his half-brother in India, where he was a high pay officer in the land service, and very wealthy. This letter had lain a month with this old *friend* of his before he thought of inquiring at anybody, or stating that we knew of it. Meanwhile, this same Lieutenant-Colonel Ovens had been home on a visit, and in taking a cross-country stroll had called here to pay a sort of feeling visit to the birth-place of his fathers; and finding his father's youngest brother, then old Willie Ovens, and family, still on the spot, was affectionately taken with the meeting. He made the old man and family some handsome presents, and ultimately settled £20 a year on him for life, which was continued to the last remnant of the family till the day of their death.

I did not see this gentleman on his first visit, and therefore, before David could receive a letter from me, conveying news to excite him to hurry home that he might meet with this brother as a generous friend ere he should again leave the country, so much delay had been occasioned that, together with his reduced circumstances in waiting to have his broken banker's affair wound up, my plan of the brothers being brought to meet could not be effected.

I saw this brother, indeed, afterwards, on his next kindly call on his old uncle, and, by the best representation of the case I could possibly make, endeavoured to influence him in favour of David, whom I understood he had likely never seen. I described him to all fair advantage, even showed him some of his beautiful letters to me, in endeavour to excite his admiration and sympathy. But the previous representations he had had of his having *so sillily* lost all his original property, together with this home uncle's coldness on that point—the uncle rather wishing, of course, to find the floating favours take an inward direction towards himself—the young officer never became so decidedly influenced in his absent older brother's favour as to decide on any plan of relief towards poor David.

Meantime, the wanderer had come down to the lower district to sojourn with his American uncle's son, his cousin, then out on a farm of his own, some ten or twenty miles up from Montreal, on the St. Lawrence, where poor David, unable to make other shift, was forced to live, poor and dependent.

The last account I had of him was this, that when riding one day between his uncle's and his cousin's place, the horse called at an inn with David sitting on its back speechless. Upon the landlord observing this, he had him taken in, and information sent down to his uncle, who, on going up, found him labouring under a severe stroke of palsy, of which he died the third day thereafter. His uncle had his remains taken down and interred at his own place of Cot, St. Paul's, near Montreal. I felt the more struck by his death, from the consideration that he had certainly fallen a prey to disease greatly superinduced by his pecuniary misfortunes.

According to my idea, or rather natural feelings of morality, his brother ought to have interfered for his relief, and that timeously. But we cannot impress others, particularly those above us in pride of worldly circumstances, with our beliefs and sympathies. This is a kindly law of nature which ought to be followed even at all risks of our apparent or immediate self-interests, and for the neglect of which, if there is no punishment of Heaven, either in threatening or future award, there is yet a blessing specified, for obedience to it, which begins its operation on the human spirit the moment the good deed is effected, or even decided on in the mind. It keeps alive, as a mild light on the soul, through the shadows of worldly grief, and may likely tend to illume the dark passage from this to another life, and flame still brighter in the more genial atmosphere of a celestial paradise. Though the negation of such delicate virtue be not positive vice, yet it is indicative of an unenviable sterility of soul. A friend dying in our debt may be occasionally distressing to us; but a mild friend dying in lack of certain relief, which we knew it to be in our power to have supplied, is still a worse matter, and must leave a most Novemberish feeling on the nerves of the survivor, if he be not of a very fish-like temperature of blood, calculated to sport, spawn, and rejoice amidst the icy waters of a dull wintry climate.

CHAPTER XXXII.

ON our life's journey we here and there fall into "a den," as old John Bunyan, my friend and brother, did into Bedford jail, where, as all the world knows, instead of fretting at finding himself so situated, he lay down to sleep and delighted us with his dreams. At other more favourable points and turns of our life's path, even amid the common storms and wrecks of our circumstances, we do also occasionally arrive at quiet nooks, fairy knolls, or daisied plots, which are illumined by the sunlight of what may comparatively be called prosperity.

I had at this time arrived at such a green spot in life's walk, and in the full capacity, bodily and mentally, of enjoying it to satisfaction; for as "rest to the labouring man is sweet" in a bodily sense, so rest to a shoemaker's mind, from finding himself in circumstances of ability to honour duly his leather bills, is to him a central point of comfortable feelings.

Though my work required constant attention and vigorous application, yet while it was found, by proper arrangement, equal to the means of yielding something like a comfortable subsistence, with no dread of a jail thickening the gloom of the mind, nor even causing me to be afraid of taking an opportunity of spending a favourable afternoon in a manner somewhat more agreeable to one's feelings than the incessant every-day drudgery of sedentary application could afford, and as fishing was always a first favourite pursuit, particularly along with any friend, such as John Haliburton, first of Dryburgh, then of the Mertoun water, I took the liberty with Mrs. Fortune of a frequent indulgence, which I enjoyed, as people are apt to do many things, even at the risk of prudential reflections.

But a slight sketch of John Haliburton, as my old fishing friend, may be necessary to clear up some matters. On the death of old Andrew Shiel, who had long been tenant of the Dryburgh water, the fishing there was advertised to be let, along with the ferry-boat and a cow's grass. John Haliburton (a *Scotch cousin* of the now distinguished *Sam Slick*) was then a day-labourer, with a wife and two young children, and desiring a cottage to live in, he thought that if other people had lived by fishing, there was nothing to hinder him doing so, although he had then never handled a rod or thrown a line around his head. So he took the premises at a moderate rent, there being few gentlemen fishers in those days to raise waters to foolish rents, said gentlemen being then generally engaged in other pursuits, such as the French wars, and trying to make fortunes on the spoils of common life. On John's entering his fishing at the Whitsunday term, when the water was summer-low and clear, he came over to me, having heard that I dressed flies, and bought a dozen for eighteenpence. They were of such large-sized, brown trout flies as I recommended to him to try for a salmon, in that low state of the river. These were the first flies John ever threw in water. He then commenced, and, through diligent application and perseverance, became eventually a first-rate fisher, while he and I were drawing gradually into such friendly terms as to become like brothers.

There was no bad ingredient in John's character, nor did he seem to have any suspicions of mine, so that from the time of his initiatory practice down through the course of his fishing years, no first conception, observation, or experience of either of us, in fishing matters particularly, could escape the notice of the other.

John was an ingenious fellow, naturally inclined to action, observation, and experiment. He in daily practice, and I in theory, and occasionally in practice together, soon found the propriety of reducing the undetermined confusion of varieties of our Tweed salmon flies then in use to a very few standard ones of never-failing success.

While Haliburton was on the Dryburgh water, Mr. Scrope came here following his fishing tastes. He had been on a jaunt around a number of the fishing stations in Scotland, and, calling in for some days with John at Dryburgh, became quite delighted with the river and John together. As he then expressed it to Philip Garrat, his chief servant, he found John the most able, handy, and ingenious fisherman he had ever met with.

Scrope, supplanting George Sanderson and old John Wight of Kipper Hall and Crago'er, took the Mertoun water at a rent double or treble of theirs, and engaged Haliburton at a guinea a week to leave Dryburgh, and become his fisherman attendant at Mertoun. John hesitated a little on this, as he had succeeded so well in Dryburgh as to have saved £60 in the few years he had been there. But with a blaze of generous appearances Scrope prevailed, and John left Dryburgh (where, through his advice, George Johnstone* succeeded him), and went to the Mertoun water with Mr. Scrope, whose first seven or ten years of regular training on the Tweed here was under Haliburton's regular tuition. John regularly dressed his standard flies, and every day directed their particular application, carried him for some seasons out and in to the boat on his back over the shallows every time a fish was hooked, before either of the two had contrived that I should make him light leather boots, which he could find comfortable in which to wade dry.

In fine fishing days he used to keep two rods in the boat, with an extra rower. He pleased himself by hooking the fish, when he handed the rod to Haliburton to wade ashore with it, there to run and kill the fish, while he should angle for another, in order to see what number he could be said to murder in a given time; for, of course, the main manager and worker in this case, as frequently in similar cases (even in the taking of towns and kingdoms), stood only as a nameless auxiliary:—all this while Haliburton and I happened to keep in such friendly intimacy that we generally agreed to the most minute speck of tip, spot, shade, and spreckle in hair, wool, and feather in the dressing of hooks.

* Many years afterwards unfortunately drowned.

When, therefore, in late years I had occasion to please a new friend (my late lamented Martin Müller of Edinburgh), to describe my favourite salmon flies, I reduced all strictly to five, which I perceived, or at least fancifully conceived, to resemble, in some degree, the five pristine colours of the rainbow, or the five human senses.

In thus writing on the subject, as an article by itself, which came to be published under the name of "River Angling," I described these five flies numerically, 1st, 2d, 3d, 4th, 5th, adding a sixth as a favourite variation of my first. Mr. Scrope, some year or two thereafter, published a splendid book on fishing, under a show of plates, and price as great in proportion to mine as the amount of his original fortune in life was above mine, not as he stood higher in knowledge of his subject or in manual ability, but in worldly circumstances, and consequently in the world's eye. Thus the world goes generally—while I am valued at eighteenpence, Scrope sells at two guineas! God help me and the world both; we are a farce to think on—a sorry farce indeed. It is puzzling to suppose which is the most to be pitied. Scrope's six flies are mine, of course, to a shade; they could indeed be properly no other, only that he has described them in other words (even figured them in painted plates), with perhaps more quaint punctuality in tufts and toppings, and under fanciful local names of designation, such as "Meg in her braws," "Kinmont Willie," "The lady o' Mertoun," and so on. He is out in one point, however, of his description of these flies, which may be here worth observation, for the correction of those who may be led to dress from his description. He recommends these six flies to be mostly all dressed with hackles, laid over bodies made of bullocks' hair. Now, this is rather incongruous, springing from a mistake, as I will suppose, since I cannot conceive that he ever used them of that style in his practice on the Tweed here; and the mistake has probably arisen thus:—He had, properly speaking, left the regular fishing here, just previously to the time that Haliburton and I settled on the propriety of using cow hair for bodies, to supply the place of hackles laid over soft wool bodies, thus making a fly equally pretty and useful, and much more substantially solid, than with a hackle over the soft wool body, which proved often so troublesome by its breaking loose at the small end of the hackle on the first fish being hooked with it. This was what we considered a grand improvement upon former methods, and Mr. Scrope might afterwards have only partially seen or heard of it after he had removed from here up to the Pavilion water, near Melrose. He therefore made a mistake in conceiving that cow hair (or bullocks' hair, as he perhaps more properly called it) should be used only in place of soft wools for the body, with the old wool-bodied habit of a hackle laid over it, as this, if not quite incongruous, is at least altogether unnecessary, the bullock hair being calculated to make both body and hackle of itself, ribbed with the tinsel, as may be seen necessary, the same as hackles used to be. To this day, in dressing flies for others who are yet positive in their taste for using hackles, we still use soft furs or wools for body, with the hackle laid over it, as over a rather smooth surface, but seldom think of using bullock hair and hackles together, which makes a fly too rough and unshapely, of quite a heather-bush appearance, and, properly speaking, characterless.

One point is worthy of observation, that many who can dress hackle flies well cannot readily succeed in making the cow-hair body, and therefore disclaim it. Except ourselves, I know only two brothers, who were hired fisher lads with Haliburton after Scrope had left him to rent the Mertoun water for himself, who ever succeeded well in making the real cow-hair body.

The sequel of John Haliburton's history may lie rather out of my present way, yet it may be as well to relate how Scrope drew up from continuing to pay him the guinea a week, and translated the terms of the verbal agreement to have meant that he was to pay him that wage only for the weeks or months he should himself be down on the water, when he would require his attendance personally. This he did; and, as the river in those days opened for salmon fishing on the 10th January, he made his man of business here let the fishing for the spring months to the highest bidder, leaving John in such intervals to shift for himself. Haliburton then, instead of sickening on the subject, became at every time of let the highest bidder, thus securing the water to keep himself at least employed. The two following seasons of the most plentiful run of fish ever seen by living eye just succeeded, while the London market was yet open for fish of all seasons, kelts, foul fish, and so on; for all then went under the general name of salmon, with only a little variation of price, agreeably to the appearance or the quality.* John cleared something like £150 or £200 in the course of the two successive years of (I think) 1816 and 1817. But these savings he was again doomed to leave to the landlord in the years following on the expiration of Scrope's lease, as John felt obliged either to become annual tacksman himself, and to pay Scrope's advance of rent (some £50), or to leave the place under great disadvantage, with a very large family to be provided for—to wit, his wife's old father and mother, and his own mother, over and above a swarm of children. This necessitated John to stick fast to this fishing from year to year, through succeeding bad seasons, until all his gains on the waters were again swept off on the floods, when he once more, like a hunted otter, took to the dry lands, and somewhere west about Lanarkshire, tugging on in a small farm, has been faring variously since.

I might make up a book of fishing matters, anecdotes, and so on, as thick as Foxe's "Book of Martyrs" in octavo, and tell over all the high-winded stories that have been sported on the Tweed here throughout the course of the last one hundred and

---

* The lower-down and higher-up proprietors of the Tweed then, differing amongst themselves about the terms of appropriation and preservation of the river, stupidly altercated about *foul* and *clean* fish till they "let the cat out of the pock" in regard to the proper season for salmon. The Londoners then got hold of a notion, new to them, that nearly all the fish of the salmon kind were unclean or out of season through the winter and spring months, and hence, of course, the sale was done up for our poor tacksmen on the river here, as the fish that went formerly from them at from 3d to 6d per lb. could not then be taken in at Berwick for the London market, but fell to be hawked around the country here for sale at 1½d and 1d per lb., many of them dear food at that, the poverty of our country people rightly considered.

thirty years, which would, of course, comprise all the dreamy wonders of even old David Kyle, the village blacksmith of the seventeenth century, of fishing and shooting notoriety and Baron Munchausen exploit and anecdote. But such book would not likely sell, without some titled offset or addition, by way of head or tail to my Christian name or surname; and it would be idle to repeat lying wonders for nothing.

Discarding, then, these old stories, there are yet several points on such a subject as river fishing which may be well worth observation, which are not yet generally understood, and happen to have been hitherto ill-managed, even in point of legislating on the subject, to which I feel impelled here to devote a page or two by way of illustration.

Our landlords for long have held the dry land, with all its rocks and springs, rivers, streams, and pools of water, even to the bill and claw of wild bird and feathered fowl, snipe, and woodcock, every individual hare to the bunt, and every fish to the murt-fin*—a claim, indeed, more than, with all their game-law legalities, they can conjunctly supply the genius to devise the means of duly protecting, while far less can they claim the countenance of the general law of God to sanction such unnatural assumption and mischievous appropriation. For the preservation of the salmon species of fish to themselves exclusively, it is needless now to repeat what laws these gentry have got enacted, tried, abandoned, and superseded, every succession of new heirs to estates having found fault with the old, and legislated anew for themselves; while these enactments in their turn, having also been

* The second dorsal or adipose fin.

found inefficient to serve their purpose of satisfying the avaricious, are again thrown aside to the family vault, along with the bones of their ancestors—(such are the works that follow them)—and still something nothing less ridiculous established in their place.

Our last discarded Tweed law was this:—The river to be closed for all sorts of salmon fishing on the 10th October, and opened again on the 10th January, those who procured the passing of this enactment vainly imagining that they would enclose the spawning season within these three months. They found out, by-and-by, that the best of the fish were still left unspawned at the opening, and that these were at that season leistered promiscuously.

The latest act of legislation in the case is, that the river be closed for *net* and *leister* fishings on the 15th October, and for *rod* fishing on the 7th November, and open on the 15th February.*

Protection under these Acts is attempted by some sort of association of the proprietors of waters clubbing to keep up a constabulary force under the local name of *water bailiffs*, to go about day and night for the purpose of preventing, seizing, and convicting poachers.

The public conceive (however misconceivingly) that their natural rights are at all times rather arbitrarily abridged by a mere assumption of claim and privilege, and therefore consider *close-time* as the time when the claiming proprietors agree to suspend their personal outlook, and merge their individual protection in the care of their substitutes, the bailiffs. Hence, close-time is considered the poor man's, or

* This Act has long been superseded, and leistering is now illegal.

poacher's, open-time, as he finds that he can always more easily mislead or evade a watching bailiff than a local laird or tenant.

The department of fishing most easily found preventible by bailiffs is the simplest mode, that which can do least harm to the spawning fish, the rod, while cairn and strake-net poaching is difficult to detect in the dark of night.

But the worst of all fresh water piracy—desperate, daring, cruel, devilish—is the leistering or spearing with night lights; and being prevented from all other more sportsman-like methods, this the poacher falls back upon, and manages to effect his purpose by its means, in despite of all the police force that can conveniently be organized against him. This can be done on spawning beds by two or three individuals, one to hold the torch, and another to use the spear; but as, in this case, they have no sufficient protection from a surprise by bailiffs, they associate in bands of twenty, thirty, or fifty (poor fellows! being often at the season by enforced idleness rendered daring and desperate) from all the districts around, and, disguised in rags and blackened faces, proceed, like tribes of Indians, to a massacre. Thus, rushing to the spawning gravel beds, over which the flaming lights are kindled, behold fifty or a hundred pairs of fish all promiscuously slaughtered in the very act of spawning for the present, and (I presume) impregnation for the succeeding season. A dozen of hired bailiffs, who may steal on the spot, in the name of prevention, look very stupid standing in the chill of a winter night as witnesses of a scene like this—more bewildered than Tam o' Shanter looking at the witches' dance with the devil piping to them. This has long been, and still is, the prevailing practice in the higher districts of the rivers, where the greatest masses of fish have got up in the autumn and early winter floodings for the purpose of spawning. And the greater facility with which these poachers get forward in such cases is by the blinking of the smaller proprietors or tenants, who find less interest in preventing them than in obtaining a share of their spoil. This practice occurs the more readily in consequence of the great trade of net fishing at and near the river mouth, where the clean fish are mostly all caught in the summer, with little chance of many getting up the river till the high floodings in the fall, when the nets are laid off working either from the cause of high floods or the close-time having commenced. Then the fish get run up in shoals to spawn under protection of upper-water proprietors, to whom, properly speaking, protection is no special benefit.

It may be supposed a very natural dialogue to hear a farmer's servant in close-time say—"Master, twa or three o' us are thinkin' o' lichtin' a bit bleeze at the *redds* the night up at the Shaw-braefords, where we saw them tumlin' up this afternoon, like brewers' swine drunk on maut 'draff.'" "Well, Davie, I daresay, for my part at least, ye may just take what ye can get when ye have them here, as I'm sure I havena seen three good fish in our water down through the summer. They kep them a' about Berwick and Norham now wi' these lang nets, except just a-while in the tail o' the season, when the floodings get ower heavy for their net wark." So under this, to Davie, supreme permission, he raises a band of comrades, with leisters, and staves of tar barrels for lights—a band perhaps nearly as strong as Rob Roy's black-mail clan, that a regiment of dragoons might scarcely be expected to capture, kill, or disperse. Hence the havoc proceeds indiscriminately on fish in all respects out of season, as a half-spawned or a newly-spawned fish is certainly most disgusting food, though, as one of these poachers will say, "a fish is a fish if you can catch it, when, where, and how you can." In this mind he pursues his purpose recklessly, regardless of the depreciation of value or the destructive effects on the species to future generations.

This is bad enough as the practice in such a "free, glorious country" as ours; but the next scene that follows on "bonnie Tweedside," notwithstanding that it is agreeable to law, is little better, if anything. On the 14th of February the fish, which are held by the authorities as previously unclean, are, on the morning of the 15th, all understood to be duly purged and cleansed *by law*, fit tit-bits for the tables of the rich and for the London market. Hence the gentleman's *sport* begins, which, in many instances, is not so very much of a super-refinement on the before-mentioned mode of procedure as a London lady, in the gentility of her imagination, might be led to suppose, or at least to suspect to be legalized in the statute-book of this "greatest nation under the sun."

Some of the fashion-leading Lord Johns of the age even delight in pursuing this blood-letting method of "the sport" by boat-lights and leisters, dashing that vile instrument through the body of the unguarded creature whilst in the most interesting act of its nature, the propagation of its species, and then most unfit for human food.* Indeed, every means so much reprobated when used by the poor poacher, are then by themselves resorted to under the general designation of *sport*, without even the poacher's plea of something akin to necessity.

Now, if our great landholders may still persist in adding all the running waters to their other appropriations of the solid lands, one would think that some generation of them might surely contrive how to make these rivers most conducive to their own interest, teeming and beneficial, as well as to their general and individual amusement of a more gentle description. This might easily be done by proprietors agreeing amongst themselves to make a law to do away with the practice of all net and leister fish-

* And only think of a *leister* of five or six long barbed prongs, like the forks in the devil's pictured tail, or like the outstretched fingers of the "Iron Duke's" red right hand as it may be extended forth in a dreaming grasp at the fancied shadow of his old friend, or rather foe, of the hundred battles, or rather just now (December, 1845), for a last clutch and retentive hold of the passing Corn-law Bill, which, in despite of that lumpish hero-god of our present nobility (who brings one in mind of the big, clumsy, metal image of Juggernaut), will soon be a fearful ghost, fit only for quieting the supperless children of the coming age in words like these—"Lie still an' sleep, or else the big Iron Man's Ghost will come back, and Corn-Bill ye to cauld hunger and death—him that killed the French, an' then came hame, and was set up to be worshipped as the hero-divinity o' our British gentry, and under that godship kept a seventy-lord power stamach bill-trap in his greatcoat pocket, wi' which he catched an' hungered a' the poor bairns in his ain country, to please the big-bogle man o' Buckingham, till their wee, starved spirits were heard *yeaing* an' *pleening* through a' the blasts o' winter; an' ye wadna hear a souch o' frost wind through the keyhole o' your outer-door, but there was the voice of a dyin' creature's last curse in't."

ing on these rivers, from the sea upwards to their sources; and instead of the application of any public or county money, or of clubbing their own for the purpose of keeping a bailiff force, as under the present Act, let them lay such funds out the rather in purchasing or leasing the special net waters at the river mouth, and thus preserve a free run of fish throughout the whole year.

If these net waters are worth the rent to individual tacksmen, they are certainly worth it (even in *value*, overlooking the pleasure,) to the whole proprietors of seventy miles of the Tweed. It would be, individually, a mere fractional consideration to the rents that might be drawn if let in mile-lengths to gentle rod-and-line anglers, who cannot, under present arrangements, be one-hundredth part accommodated, besides the benefit it would be to the localities where these individuals might be thus drawn for their amusement. We starve under our present lairds, and they will not allow the means by which money would get circulated in our way.

The distribution of fish, then, through the rivers generally would depend solely upon the casual floodings of these rivers throughout the round year. There would then be always plenty of fish for the rod, and many would live to grow to a great size; while the amusement of rod-fishing would be one of the most pre-eminent, healthful, and exhilarating amusements of our country. It would beat Grecian games, as well as English horse-racing and hound-coursing, all to nonsense. The bodily exercise which it causes is just on the top calculation of the bill of health; the excitement on the most nourishing principle of mind, without any engrossment of the faculties from higher pursuits. It is a charming relaxation from sedentary employments and severe studies. It would besides provide an honest source of livelihood for a few poor fellows like myself, who, living by the waters, have, from observation and practice, acquired a taste and use of hand in practical fly-dressing and the preparation of other necessary tackle, rods, lines, and so on, so that we could supply our richer amateurs of the high fancy taste with what they need for "gentle angling."

No close-time would then be necessary, only just such as the river proprietors might mutually agree on as a sort of understood or partial forbearance amongst themselves, always having it in their power to restrict non-proprietors, as they already have all the season through on what they claim as their own waters.

Indeed, in rod-fishing the spawning fish are less liable to be taken than the fish in a more seasonable state, as those second best to the winter clear salmon in his splendid silver beauty are those which come up with the late November, December, and even January floodings, for the natural purpose of a fresh-water excursion as well as the ultimate innate object of spawning before their return to the sea. These are then in a much better state for slaughter than in the months of February, March, and April, when only partially spawned, or on the eve of spawning. All these we have in December and January in excellent state, the transient clear salmon, the brown twenty-pounders of the "grey-school" tribe, without eight ounces of milt or roe in them. They may be regarded as in as good condition as a grass-fed ox, and in excellent state for eating. All these live in the same pool together, while another pair of the more early fish are spawning on the gravel ford above, and thus the most easily got at by the poacher's spear, who, rather than want all, will take what he can get at with least trouble.

By the time the water opens, those fish that are in the present close-time in good season are getting full, and ready to spawn in the spring months (many are not spawned till April, and even May), and here they are slaughtered in a *full* state, agreeably with law, on the opening of the river.

Here is a blundered and ill-weighed state of matters, while a pound sterling's worth of liberality of principle thrown into the scale would effect more of rational protection than a restrictive bailiff's winter fee of £10 or £15; and though I am not acquainted with any of the present occupants of these *most honourable* posts of trust, I am yet certain that their predecessors in office, twenty or thirty years back, were in several instances understood to have acted as the slyest poachers to be found. We have known them blink at the setting-in of nets, on condition of kidnapping a draught as their own perquisite ere the morning, and there seems little alarm to Satan yet of the world's much mending.

But our land and water holders generally seem to have a mortal antipathy to the idea of any liberality of principle whatever, and always bring me in mind of the thief who declared that he thought more of sixpence of plunder than of eighteenpence earned with credit and honour. I have therefore no hope of their adopting any measure which may happen to bear the least semblance of an approach to liberality of principle or sentiment, though I am convinced that such would very much improve their already good fortunes, as well as those of their poorer neighbours.

The waters have certainly brought forth abundantly, agreeably to divine promise, for the use of all human beings. This would be acceptable, indeed, and received with thankfulness, if it could reach us. But, alas! it is too often arbitrarily intercepted in its proper direction by the appropriation and misapplication of those who have assumed the stewardship of God's common providence, of which, most unhappily, they give no account, and seem to be called to none, on this side the grave at least—the more shame to them and to us; while as to the next state of existence, I hope that the paradisical "rivers of life" will not be patched and parcelled out in pools and streams amongst a very few exclusives—assumptive, selfish, gripping, and despicable—but flow free for the comfortable refreshment of the happy general community.

CHAPTER XXXIII.

IN the remainder of this homely narrative, I could fain imitate the improvements of the present age by trying my hand at some sort of mental railway movement, giving only a passing glance at objects already falling behind into the shadow of memory, while new scenes are coming ever in view, dancing around, and forming fairy rings with the rapidity of thought, as objects, such as a tree, a windmill, or a steeple, are seen to do in the varied distance from a railway carriage window.

The relation of commonplace affairs can only be interesting from the rarity of their occurrence in history, or even in biography, as writers generally incline to deal in the marvellous, leaving the homestead of their thoughts whenever they set about to write what they suppose other people may see, and, groping in the dark for the marvellous in order to give what they suppose effect, find only the ghosts of life in place of flesh and blood realities.

I had at this time begun to feel more and more the necessity of curtailing vague desires of out-door amusements, so as to make every hour tell to the value of its own necessary expenditure, and a harassing tug this certainly was, adding stitch to stitch in constant repetition, like the monitory tick of the jail-clock over the prisoner's weariness.

The vigour of life is essential to the effective maintenance of this toil, while the same vigour of the mind of life would often require a broader field of action in which to

> "Expatiate free o'er all this field of man,
> A mighty maze, but not without a plan."

I have often thought deeply of the maze—which thought is bewildering enough; for the plan, so certainly as it is there, is too multiform and complex for all our powers of investigation.

The best philosophy on this subject appears but a speculation, since bishops, doctors of divinity, *et cetera*, who seem to discern something real somewhere, so disagree about the spirit and meaning of the vision, the history of the past, and the prophesyings of the future respecting the grand phenomenon of creation, or the present position or ultimate destination of man as a specific part of it, as to leave the simple mind of the humble inquirer mystified in a fog of inexplicable reflections. But the only way to get over this I found was to leave it as usual, after having spoken something unintelligible about it, and return to my explicable thoughts, such as those in which I used to indulge at that time, that, hard as the world was, I felt strong in the hope of being now a match for it.

I had seen through the general selfishness, and conceived the imperious necessity of guarding against imposition, not supposing myself in anything like the state that Satan perceived Job to be in, hedged about with blessings of the divine favour, both for supply and for protection. I tried, therefore, to make up my mind to commence with some plan of self-defence on the general principle, not to try to over-reach, but to maintain a prudent caution in guarding against the consequences of that disposition in others; for bad as the world is, or as we may think it, necessity in some degree is urging us to an assimilation with it. I could never, however, maintain this resolution in practice, always finding that the balance between common prudence and an intuitive generosity of sentiment was extremely nice, and that the latter must submit to sad taxation in a world like this, where he who might literally comply with the Christian injunction of giving his back to the smiter may lay his account with a tanned hide in the course of a sixty years' pilgrimage, if under such circumstances he might possibly attain to that age.

Though at this stage of life I could not calculate upon any advantage gained, or in clear prospect, yet matters seemed, upon the whole, to bear a rather clearing-up appearance in our family circle.

My father was working diligently for his living, and realizing *it* barely—that is, he was not saving anything, which might have been done to a small extent had he been under a full first-love marriage. I estimated the matter thus—that, had my mother been spared to have been then his housekeeper, or, indeed, had that office been assigned to any of my three sisters, there would have been saved some ten or twelve pounds a-year for nearly thirty years of that time, as this much was baken and brewed over and above the way he had ever formerly been accustomed to live, or even then desired to fare, for he was a gently-temperate being. But being also of a quiet, easy disposition, he inherited a spirit of peace; and so the means being produced, and no harassment being in prospect, he left the stewardship of his house entirely to its mistress, as in such circumstances is generally the most proper, as well as the most convenient; while she considered—and even unwittingly said so—that it was needless for her to save penuriously, since she was assured that if she outlived him she would be looked to by the family by whom she had been brought to this part of the country, and had been so long in service with before her marriage, and that in this way her own living was all she had to take concern about. This was so far from the disposition of the family with whom she had come into connection that we certainly could not help disliking it, although prudence required that we should not seem to observe it. What we principally wished then was that our father might still have the peace he had always so much prized, and might be enabled to do for himself, and get a creditable throughbearing without requiring that assistance which we found it would have been hard for us to have afforded, set as we then were in the world. With a journeyman and himself he was gaining more than I was able to do under the same arrangement of work. One principal cause of this was that, though I wrought as diligently upon the whole, yet I lost profit in following my finer tastes in my work, he being past that time of life when such fanciful notions predominate in the mind over more judicious considerations. Perhaps, indeed, he never was, even in his prime days, troubled with them, to the same extent as I was, but just did his work plainly, pleasing his customers well enough, and getting his payments as well as I did for a third less labour and cost. Besides, I was often following other fancies, and attending to other people's affairs to no profit, and generally receiving no thanks for myself.

I may here remark, in passing, that this has been a prevailing error in my life, and one which I do not think I could correct, though I had just now to begin to live it over again. Some of these things are so constitutional that our heart quite overcomes the philosophy of our head. My father had as good a heart as I ever had, with a leniency often extending to even greater simplicity, yet he was shrewd in perception, and could take up his ground and move timeously, which prevented various troubles that fell to my share. My sisters were all come to their full senses, besides being all hale and out-stout for the push and tug of life, the oldest keeping house on the remnants of her former means, with her spinning industry to eke it out, and keeping our nephew, our second sister's son, still at the neighbouring parish school of Bowden, where he was getting on with his Latin and mathematics, while his mother kept out in good service, gaining and saving the additional means necessary for their house-keeping. My third sister was married about the same time that I was; her first child and mine were both born on the same day. Her husband, John White, was a hale, stout man, a farmer's hind, while she made as useful a wife, and they have wrestled through hitherto, living upon their small wages comfortably in a plain and simple way, after the manner of thousands.

We were all alike fond of our nephew, the young lad, George Knox; indeed, he was quite a favourite with everybody—a splendid specimen of a human being both in mind and body; and although, as the vulgar saying is, "he came unsent for," he now gave promise of great usefulness, coming fast on to be an excellent scholar, taking the lead at the then duly famed Bowden Parish School, and tugging his fellows along with him. As I have before said, I had been sorry at having missed education for myself, and I then felt a keen desire of bringing him forward to the point of bettering his situation in life. This wish arose as much from my desire of information as from the way I found myself left in the world. I thought that some generation of us should again escape out of the double drudgery of the cobbler's situation, and assume, if not a more useful, at least a more reputable as well as a more congenial station in society.

I therefore made proposals of binding George an apprentice with Mr. Archibald Rutherfurd of Kelso, a stationer and bookbinder, when Mr. Rutherfurd advised me that far less means would bring him forward as a teacher, which he considered at that time a preferable occupation. For this purpose I then set to thinking about plans of getting him to Edinburgh College, when an accidental occurrence determined the case.

Mr. Craw, then our parish minister, had been at the annual examination of the Parish School of Galashiels, where, at their after-dinner party, great admiration was expressed at the figure a certain youth had made at that examination, who was the son of a shepherd on the farm of Crosslee, on Gala water. The farmer there at the time happened to be no other than Ebenezer Knox, the father of my nephew. "Well," says Mr. Craw, "this lad makes a fine figure for his age; but on Friday last, at the examination of Bowden school, I met with a youth there whom till then I had not known as a parishioner of my own, who is far further advanced as a parish scholar than this Redpath—that is George Knox, a son of Ebenezer Knox himself. I have since been speaking to his uncle, his mother's brother, in our village, with whom he has been brought up, to try if possible, as a duty, to make an effort and get him to college this coming winter, as he should have been there a year since, for it would be a sin not to make him follow it out. His uncle informs me that their mutual family means are so nearly exhausted that he doubts of being able to match it, and that Ebenezer Knox, his father, has never done anything worth naming for him, only giving some small allowance for him when he was a child, and once a suit of boy's clothes to the value of thirty shillings." Mr. Milne of Faldonside being one of the party, observed that, from his knowledge of Ebenezer Knox, he would take in hand, and indeed he would warrant the effect, to advise Ebenezer to raise a given sum, say £10, to assist in getting his son to college that season. Mr. Craw, who was a kind-hearted man, as particularly shown in such cases, said he would keep him strictly to his promise, and as Mr. Milne desired to see this son of Ebenezer Knox, he would send him up to

Faldonside. He then called on me, and submitted the matter, of which, of course, I highly approved, cordially thanking him for his friendly interference. Accordingly, on a given day, choosing our way over Eildon Hills to Faldonside, we saw Mr. Milne, who admired the stripling, and told us that he had got the promise of the £10 from his father, and that with such assistance I must make a strong effort to get him to college at the opening of the session. Though I had been pre-determined to do this at risk of all personal conveniency of means, yet I felt it prudent not to boast of my purpose, but said that if I should be disappointed in Ebenezer's performance of this promise, it would go near to wreck me on my voyage of life. "It is Ebenezer's poverty," says he, "not his unwillingness, that keeps him from doing more in such a case." "That might perhaps stand an excuse with his Maker," says I, "though it would not do so with his farm landlord; but I think I understand him as well as anybody does. I'll take his word through you, sir, as sure in that way as if given solitarily to myself, and run chance of the matter in the first instance." So I set about getting George fitted out for college. A schoolfellow of his—to wit, Thomas Aird of Bowden, a man who has since made a considerable figure as a scholar and an author—was then also on the point of being sent to college, when his father and I agreed that my eldest sister, George's aunt, with whom he had been brought up principally, should take a room and keep house with the two lads through the winter, and in this way the matter would be managed most economically. After they were gone, and entered to their classes, I was one day at Kelso on necessary business, when, trudging home after dark, and ruminating on all the chances and changes of life, past scenes, and future prospects, it came to my recollection that a meeting of Tom Kyle's creditors was that evening to take place at the inn at St. Boswell's Green, and that Ebenezer Knox would be there. I then hurried on for the five remaining miles, went straight out to the inn about ten at night, heard them all up stairs, and sent a message requesting Ebenezer Knox to see a friend in a down-stair room. He came, when I plied him about his promise of the £10. He stated that he was very willing to give it as he had promised to Mr. Milne, but could not raise it at the present time, as he was lying out of all that was his own, having sold his lease of the Thornilaw farm to Tom Kyle, besides other moneys, amounting in all to £2100, and could at the present scarcely keep credit. He took £2 from his pocket, which he gave me. "A poor man must be thankful for any little he can get," says I; "but this will do little indeed to the matter I have in hand, and on the faith of your word to Mr. Milne I have staked my credit. But you can give me a bill at three months; I have accidentally a stamp in my pocket," which was truth, as I was frequently paying my leather by bills. "No banker will discount a bill just now," says he, "and that is threatening to be my ruin, as the present farming system is knocked up by the fall of Buonaparte." "Tut, man, the fall of Lucifer, hurling a third part of heaven after him to deepest perdition, was over-ruled, and renovation of general circumstances gloriously effected, to Satan's utter consternation. How, then, can you think that farming is done up by the fall of a single creature dependent on animal pulsation and a digestible dinner, which was not, I suppose, the case with his great prototype in ambition, insolence, and cruelty, who is bound in everlasting chains, to eat and digest fire as he may. It is a poor keeping up of a few silly farmers by the raising of markets through the destruction of food by wars and waste, and three-fourths of the population under starvation. Buonaparte's fall is a world's blessing, and do you not understand that the corn-ridges will grow beautifully green over Europe when the worms will have consumed all the generations that shall ever hear of his infernal insolence. You farmers have been the landlords' dupes and the country's fools, and you have worn your fools' caps, too, and are still not doffing them, though they may likely fall, with the heads in them. Bankers will not just now discount bills to your class, considering you a pack of adventurous 'tumblers,' whom they see on the fall from the slack rope; but they will yet accredit an honest shoemaker, for I had a bill discounted to a currier last week. If you are willing to give me that money, then signing this bill will keep me in credit with William Aitkin, currier in the West Port, Edinburgh, for three months to come." So he drew it for £10. "You have forgotten you have given me £2 already," says I; "I suppose I must return you that now?" "Oh, no," says he, "keep what you have; it is all too little; but my excuse is my being so hard set." "God help us all!" says I. So in a single glass we drank good night; he went to his company, and I home to my bed.

The three months had nearly slid past, when one day I heard that amongst a list of the failing farmers Ebenezer Knox, in Crosslee, was broken down. I instantly wrote to William Aitkin, who held the bill, stating the nature of the business, and advising that he must deal delicately with the subject, and write Ebenezer in a very discretionary manner, as nothing could be got by force of law, and I knew the nature of his constitutional pride. This Mr. Aitkin attended to, when the answer by return of post was £10, sent enclosed in a letter. Though I had often felt angry at Ebenezer previously, yet his honour in this last action just before leaving Crosslee, and fugitating himself, touched my heart so powerfully that the impression is not effaced now, after the tear and wear of forty winters.

> "Far as this little candle throws its beams,
> So shines a good deed in a naughty world."

The rest of this man's history is strange, arising not less from peculiarity of disposition than casualty of circumstances. His self-esteem had been developed to an overbalancing extent, causing an improper pride of spirit, which he wanted the necessary means to support according to his taste. These, with some other propensities, pulling, like wild horses, the opposite way of what his better judgment approved, kept him in continued trammels and distress of thought, and drawing him into troubles far beyond the ordinary lot of life. From a first seven years' banishment to New South Wales for some sort of half-proven forgery in the times of his distress of circumstances, he there, from his abilities and honourable usefulness, combined with a winning kindness of natural disposition, rose to credit, wealth, and respectability under three governors, getting free grants of land from each, to the amount, in all, of 1000 acres—which lands he got into cultivation and stocked, so as to be able to declare himself, in writing home to his son at the date 1834, worth £4000, which he then saw would double itself in a year or two. A will of this property he then made in favour of his son, my nephew, here; but he immediately afterwards fell into another scrape by branding as his own some out-field cattle which had not properly belonged to himself, so that under a then new astringency of the law in that case he was tried and condemned, his property confiscated to Government, and himself put under a second banishment. While his natural abilities were remarkably good, for want of a stronger sense of moral propriety, he had, upon the whole, a disgraceful as well as disagreeable life and a sorry ending.

I may have occasion to revert to that man again in the course of this narrative; but in case not, it may perhaps be as well in brief here to say that his was one particular instance of the folly of an attempt to fight the battle of life with the wrong weapons; and that after a variety of the most honourable and dishonourable actions, his bones lie wasting in a convict's grave in Norfolk Island.

CONCLUSION.

HERE ends abruptly John Younger's "Autobiography," or at least that part of it which the publishers have been able to recover. We have reason to believe that it was brought down to a later date; but, if so, the rest has been lost. In a letter to an old friend, dated 23d December, 1856, John gave a most interesting account of his life's experience up to that time; but this letter, too, has gone astray irrecoverably, having been sent by its recipient to a certain noble duke, in the hope that a perusal of it might induce his Grace to do something substantial for the writer, who described himself as having been on the "back-thraw" for twelve years then past, "straining to keep a footing and maintain a position." His Grace, however, made no sign—did not even acknowledge receipt of the letter—perhaps never saw it, as it might have been intercepted on its route to him, and flung aside, by some underling employed to open his letters, and who looked upon it as an ordinary begging letter. When made aware of this miscarriage, honest John, who had had no inkling of the use his perhaps indiscreet but well-meaning friend had made of his communication, wrote as follows:—"Land-logged in this life, I am making gravewards very heavily. I can see no substantial point of dependence before me. I am 73; my father cobbled on every day till 90, and lived till 94; and I am as strong as he was at my age. He was never in life so wealthy as I have been; but never so poor as I am now. I could work for my daily bread yet, if I could only get the means of a moderate new commencement. But you see it is needless to look to dukes and their dogs except to get worried." "Not a single duke on earth, or ever on earth, would I know or he me, should we meet face to face, either here or in the Elysian fields. We have no natural sympathies, save eating, when we can get to eat." "How can I read Shakspeare, Milton, and Burns, and think of dukes and dogs?"

It is the revelation of the inner life of such a man as John Younger that has abiding interest to thoughtful readers. His life-long residence in a quiet country village, his monotonous daily occupation, and his every-day relations with commonplace, unappreciative neighbours, furnish little or no matter for any but the ablest and aptest autobiographer, who can lay open, to such as have ears to hear and an understanding heart, the secrets of his own great soul— his gropings towards truth—the growth of his master mind, ever onward, upward, heavenward. And so it would not tend to edification to detail here at any length the events of the St. Boswell's shoemaker- poet's life, from the period when his own genial record closes till the day of his death. Suffice it to say, that, with all his rare philosophy and sagacious saws, he remained to the end a son of toil, hammering and stitching at the trade of cobbling the shoes of the village rustics, though as a maker of fishing boots and dresser of flies he was famous from Berwick to Drumelzier, and far further. He was described, when verging towards his seventieth year, as "still active and athletic, of tall and commanding stature, and with the mein and presence of a nobleman; his stalwart frame, the correct and yet imperfect embodiment of his powerful mind; simple and unsophisticated as an infant, though rich in both joyous and sad experience; not unread in books, and of men and things an incessant, deep, and successful student; his workshop the village forum, himself a true oracle; the well-worn joint-stool fronting his own occupied day after day by listening visitors of all ranks, down to the sauntering angler and muse-struck ploughboy; a keen politician, without a spark of partizanship; a caustic satirist, who never made an enemy; a true philanthropist, without sickly sentiment; a real Christian, without sectarianism." That he was supremely original in some of his conclusions, and bold in his publication of them, may be seen in his sentiments upon Sir Walter Scott, for whose writings he, a Scotsman to the very tips of his nails, "did not care at all." He looked on the Waverley literature as "old piper stories," "dwarf and witch tales," and "monstrous caricatures of Scottish manners;" and he could never be induced to read one of the novels or romances through, or, indeed, to look at it twice —the circumstance of Scott being an anti-Reformer giving emphasis to his feeling of contempt for all laudation of the bad old times, when might was held to be right, superstition to be religion, and prejudice principle. The Reform Bill he hailed as a great and just measure, constituting "an inestimable general privilege," which he felt confident "would exercise a wholesome influence over the tergiversations and abuses of public trust by the governing few." On the Corn Laws he naturally vented his hottest ire, summing up their evils in a "Scotch Corn-Law Rhyme," published in 1841—a rugged rhapsody truly, yet instinct with sterling truths. He was opposed to war in all its phases, as the following sentence will show:— "Has humanity not yet been long enough debased, running with dirks at their hips, after their worse than wooden gods, whom they call their chieftains? —ready at their paltry bidding to rip the life-blood out of the man whom God has created to be their rational neighbour, and then sent home to starve with their poor, degraded wives, and those who should have been their rational offspring; yes, and in cottar-hovels, scarcely deserving the name of a shelter! Were men not stone-blind, blank, and morally ignorant, could they submit to such things, or follow the wicked to war, when they have simply to agree in saying, 'We nourish the Christian principle of peace and good-will to men, and decline to kill each other?' And in such case, what profane and dominant ruler could force them? What could an emperor of here or there say, should the millions say, 'We will not fight; so keep the peace yourself, or we will choose another servant to administer an equitable government to us?'"

In 1834 John gave to the world a small publication, entitled "Thoughts as they Rise," a poem in Byronic metre, but "without an imaginary hero romanting through its cantos, out of all the ordinary tracks of real life." In his preface he said:—"Plain truth in rhyme has been so long out of fashion, I have no doubt of its being well received, even as quite a novelty." But, alas! he was doomed to be wofully disappointed, as of the thousand copies printed only a few were sold. In plain terms, the work fell still-born from the press, and the insouciant world was saved the promised periodical gift of a succession of cantos of the same description, which John, who went on still thinking, would have presented it with had the reception of the first been encouraging. Although not void of the usual blemishes overlooked by impulsive, sanguine writers, whose idiosyncrasy does not permit them to see or acknowledge that the great world's work is carried on by compromise between conflicting principles, these "Thoughts" were really remarkable for keenness of insight, depth of feeling, logical acuteness, and chaste expression—they were, in fact, the result of his working as well as meditative hours. Whenever he had got an idea moulded into consistency and shape, he was in the habit of writing it down before it escaped from memory. Hence the brief sententiousness of his style in this poem, which, as a kindred spirit said of it, "reminds one of bits knocked off at odd moments, with the marks of the fire and the steel upon them."

In 1840 John made his *debût* as a prose writer. His "River Angling for Salmon and Trout," published by Messrs Blackwood, brought him somewhere about £30 in clear cash, and a wide and high reputation among lovers of "the gentle art," being, as far as it went, a most admirable treatise, both plain and practical in its directions, and racy in its matter and style. John held fly-fishing to be the next best thing to "sweet-hearting;" and it is evident that he entered with almost equal heart and soul into both occupations at fitting time and place—one hour rivalling the best Scottish song writers in inditing exquisite little love lyrics, and another hour coping with old Izaak Walton in the description of the sports of his green years, when "a boy, so poor as not to be master of a hook or a halfpenny," he sallied out to the small burn, which, at that time yet unrestrained, like himself, "chose its own vagrant way from Elliestoun House to the Tweed, circling through the low rushy leas, forming dimple, pool, and ripple, and *gumped* out half a stone of speckled trouts, where the neighbours never suspected such a thing existed." Even then, he tells us, "when a hungry laddie," he often enough got into fits of extreme sensibility, returning the small trout to the stream,

> "As piteous of his youth, and the short space
> He had enjoyed the vital light of heaven."

"I would suspend my angling pursuits," he adds, "and admire the trouts tumbling up in the streams, suppressing the desire to cast a hook amongst the freebooters. And the same sympathies," he goes on to say, "have at times unfitted me for some necessary employments of life—yes, even to the length of requiring an effort of my strongest philosophy to bring me to prune a rose or pluck a flower!"

In a sketch of the author's life, prefixed to a new and much enlarged edition of the "River Angling," published in 1860, we are told that "with friends at a distance, men who had left St. Boswell's for the broader field of adventure and pursuit of what it could not supply, or friends of a chance intimacy, he maintained an extensive correspondence, making his epistles so much the record of his careful thinking that he took copies of them. In this way an immense quantity of manuscript accumulated in the course of years, significant of the ceaseless mental activity which characterized him. At his death there were more than seven hundred copies of letters which he had addressed to friends. Many of these had been written to men of literary eminence or public distinction, giving his views on opinions associated with their names. This collection he cherished as the treasure of his mental history. Sometimes, when leaving home, he used to warn his family that if the house took fire in his absence, next to saving themselves they should save these writings." Two volumes of this correspondence are in the possession of the publishers of the present volume. They contain a rich omnigatherum of facts and fancies, opinions and speculations, on all sorts of subjects, and to all sorts of persons, which, according to the judgment of a perhaps too friendly critic, who has been favoured with a cursory perusal of their contents, would, if printed in whole or part, "cast Burns's correspondence far into the shade, and take an honourable place on the library shelf beside those of Cowper and Kirke White."

In his sixty-fourth year, John Younger succeeded in gaining the second prize for an essay on the temporal advantages of the Sabbath to the labouring classes. His paper was entitled "The Light of the Week." It showed him to be no maw-worm. In it he expressed his wish that the sacred day should be protected from the invasion of mammon worship; but he had evidently a similar dread of the intrusion of the civil power to enforce its strict observance. "Moral force," he says, "is the true agent to be employed in this work, as physical coercion always fails of effect in moral or religious matters. The mind is never subdued by pinching the body into forced circumstances: we have proof enough of this from the Cross downward. Under despotism men may take the colour of the evil time, but the immortal mind will have its own range—will never be bound in earthly chains, nor in fettered circumstances ever sit easy." In a brief autobiographical sketch prefixed to the essay, for which he received £15, John says:—"I have my good wife still spared to comfort me, and to be comforted, after having been joined above thirty-seven years. Of eleven children we have only the three first born alive, two daughters and a son, all married, and from whom have arisen to us twelve grandchildren, all loved little ones, in present health and good liking. I have had a feeling of deep interest in four generations: first, in my father's pecuniary straits in the time of my youth; next, in my sisters' concernments; again, in our children's; and now 'life's cares are comforts'— my little grandees are as interesting, and claim as much attention, as any of the preceding. I see it would be the same should I be spared to the age of Methuselah."

When John returned from London, whither he had

gone to receive his guerdon at the hands of the Earl of Shaftesbury, gentle and simple on Tweedside gave the rustic philosopher a complimentary banquet, and a purse full of money, which more than defrayed his expenses to the metropolis and back. Shortly afterwards, a vacancy having occurred in the village Post Office, the appointment was, on the recommendation of the Hon. J. E. Elliot, at that time member for the county, conferred upon John, in the belief that his advancing years would thus find an easier living than in toiling at his old trade. The result, however, proved different from what was expected. The rigid exactitude of rule, and the perplexing net-work of forms and business routine, were more than one accustomed to the simple machinery of making shoes could overtake; and after his life had been nearly vexed out of him, John threw up the appointment in disgust, in January, 1856. He had felt himself, he said, when postmaster, just like a caged squirrel running over its never-ending wheel; whereas, now that he was again free, he felt like the squirrel on the top of a tree, ready to jump wherever he liked.

At his old trade and at the angling—which latter, in conjunction with the sale of fishing requisites, and the perquisites given by gentlemen anglers from a distance, to whom his company and advice were ever welcome, was perhaps the more lucrative source of income of the two—John worked on cheerfully till the centenary of Burns came round. In that celebration he took a prominent part, delivering lectures, described to have been a real intellectual treat, in most of the towns and villages in the Border district, and afterwards in Glasgow, to which he was invited by a few admiring friends. His visit to the city of St. Mungo, however, turned out unfavourably, in that he was exposed during his stay to extremely severe weather, which brought on an attack of rheumatism that prostrated and confined him to his lodgings for several weeks. The consequent doctors' and other bills absorbed the profits of his lecture, and he came back to St. Boswell's as poor as ever.

During the long and severe winter of 1859–60, he was seldom seen abroad, and did not regain much strength. Generally cheerful and unrepining, he began to confess himself as growing old, and less able for active work at his ordinary trade; but stern necessity still impelled him to gird himself with his leather apron, and make or cobble shoes to the best of his remaining ability. On the eve of the 18th of June—Waterloo day—he was apparently in nearly his usual health and spirits, and those about him had no premonition of what was soon about to happen. He had been engaged in reading "The Journal of a Poor Vicar," a work translated from the German, which was a great favourite with him; but shortly after daybreak, on the forty-fifth anniversary of the great battle, in which Buonaparte succumbed, death struck him suddenly with a paralytic stroke. Twenty-three hours afterwards, at half-past four o'clock on the morning of the 19th, he fell asleep, after a brief struggle. He had, we are told, ever cherished a wish that his end might come under circumstances in which he would leave the world without being a tax or trouble to any. The wish was gratified. For only a short week before his mortal remains were laid in St. Boswell's churchyard, close beside his

Nannie, he had been standing entranced on the romantic "brae-heads," behind Lessudden, looking over to Dryburgh, and Bemersyde, and Gladswood, and The Holmes, and up to the Eildon Hills, that recalled so many fond recollections of pleasant days spent on the silver Tweed, and quiet strolls among the mantling woods, and kind friends gone away to all the ends of the earth, but dearer than ever in the dim distance. For to the very last he had cherished

> "Love's youngest hopes, and downy dreams,
> In memory's light, like glowworm gleams."

Mr. William Henderson, of Durham, in his "Life of an Angler," tells us how, many a time, when seated with John in his workshop, he has seen him steal away as secretly as he could to the adjoining room, where, in her chair by the ingle-neuk, sat his poor, helpless life-partner, totally blind from cataracts on both eyes, listening always to the sound of the step she knew and loved so well. The old man, he says, would take her hand, whisper some tender words, and, bending down, bestow the longed-for kiss. Then, wiping away the tear that would gather in his eye, John would return to his lapstone and his labour, leaving the loving heart to count the minutes till he would return again. The good woman went away to "the land of the leal" about four years before John, Providence thus fulfilling the wish he had pathetically expressed years before in one of his sweet songs:—

> "'Mid a' the thoughts that trouble me,
> The saddest thought of any
> Is wha may close the other's e'e—
> May it be me or Nannie?

CONCLUSION. 457

> The ane that's left will sairly feel,
>   Amid a world uncanny;
> I'd rather face auld age mysel'
>   Than lanely leave my Nannie."

Writing to a friend about two years after his wife's death, he concluded thus:—"Besides your love-kissings, give your wife a friendly kiss for my sake. I was once, and long, myself a kindly husband, though now, alas! all is fled but the sad yet pleasant reflection."

> "I like an owl in desert am
>   That nightly there doth moan!"

Price 2s 6d, Bound in Cloth, and a proper size for the Pocket,

A NEW EDITION OF

RIVER ANGLING FOR SALMON AND TROUT.

BY THE LATE JOHN YOUNGER, ST BOSWELLS.

With additional Chapters on CREEPER, STONE-FLY, and WORM FISHING, by the EDITOR; and a Portrait and Short Memoir of the Author.

"This is a new and improved edition of one of the most pleasant and useful little books on this pleasant subject. It is needless to say what we have said before, that John Younger's instruction and advices as to angling are most valuable, as the fruits of long experience and great shrewdness."—*Scotsman.*

"To the young Trout fisherman we say, get Younger's little book and study it, and you have the whole art of Trout fishing. To old fishermen we can say that it is the best and most practical book upon this class of fishing ever published."—*The Field.*

"'The Shoemaker of St Boswells,' as he was designated in all parts of Scotland, was an excellent prose writer, a respectable poet, a marvellously gifted man in conversation; and in all that related to the 'gentle art' of fishing, the very highest authority of his day. . . . His is the Angling Book for Scotland. . . . It is a genial pleasant book to read, independent of the information contained in it. There is one part of the book that will be read with interest; that is, the biography of the author, the simple heart-stirring narrative of the life-struggle of a highly-gifted, humble, and honest mechanic—a life of care, but also a life of virtue."—*London Review.*

"Taken altogether, the book must assume a high position as an original piscatorial authority—the result of many years' keen observation."—*Border Advertiser.*

"On all subjects of interest in the art it will be found full of information of the soundest and most ingenious description. The adept and the inexperienced will alike esteem it. On the subjects of when, where, and how to fish, as well as what to fish for and what to fish with, will be found sage advice, grounded on long experience."—*Kelso Chronicle.*

"The publishers of this little volume deserve the highest credit for its handsome and elegant appearance. It contains an excellent portrait of Younger in his cobbler's apron. It is printed in a clear type, on good paper, and is very tastefully bound. We are glad to see such a production emanating from a publishing office in Roxburghshire."—*Hawick Advertiser.*

A few copies of the 1861 edition, containing Younger's "Fresh Hints on the Nature of the Salmon," &c., price 2s 6d, are still to be had.

"To us who leave the gentle art to more patient and painstaking spirits than our own, the best part of the book is that which contains some 'Fresh Hints on the Nature of the Salmon,' and for conducting the Salmon Fisheries of the Tweed."—*Sunderland Times.*

KELSO: J. & J. H. RUTHERFURD, 20, SQUARE.

WORKS PUBLISHED BY

Lately Published, Price, Post Free, 8s 6d,

BORDER BREEDS OF SHEEP,

By JOHN USHER, STODRIG, KELSO,

SECRETARY TO THE BORDER UNION AGRICULTURAL SOCIETY.

Special Edition (of which very few copies now remain), containing the following first-class Photographs:—

- The Author.
- Group of Blackfaced Ewes.
- Blackfaced Tup.
- James Archibald, Duddingston.
- Blackfaced Tup Lamb.
- Scenery of the Cheviots.
- Group of Cheviot Gimmers.
- Belford Old House.
- Thomas Elliot, Hindhope.
- Cheviot Tup (Mr. Elliot's).
- Cheviot Yearling Tup (Mr. Archibald's).
- Group of Border Leicesters and Scene on the Tweed at Mertoun.
- Border Leicester Tup (Mertoun).
- Border Leicester Shearling Tup (Mr. Lees').
- Andrew Paterson, Mertoun.
- Border Leicester Ewe (Mertoun).
- Late William Aitchison, Linhope.

Editions with fewer Photographs, prices 5s 6d and 2s 6d, and with Frontispiece only, 1s 6d.

Lately Published, with Portrait of the Author, Price 1s 6d,

HINTS TO STOCKOWNERS.

By WILLIAM ROBERTSON,

Principal of the Royal Veterinary College, London (formerly of Kelso).

Lately Published, Price 3s,

LIFE and TIMES of WILLIAM THOMSON,

LATE FARMER, OVER-ROXBURGH.

BY HIS SON, THE REV. J. THOMSON, HAWICK.

COMPANION VOLUME TO AND UNIFORM WITH THE ABOVE.

Lately Published, Price 2s 6d,

LIFE OF JAMES SCOTT, ESQ.

Of Allanshaws, Roxburghshire, and Pastoral Farmer, Ross-shire.

BY HIS SON-IN-LAW, THE REV. J. THOMSON, HAWICK.

KELSO: J. & J. H. RUTHERFURD, 20, SQUARE.

Lately Published, Alexandra 8vo, handsomely bound in cloth, gilt edges,

THE POETICAL WORKS OF DR. JOHN LEYDEN,

With BIOGRAPHICAL MEMOIR by Sir WALTER SCOTT, and Supplementary Memoir embracing many new facts in Leyden's Life, and a full account of the Centenary Celebration at Denholm; and illustrated with Portrait, Views of Leyden's Birthplace and Monument at Denholm, *fac similes* of the Poet's Handwriting, and Steel Engravings, &c.,

Price 3s 6d.

"This is incomparably the best edition of Leyden's works that has yet appeared. . . . Whether or not the portrait is correct in all its features, it was undoubtedly sketched from life, and it is the only one known to be in existence, and it is uncommonly well executed. The engraving of the poet's birthplace, from a photograph by J. Y. Hunter, Hawick, is a great improvement on all former pictures of the cottage, for it exhibits the house as it really is, with no fantastic or imaginary figures or features about it. The engraving of the monument on Denholm Green is likewise remarkably like the original. But the most novel and interesting of all the illustrations is a *fac simile* print and inscription from Cardonel's rare picture of Hassingdean Church, showing the ruin as it existed subsequent to the year 1700. . . . It is obvious that no expense and no trouble have been spared to make this a really splendid reprint of Leyden's works, and we feel warranted in saying that it not only has never been, but never will be surpassed as a memorial of the true-hearted Border bard, Dr. John Leyden."—*Kelso Chronicle*, Nov. 19, 1875.

"We have only to add that considerable credit is due to the printers of Kelso for turning out so excellent a specimen of typography, and for getting up the book in so handsome a style."—*Glasgow Herald*, Dec. 11, 1875.

Lately Published, Price in Paper Covers 1s 6d; Neat Cloth, with Photo Portrait and View of Obelisk, 2s 6d,

MEMORIAL of the Rev. HENRY RENTON, M.A., Kelso,

Containing the Funeral Sermons by the late Rev. JAMES ROGERS and the Rev. Dr HUTTON of Paisley, Biographical Notice, Account of the Funeral, and Pulpit and Press Notices.

Preparing for Publication, a New and Enlarged Edition, handsomely bound in Cloth, semi Antique, Price 1s 6d,

THE COLLECTED ADDRESSES OF LORD POLWARTH.

KELSO: J. & J. H. RUTHERFURD, 20, SQUARE.

Published July, 1880,

KELSO AND ITS ASSOCIATIONS:
A HISTORY AND A GUIDE,
TO WHICH IS ADDED THE

History of the Rise and Progress of the Kers of Cessford (now Dukes of Roxburghe), Notes on the Plants and Birds of the District, Map of the Town, and many Illustrations,

In Paper Cover, 1s (postage 3d); Cloth Boards, 1s 6d (postage 4d).

SUPERIOR EDITION WITH EXTRA VIEWS,
2s 6d (postage 6d).

CONTENTS.

KELSO: Name and Derivation—Antiquity and History.
ROXBURGH: Mint and Coins.
BRIDGES: Sir William Fairbairn—Bridge Riots—Show Ground—"Edie Ochiltree."
THE ABBEY: Rise of the Douglas Family—The Abbey Ruin—The Boy Walter Scott, and the Ballantynes—The Knoxes.
THE CHURCHYARD: Former Disgraceful State of—"Beardie's" House and Grave—Hanging of Hislop and Wallace.
MODERN KELSO: Palmer the Printer, a "Blackneb"—Prince Charlie at Kelso.
THE TOWN HALL: "John Anderson, my Jo"—The "Cunzie Neuk"—The "Bull Ring," &c.
ROXBURGH STREET: The "Horse Shoe"—Terrace, Museum and Library—Site of Wester Kelso and its Cross.
FLOORS CASTLE AND GARDENS: Incidents—Montrose at Kelso, &c.
BOWMONT STREET: Dr Horatius Bonar.
HORSE MARKET (Theatre, &c.)
WOOD AND COAL MARKETS.

SHEDDEN PARK, CEMETERY, AND ROSEBANK.
THE CROSS KEYS AND EDNAM HOUSE: Dickson of "The Havanah"—Burns at Kelso—Kelso Races.
SOME FRAGMENTS OF HISTORY: Queen Mary—Covenanters—Jacobites—Fires—Queen's Visit.
"MOBBING AND RIOTING:" Kelso's notoriety for—Antiquity of its Burghal Constitution—Its Galalaw.
THE BORDER CAVE OF ADULLAM: Chevalier Johnston—Murray of Broughton Episcopalians—"Black-Nebs"—Quakers—Border Bowmen—Stage Players, &c.
BURNING OF THE ROMAN CATHOLIC CHAPEL, STORY OF THE.
TRADE AND MANUFACTURES.
CONVEYANCE: Early Coaches, &c.
THE NEIGHBOURHOOD AND WALKS AND DRIVES: Ednam and Lyte the Hymnist—Newton Don—Hume Castle—Wooden Glen.
THE KELSO ARMS.
POPULATION.

APPENDIX.

PLAN OF THE TOWN.
THE STORY OF THE HOUSE OF ROXBURGHE: Illustration, "*Cessford Castle*"—The Kers of Cessford—Floors and the House of Roxburghe—Cessford Castle.
NOTES ON THE PLANTS AND BIRDS OF THE DISTRICT.

Extra full page Illustrations in 2s 6d issue.

BURNING OF THE ROMAN CATHOLIC CHAPEL.
SLEZER'S VIEWS OF KELSO, 1690, AND OF THE ABBEY, 1690 *(reduced).*
CARDONEL'S VIEW OF ROXBURGH CASTLE, 1788 *(reduced).*
SUBSCRIPTION LIST—BUILDING OF THE FIRST BRIDGE OF KELSO, 1752 *(reduced).*

KELSO: J. & J. H. RUTHERFURD, 20, SQUARE.

Preparing for Publication, in Small Octavo, Prices 1s and 2s,

A NEW AND COMPLETE
HISTORY OF THE GYPSIES,
IN SMALL COMPASS, FOR THE USE OF TOURISTS AND VISITORS TO THE
GIPSY VILLAGE OF YETHOLM.
BY JOSEPH LUCAS,
AUTHOR OF "STUDIES IN NIDDERDALE," ETC.

THIS hand-book is specially designed to meet a want experienced by the author, when, on crossing the marches among the green fells of Cheviot, he suddenly found himself in the Gypsy Village of Yetholm, which lies snugly ensconced beside the broad alluvial meadows of the beautiful valley of the Bowmont.

Enquiry at Kelso failed to supply the book which would go into the pocket and contain everything about the Gypsies for 1s. The subsequent labour of months showed that the information required was only to be gained by wading through piles of volumes, many of which are scarce, most are old, and several written in Latin, French, and other languages. The first result of this investigation consisted in an article which appeared in the *Nineteenth Century* for October, 1880, under the title of "Petty Romany." This article gave in chronological order nearly all the facts recorded about the Gypsies in the various countries in Europe, so as to show the reasons of the ebb and flow of the tide of Gipsy migrations from one country to another. There is little to add to this summary, which is the most complete as yet published; but several works escaped notice from want of space which will be mentioned in the present volume. A Glossary of more than 500 Gypsy words still in use, referred in most cases to their parent tongues, will be added. A few fragmentary sentences, remembered but not used by the Gypsies, and two fragments of songs of genuine antiquity, with other matter of local and general interest, will also form part of the work. The Author has spent much time and picked up all the words, songs, and sentences in the Glossary in personal intercourse with the Gypsies in the South, and has also visited those at Yetholm, and learned upwards of 100 words from their venerable Queen, Esther Faa-Blyth, to whom this little handbook is respectfully dedicated.

Lately Published, Price 3s,

RAMBLES IN THE NEW WORLD,
BY JOHN CLAY, JUN., ESQ.:
Being a Series of Papers contributed to the *North British Agriculturist* and the *Kelso Chronicle*.

KELSO: J. & J. H. RUTHERFURD, 20, SQUARE.

THE LATE THOMAS TOD STODDART, Esq.

J. & J. H. RUTHERFURD

RESPECTFULLY announce that they have issued a new Edition of the late Mr. STODDART's most recent work, "Songs of the Seasons and other Poems."

At the request of the Publishers, Mr. STODDART wrote an Autobiography for this edition, the final revision of which he completed a few days before his death.

The Autobiography extends to 40 pages, and contains many characteristic reminiscences and reflections, and an enumeration of his remarkably wide acquaintance with men of note in various walks of life.

The Autobiography is illustrated by the following Photographs:—

THE AUTHOR	*(Misses Brocklehurst and Booth, amateurs.)*
SHERIFF GLASSFORD BELL	*(Annan, Glasgow.)*
JOHN WILSON (Son of Christopher North)	*(Mackintosh, Kelso.)*
AULD ROB O' THE TROWS	*(From Frain's Subscription Picture.)*
A FAMILY GROUP	*(Mackintosh, Kelso.)*
THE WINDINGS OF THE TEVIOT	*(Mackintosh, Kelso.)*
THE TWEED AT KELSO	*(Wilson, Aberdeen.)*
THE AUTHOR'S FAVOURITE DOG "OBIE"	*(Mackintosh, Kelso.)*

Mr. STODDART took great interest in these illustrations, putting himself to no little trouble in obtaining the best negatives, so as to procure satisfactory pictures. The last meeting between him and the publishers was about the Photos at Mackintosh's Studio on the day he lay down to die.

The impression of the Autobiographical Edition of the "Songs of the Seasons" was limited to 250, and of these 200 have been sold.

Net Price, 6s 6d; Postage, 6d extra.

20, SQUARE, KELSO, *October*, 1881.